Advances in Organizational Psychology

Advances in Organizational Psychology
An International Review

is published in cooperation with the Division of Organizational Psychology of the International Association of Applied Psychology

● CONTRIBUTORS ●

Jen A. Algera
Neil Anderson
Bernard M. Bass
Walter C. Borman
Xu Liancang
Pieter J.D. Drenth
Charles J. De Wolff
Dov Eden
Göran Ekvall
Jaime C. Filella
Hisataka Furukawa
R. Bruce Gould
Jerry W. Hedge
Frank A. Heller
Luc Hoebeke
Karl Hofmeyer

Michael J. Kavanagh
Rajesh Kumar
Frank J. Minor
Jyuji Misumi
José M. Peiró
Mark F. Peterson
Simcha Ronen
Vivian Shackleton
George Shouksmith
Jean-Claude Sperandio
Donald Super
Tharsi Taillieu
Leopold Vansina
Peter Weissenberg
Bernhard Wilpert
Jacques A.M. Winnubst

Advances in Organizational Psychology

An International Review

•

EDITORS

Bernard M. Bass / Pieter J. D. Drenth

Associate Editor PETER WEISSENBERG

SAGE PUBLICATIONS
The Publishers of Professional Social Science
Newbury Park   Beverly Hills   London   New Delhi

For information address:

SAGE Publications, Inc.
2111 West Hillcrest Drive
Newbury Park, California 91320

SAGE Publications Inc.
275 South Beverly Drive
Beverly Hills
California 90212

SAGE Publications Ltd.
28 Banner Street
London EC1Y 8QE
England

SAGE PUBLICATIONS India Pvt. Ltd.
M-32 Market
Greater Kailash I
New Delhi 110 048 India

Printed in the United States of America

Library of Congress Cataloging-in-Publication Data

Main entry under title:

Advances in organizational psychology.

1. Psychology, Industrial. 2. Organizational
behavior. I. Bass, Bernard M. II. Drenth, Pieter
J. D. (Pieter Johan Diederick) III. Weissenberg, Peter.
HF5548.8.A58 1987   158.7   87-9484
ISBN 0-8039-2802-5

CONTENTS

PREFACE

Since its formation in 1978, the Division of Organizational Psychology of the International Association of Applied Psychology has grown to 1,300 members from approximately 40 countries. Partly to celebrate this growth as well as to provide a contribution to them and others interested in an international perspective on recent work in the field, the publication of a compendium of original articles was proposed and endorsed by the Executive Committee of the IAAP with all royalties to contribute to the work of the Division.

Leading authorities drawn from a worldwide slate were asked to complete chapters that would focus on developments in their specialized areas of interest. Special attention was to be paid to accomplishments and trends in their own country or region of the world.

As will be seen, the plan generated a partial matrix of topics by countries. North America, Europe, and Japan are well represented, and, as in the membership of the Division, Africa and Latin America are not. We are represented down under by New Zealand rather than Australia. And we succeeded in crossing East-West boundaries with contributions from the People's Republic of China but not the USSR. We also addressed some of the special problems of the developing world and of the workers coming from industrialized backgrounds, such as the Maori of New Zealand and the blacks in South Africa.

At the same time, a broad spectrum of topics are included, ranging from work motivation, selection, and training to sociotechnical analysis and the impact of the new technologies. Organizational psychology is conceived here as a discipline encompassing a broad array of issues concerning people and work. Again, uncontrollable circumstances caused the loss of contributions to some important topics such as compensation.

Each editor was responsible for reviewing all of the manuscripts. At the same time, the editors wish to express their appreciation to

Roberta Diamondstein for much of the typing, record-keeping, and follow-ups, Karen Schramm for copyediting, and Lois Foulke for assisting with organizing the bibliography.

—Bernard M. Bass
Binghamton, NY

—Pieter J. D. Drenth
Amsterdam

—Peter Weissenberg
Camden, NJ

1

INTRODUCTION

BERNARD M. BASS
State University of New York at Binghamton
Binghamton, NY, USA

It has been a little more than two decades since Harold Leavitt introduced the label "organizational psychology" at a Walter Van Bingham lecture at Carnegie-Mellon University and since the first books with the title of organizational psychology were published in the United States (Bass, 1966; Schein, 1965).

Nevertheless, organizational psychology has developed rapidly both in depth and in scope. This book is evidence of its rapid spread internationally as a discipline.

The book represents the work of 31 scholars and professionals from 20 countries. Each chapter not only attempts to highlight recent developments of importance in a particular subject of organizational psychology but also tries to emphasize research completed in the country or region in which the author works. Those of us who are privileged to meet and work with our counterparts in other countries are often amazed at how much we do not know about what is going on abroad in our own field of interest. A central purpose of this book is to help familiarize readers with many recent developments and applications of organizational psychology in many parts of the world that they may not have already seen in their own national publications.

When I tried recently to send a package from the United States to New Zealand, the international shipping agent asked me if New Zealand was someplace in Canada! In spite of this ignorance about New Zealand, as a self-centered, modern society with similar problems as elsewhere but on a smaller scale, it is an important laboratory for the larger modern countries. With Chapter 2, George Shouksmith begins our exploration of recent developments in attitudes toward work by pointing out that despite its large Pakaha (European) ethnic majority, work had a much different meaning for the New Zealanders than for the British and Europeans they left behind. Even what *masculinity* means in Europe fails to capture New Zealand's strong masculine norms.

George Shouksmith looks at what is occurring in the work force in New Zealand, a country that is a microcosm of the larger industrialized countries, all of whose work forces are changing as well. The meaning of work itself is changing for numerous reasons. First, it becomes only part of the life space in a consumer-oriented society. Second, women are becoming an important part of the work force. Third, the social values of non-European cultures, such as those of the Maori in New Zealand, are becoming increasingly important. Fourth, jobs are becoming increasingly difficult to find and hold for significantly larger portions of the disadvantaged, the older, and the unskilled. Fifth, jobs are being deskilled with increasing automation. The effects of all of these trends (not all negative) in New Zealand are dramatically unfolded by Shouksmith and the implications for industrialized societies everywhere can be seen.

In Chapter 3, Hisataka Furukawa moves the examination of recent developments in motivation to work to consideration of current research and theory on approaches to increase worker commitment, effort, satisfaction, and productivity. These include goal setting, modifying expectancies, and providing a possible better mix of extrinsic and intrinsic rewards. Results recently with more generally useful programs such as behavior modification, participation, and job redesign are then reviewed. Finally, special focus is laid on the use of small group efforts in Japan such as the Quality Control Circles. Furukawa acknowledges that Quality Control Circles have fit with traditional Japanese values but warns that since these values are changing, we may expect to find increasing problems with these group efforts.

What continues is the failure of needs to be satisfied in the workplace and this may result for many workers in disabling stress. In Chapter 4, stress in the workplace is the subject of Charles de Wolff's and Jacques Winnubst's detailed review of theory and research in North America and Europe on stress and work disability, with particular attention to the Dutch experience.

The authors examine the major methodological problems and the division of labor that is needed between organizational psychologists and stress investigators from other disciplines (e.g., psychology, neurology, immunology). They proceed to review the sources of stress in the workplace and effects associated with occupation, socioeconomic status, organization, technology, career, unemployment, social support, individual personality, and coping strategies. They conclude with what we know about prevention and intervention strategies to combat stress in the workplace.

Michael Kavanagh at the State University of New York, Albany, and his coauthors at the Air Forces Human Resources Laboratory (W. C. Borman, J. W. Hedge, and R. B. Gould) present a model for describing the variables of consequence on performance appraisal. They examine current trends in research on performance appraisal with the model as a basis. They note that, in the past five years, research reports about performance appraisal increased generally, particularly about its quality. Within this, they have seen an increase in focus on cognitive process, measurement accuracy, feedback, appraisal interview, legal aspects, rater training, and the gap between practice and research. At the same time, concern about rating formats has decreased.

Viv Shackleton and Neil Anderson complete a detailed review in Chapter 6 of the state of the art of recruitment and selection outside of psychometric testing. Although much American and European research is examined, the chapter is clearly focused on recent experience in Britain.

The authors begin with considering four of the major forces of consequence to recruitment and selection: the law, massive unemployment, the computer, and the perversity of human resources managers. They then note that much more research effort still tends to be invested in selection rather than recruiting, and in the reliability and validity of alternatives to testing, such as self-evaluation, biodata, assessment centers, the reference letter, graphology, and lie detector testing. There seems little relation between the validity of these techniques and their popularity. Graphology, lie detectors, and reference letters lack supportive validations, for instance, yet remain widely used. The interview may also be unable to pass muster in terms of traditional validation analysis but the authors suggest that the interview serves a variety of additional purposes beyond providing opportunities for assessment. Moreover, it may be found valid if the interview is seen as a social linkage of training to such diverse considerations as performance evaluation and strategic management. Other issues reviewed include reports about stress training management and organizational development and human factors training.

In Chapter 7 Donald Super and Frank Minor note that employees go through recognizable stages in their careers: *exploration* to learn how their abilities and interests fit with organizational demands; *establishing* or consolidating their position and laying the groundwork for career advancement; *maintenance* in the middle of the 40's to settle for what has been attained and a final *deceleration* toward retirement and afterward. Organizational programs for career development are described which help career planning and career management. Closely associated is the organization's own succession planning. Several trends are seen by the authors. Management is becoming increasingly aware that career development contributes to employee satisfaction. Advances in information-systems and computerization make possible individual employee responsibility for career planning as well as the integration of the organization's human resources data files with career planning systems.

"Plus ça change; plus c'est la même chose" (The more things change; the more they stay the same). Like other reviewers of training, Dov Eden, writing about training developments in the less developed world and in Israel laments like his reviewer predecessors from North America and Europe on the lack of evaluation, the inattention to organizational factors and the continued receptivity of training to fads. Nevertheless, he goes on to introduce a number of newer ideas that have blossomed recently such as the use of the Pygmalion and Galatea effects on learning of building positive expectations, applications of behavior modification, and the interaction of training and corporate culture.

In discussing training developments in Israel, Eden notes the linkage of training to such diverse considerations as performance evaluation and strategic management. Other issues reviewed include reports about stress training, management and organizational development and human factors training.

In Chapter 9, Karl Hofmeyer provides a critical essay on the South African experience in upgrading black employees into management positions. The presentation points to both the parallels with and the differences for U.S. affirmative action.

Four reasons are offered by apologists for failure of larger numbers of blacks to achieve managerial positions in South Africa. Blacks are seen to be unprepared culturally and educationally. Job openings, legally restricted to whites only, prevented blacks from moving into skilled positions as a step upward toward management. Even without such legal constraints, racial prejudice was enough to bar much upward mobility for blacks. Finally, potential black managers must function in a world with apartheid rules for separate community living while working alongside whites. Conflicts and ambiguities abound in a similar way for many U.S. black managers.

South African firms use the above to justify maintaining the "white only" status quo. Change could be too difficult, expensive, and likely to bring on a white backlash. Nevertheless, there has been some progress. Behavior modeling, achievement training, and bridging education have been tried as ways to overcome the disadvantaged black's deficit in education and experience with only modest success.

Needed, Hofmeyer feels, to make such efforts work better, are attention and support by top management "dictating the direction and pace of advancement plans" instead of delegating the problem to human resources specialists. Affirmative action will also need to reduce the inconsistencies, ambiguities, and conflicts in the black-white arena.

Based on three decades of service in management development in India matched by comparable efforts in Spain, Jaime Filella was in excellent position in Chapter 10 to provide us with a contrast in management training needs and approaches in these two traditional countries in which modernization has come late.

Indian managers seem frustrated by their well-read command of the modern management literature that they cannot put into practice; Spanish managers seem to many trainers to be fundamentally sound but lacking in the right tools and knowledge of the right techniques.

In Chapter 11, Jen Algera presents a quite thorough review of the current state of the art of job and task analysis in the United States and Europe. He first looks at the four conceptual bases for task analysis: behavior description, behavior requirements, ability requirements, and task characteristics. Issues of consequences are to describe how information is transferred and the strategies used by the human operator. Taxonomies are required that will capture empirical as well as logical relationships.

Methodological and psychometric problems abound dealing with the sources of information and the type to be collected. Algera sees that the older instruments such as the PAQ need to reflect more of the increase in the detailed mental requirements of new technology jobs.

Controversy continues on whether validity generalization means a decreased utility in specifying some of the details of job differences in different situations as well as the increased utility of job clustering. The international nature of the field is seen in parallel connected developments in Britain, Holland, Germany, and the United States.

For those in U.S. business schools who have been wrestling with how to organize the curriculum and research efforts of Management Information Systems, Jean-Claude Sperandio's Chapter 12 provides many fertile ideas for how to structure the solution. The applied science of computer ergonomics, a common European approach, goes a long way to fulfilling what is needed. Sperandio begins by describing the ergonomic approach and points to the critical demand for task analysis as fundamental to any efforts to improve man-machine interfaces. The field of technology-based problems is presented. Finally, Sperandio details how team research efforts have been organized in institutes and universities in France rather than in the private sector.

In Chapter 13, Leopold Vansina, Luc Hoebeke, and Tharsi Taillieu launch a critical review of what is wrong with sociotechnical interventions. They see that the democratic, humanistic desires of theorists and practitioners often stretch beyond economic realities. We still are unable to design work or the workplace from solidly tested principles. In the last analysis, most sociotechnological interventions are some form of joint-optimization efforts. Vansina and his colleagues see the need and the potential to better mix and match the human contribution with the technological imperatives in attending to the development of the organization. They show the correspondence among various schools of thought in this endeavor that have developed in Europe.

Göran Ekvall's insightful view of the current status of the concept of organizational climate provides a picture, in Chapter 14, of the various distinctions of use. Climate can be an objective pooling of sense impressions or phenomenological. It can be organizationwide or suborganizational. It can be strongly a function of the eyes of the beholders or an organizational characteristic transcending any one individual. It can even be associated with a particular informal group of organizational members. It can be distinguished from psychological climate as well as from the values and core beliefs that make up an organization's culture. At the same time, in whatever way it is formulated for use, it serves as a powerful predictor (or consequence) of a wide variety of individual and organizational measures of performance. The blending of theory and empirical results is matched equally by the blending of Swedish and American research literature.

In Chapter 15, José Peiró takes on the difficult challenge of presenting a brief review of the major approaches to understanding how organizations are structured. After describing the dimensional approach to organizational analysis, he notes that the original Burns and Stalker twofold categorization of organizations as mechanistic or organic has been expanded considerably by subsequent investigators. Particularly interesting are his conclusions about the need for intermediate variables inside the organization to link the macrowith the micro-level of analysis, and the need to see that individual job holders may influence structure just as structure influences them. The Spanish Civil War retarded developments in Spain but, increasingly, both imported and home-grown programs of research have been seen in the past decade, and Peiró expects that the entry of Spain into the European Common Market will accelerate such programmatic research efforts on organizational structure because of the contention that subsequent understanding will make for better organizational designs.

Frank Heller and Jyuji Misumi, in Chapter 16, see rationality and predictability as the two basic issues in organizational decision making. With this in mind, longitudinal results are reviewed in seven firms in Britain, the Netherlands, and Yugoslavia, using in common a contingent decision-making model. Looking at the organizational decision according to whether it was in the early or later phases of its development was seen as important to understanding and prediction.

The competence of the individuals within the process was seen to be underutilized. The status of one's position gave power, which continued extra de facto influence in supposedly shared participation. External power sources also had to be considered to appreciate the participative process.

Participative decision making in Japan was also the subject of review. Here the *ringi* method was seen in practice early in the Meija era. The current practice of the *ringi* method is described in detail both as a method of bottoms-up communication as well as of organizational decision making. Consensus is sought as an idea filters slowly upward in the firm, but the interpretation of the decision reached can be very rapid as a consequence of the earlier participation in moving it along in the system. Problems caused by the *ringi* method are also examined as well as another Japanese decision aid, *nemawashi*—an informal sounding of opinions. The ability to use the *ringi* method or *nemawashi* requires a high degree of frustration tolerance.

Jyuji Misumi and Mark Peterson, in Chapter 17, look at leadership research from two contexts: recent work in Japan and Misumi's P(erformance) M(aintenance) Theory. Misumi's theory has generated a great deal of laboratory and field study, primarily in Japan. It parallels the vast array of studies in the United States and Europe on task versus relations orientation and initiation versus considera- tion but specially enlarges understanding of various aspects of performance and maintenance emphasis. For example, Mainte- nance can be seen in ethical, rule-abiding behavior in government agencies, and in recruiting efforts in voluntary college sports groups. It can be situation conserving. Similarly, Performance can emphasize pressure on planning. Different consequences emerge depending on whether P or M is emphasized.

American-based theories and models such as Fiedler's contin- gency theory and Graen's Vertical Dyad Linkage Model have been tested in Japan with mixed success. Another international topic, crisis leadership, has also been the subject of numerous studies in Japan. Chapter 17 concludes with the suggestion that we are in for some sharp shifts in leadership research paradigms as a conse- quence of the recent increase in managerial interest in the issue.

In Chapter 18, Bernhard Wilpert's examination of participation and industrial democracy first brings up to date the de jure and de facto state of affairs in West Germany and in Norway. Then he examines managerial participation practices and beliefs seen in a variety of comparative studies such as in a multinational's 39 subsidiaries, in an eight country comparison of approaches to specific decision making by managers and their subordinates, and in a twelve country comparison of normative prescriptions about participation and external and internal factors associated with them. Both differences and convergences are noted across national boundaries.

The People's Republic of China is truly an awakening giant of opportunities in organizational psychology. In Chapter 19, Xu Liancang reviews the sizable developments that have occurred in China since the end of the Cultural Revolution in 1976. He shows how research in organizational psychology in China is emerging as an important element in economic reform. It should import Western principles of organizational psychology for examination in the Chinese context. But applications and theory development in China must also be consistent with the collective principles of Marxism. Moreover, the rich Chinese cultural heritage, which for 3,000 years has provided a scholarly outlook on behavioral ques- tions, will also provide a source for modifications of Western-based propositions and new ideas about individual, groups, and the organization.

Most impressive are the opportunities to discover, test, and verify in replication particular ways to improve individual, group, and organizational performance using action research involving what may come to be hundreds of factories and hundreds of thousands of workers.

Just as Japan in the third quarter of this century provided us with the *kanban*, Quality Control Circles, and theory Z, so China may provide the world with comparable innovations in the last quarter of this century.

Simcha Ronen and Rajesh Kumar take up the broader issues in the international area of comparative management. Psychology is seen as the preferred discipline among the social sciences for greatest potential accomplishments. Two subjects in organizational psychology are reviewed at length: leadership style and attitudes toward work. Particular attention is paid to the differences in cultures in attributional pressures as well as values, needs, meanings, and beliefs.

Methodological and conceptual problems discussed include the problems of transferring models and measures across countries disciplines, the nation/state as a unit analysis, sampling of cultures, and the need for more cross-cultural internation research.

In just 25 years, the field of organizational psychology has spread worldwide. As can be seen, the authors of the chapters that follow reflect this spread. North American, Western Europe, and East Asia are well-represented along with South Africa and New Zealand. However, plans for chapters from Latin America and Eastern Europe failed to materialize and are unintented omissions.

Part I

Personnel Psychology

2

EMERGING PERSONNEL VALUES IN CHANGING SOCIETIES

GEORGE SHOUKSMITH
Massey University
Palmerston North, New Zealand

The industrial revolution institutionalized work and changed the work force from a rural craft-based one to an urbanized laboring group in large mechanized, productive enterprises. In these enterprises, work was planned to make the most efficient use of machinery and materials. The organizational tasks became the focus of the employers and managers who provided the capital base for the enterprises. The new industrialized work force provided the labor to achieve the aims and goals of the enterprises for which they worked. For these "new" societies of the nineteenth century to succeed, the whole population needed to be committed to regulated, disciplined, and productive effort. These concepts became central to society, focused in a positive endorsement of the value of work for its own sake, a value essential, one might argue, to the motivation of assembly line workers who, all too frequently, saw neither the raw materials nor the end products of their labor. Dubin (1976), reviewing the nature of work in modern society, concluded that it was still true of all societies, whether capitalist or socialist, that formal education was tied to the preparation of the youngster for a productive role in society. Schools are assumed to aim to reinforce desirable worker behavior and attributes, such as discipline, regular attendance, and obedience to authority. New workers arriving from this educational background are assumed to evaluate themselves in terms of accomplishment and production and to seek satisfaction of these goals through work. Dubin comments, somewhat cynically, that the modern affluent society has developed new ways of judging the worth of its citizens, other than by their productivity and their accomplishments. They are valued, he suggests, by their consumerism! If consumerism has replaced achievement in traditional industrial societies, others with recent exposure only to industrialism might well be expected to have very different expectations. In New Zealand, for example, the indigenous Maori population has joined a Western-type industrialized society only in the last hundred years or so. Their background as highly mobile seafaring Polynesians was not even in rural crafts and agrarian industries, but rather as fishermen and explorers. Their strong tribal ties make it difficult for them, even today, to accept working in mixed groups among other Maoris (Kawharu, 1968) and these same traditions predispose them to avoid seeking self-advancement through achievement. Ritchie (1973), reviewing the employment of minority groups in New Zealand industry, has put it more picturesquely, "Maori and Islander attitudes of community, of sharing, caring and generosity, of using rather than valuing money and material goods, of placing affiliation needs ahead of those of acquisition or achievement," he writes, "are simply and frankly incompatible with the economic system [materialistically motivated toward achievement and power] that constitutes the truncated and decaying core of our national culture."

The evaluation of "work" as something to be valued in itself owes much to the development of Christian ethics, again a heritage not shared by many more recently industrialized societies. Notwithstanding Adam's fall from grace and his being driven from the Garden of Eden to work for a living, the early Christians still held that work was good for a man while idleness was not. In retrospect, the industrial revolution stripped work of its religious connotation. As Dunnette (1983) points out, materialism became the order of the day. Work became "labor" in the sense of activity imposed by necessity and lacking any element of free choice (Auden, 1972). When people could no longer see the fruits of their labors, where their endeavors were just one step in a chain or assembly line, and where the time clock and production units became the arbiters of acceptable activity, it is not surprising that people's attitude to work also became less positive. Indeed what is surprising is that the Protestant work ethic should remain central for so long in so many societies and still be seen predominantly in sound correlative research (Furnham, 1984). But perhaps this work ethic may be just a convenient assumption of organizational psychologists and personnel managers, a modern day "myth," bearing little relation to the reality of the situation. A closer look reveals that, in some societies at least, newer roles for work in the life cycle of the individual, increases in leisure (both voluntary and enforced), changing technologies, and the impact of unemployment have all led to the development of new values, both for employed personnel and for the unemployed. In other societies, the Protestant work ethic never existed. In such societies with differing value systems the whole meaning of work and paid employment is altered.

CULTURAL DIFFERENCES

Work does not exist in isolation, nor is it carried out in a vacuum. From the days of the Hawthorne investigations, the influence of social variables on work behavior have been recognized. Surprisingly, only recently has belated recognition been given to the possibility that such social factors could vary greatly, both qualitatively and quantitatively, from one country to another. The English *tomorrow* and the Spanish *manana* reflect great differences in expectancy in terms of job completion. In New Zealand it is not uncommon for someone to speak scathingly of "Maori time," contrasting it with "real time." Other and deeper value differences arise, as Ritchie suggests, reflecting major underlying differences in attitude to work as Western society knows it. Lack of recognition of such differences can be a major problem for those establishing management policies for multinational organizations.

Hofstede (1984) contrasted attitudes and values of work personnel of a large multinational corporation between 1967 and 1973 in 40 countries. Culture was defined as "the collective programming of the mind which distinguishes the members of one human group from another." It may be seen as the impact a society has on its members and can be measured, through the common attitudes and values expressed by those members. Inferences that could be drawn in the cross-country comparisons were limited by the restriction of data gathering to one firm and its marketing and servicing divisions. Nevertheless, the research presents an important data base of information on similarities and differences in values held by personnel from a large number of disparate countries. That all the personnel belonged to one corporate organization and so, presumably, were carefully selected to fit its own self-ideals make the differences that emerge even more significant. Hofstede tapped demographic data and questioned respondents about their personal evaluation of different aspects of the work situation, their perception of various work settings and of management, and their personal goals and beliefs. Responses were found to stabilize into four dimensions or factors, which showed both ecological stability and stability over time.

Hofstede named four factors he extracted from his questionnaire data "power distance," "uncertainty avoidance," "individualism," and "masculinity." This last dimension illustrates the difficulty of using general descriptive terms for factors that consist of specific response patterns to a limited number of items. Scanning Hofstede's table of Masculinity Indices by country, I was surprised to find Australia and New Zealand with only median-range MAS scores, 61 and 58, respectively, falling behind the United States (62), Great Britain (66), and well behind top-scoring Japan (95). In Australia and New Zealand the pattern of life is traditionally masculine with its emphasis on sport and outdoor pursuits. Problems of the "naming fallacy" appear to be reflected in Hofstede's work and one has to be careful not to interpret the findings too broadly, or out of context. Hofstede uses the term "masculinity" and its opposite pole "femininity" to refer to the dominant sex role pattern in the vast majority of both traditional and modern societies. This in itself, it seems to me, begs the question. From experience of working for many years in New Zealand, for example, and from organizational and personnel analyses made in a number of organizations, a different pattern emerges for the general worker in that country. The typical New Zealand male worker is concerned much more with coworker compatibility and pleasant working conditions than he is with advancement or achievement, which, in Hofstede's terms, places him at the female end of the masculinity-femininity dimension. It may be concluded that less value is put on work itself in New Zealand than is the case in many Western communities. As one Austrian migrant commented to me, New Zealanders' work commitment is higher in weekend do-it-yourself activities than it is in weekly paid employment. If you ask workers, who are members of a multinational work force, with its own well-accepted cultural ethics, about "achievement," the response they give is likely to be a reflection of their perception of that ethos. It is also likely that the Australian or New Zealand worker concerned will be atypical for their cultural groups having been carefully selected to fit the multinational image.

The problem of naming a statistically derived variable may be seen again in the Uncertainty Avoidance Index. The three correlated measures producing the overall score—stress, employment stability, and rule orientation—could be related in a number of ways. In New Zealand, for example, employment instability is a recent phenomenon, produced by a change from overfull employment to a medium-level employment. A personnel officer in the Hutt Valley, the New Zealand capital city industrial area, related to me how, some twenty years ago, employees would move every year or two to a similar industry, requiring the same skills, simply to get "a change of scenery." That this seems to have changed reflects not so much a change in attitude or values but rather a change in circumstances. Jobs are no longer so readily available and thus job changes are not possible. It also follows that stress levels are higher, but, as I have argued elsewhere (Shouksmith, 1985), this reflects a number of relatively rapid changes that have taken place recently in New Zealand society. In part, this increase in societal stress was seen to derive from a sectionalizing of society in which "individuals in their separate groupings have taken up different attitudes and positions, leading to inter-group conflict and personal feelings of ambiguity." It seems likely, therefore, that the strong rule orientation found in Hofstede's analysis is more a reflection of the group identity of this particular set of workers. Others within New Zealand society with other allegiances may be much less rule oriented, but, at the same time, may be equally highly stressed.

On all the indices, New Zealand shares a pattern along with the traditional Western countries, the United States, Great Britain, and the industrialized European nations. On the surface, strong similarities within the groupings do exist. But the comparison along these major dimensions serves to hide or disguise underlying differences. Many of these differences are qualitative rather than quantitative, or lie along dimensions that were not tapped in Hofstede's survey. The problem is the old dilemma of ideographic versus nomothetic research.

Although it take longer to operationalize and is more difficult to analyze, the intensive "case study" approach may well be better for investigating values and attitudes, especially where cross-cultural comparisons are involved. Such work may well be theory guided and so combine the benefits of the ideographic approach with nomothetic comparisons. Inkson and Gidlow (1981), for example, used a structured interview approach to collect data on life history, attitudes to work, and the work-group and leisure time activities and aspirations among watersiders (longshoremen or dockers) in two major South Island ports in New Zealand. The data was gathered as part of a wider study of New Zealand manual workers, and this study was then used to test the "fit" between waterside workers and the theoretical "traditional proletarian" model suggested by Lockwood (1966). The results reveal both differences between New Zealand watersiders and their British counterparts and between them and other New Zealand workers. Changing patterns were indicated, suggesting that among New Zealand watersiders in the seventies, an increasing affluence and altered leisure patterns were moving them away from the pattern of other New Zealand workers and from the theoretical model. The influence of Maori norms and values may well be a further contributing factor to the watersiders' position, since many of them work on the docks. Just as work attitudes and values of work, and affecting work and change, so theoretical models of the personnel involved needed to change. Seen in this context, the value of Hofstede's (1984) contribution may be seen to lie in providing a theoretical model of personnel values that can be studied across cultures and from which divergencies and changes may be measured.

CHANGING VALUES RELATED TO WORK

Changing patterns of reaction as circumstances and society changed, noted in watersiders by Inkson and Giddow (1981) were also reported in other New Zealand studies made by Cammock and Inkson (1985). Trade apprentices in the engineering and travel industries were surveyed and their long-term plans and aspirations questioned. Cammock and Inkson interpreted the findings as revealing a significant shift in the attitudes and values of these future skilled workers. Significantly for management, they rejected staying with their training organization or working in any large institutional settings at all. All wanted to travel overseas following completion of their apprenticeships and saw themselves as looking for long-term employment in areas not directly connected with their trade. Cammock and Inkson (1985) conclude that these findings reveal a "direct contradiction to fundamental assumptions concerning employee commitment on which the apprenticeship system is based." This they see as suggesting that the nature of society is changing in the trend among young people to alter their work attitudes and adopt "postmaterialistic" values. New personnel enter the work force with values differing from those of both their parents and their grandparents. These young workers will make decisions about their futures in terms not of the traditional commitments to achievement, independence, self-control, and endurance of distress common under industrialism; rather, they will in a "postindustrial environment," as Emery and Trist (1965) have referred to newer emerging work cultures, choose self-actualization and self-expression as more appropriate goals.

Values, norms, and roles are inextricably linked in any social grouping. As a result, one factor influencing the attitudes and values of work personnel is the women's movement, which has come to the fore over the last few years, resulting in pressure to change women's roles. In a number of earlier studies of women at work, Cromie (1981) points out, "there has been an assumption that women are less committed to work than men and have lower career aspirations." Cromie's study of middle managers, professional tertiary teachers, and librarians in Northern Ireland shows that working women have just as strong a commitment to work as their male counterparts. What does emerge from this study is that "many men perceive women as lacking in managerial attitudes." If men with these perceptions predominate in higher management and so predominate also in decision making, including the selection of personnel for management positions, then it is not surprising that women tend to have lower probabilities of being accepted for management positions. But more and more they are being selected for and accepting such positions and in so doing introducing fundamental changes into the structure of society and in its values. A recent New Zealand study of 95 engaged couples (Abbott & Koopman-Boydon, 1981) revealed that, in comparison with the actual practices of their parents, these couples envisaged a greater sharing of tasks, if only partial. Significant changes in family values related to work are taking place at the same time that females are beginning to occupy more and more supervisory and management roles in industry and commerce. Sekaran (1985), summarizing data from her own study of dual-career families, points to the different values in terms of seeking satisfaction, which husbands and wives in this study had. Whereas the mental health of the husbands was affected by their job-satisfaction levels, this was not the case for wives for whom general life-satisfaction was significant to their mental health. Women may be just as dedicated to work as men, as Cromie (1981) points out, but the impact of work on them is less positive unless it adds to their total life satisfaction. Sekaran (1985) concludes: "It's quite possible that the next generation of working wives who are currently being exposed to a different set of values and life styles and who are training themselves for professional careers will be different from the present population of wives."

The young and working wives are not the only forces producing change in society, reflected in changing conceptions of work. Both technological and social changes are taking place in many societies and both have an impact on work personnel. Changing technology can offer increased potential for producing better quality jobs. Furthermore, new technologies can lead to a deskilling process, which has to be countered if work values are not to suffer. With increasing degrees of automation, knowledge or skill may deteriorate through lack of use. Airline pilots employed by QANTAS, the Australian airline, fly Boeing 747s that use advanced flight decks capable of being computer controlled for complete flights from take off to landing. The airline insists that in spite of the on-board computer, all pilots must fly manually, hands on, for at least one "leg" in four. Not only does this procedure avoid "deskilling" but it also increases the satisfaction pilots have in carrying out their jobs. As Alderfer (1983) has pointed out, programs of planned change, technological or organizational are successful only if they satisfy at least one human need and are compatible with the value systems of the groups affected by the change. Commercial pilots value highly both safety and being involved in the operation of the latest equipment. At the same time, they set an equally high value on their individual skills and practical flying experience. New "advanced cockpit" technology is in tune with the former while the system directive for manual flying of one leg in four satisfies the latter.

CHANGE AND LACK OF EMPLOYMENT

Although formal education in most societies tends to focus on preparing the youngster for a productive role in society, more and more societies are finding it impossible to provide opportunities for all their members to engage in such work. Shorter hours, glide-time, (flexible working days where the employee has to complete a certain amount of work, but only has to be at his or her work area for limited and specified times), job sharing, and other flexible work patterns common in the South Pacific have, in the wake of more effective technology, taken the emphasis from manual labor and begun to change concepts of what constitutes work. Overriding this and causing even greater changes in people's conceptions of work has been the increase in unemployment affecting most

Westernized societies in the late 1970s and early 1980s. For example, in the past, New Zealand has always been a country of overfull employment, with too many jobs needing to be filled by the work force available. Anyone not in a job was regarded as a "dole bludger." The traditional concept of productive work in New Zealand, as in many societies, was to equate it with "paid employment" (Shouksmith, 1985), thus "those without paid employment arouse negative attitudes and [are] accorded low self-esteem." With older, well-respected members of society, including managers and executives, becoming redundant as has been the case both in the United Kingdom and, to a lesser extent, in New Zealand, and with many school leavers in both countries having to contemplate adult life with no job, unemployment has become a topic of public debate. In these new circumstances, to have a job certainly confers status and self-respect, and to be unemployed means to lose these desirable characteristics. Unemployment can lead to an increase in vandalism, antisocial feelings, and petty crime. As a result, political and social leaders of the many countries affected both by changing employment patterns resulting from changes in technology and by increased unemployment, from whatever the cause, have become concerned not only about the quality of working life, but the quality of life itself. Dubin (1976), almost a decade ago, remarked on the fact that a redefinition of work in the life cycle of the individual had begun to take place. Writing at the same time, Parker and Smith (1976) used the concept of "life-space" to replace the older, twin concepts of work and leisure used to contrast major components in an individual's life history. "Life-space," as Parker and Smith use the concept, refers to the ways that people have of spending time. "Time" and "activity" are present in all categories of life-space and what becomes important is to ensure that all members of society, whether they are employed or not, can engage in activities that they value highly. In New Zealand, not only have later starts to working life been encouraged but "golden handshakes" as a way of encouraging early retirement have been introduced. Both policies make additional jobs available for the reduced number of job seekers, but both also have social consequences. Many of those who retire early share with those made redundant a feeling that they have been put "on the shelf." To be adjusted in retirement a person has to change his or her attitudes to "work" and "leisure," as Lassen (1978) found in a major survey of retired persons in the Manawatu area of New Zealand. Those who had not reassessed their life values and had not developed personal resources to cope with their increased free time were the least well-adjusted in retirement. Aston (1978), writing on "Planning Your Retirement" after he himself had retired quite successfully, concluded that new interests, voluntary work, or social activities were necessary to produce an adjusted lifestyle in retirement. The change in approach to life, required for satisfactory adjustment, requires the retired individual to modify his or her values relating to the use of time.

The impact of an extended period of nonwork on the unemployed school leaver can be even more traumatic. Many of the problems facing the young unemployed arise, as Tiggeman and Winefield (1984) have pointed out, from the fact that since "getting a job" is still the valued goal it gives the employed a positive sense of identity and a raised self-concept. The unemployed individual, in contrast, "is not given the same opportunity to grow and develop as his employed counterpart." Tiggeman and Winefield's study shows significant mood changes between the two groups, the unemployed being more bored, angry with society, helpless, and depressed. The way out of this situation for the young person is to find a job, a course of action not always possible and, unfortunately, an undiscriminating job search may not be the universal panacea it is assumed to be by those still classifying the unemployed as "dole bludgers." O'Brien and Kabanoff (1979), in their study of work values among the employed and unemployed in Australia, found that stress levels among their subjects were positively correlated with the amount of time spent in looking for work. The dilemma that the unemployed face is that they must continue to apply for jobs and accept employment interviews whenever these are offered. At the same time they must not let failure adversely affect their evaluations either of the job-search process or of themselves. Hesketh and Shouksmith's (1982) longitudinal study of the job-search processes adopted by the long-term unemployed in New Zealand showed that although an active job-search strategy, if persevered with, produced feelings of low well-being, it is, by its nature, the strategy most likely to obtain work. However, those who initially blamed their unemployment on a lack of jobs and who thought that success in the past was due to their own efforts, retained their self-esteem, continued the job search longer, and were found to be more likely to obtain a job. A further finding in this study shows the complexity of the meaning of work for many young people. Unemployed subjects rated work as significantly more important in their lives than did those subjects who were working. One respondent, "although assigned to periodic detention as punishment, simply longed for Saturdays when he had something meaningful to do." Others, in unsatisfactory jobs, reported work as being of much less importance in their lives and such work was not always related to independent measures of well-being. As the authors conclude, "Work may be better than non-work, but it is not the whole answer."

The continuing absence of job opportunities for a large proportion of the population has led to a number of new conceptions of the nature of work and new approaches to creating work being developed. In the small North Island, New Zealand town of Patea, for example, the closure of the old meat freezing works in 1982, the town's one major industry, brought high levels of unemployment to the whole surrounding area. The former meat workers were affected directly and so were many other businesses that depended on the incomes of the freezing workers for their trade and turnover. No new employment or businesses of the traditional kind have come to Patea since the closure of the works, but few of the workers have left. House prices were low and houses almost impossible to sell, making it economically unattractive to consider leaving; many of the freezing workers, particularly the older ones, hesitated to leave the established social contacts of the area in which they had worked. To this situation "the community of Patea responded . . . even before the closing of the works" (Pirikahu, Macpherson, Gibbs, Kahu, & Ponter, 1984). The focus for the new commercial activity is in the Rangitaawhi Marae Enterprise Trust, whose concepts and values are based on those of the "Turangawaewae" (the culture and traditions) of the "Tangata whenua" (the people of standing) in the local residential groups or maraes. The stimulus for bringing together in one Trust these various subgroupings of the local Maori came from the Patea subbranch of the Meat Workers Union. The majority of the freezing workers were Maori, as were the Union's executive. This fact, without doubt, contributed to the group orientation of the Trust. The group, who formed the early leaders of the Trust, wanted to replace meaningless, mindless work by something different. They approached the task from an entirely different value position, based on the traditional Maori concepts of "community." Pirikahu et al. (1984) write: "The leaders had little experience in running a business" and "their knowledge of the problems associated with the management of labor was the view from below, from the union." Rangitaawhi's strengths, the authors record, were, "a commitment to courtesy and equable treatment for all men" and "a solidarity reinforced by . . . their being, literally, an extended family." From these unpromising beginnings, the Trust has developed a number of enterprises, which as well as giving purpose and dignity to its unemployed members are now beginning to show a profit balance. Among them the Producers' Cooperative is notable as an attempt to form a low-cost industry producing rabbit meat and processing and marketing unusual meat "cuts" that are not possible within the production line, carcass-oriented, national meat industry. More striking has been the formation of the Patea Maori Club, originally as a social group aimed at providing time-filling activities for unemployed life-space periods, but eventually producing an internationally recognized and economically viable singing group with a pop record that held number one on the charts longer than any other had ever done. This latter success undoubtedly stems from the way in which the Patea Maori Club and its membership became an integrated societal group composed of Maori and European New Zealanders, which through new music combined the values of "Maoritanga" or traditional culture with the modern idiom.

The work of the Rangitaawhi Trust has, according to Pirikahu et al. (1984), demonstrated three things. First, that Government handouts of unemployment benefits are no substitute for employment itself. Second, as writers comment, "government interventions weaken rather than strengthen (local) resources" because they try to strengthen established employment practices and "largely the potential of the unemployed's own efforts." In the case of Patea, traditional employment has failed, but the third conclusion to be drawn from the Trust's endeavors is that the unemployed themselves can adopt new entrepreneurial values and put them into practice through cooperative endeavor. In this new form of entrepreneurial activity, those making up the cooperative share activities, responsibilities, and decisions, each according to their skills. Particularly in those cultures where, as Bradaway (1980) points out, leadership, participation, and information sharing is based on kinship groupings, such cooperative, entrepreneurial approaches may well fit better than traditional, Western "master-servant" working relationships. Bradaway concludes that neither leadership attitudes among personnel nor their perceived importance of needs are culture free.

Even where there are not traditional kinship ties, the changing values in work, noted earlier, have led to the development of a number of cooperatives in many societies. Reviewing these cooperatives in New Zealand, Hutchinson (1984) has suggested that much of their development is due to "the increasing desire in many people for a work-style that reflects more human values." "Many people," he adds, "also see cooperative enterprises as a positive response to unemployment and the destructive tensions in industry between workers and employers." Following a review of the work of a number of cooperatives, including a highly successful nine-woman strong sewing factory named "CHATTERS," the Te Whanai Trust, which runs a cooperative wholesale feedstore and a local dairy, and the Whakatu Freezing Workers who cooperatively planted and own their own forest, which provides them with off-season work, Hutchinson concludes that the cooperatives evoke, "in our wider communities an equal force for change as we look anew at the competitive values of our majority culture and the economic system which has created many of our difficulties today." None of these cooperatives are eligible for government subsidies since these are given only to established industries with a proven track record. Operating as self-employed or as groups of workers on a profit-sharing basis, however, with, in some cases, no wages paid, many cooperatives do have the option of offering tax benefits to the workers involved. Not all cooperatives are successful, Hutchinson writes, and members of cooperatives find that they need to learn a whole new range of skills based on cooperative values. They need to learn "how to make group decisions, how to resolve conflicts and how to shape, together, a worker enterprise," social skills not generally part of traditional educational philo-sophies and values. It is worth noting also that these newer cooperative approaches are in line with newer concepts of work and its meaning. It is not so much paid employment that is essential for psychological well-being as some form of productive activity to fill a significant proportion of time available.

JOB AND LIFE VALUES

The influence of different traditions and value systems in more recently developed and emerging countries, the significant impact of women in the work force, changing technologies and changing social situations have all played their part in altering and developing the attitudes and values of work personnel. Work of any kind is insufficient to offer complete satisfaction and produce a mentally stable and adjusted person simply because he or she is employed. Even among professionals, as a recent study of veterinarians has shown (Shouksmith & Hesketh, 1986), employment satisfaction patterns vary and a significant number think of changing their jobs in midcareer. The results of the above study showed that within veterinary practice different job roles could be distinguished in terms of their component activities and that the scales could also be used to describe nonjob activities. The nature of the job was found to be related to mental health, with certain elements (for example, variety of activities, control over what was done and how and when the job was carried out) being positively related to both job satisfaction and positive mental health. Conversely, however, a lack of these factors inherent in the job and a consequent lack of job satisfaction did not imply lack of overall adjustment. Subjects were able to compensate in their nonjob activities, producing both life satisfaction and overall adjustment. Adjustment depended more on the ability of the individual to satisfy his or her needs, which in turn depended on how they valued job aspects of their total lifestyles. Among veterinarians working for the Meat Division of the Ministry of Agriculture and Fisheries, a role for veterinarians that was lacking in both variety and individual control, there were many who showed, nonetheless, high overall adjustment. These veterinarians produced high "life-satisfaction" scores, valuing highly the additional free time inherent in the Meat Division job and using this for nonjob activities that they also valued highly.

This large-scale study of veterinarians in New Zealand (Shouksmith & Hesketh, 1986) suggests the need for a new two-part approach to analyzing the nature and meaning of life-space activities, both work and nonwork. Attitudes and values held by personnel toward and about work, and about nonwork time differ. For an individual, adjustment and psychological well-being depend on total life activities being congruent with and satisfying that individual's predominant needs. The evidence of the study of veterinarians, although it does not support Broadbent's (1985) suggestion that social activities can alleviate depression, does suggest that for this group, at least, balanced variety in both job and nonjob activities will do this. These findings do support Broadbent's conclusion that leisure activities can act as a buffer if job activities are unsatisfactory.

The relationship between peoples' value systems and their general well-being and adjustment are complex. For some, the nature of the job, particularly if it gives them variety, control over their job activities, and discretionary power, produces a high degree of job satisfaction and a generally adjusted state of well-being. For others, including many females (Comie, 1981), a generally satisfying lifestyle is required. Still others, particularly the un-employed, the redundant, and the retired, must seek satisfaction and adjustment outside work. There is evidence too that in some cultures, particularly those like New Zealand that are influenced by multicultural norms, value systems are no longer traditionally or necessarily work centered. A balanced lifestyle, with acceptable job and nonwork components, is more likely to be sought.

3

MOTIVATION TO WORK

HISATAKA FURUKAWA
Railway Labour Science Research Institute,
Japanese National Railways, Tokyo
and
Faculty of Education, Kyushu University
Fukuoka, Japan

This chapter covers studies that were published for the last 6 years since 1980 and begins with a discussion of some of the antecedents of work motivation and organizational commitment such as goal setting, employee expectancies, and their cognitive evaluations. Here the aim is to review current research on motivation to work and such related variables as performance and satisfaction. Then strategies for increasing work motivation such as behavior modification, participation, and job redesign are introduced. Following this, attention is turned to the use of small group activities in Japan, and finally future research needs are addressed.

ANTECEDENTS OF MOTIVATION TO WORK

Despite the continuing lack of agreement on one standard, reliable, and valid way of measuring commitment (Cook & Wall, 1980; Ferris & Aranya, 1983; Gordon, Philpot, Burt, Thompson, & Spiller, 1980; Meyer & Allen, 1984), several studies examined the antecedents of organizational commitment measured in somewhat different ways. Welsch and LaVan (1981) revealed, as might be expected, that role conflict and ambiguity are detrimental, while a participative climate, teamwork, satisfaction with work, and promotion are positively related to commitment. Oliver (1984) stressed the necessity of a close match between goals of the members and what

Author's Note: *I would like to thank the editors of this book and Michael R. Manning for their comments on an earlier version of this chapter. Partial support for the preparation of this chapter was provided by a Grant-in-Aid for Scientific Researchs, Ministry of Education, Science and Culture, No. 60301015.*

the corporation provides. Gould and Werbel (1983) compared the degree of commitment between dual and single wage-earner families and found that commitment was lower among male subjects whose spouses were employed. Culture, as such, could not account for these kinds of results, for Luthans, McCaul, and Dodd (1985) presented data to reveal that Japanese workers are not always more committed to the organizations than are their U.S. counterparts.

The major antecedents of motivation to work are employees' goal setting, their expectancies, and their cognitive evaluations.

GOAL SETTING
AND MOTIVATION TO WORK

Motivation to work is enhanced by having specified goals toward which to work. Goal setting theory has evoked a number of questions about this, mainly in laboratory experiments (Locke, Shaw, Saari, & Latham, 1981) and has become one of the most influential theories on motivation to work. Recently, however, some field research results are also available in support of laboratory-based explanation. In a review of the goal setting research literature, Campbell (1982) concluded that both situational and personality factors affect an individual's preference to work on easy or hard goals. Situational factors include such variables as prior success or failure on the task, monetary and verbal incentives, feedback, participation, and competition. Personality factors are need for achievement, higher order require strength, self-assurance, and maturity.

A positive relationship between previous performance and difficulty of the goal chosen has been confirmed consistently (Garland, 1982). Thus Locke, Frederick, and Bokko (1984a) reported that experimental subjects tended to choose more difficult goals if their earlier assigned goals had been easy, and to choose easier goals if their previously assigned goals had been difficult. The subjects' performance was heavily influenced by their self-set goals. At the same time, Erez and Zidon (1984) revealed that goal acceptance moderated the relationship of goal difficulty to task performance.

Several studies examined why goal setting works. Campion and Lord (1982) proposed and confirmed a control system model of motivation in which a goal is considered a referent or desired state by which performance is compared. Then the discrepancy between the goal and actual performance creates a corrective motivation. Again, Locke, Frederick, and Bokko (1984b) introduced the concept of self-efficacy and suggested the possibility of integrating goal setting and social learning theory approaches to task performance. Also attempted has been the effort to relate the goal setting theory with the job characteristic approach (Jackson & Zedeck, 1982) and with expectancy theory (Garland, 1984; Matsui, Okada, & Mizuguchi, 1981; Mento, Cartledge, & Locke, 1980). For example, a job with clear instructions and rewards may generate goals set with more confidence, hence contribute more to task motivation than a job with ambiguous instructions and uncertain rewards.

Goal setting combines well in its effects with feedback appraisals. Ivancevich (1982) conducted a field experiment to compare the effectiveness of three appraisal interview conditions (feedback only, feedback plus assigned goal setting, and assigned goal setting) with a control group. Results indicated that the appraisal interventions were superior to the control group with regard to subordinates' reactions. Training also made a difference. Ivancevich and Smith (1981) showed that the goal setting training relying on role playing and videotaping had a positive effect on increasing salespersons' productivity. At the same time, Latham and Saari (1982) stressed the necessity of union acceptance for productivity improvement through goal setting.

EXPECTANCY AND MOTIVATION TO WORK

While expectancy theory has been widely accepted in contemporary organizational psychology, the number of studies using this theory as their basis seems to have decreased compared with the 1970s. As for the validity of the expectancy model, Kennedy, Fossum, and White (1983) and Teas (1981) examined within-subject and between-subject predictions. As predicted by the model, within-subject predictions were of greater magnitude than between-subject predictions. In predicting work effort using expectancy theory, the role of its components of expectancy, instrumentality, and valence were investigated (Ilgen, Nebeker, & Pritchard, 1981; Shiflett & Cohen, 1982). Effects tended to be modest. Clarity of linkages contributed to the observed efforts. Thus in a 32-week field experiment to study the effects of participative decision making, Neider (1980) found that increments in productivity and effort levels occurred only when the participation process clarified the effort-performance linkage and when valued outcomes were attached to high-performance levels.

COGNITIVE EVALUATION
AND MOTIVATION TO WORK

Cognitive evaluation theory has recently been receiving increased attention from organizational psychologists. The impetus for concern seems to stem mainly from the practical possibility that the introduction of extrinsic rewards for a behavior may decrease intrinsic motivation rather than add to it, because the extrinsic rewards decrease the perception of intrinsic causation (Deci, 1975). In a comprehensive review of cognitive evaluation theory, Furukawa (1982) suggested that, for extrinsic rewards to have an inhibitory effect on intrinsic motivation, the task needed to be inherently interesting, and the reward had to be administered in a contingent and salient manner under the strong situational norm of nonpayment for work. Suggesting that industrial work settings do not provide fundamentally those necessary conditions, Furukawa concluded that more research is needed to test the detrimental effect of extrinsic rewards on work motivation in actual organizational settings. A variety of other task and situational factors affect the impact of extrinsic on intrinsic motivation (Daniel & Esser, 1980; Freedman & Phillips, 1985; Pearce, 1983; Porac & Meindl, 1982). Also important are such individual differences as need for achievement (Vecchio, 1982). Moreover, a number of the studies failed to find support for the theory (Boal & Cummings, 1981; Phillips & Lord, 1980).

PROGRAMS FOR INCREASING
MOTIVATION TO WORK

So far, we have looked at the important elements in the motivational process as goals, expectancies, and combining of extrinsic and intrinsic rewards. Now we turn to specific programmatic interventions that have been seen to have an impact on motivation to work.

BEHAVIOR MODIFICATION
AND FEEDBACK PROGRAMS

The theory and application of behavioral techniques in work settings also has received renewed attention. Luthans, Paul, and Baker (1981) conducted a field experiment to investigate the effect of reinforcement technology on service employee performance. Both experimental and control groups were informed of the specific standards against which they would be measured, but only the experimental group was told of and received the contingent reinforcement, which consisted of paid time off, equivalent cash, and a chance for a paid vacation. Results showed that the experimental group had a significant improvement in performance behavior, whereas the control group's behavior remained the same.

Komaki, Collins, and Penn (1982) examined the role of performance antecedents and performance consequences. The safety performance of employees of a processing plant was monitored three times a week over 46 weeks as a baseline period. Following this, the antecedent condition was introduced involving frequent supervisor interaction and presentation of photographs on safety. Then the performance consequence (feedback) condition was followed. The results strongly confirmed that in the antecedent period there were no improvements in safety performance. However, during the consequential conditions, safety performance improved over the baseline and antecedent conditions.

The impact of the scheduling of feedback was investigated by Chhokar and Wallin (1984) who assessed the effect of varying the frequency of feedback on safety performance. The results indicated that more frequent feedback (once a week) did not always contribute to more performance improvement than less frequent feedback (once every 2 weeks). Also dealing with the feedback schedule, Saari and Latham (1982) examined employee performance and reactions to a monetary incentive administered on continuous and variable ratio schedules of reinforcement.

PARTICIPATION AND MOTIVATION TO WORK

Employee participation in decision making is believed to be a strategy to increase their motivation to work and job satisfaction. Research on whether, when, why, and how participation works have been accumulated. Schuler (1980) found support for his prediction that participation is associated with employee satisfaction when it reduces role conflict and role ambiguity, and clarifies the expectancy from performance to reward. Similarly, Neider (1980) and Lee and Schuler (1982) revealed that participation worked when it could make clear the employees' perception of effort-performance linkage.

JOB REDESIGN AND
MOTIVATION TO WORK

The job redesign model has became a dominant research area in enhancing work motivation. This approach generally includes: (1) measuring employee perceptions of task attributes in terms of skill variety, task identity, significance, autonomy, and feedback, (2) associating these perceptions with relevant outcomes such as motivation, and (3) examining certain hypothesized moderating variables. Besides those paradigms, researchers aided by the work of Terborg and Davis (1982), who proposed and evaluated a retrospective method of assessing job change, have recently begun to investigate the effects of job change caused by advanced technology. Some fundamental questions are involved. For example, incumbent's job perceptions are often assumed to reflect the objective characteristics of the job. However, when both characteristics and outcomes are addressed by an incumbent, a within-person consistency problem may arise. Algera (1983) used both independent objective assessments and incumbents' perceptions of jobs. His results showed a reliable convergence in the patterns of correlations between job characteristics and outcomes in the two forms of assessment. But, O'Brien and Dowling (1980) reported that job satisfaction was more strongly associated with congruency between desired and perceived job attributes than with perceived job attributes alone.

While it has been continuously shown that job attributes have significant influences on incumbents performance, motivation, and satisfaction (Bhagat & Chassie, 1980; D'Arcy, Syrotuik, & Siddique, 1984; Griffeth, 1985; Griffin, 1982), studies have emerged that advocate that the causality may actually be reversed. For instance, Adler, Skov, and Salvemini (1985) found that subjects given satisfaction feedback, as compared with those given dissatisfaction feedback, rated the physical environment and task characteristics as being more positive. Keller and Holland (1981) also reported that increases in performance and job satisfaction were reflected in higher ratings of job variety and autonomy. Several studies confirmed growth need strength (Griffin, 1982; Jackson, Paul, & Wall, 1981) and job longevity (Kemp & Cook, 1983) as moderators of the job complexity-satisfaction relationship.

Buchanan and Boddy (1982) examined the impact of word processing technology on the typing job. Interviews with typists revealed that the new technology had reduced task variety, meaning, control over work scheduling, feedback of results, and communication with authors. These changes were determined more strongly and directly by management decisions than the technology itself. Recently, Brass (1985) investigated the relationships among technology, job characteristics, and employee performance and satisfaction. Job characteristics influenced satisfaction and performance to the degree that appropriate matches were made with technology and job characteristics.

SMALL GROUP PROGRAMS:
THE JAPANESE EXPERIENCE

It is widely known that such small group activities as quality control (QC) circles, zero-defect (ZD) program groups, organizations of semiautonomous groups, and suggestion system groups have been contributing to enhancing workers' commitment and motivation to work in many Japanese organizations of the participating rank and file employees. The overall success of small group activities in Japan, supported by such factors as Japan's strong tradition of group importance, of lifetime employment, of promotion and wage based on seniority, of vagueness of job content, and of labor unions within the company, has led organizations in the United States, Europe, and Asian countries to introduce these activities without the present necessity of these Japanese culture-based traditions (Japanese Industrial and Vocational Training Association [JIVTA], 1982; Ross & Ross, 1982).

It was soon after the end of World War II that group dynamics, as a small group behavioral science, were introduced into Japan (Misumi, 1986). In 1949, the Japanese Group Dynamics Association was established at Kyushu University in Fukuoka. Since then, many laboratory experiments and field researches on the effectiveness of leadership and of participative decision making upon employees' motivation to work have been accumulated (Misumi, 1985). Small group activities like QC circles and ZD groups that have current popularity in Japan, however, is not necessarily matched by the available basic research on the subject. Nevertheless, the past five years have seen the publication of a variety of interesting suggestive findings. Thus Onglatco and Matsui (1984) investigated the effect of QC circle involvement upon performance effectiveness of the branch office, and work motivation and satisfaction of employees in a commercial bank. The analysis by cross-lagged correlation suggested that a high level of quality circle involvement led to improved performance at branch and section levels. And, for higher circle involvement, such factors as a cooperative atmosphere among members, a high level of performance orientation, appropriate behavior of the circle leader, and management attitudes toward circle activities were needed. It was also revealed that the effect of circle involvement on work motivation and satisfaction was moderated by circle members' growth needs.

Onglatco (1985) also contrasted 149 QC circles of a commercial bank in Japan and 66 circles of a manufacturing company in the Philippines. Circle activity had been ongoing at an average of more than 6 and 1.25 years for the Japanese and Filipino samples, respectively. Both Japanese and Filipino managers tended to see a positive contribution of circle activity toward the attainment of organizational goals. As for employees, Japanese members evaluated favorably the circle activity as a chance for work review, as enhancing thinking and judgment, and as self-beneficial. On the other hand, a majority of these same Japanese workers regarded participation in circle activities outside the scope of their work and expressed as their opinion that these activities were not voluntary, but compulsory. This was contrary to the widespread belief that activities with respect to quality circles are voluntary activities. At the same time, the majority of Filipino members were more favorably disposed toward QC activities. They preferred to continue being engaged in circle activities that were seen to be self-beneficial and interesting. The clear differences in attitudes toward QC activities between Filipino and Japanese can be interpreted in terms of the shorter duration of circle activity among the Filipinos and the higher discretion they had on whether or not to participate.

Onglatco's work points to some of the problems with small group activities in Japan. The first problem concerns the self-effacement of the individual that the small group activities may have. Continued group activity brings accumulated work improvements that lead to the optimization of the work procedures and to minimum costs. As improvement approaches near the maximum level, the room for further improvement disappears. A number of employees indicated in Onglatco's study the difficulty of continuing to generate themes that they handle.

The mannerism and formality in their activities (JIVTA, 1982) is another problem which contributes to the loss of vitality as time elapses. The clear differences of attitudes toward group activities between the Japanese and Filipino sample seems to have emerged partially as a consequence of this.

A further problem involves compulsory attendance. As noted

before, Japanese members tended to consider the activity as compulsory. Employees stated that they were forced to engage in the activity only for the sake of the requirement from management. As a result of compulsory implementation, Onglatco (1985) warned that mental health problems among members have begun to appear.

Another problem has to do with the rewards distributed by a company as a return for employees' contribution through small group activities. Employees make an effort in activities that often leads to enormous cost savings on the part of organizations. In Japan, however, employees are seldom provided any kind of financial rewards for their contribution. This is likely to make employees less motivated to engage in QC and related activities in the long run. Associated with this, Sekimoto (1985) recently found that the psychological bond between Japanese workers and organizations has been changing in its nature and is becoming weaker compared with a decade ago. This weakening will be accelerated by the accompanying collapse of traditional lifetime employment and the importance of seniority systems. Organizations will face a future in which they cannot expect employees' self-sacrifice and continuing employee effort immensed in group activities because the individual goes unrewarded for group efforts and successes.

COMMENTS FOR FUTURE RESEARCH

Motivation theory has tended to focus on individual processes. The performance of organizations, however, is frequently misunderstood, not for lack of study of individual motivation, but for lack of study of motivation at the group level. Major emphasis of future research should go into investigating how specific individual motivation combines to create collective motivation at the group level. Lawler (1982) made one step in this direction and suggested that collectively oriented behavior is motivating if it contributes to organizational performance that, in turn, is linked to intrinsic and extrinsic rewards received by the individual. Then, we may also be able to acquire useful suggestions from social psychological studies of altruistic behavior (Rushton & Sorrentino, 1981), social facilitation (Zajonc, 1965), and social loafing (Latane, Williams, & Harkins, 1979).

4

STRESS IN THE
WORKING SITUATION

CHARLES J. DE WOLFF
JACQUES A. M. WINNUBST
Katholieke Universteit
Nijmegen, The Netherlands

Stress is a relatively new field of study for work psychologists. Although the pioneering work of Kahn, Wolfe, Snoek, and Rosenthal (1964) and Kornhauser (1965) was done in the early 1960s, and some interesting studies took place during World War II (Stouffer, *The American Soldier*, 1949), the field mainly started to develop in the second half of the 1970s. Nowadays there is great interest in the subject. Out of 83 European university departments for work psychology, 21 claim to be involved in stress research; seven of these are in West Germany, five in the United Kingdom, three in the Netherlands, and two in Sweden (De Wolff, 1985).

The Annual Review on Public Health featured a chapter on "Stress and Health" by Kasl in 1984, while the *Journal of Occupational Psychology* published its first review article in 1976 (Cooper & Marshall, 1976) and *Personnel Psychology* did so in 1978 (Beehr & Newman, 1978; Newman & Beehr, 1979). Dunnette includes a chapter by McGrath (1976) in his well-known handbook.

Stress is a subject without clear boundaries. It is not only work psychologists who study the subject; the interest is not even restricted to psychologists. All types of medical and social scientists conduct research on stress and related subjects. Selye (1976) mentions that more than 100,000 publications on the subject have appeared. It is impossible for any individual to have an overview of the whole subject, and to monitor even the main publications.

This broadness has to do with the nature of the subject. Researchers are often forced to extend their studies to areas they feel are not part of their field, but belong to the domain of other disciplines. So it is not uncommon for work psychologists to include variables such as blood pressure, heart disease, epinephrine, and cortisol excretion in their studies, but pharmacologists also use models that include anxiety. The domain of stress studies includes elements of many disciplines, not only of psychology but also of physiology, neurology, endocrinology, immunology, and others.

Stress is very much an interdisciplinary field, one in which researchers can benefit from collaboration with others. Fortunately, cooperation and exchange of information is fairly common. One often finds representatives from different disciplines in laboratories, while papers by researchers from different fields (e.g., Gentry, Benson, & Wolff, 1985) are presented at many conferences. The "Dutch Stress Foundation" has been established in the Netherlands, with a scientific board of six professors in psychology and six in medicine, representing such different disciplines as immunology, pharmacy, physiology, experimental psychology, clinical psychology, and work psychology. This foundation organizes workshops and stimulates research; but it also informs the general public as well as policymakers involved in health administration and in organizations about developments in stress research (Boer, Verhage, & Wolff, 1983).

There is much exchange taking place between work psychologists and clinical, experimental, and social psychologists, as well as researchers from the rapidly expanding field of health psychology. Contrary to the differentiation process, which usually follows the establishment of a new field, stress appears to be a subject leading to some integration and at least an increased cooperation among representatives of different disciplines.

An important reason why stress has attracted so much interest has to do with the assumed consequences of being exposed to stressful conditions. In the literature many such consequences are mentioned, particularly emotional problems, mental illness, physical illness, and social deviance. Stressful conditions are assumed either to have a direct effect on these consequences or to moderate the relationship between other factors and these consequences. Statistics show that these consequences are of an appalling magnitude, which has tended to increase in the past two decades (De Wolff, 1981, 1982). Estimated costs are usually expressed in billions of dollars. The consequences cannot be attributed to a single stressful condition, but are the result of complex processes in which stressors play a more or less important role. One such issue is work disability—often stress-related. Most European countries have adopted legislation to insure workers for work disability. In the Netherlands this took place in 1968. Since then the number of individuals receiving social disability benefits has grown to about 670,000, equivalent to approximately 15% of the work force. The increase is primarily the result of illnesses of the neuromuscular system (lower backache in about 30% of the total number of cases) and mental problems (about 25%). It is particularly those workers over the age of 55 who are vulnerable; almost 50% of this category receive social benefits (GMD, 1983; De Wolff, 1981). So it has become rather uncommon that workers continue with their careers until the "normal" retirement age of 65.

Germany has similar statistics, although the figures tend to be somewhat lower (Margin, 1983). For other European countries, no data giving a satisfactory insight into these problems could be found. The Dutch and German statistics have much to do with the way social insurance is structured, and also with how the law is administered. In these respects there are substantial differences between countries. But these figures point at important developments in organizations, whereby workers experience very serious limitations in their careers, forcing them to leave the organization earlier than originally intended.

Noteworthy in all statistics about possible consequences of stress is the strong relationship to socioeconomic status. Unskilled workers suffer considerably more than skilled, clerical, and professional workers (De Wolff, 1981). Even death rates indicate substantial differences for all causes (Social Trends, 1977).

Government agencies have shown considerable interest in the subject of stress in the working situation. A number of official studies have appeared in the past 15 years. In 1973, a report entitled "Work in America," sponsored by the Department of Health, Education & Welfare in the United States, was published. In 1982 the Institute of Medicine prepared a report, "Stress and Human Health" (Elliot & Eisdorfer, 1982). In Europe, the European Community has stimulated similar studies. The Foundation for the Improvement of Living and Working Conditions in Dublin commissioned a study on stress at work (Lawrence et al., 1981). Additionally, the Commission of the European Communities began a special program ("concerted action") on "Breakdown in Human Adaptation to Stress" (1983). And in 1985 the Dutch Health Council established a committee on Stress in Organizations. Furthermore, the World Health Organization has asked several international psychological associations to prepare a report on health and psychology (Holzman et al., 1985).

Stress is a multidisciplinary field. Since so many disciplines are involved, each having their own ideas and approaches, there are many definitions of *stress*. Van Dijkhuizen (1982) counted more than forty. No one has formulated a definition that satisfies even a majority of stress researchers (Elliot & Eisdorfer, 1982). One can, however, distinguish three major approaches. In the first approach, stress is seen as a response. Selye (1936, 1976) defined stress as the nonspecific response of the body to any demand upon it. Researchers adopting this approach can be found among experimental psychologists and physiologists; they are particularly interested in physiological responses. A stimulus is seen as a stressor only if it evokes a stress response. The advantage of this approach is that it has given more insight into physiological processes. It has, however, contributed little to our knowledge about what makes a particular stimulus stressful.

The second approach has concentrated on stress as a stimulus. Kahn et al.'s 1964 study is a good example. This study addressed itself to the question: What characteristics of the job environment pose a threat to the individual? Another example is offered by Greiff (1974), who said, "Stress is used to mean those environmental factors which stimulate unhealthy, individual reactions." Many such factors such as role conflict, role overload, and role ambiguity have been identified. The studies about stressful life events (Dohrenwend & Dohrenwend, 1974) belong to this category. This approach can be seen as the complement of the first one; as it focuses on stimuli it has thus contributed to greater insight into how the environment influences the individual.

The third approach was stimulated by Lazarus (1966), who presented the viewpoint that an event can be stressful only if the individual perceived it as such, adopting a transactional view whereby stress refers to the entire phenomenon of stimuli, response, and intervening variables. This approach has been accepted by many researchers, particularly work psychologists and social psychologists. The one developed by researchers of the Institute for Social Research (Kahn, 1981) indicated how environmental factors are supposed to evoke strains and how relationships are supposed to be moderated by individual and organizational variables. Researchers at the Institute for Social Research (ISR) developed a questionnaire to measure these variables (Caplan, 1975) with psychometric properties which are quite satisfactory (Van Bastelaer & Van Beers,

1983). The ISR model of stress has been the basis for many work psychological studies. There have been many attempts to validate it, that is, to find out if stressors lead to illness (e.g., Van Beers & Van Bastelaer, 1983; Van Vucht Tijssen et al., 1978). In doing so, a number of methodological problems became apparent. Three major ones are

(a) Studies rely heavily on self reports. Questionnaires are generally used for measuring stressors as well as affective and behavioral strains. This might lead to contamination, meaning that correlations between stressors and strains cannot be attributed to stressful conditions leading to emotional and behavioral strains, but concern individual characteristics, for example, the tendency to complain. There is at least one study supporting this idea (Fineman & Payne, 1981). However, there are other studies indicating that self-reports of strains show high correlations with physiological measures such as blood pressure and heart rate (e.g., Frankenhaeuser, 1980), suggesting that these measures do have validity.

(b) A second problem concerns the time factor. The model does not specify how much time it takes before stressful conditions lead to behavioral change and change in physiological variables such as blood pressure and cholesterol level. But time is evidently an important variable. It seems likely that individuals have to be exposed for a considerable period of time before a significant change may occur. If that is the case, cross-sectional studies, whereby variables are measured only once within a relatively short time span, may not be adequate to show relationships between stressors and strains.

(c) A third problem has to do with the complexity of the model. Relationships are influenced by individual and organizational variables; for example, a stressor will lead to a particular strain when there is lack of support from relevant others. It is particularly when one studies relationships between stressors and illness that one has to deal with complex chains of relationships. Stressors might evoke different responses, depending upon different intervening variables. In such a case, correlations may be very low and nonsignificant.

As far back as 1978, Kasl stated, "Longitudinal studies will get us away from the plethora of hopeless cross sectional studies, which attack extremely complex issues with the weakest of research designs. They are found to yield uninterpretable findings in spite of the extensive effort that may go into collecting the data." He was particularly referring to correlational studies. Others have also expressed their dissatisfaction (e.g., De Wolff, 1981; House, 1980; Kahn, 1981, 1984).

Longitudinal studies have been viewed as a solution and some researchers have begun such projects. A well-known example is the Framingham study, which explored the relationship between A-type behavior and heart disease (Haynes, 1978, 1980). A few years later Nijmegen's stress research group conducted a longitudinal study among employees in a region in the Netherlands (Marcelissen, Weel, & Winnubst, 1983; Marcelissen, Weel, Winnubst, Wolff, & Leufting, 1984).

Longitudinal studies are, however, large projects posing many organizational and methodological problems to researchers. There seems to be an important strategic question: What should work psychologists attempt to accomplish through their studies?

The ISR model was introduced in the early 1970s, and, initially, discussion and research focused on the demonstration of the validity of the model: Do stressors lead to illness? Now, more than a decade later, it has become clear that we are confronted with highly complex issues, and that correlating stressors with illness is too simple an approach. Work psychologists should ask themselves to what extent they can contribute. Should they concentrate on the entire model, or limit themselves to particular areas? Since the subject is also studied by other disciplines involving other expertise, it appears that work psychologists would be better off if they directed these efforts at studying the relationships between the environment and affective and behavioral strains (i.e., the relationships in the first part of the model). Other disciplines (e.g., experimental psychology, physiology) should concentrate on the latter part (e.g., why do stressors lead to hypertension and increased level of cholesterol, and how can this lead to heart disease or ulcers). Additionally, there is still room left for collaborating studies to test larger parts of the model.

It appears that such a division of labor has more or less taken place. There is growing cooperation among experimental psychologists, neurologists, and immunologists. It has been advocated that the psychological system, the endocrine system, the brain, and the immunological systems be integrated into one large system. Insight into how stressors might lead to illness has to derive from such an approach. There are also studies by sociologists about the relationship among macrovariables such as economic conditions and cultural variables and strains.

There are, however, many other questions left for work psychologists. The past decades witnessed the appearance of a number of approaches:

Exploring stressors. Many studies have been carried out to determine which stressful conditions exist in certain occupations. Examples of these studies include those concerning middle managers (Van Vucht Tijssen et al., 1978), personnel officers (Van Beers & Van Bastelaer, 1983), nurses (Jacobson, Sharol, McGrath, & Marie, 1983), head nurses (Van de Bergh-Braam, 1981), dentists (Cooper, Mallingen, & Kahn, 1978), firemen (Kalimo, 1980), teachers (Payne, 1983), prison officers (Kalimo, 1980; Shoucksmith, 1982, 1985; Voges, Long, Roache, & Shouksmith, 1982), and women managers (Davidson & Cooper, 1983).

Such studies, most of which are field studies, using questionnaires and interviews, explore tasks as well as relationships between job incumbents and their role senders.

Relationship between technology and stress. Technological developments contribute substantially to the turbulency of the task environment. Most of the university departments studying stress also study the effects of automation and the introduction of computers. It is therefore not surprising to see that there are many studies concentrating on the impact of technology on health and well-being. Alcalay and Pasick (1983) present a review of this area. They point out that it is important to distinguish between effects on lower socioeconomic level and professional workers. For blue-collar and clerical workers, technology is often a controlling element in their work, with negative consequences. For professionals, new technology often facilitates output and may improve conditions.

Turner (1980) found that computer-based systems make the task environment more demanding and anxiety provoking, thus leading to more mental strains and a decrease of job satisfaction. Johansson and Aronsson (1984) studied the introduction of visual display units. They found that unforeseeable breakdowns in the computer system were related to a significant change in adrenaline production, blood pressure, irritation, and feelings of tenseness.

Studies on repetitive work, monotonous work, and machine-paced work have also been conducted (e.g., Cox, 1980; Frankenhaeuser, 1980; Gardell, 1976; Salvendy & Smith, 1981). Karasek makes a distinction between job demands and job decision latitude. It is particularly the combination of high job demands and low decision latitude that produces such strains as exhaustion, depression, and distorted sleep. Since decision latitude depends on the way organizations and tasks are structured, this offers opportunities for stress management. Job enrichment programs might be useful in reducing strains.

Relationship between stressors and physiological responses. Mary Frankenhaeuser and her coworkers investigated the relationship between stressors and physiological responses such as cathecholamine production, heart rate, and blood pressure. She was able to demonstrate that subjective estimates of stress by the individual concerned are substantially related to the physiological responses. Particularly interesting are the stressors she has studied, for example, defending a thesis, working overtime, using the subway in a crowded area, as well as the effects of machine-paced and monotonous work. With her experiments she has convincingly demonstrated that stressors evoke immediate physiological and endocrine responses, firmly establishing one link in the long chain between stressors and eventual illness.

Organizational variables. A considerable part of the variance of stressors and strains, including physiological strains, can be attributed to organizations and departments (Van Bastelaer, 1980). There are substantial differences in mean scores between organizations and departments. Studies have concentrated on differences between occupations, but much less upon differences between organizations. Stor (1985) reanalyzed data from a study among personnel officers working in 42 organizations. He categorized organizations on the basis of two dimensions of their task environment: simple-complex and stable-dynamic (Mintzberg, 1979). He found that personnel officers working in machine bureaucracies experience less stressors and strains, more support, and a higher level of satisfaction. In professional bureaucracies the workload is high, as are the scores on stressors and strains. The workload in all bureaucracies is high, but this is perceived by personnel officers as being meaningful. The main problem in these organizations is ambiguity. In the separate samples much stronger relationships were found between stressors and physiological strains (blood pressure and cholesterol level) than in the total sample. Studies such as this might improve one's insight into the relationship among organizations and stressors and the coping techniques developed by individuals.

Relationship with career. Several psychologists have pointed out that pursuing a career leads to demands upon individuals (Levinson

1974, 1978; Super, 1957). Within careers certain periods can be distinguished, such as "entering the adult world," "settling down," "becoming one's own man" (Hall, 1976), each period posing its own problems. It is particularly the change from one period to another, the period of transition, that is seen as difficult. Such a transition period—which has been labeled "the midlife crisis" or "midcareer crisis"—is supposed to occur at the end of the thirtieth or early fortieth year. As far back as 1967, Jaques observed a higher suicide rate among artists in that age group. He attributed it to a change in their creativity; many artists could not cope with this change.

By the time individuals in management positions and in professional work reach the age of 40 they have become settled and ask such existential questions as: What do I want to accomplish and what is the sense of spending so much effort on my work? They seek confrontation with new challenges, and might worry about what they can achieve. There might also be conflicts between the demands of work, which require them to spend long hours at the office, and the demands at home, where they are asked to spend more time looking after the children (Selles, Gerrichhauzen, & Wolff, 1985). The importance of studies about careers is that these show that demands made upon individuals and expectations that individuals have about subsequent rewards from their superiors are related to careers. Therefore, stressors and strains are also related to careers.

Unemployment. Unemployment has grown considerably in European countries over the past five years, and much concern has been expressed about its effects upon mental and physical health. Back in 1973, Gore conducted a study on the consequences of job loss. Warr also published a chapter on the subject in the *Handbook of Work and Organizational Psychology* by Drenth et al. (1984). In the United States, the National Institute of Mental Health has supported a number of studies. A bibliography about unemployment and occupational stress was written by Price and Bronfman (1984), and a detailed review of the impact of unemployment on mental illness, physical illness, and social deviance was conducted by Gordus and McAlinden (1984).

Social support. In the *Annual Review of Sociology 1979*, Goldstein wrote that social support was a subject "just beginning to be addressed by researchers, and maybe a focal point of future work." Social support is seen as an important variable, one not only influencing stressors and strains, but also the relationship between the two. Researchers utilizing the model by Kahn have used social support as a moderating variable. House (1978) gives a good overview of the subject, including a description of relevant social psychological experiments. Another review of the literature was written by Leppin (1985). Studies about moderating effects have been conducted by Reiche (1981), Winnubst, Marcelissen, and Kleber (1982), and Katz (1981).

Individual characteristics. Individual characteristics are seen as important moderator variables. Psychologists have been intrigued by type-A behavior, which is characterized by competitiveness, time urgency, and hostility. It is associated with coronary disease (Friedman & Rosenman, 1974), but recently there is also some doubt about the coronary risks involved (Appels, 1985; Myztek, 1985). It appears that this type of behavior is reinforced in organizations, particularly in management positions. Reiche (1981) found that middle managers in organizations having economic problems, score lower than those in organizations that are profitable. Several studies show the importance of A-type behavior as a moderator variable (LaRocco, House, & French, 1980; Reiche, 1981; Winnubst, Marcelissen, & Bastelaer, 1984; Winnubst, Marcelissen, & Kleber, 1983).

Coping strategies. Coping is defined in different ways by different authors. Some see it as a kind of stress management, aimed at the reduction of stress, that is, "What can be done about stress?" (Marshall & Cooper, 1981). Others see it as a process of analysis and evaluation in deciding how to protect oneself against the adverse effects of any stressors and their associated negative outcomes, yet taking advantage of its positive outcomes (Schuler, 1985). This definition concentrates on coping as a transactional process. Lazarus and Launier (1978) also take this view. Still others concentrate on the preservation of self-identity and self-esteem. There is a growing consensus that the way in which one copes with stress is an important modifier of the stress-illness relationship (Elliot & Eisdorfer, 1982). Research in work psychology is concentrated on strategies that might be useful. Schuler (1985) presents a list of 40 strategies. As many of the demands people have to meet stem from the work situation, it appears to make sense to study how people try to meet those demands. How does one cope with role conflict and role ambiguity, and with a demanding boss? Learning more about this might enable us to enlarge individual behavioral repertoires, enabling one to be better able to cope with stressful conditions.

Work psychologists have taken up different areas of stress research. They do not attempt to test the complete model, but concentrate on parts of it, particularly on questions such as "What are potentially stressful properties of organizations and of tasks?" and "What is the effect of external conditions?" Complicated problems, requiring studies on homogeneous samples, taking interactions and moderator effects into account have already arisen. The relationship between psychological variables and illness is still an interesting subject, but to prove that such relationships exist demands complicated longitudinal studies, which requires the collaborative effort of several disciplines.

PREVENTION AND INTERVENTION

Stress is not only an area of research; there is a strong need to apply the knowledge obtained through studies. Particularly since the effects of being exposed to stressful conditions can be very serious for the individual as well as for the organization and society, there are many questions about what can be done about prevention and intervention. In the last half of this chapter we will address ourselves to these questions. Thereby we will base ourselves partially on literature, but also on personal knowledge, since much of what is going on is not well documented. What we will describe is primarily the situation in the Netherlands, although we will refer to some developments in other countries. We realize that there are substantial differences between countries, due to differences in socioeconomic structures (e.g., social insurance, legal provisions) and culture. Nevertheless, we feel it is of interest to describe how the situation develops in a particular country, as this might point at what can be accomplished by using psychological expertise.

During their working life, individuals experience situations in which they have to cope with serious emotional problems. This can be due to many causes: conflicts with superiors or with colleagues, tasks that are too demanding or not challenging enough, marital problems or problems with children that interfere with doing a good job, and so on. Miner (1967, 1976) has presented a good scheme for diagnosing problems. In many cases, employees are able to solve their problems alone, or with help from friends, colleagues, superiors, or others. Occasionally, however, this is not enough, and there is a need for help from a professional. In most organizations it is not clear where such help should come from. When the ineffective performance aspect of the problem is stressed, the personnel officer usually becomes involved. Personnel management courses advocate doing so, underlining that a personnel officer can act as a third party, discussing remedial action but also keeping a file in case remedial action is not successful and legal actions (e.g., changing the employment contract) are needed.

The situation is much less clear when the emotional aspects of the problems are stressed. Personnel officers do not usually regard themselves as specialists in counseling. Many organizations do, however, employ psychologists for selection work or other services. Although managers and personnel officers often feel that these psychologists could deal with these problems, the psychologists themselves feel they are not qualified to do so, since they have had no training in clinical methods. In a number of organizations, social workers have taken on this role. External mental health institutes are, in principle, qualified to do this type of work. But psychiatrists and clinical psychologists working in these institutes have little knowledge of organizational processes and are inclined to address themselves to clients with problems of a more severe nature. Industrial health officers see such cases during their consultation hours, when the somatic complaints are usually stressed (headache, fatigue), but they also often feel inadequate in dealing with these cases (labeled as "psychosocial" cases).

There is a tendency in organizations to deny and suppress emotional problems. However, there has been a gradual recognition that individuals may be suffering from stressful conditions and may need special assistance. It appears that a "clinical work psychology" field is developing. The Netherlands Institute of Psychologists recently began to stimulate activities in this field. Several firms now employ specialized psychologists. To some extent this was stimulated by clinical psychologists, who, not being able to find employment in their own field, applied for jobs in organizations, particularly for personnel selection. Having established themselves in work psychology, they also began to take up clinical work psychology. A large multinational firm recently discussed its personnel politics in this regard. The personal responsibility of employees to solve their own problems has been stressed, but the firm is prepared to offer assistance when needed. This firm wanted to avoid any form of paternalism, as was often associated with human relations programs.

Psychologists offering such assistance stress that it should be restricted to brief periods, for example, the psychologist should limit himself or herself to approximately six sessions. In cases where more assistance is needed, clients are referred to outside mental health services by industrial health officers, social workers, and personnel officers. The methods used stem from clinical psychology and counseling psychology, and include counseling, relaxation, meditation, behavioral skill training, and cognitive restructuring. A recent review article (Murphy, 1984) presents evidence that stress management programs offer workers help in coping with stress.

Stress management can be approached from the viewpoint of the individual seeking professional help, but also from the viewpoint of the organization being concerned about the preservation of employees' competence and the quality of output. Over the past decade, many executives have expressed their concern, for example, in formal addresses, and have investigated what could be done about stress management. As a result, many companies have started programs aimed at dealing with this problem. *The Economist* recently mentioned that 20% of the 200 largest U.S. companies now have some kind of stress management program. Although many of their policies and activities are not necessarily seen as stress management, an increasing number of firms are involved in establishing sound personnel management procedures. Many of the procedures that have been developed to improve personnel management may also have a strain reducing consequence. In the next few paragraphs we will describe these activities, organizing them around a number of principles.

Early identification. It is important that problems of ineffective performance, and suffering from strains, be identified early. Intervention at an early phase is usually more successful. Studies show that changes in attitude and behavior take place in the period before employees become disabled (Van 't Hullenaar & Koningsveld, in press). It appears that periodic medical examinations and performance appraisal programs might be useful in this respect. Some industrial medical departments have used questionnaires to identify employees with complaints of a psychosocial nature.

Improvement of person environment fit. Some time ago, researchers from the Institute of Social Research in Ann Arbor suggested that improving person-environment fit might be beneficial in reducing strains. In many definitions, *stress* is seen as the result of demands that cannot be met by individuals. Thus it makes sense to pay attention to balancing demands and capabilities (e.g., Lofquist & Davis, 1969). Many organizations have programs, for example, selection, career development, training, and performance appraisal, aimed at attaining this balance.

Social support. Studies have demonstrated that social support reduces the stressfulness of conditions and that individuals experiencing support suffer less from strains. The support of one's superior and colleagues is particularly important in organizations. Leadership studies have given much attention to support and consideration. Many of the findings can be applied by organizations, for example, in the structuring of management training programs. Examples are the behavior modeling program developed by AT&T and General Electric (Burnaska, 1976; Goldstein & Sorchez, 1974; Moses & Ritchie, 1976). Self-help groups constitute another approach. These have been developed by community psychologists. These groups are very common in the United States; it is estimated there are about 500,000 of them. In Europe this approach is much less common. However, they appear to be good examples of organized support.

Reducing role ambiguity. Role ambiguity and future uncertainty are stressors with the strongest negative consequences (Kahn et al., 1964; Van Vucht Tijessen et al., 1978). Thus programs directed toward reducing ambiguity may have beneficial consequences. Ambiguity is the consequence of organizational change (restructuring, merger, close down), but also of leadership processes. Therefore, programs to facilitate organizational change (e.g., organizational development), but also personnel management programs such as goal setting and management of objectives, may lead to reduction of ambiguity.

Improving coping techniques. Individuals operating in a turbulent environment may experience that coping techniques that were successful in the past are no longer adequate. Enlarging the behavioral repertoire by learning how to deal with pressure from the environment may be a fruitful approach. A report *The Executive Under Stress* (1976) mentions that some 1,500 American firms participate in a program whereby employees attend a mental health assessment program, which includes an assessment of coping techniques.

Kahn and his coworkers kicked off their 1964 book with a bold introduction. They placed organizational stress in the perspective of modern man struggling with preserving identity in a society where organizations seek to control behavior in order to achieve its goals. When this has to be done in a turbulent environment, it inevitably leads to ambiguity and conflict. Not only do the organizations one works for demand conformity to organizational requirements; government agencies and others also require it. They do so, as this is thought to be important for a common goal, which is associated with survival and well-being.

There is now an extensive literature on stress that has made it clear how difficult it is for individuals to cope with organizational demands. In 1964, the consequences were primarily seen as mental ones; now, more than twenty years later, it is also clear that it influences health.

For work psychologists this means they should concentrate on studying the relationship between demands and individual behavior, but that they should also continue to develop intervention techniques using methods and knowledge developed in the total domain of psychology.

Stress is an interdisciplinary subject. Work psychologists have much to learn from other disciplines to understand this field; they also have something to contribute.

5

PERFORMANCE MEASUREMENT QUALITY

MICHAEL J. KAVANAGH
State University of New York
Albany, NY, USA

WALTER C. BORMAN
Personnel Decisions Research Institute
Minneapolis, MN, USA

JERRY W. HEDGE
R. BRUCE GOULD
Air Force Human Resources Laboratory
San Antonio, TX, USA

The measurement of job performance measurement is perhaps the most frequently researched topic in the behavioral sciences. Nevertheless, no comprehensive conceptual framework exists for it. One purpose of this chapter is to present such a model. It is focused on the quality of the performance measurement. We will review the major trends in the literature, such as the work on cognitive processes of raters (Ilgen & Feldman, 1983) in terms of the model.

The lack of a comprehensive conceptual framework for the measurement of job performance (Kenny, 1979) leads to numerous inconsistencies across research studies in terms of the selection of research variables, the operationalism of the levels of the variables, and the measurement of the variables. Given this state of affairs, it makes it almost impossible to generalize findings across studies to arrive at prescriptive advice for either future research or practical applications. This creates difficulties, particularly for the applied researcher who is concerned with understanding and predicting the behavior of people within organizations. The problem is acute in dealing with research and recommendations for action in any of the traditional personnel decision functions. Since performance appraisal plays a central role in determining the effectiveness of most of these decisions, the need for valid measures of job performance are needed. The model described here can guide research to establish more valid measures of individual job performance.

A JOB PERFORMANCE
MEASUREMENT QUALITY MODEL

A review of the existing literature on attempts at descriptive models of the performance measurement situation (Cummings & Schwab, 1974; DeCotiis & Petit, 1978; Kavanagh, 1982; Landy & Farr, 1980; MacKinney, 1967; Ronan & Prien, 1971; Wherry & Bartlett, 1982) revealed that, although conceptually strong, none of these provided a comprehensive picture of the job performance measurement situation. Although our model is similar in orientation to those developed by DeCotiis and Petit (1978) and Wherry and Bartlett (1982), its comprehensiveness required a deductive extension and integration of these models based on the empirical literature.

A complete description of the development of this model and a review of the empirical literature in support of it are contained in Kavanagh, Borman, Hedge, and Gould (1983). In this chapter, we will summarize the pertinent aspects of the model, its conceptual basis, and the empirical support for it.

The general model of job performance measurement quality is depicted in Figure 5.1. The development of this model involved several major considerations. First, variables were included, on the basis of theoretical literature, that could affect either job performance or its measurement. Second, measurement theory (Cronbach & Meehl, 1955; Nunnally, 1978) provided a guiding perspective. Finally, the applicability of the model for use in practical settings was an overriding concern. Although it is based on the theoretical literature, the model is descriptive rather than prescriptive because, in our judgment, hypothesized causal linkages in the model are not totally supported in the existing empirical literature.

The major reason for our conservative stance in determining the empirical support for the model lies in our definition of measurement quality, the outcome variable in Figure 5.1. The following criteria have been used to assess the quality of job performance measurement: (a) psychometric effects, that is, halo, leniency/sever-

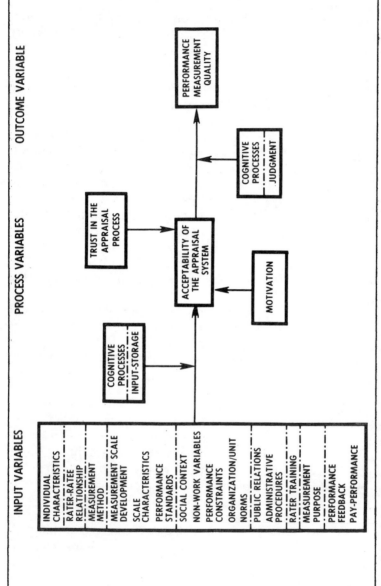

Figure 5.1 A Job Performance Measurement Classification Scheme

ity, and range restriction; (b) interrater reliability; (c) content validity; (d) rate discriminability; (e) construct validity; and (f) accuracy. Although the first four criteria are important indices of performance measurement quality in certain circumstances, our position is that accuracy and construct validity are the primary criteria to be used for the evaluation of the quality of the measurement. Thus in judging the applicability of research to test the hypothesized linkages in the model, only those studies employing these latter two criteria were totally acceptable. Research using the first four criteria provided only tentative acceptance for linkages in the model. For our purposes in this chapter, the existence of some support is all that is necessary to accept the possible viability of the hypothesized linkages in the model. Readers interested in the relative strength of these linkages are referred to Kavanagh et al. (1983).

The input variables in Figure 5.1 are characteristics of the measurement system, the organization, and the people that can affect the quality of the measurement—the independent variables. The empirical literature linking these systems and person characteristics to measurement quality is enormous (Kavanagh et al., 1983). These input variables in Figure 5.1 are, in fact, categories of variables. For example, *individual characteristics* include personality, interpersonal trust, rater sex, and rater intelligence. Based on an exhaustive review (Kavanagh et al., 1983), evidence relating all of these variables to measurement quality exists; however, some of the linkages have stronger empirical support than others.

The process or intervening variables in Figure 5.1 reflect current thinking in the performance appraisal literature (Borman, 1977; Dipboye & dePontbriand, 1981; Feldman, 1981; Ilgen & Feldman, 1983; Murphy, Garcia, Kerkar, Martin, & Balzer, 1982). The acceptability variable is hypothesized to moderate the relationship between the independent and dependent variables (Kavanagh, 1982; Lawler, 1967), and thus directly affects the quality of measurement. Although there is evidence linking this variable with the system/rater characteristics, there is no empirical evidence showing its direct link to performance measurement quality (Kavanagh et al., 1985). This is clearly an avenue for research.

The cognitive variables have been placed outside the main causal link to indicate that they could act as intervening variables. When the measurement method relies heavily on human judgment (e.g., ratings) we expect these variables to have an impact on quality. The cognitive variables have been divided into two categories. The first is concerned with the observational heuristics that people use when gathering and storing information about an individual's job performance. The second category involves judgment or decision heuristics that people use in assigning a quantitative index to the performance of a person on a job. This division of the rating process into two sets of cognitive variables may provide a solution to the search for a single cognitive variable, such as cognitive complexity (Bernardin, Cardy, & Carlyle, 1982), which relates to measurement quality. Recent work (Hedge, 1982; Murphy et al., 1982; Ruddy, 1985) indicates that considering observation and decision processes separately may help to explain better their effects on measurement quality. This is also consistent with Wherry's theory (Wherry & Bartlett, 1982), which postulates that observation and recall by the rater are two separate components of the observed score.

The final intervening variable, rater motivation, although emphasized in the theoretical literature, has received little attention in research. Only three studies, within the performance appraisal context, have included this variable (Bernardin & Cardy, 1982; Bernardin, Orban, & Carlyle, 1981; DeCotiis & Petit, 1978). We still consider this an important variable, and one that clearly is in need of further study as it relates to measurement quality.

An important aspect of Figure 5.1 is that it provides a general model on which more specific measurement quality models can be built. If one takes either the measurement method or measurement purpose variables from the list of system/rater characteristics, a separate measurement quality model could be built for differences in these variables. For example, using different types of measurement methods, one could build hypothesized measurement quality models for supervisor ratings, peer ratings, self-ratings, observational techniques, work samples, or production records. These models would differ in the weights and importance assigned to the independent and intervening variables. A good analogy would be to consider the variables in Figure 5.1 as elements in a moderated multiple regression equation. One would expect the beta weights to change for the various terms in the model as the type of method used changed. These differing regression equations would then represent the hypothesized measurement quality models for each of the measurement methods under study.

In sum, we have presented a general model of performance measurement quality that has significant support in both the theoretical and empirical literature (Kavanagh et al., 1983). We feel it can serve as a guide to both research and practice. Before discussing some of these implications, we will examine current trends in the performance appraisal literature, and how they relate to this model of performance measurement quality.

CURRENT TRENDS IN THE FIELD

In the past five years, there has been a general increase in emphasis on performance appraisal, and, in particular, on improved quality of the job performance measurement system. Perhaps this is due to a recognition that, as Kavanagh (1982) noted, performance appraisal provides the key dependent variable against which most personnel decisions are validated. In addition to this increased emphasis in personnel decisions, the following trends have appeared in the literature: (a) a focus on cognitive processes in performance evaluations; (b) increased concern with the appraisal interview and performance feedback processes; (c) reduced emphasis on rating formats; (d) more attention to quality of measures, particularly accuracy; (e) increased examination of rater training programs; (f) concerns over legal aspects in the use of performance appraisal; and (g) increased attention to the gulf between research and practice in the field of performance appraisal.

Three of these trends gained impetus due to the appearance of the Landy and Farr (1980) review on performance ratings. It led to a decreased research emphasis on differences in rating scale formats, an increased research emphasis on the cognitive processes in performance ratings, and more attention to the processes involved in the feedback of job performance results to employees. Much of the work on cognitive factors in the performance rating and human judgment is summarized in Ilgen and Feldman (1983) and DeNisi, Meglino, and Cafferty (1984), and this literature has helped provide a better *understanding* of the cognitive processes persons use when judging others' job performance. Since our model contains cognitive variables, we see little difficulty integrating this research with our model, however, the research on cognitive processes has typically used these variables as independent, rather than intervening, variables as indicated in our model. We see this as a fruitful avenue for research, and may help to clarify some of the conflicting evidence regarding the effects of both the independent and process variables in Figure 5.1 on performance measurement quality (Kavanagh et al., 1983).

Although this increased emphasis on cognitive variables in research on performance appraisal will aid in understanding, it will have little immediate impact on the practical uses of performance appraisal. As Kavanagh et al. (1983) noted, if we discover that certain cognitive characteristics are related to more accurate ratings, it is impractical to expect that we can select raters on this basis. Further, it is unlikely that training can affect the cognitive characteristics of a person, which are probably quite stable. These concerns were recently echoed by Banks and Murphy (1985) when they expressed their opinions regarding the research-practice gap in performance appraisal, a topic to which we will return.

The decreased emphasis on rating scale formats and increased attention to the performance feedback process is consistent with the argument made by Kavanagh (1982) regarding confusion between the *form* and the *system* in performance appraisal. The search for the "perfect" rating form is senseless, since the form is imbedded within the context of the organizational system. Thus changing to a new format will have little effect if the other characteristics of the performance appraisal system remains the same. The way in which feedback regarding job performance is given is part of that system. The importance of feedback processes has been emphasized recently by Stone and Stone (1985) and Taylor, Fisher, and Ilgen (1984). They indicate that the manner in which performance feedback is provided to employees may well be the most important variable in changing future work behaviors. From the standpoint of the model in Figure 5.1, feedback processes can affect measurement quality through their effects on the rater-rate interpersonal relationships.

Both of these trends in the literature can be fit into the model in Figure 5.1 as input or independent variables. As seen, all of the independent variables can affect the measurement quality, a point consistent with the argument that the total system for performance appraisal needs attention. In terms of research, the search for a more "perfect" rating form should cease. The current technology to build "behaviorally based" rating forms is well perfected, and should be used. The choice of a specific format within the family of behaviorally based forms should be made on other practical considerations, for example, whether the employees will like and use the form. This redirects effort from an overly meticulous concern with format to ease of use criteria for choice of a specific rating form.

Another trend, the increased emphasis on accuracy in performance appraisal, based on the approach promulgated by Borman, Haugh, and Dunnett (1976), has led to a redefinition of the research paradigm in performance appraisal. As noted in Kavanagh et al.

(1983), there have been multiple dependent variables used in determining the effectiveness of different types of performance appraisal systems and forms, however, accuracy or construct validity (Kavanagh, MacKinney, & Wolins, 1971) must be the crucial criterion for evaluating the quality of a measure of individual job performance. This trend is clearly reflected in the model in Figure 5.1, in fact, it is the focal point of the model. In terms of both research and practice, this means more attention needs to be paid to the accuracy of performance appraisals. Currently, most of the accuracy research is being done in experimental, contrived settings. More attention must be paid to conducting performance appraisal accuracy research in "real" settings.

The work on the walk-through performance testing (WTPT) method being done by the Air Force Human Resources Laboratory (AFHRL) (Gould & Hedge, 1983) is targeted at this issue. The WTPT method focuses on the measurement of job performance at the smallest task unit. It combines aspects of work sampling, observation, and interviewing of job incumbents to measure job performance effectiveness using predetermined scoring categories. This provides a high-fidelity measure of individual technical job competence. Comparing the results of this measure to more global ones like peer, supervisory, and self-ratings will provide evidence as to the accuracy of these latter, more subjective, measures. The practical implications of this work done on this AFHRL project should have significant effects on the types of measures chosen to assess most accurately individual job performance in our organizations.

The trends in the literature on increased emphasis on rater training and the legal implications of performance appraisal are a part of the overriding concern with the gulf between research and practice in this field. (Banks & Murphy, 1985; Bernardin & Villanova, 1986; Kavanagh et al., 1983). This orientation is completely consistent with the implications of the performance measurement quality model discussed earlier. As Banks and Murphy (1985, p. 343, italics added) observe: "We suggest that one way to achieve coordination (between scientists and practitioners) is for both to undertake the task of determining *how to increase appraisers' use of valid input data in appraisal decisions.*" The primary purpose of the model developed for performance measurement quality (Figure 5.1) is to increase the validity of the data used in performance appraisal. Thus we would argue that this model be used as a guide for both researchers and practitioners in examining ways to make their performance appraisal systems produce more valid data for use in personnel decisions.

The increased concern over meeting legal guidelines for the use of performance appraisals in organizations in the United States has provided a well-defined set of guidelines for the development and use of performance appraisals in organizations (Cascio & Bernardin, 1981). As these authors emphasize, the results of litigation have underlined what we already know to be proper practice in the use of performance appraisals in our organizations. However, with the weight of legal sanction behind it, this prescriptive advice for practice may eliminate some of the faulty and erroneous uses of performance appraisals. The prescriptions provided by Cascio and Bernardin (1981) provide a convenient checklist for anyone either developing a new performance appraisal system or revising an old one.

As can be seen in Figure 5.1, rater motivation is included as an intervening variable in this model. Bernardin and Villanova (1986) found 34 studies of rater training over the past five years. Unfortunately, as noted by Bernardin and Villanova, this increased attention to rater training has largely been concerned with student raters in experimental contexts, thus limiting the generalizability of results to real organizational settings. They further note an absence of concern over motivational variables in rater training, which may account for the weakness of the applicability of the results. This latter shortcoming was also noted by Kavanagh et al. (1983). In rater training research, rater motivation is often ignored, or treated as "noise" to be controlled experimentally. We find this not only inconsistent with reality, but also severely limiting of progress in the development and use of rater training programs in organizational settings.

These considerations underline perhaps the most important trend in the field of performance appraisal, namely, bridging the gap between researchers and practitioners. The entire purpose of the Kavanagh et al. (1983) paper was to provide practical suggestions, from an examination of the research literature, for building a performance measurement system for use in the military. The resultant model (Figure 5.1) is currently being used by the AFHRL to develop such a system. Banks and Murphy (1985), addressing the gap between research and practice, argue that much of the problem is a failure to distinguish between a rater's capability and willingness to make good quality ratings. Keeping this distinction in mind may, in these authors' opinion, help to narrow that gap.

Finally, Bernardin and Villanova (1986) propose a modal criterion setting to help assess the generalizability of appraisal research to organizational settings. By integrating features of this modal criterion setting into research, the results can be more easily used by practitioners. The common theme being emphasized by these authors, and being reemphasized in this chapter, is that we must shift our focus in performance appraisal research from the laboratory to real organizations. Perhaps we are at the beginning of a new era in research and practice in this field wherein laboratory research has matured to the point that incremental knowledge can be obtained only through applied field research.

SUMMARY AND CONCLUSIONS

We have presented a descriptive model of performance measurement quality that can be used to guide applied research in the field of performance appraisal. The results of an extensive literature review (Kavanagh et al., 1983) provided strong support for the linkages of the model, and a consideration of current trends in the field found them to be consistent with the orientation of the model. The field of performance appraisal has grown rapidly in the past five to ten years in terms of theory, research, and practice. We have covered a number of these trends in the field, but must again underscore the need to narrow the gap between research and practice. The recognition of this gap is a healthy indication of the maturity of the field, and suggests the need for a new orientation to the study of performance measurement. It is suggested that our current paradigms and methods may be inadequate to capture and explain incremental variance in our dependent variable, performance measurement quality. More controlled field research, recognition of the many organizational factors that can influence measurement quality, and comparisons of frequently used subjective measures (ratings) with high-fidelity ones, such as the WTPT method, should help in these future efforts. With these directions, we anticipate a much closer relationship and continued growth in the importance of performance appraisal to the management of our organizations.

6

PERSONNEL RECRUITMENT AND SELECTION

VIVIAN SHACKLETON
NEIL ANDERSON
*Aston University
Management Centre
Birmingham, U.K.*

Overlapping and simultaneous developments have taken place in Britain in personnel recruitment and selection in the last 5 years. There have been particular trends and themes in the academic and management literature. Concurrently, the external social, economic, political, and legislative environment have influenced and interacted with the academic and management developments. The external changes include the levels of unemployment, legal constraints, and professionalism on the practice of personnel recruitment and selection. To put the literature to be reviewed in context, an overview of the scene, particularly in Britain, will be described first.

OVERVIEW

THE LAW

Legal issues, particularly regarding discrimination surrounding selection methods in Britain, are nowhere near as important as in the United States. A number of employment law statutes have been enacted in Britain through the 1970s that conferred rights on the individual at work (Equal Pay Act, 1970; Contracts of Employment Act, 1972, modified in 1974 and 1975; Sex Discrimination Act 1975; Race Relations Act, 1976). They imposed fair practices on recruitment and selection as well as legal restrictions and constraints on dismissal. Both "direct" and "indirect" discrimination (the latter term close in meaning to "adverse impact" in the United States) on the grounds of race or sex are prohibited under law. The British

68

Psychological Society and the Runneymede Trust (1980) published guidance on how to comply with the legislative requirements.

These early Acts have in part been reversed by more recent legislation. For example, the Employment Act, 1980, restricts previously established rights to compensation and (in some cases) reemployment for unfair dismissal.

Surprisingly, discrimination in selection and recruitment has received relatively little coverage in the U.K. personnel or academic literature over the last five years, in direct contrast to the United States and elsewhere. There is some debate in the U.K. as to the extent to which employers are complying with the law. Lewis (1984) reported that organizations are prepared to operate within the spirit of the law. Also, "fair selection" is receiving greater interest judging from reports by U.K. suppliers of tests and interviewer training (Lewis, 1984). On the other hand, Keenan and Logue (1985) suggested that employers are commonly not complying with requirements of the antidiscrimination legislation as it applies to recruitment and selection procedures. Apart from mostly impressionistic evidence though, the impact of the legislation on personnel practice in Britain is hard to gauge.

UNEMPLOYMENT

Unemployment in Britain has recently reached postwar records. At the time of writing (February 1986) there are three and a quarter million people registered as unemployed. This represents approximately 13% of the work force. The same or worse is true of many countries in the European Common Market, including Belgium, the Netherlands, and Italy.

Has this recession and consequent high levels of unemployment in the last five years had an effect on recruitment and selection? The answer from a survey conducted by the London School of Economics (Wood, 1982) suggests that there have been few changes. The main effect on recruitment has been to intensify and reinforce existing methods and policies. Wood reported that "the recession has simply accentuated the tendency to use the cheapest and perhaps most reliable channel—namely social networks" (p. 40). As far as selection is concerned, there was some evidence that personnel specialists have employed more stringent definitions of job stability or age requirements, to the detriment of job hoppers and the elderly. But most of the effect has been on manning levels or working practices rather than on recruitment or selection.

Certainly it seems that the opportunity provided by high selection ratios and ease of recruitment, for those employers who are recruiting, has not been used to evaluate and overhaul existing practices.

THE PERSONNEL
(HUMAN RESOURCE) MANAGER

One might have expected greater attention to improved personnel selection in an "employers' market," with its high levels of unemployment, and greater responsivity by personnel specialists to the considerable developments in organizational psychology. This has not been the case. In fact, recruitment and selection practices within the U.K. are characterized primarily by a notable lack of sophistication and second only by considerable differences among organizations in terms of sophistication of approach.

One major study covering 335 companies (Gill, 1980) reported over 90% of respondents relied upon the interview to select executives, with only 10% using psychometric tests and an almost negligible 5% conducting some form of group assessment technique. Of those surveyed, 24% used no job description as part of their recruitment procedures; 16% did not incorporate career history into their application forms. More disturbing still is the evidence to suggest that little or no advances occurred between 1971 and 1980. A survey by Kingston in 1971 of 200 companies yielded results similar to those of Gill in 1980.

This unquestioning reliance on the interview as the mainstay of the selection process is doubtlessly nurtured by an abundance of normative, prescriptive texts founded on opinions and anecdotal evidence that are aimed at the practitioner. We can only echo the calls of Fletcher (1985a), Herriot (1985), and others (e.g., Spurgeon, Patrick, & Michael, 1984; Wingrove, Glendinning, & Harriot, 1984) for enhanced sophistication through methodical, substantiated, research findings.

COMPUTERS

There is steady development of the use of computers for recruitment and selection. Reports in the popular press (e.g., *Fortune International*, October, 1983) as well as in the academic literature (e.g., Casper, 1985) increase in frequency. Most of the applications at the present time involve candidate screening. Briefly, such systems perform the task of comparing applicant details against established screening criteria to produce a candidate short-list. However, such methods fall within the provisions of the U.K. Data Protection Act (1984). This statute regulates the storage of personal information on computerized systems and also confers rights on the applicant. For example, the applicant has the right to demand a copy of the details held on file and, more important, knowledge of the criteria of assessment. Little evaluative research has been provided as yet, but we can expect further developments and research in the next five years.

MAJOR RESEARCH AREAS

The main themes of research in the last five years are reviewed below.

RECRUITMENT AND SELECTION: A TWO-WAY PROCESS

There has been growing recognition that recruitment is a two-way process (e.g., de Wolff & van den Bosch, 1984; Herriot, 1985; Torrington & Chapman, 1983), with more research being conducted into the procedures of the employer. Herriot and Rothwell (1981) found that career information issued by organizations to engineering students had a significant impact on their intentions to apply. Quaglieri (1982), however, found that applicants tended to obtain more specific and accurate information through more informal sources such as discussions with friends already employed by the organization.

The actual extent to which recruitment procedures affect applicants' intentions is, however, clouded by contradictory findings. Powell (1984) concluded that this influence may have been overstated in the literature, but Boudreau and Rynes (1985) argued that in fact recruitment procedures "alter the characteristics of applicants to whom selection procedures are ultimately applied." This is an interesting contention in view of the concentration of current research on selection techniques to the virtual exclusion of recruitment procedures.

Significantly, in a review of previous studies into the relative influence of administrative procedures, assessment methods and recruiter behavior on candidates' reactions, Rynes, Heneman, & Schwab (1980) concluded that recruiter behavior is the most important.

Thus, in general, the quality of new recruits depends on an organization's recruitment practices. If one also considers the conclusions of research into interviewer behavior (to be dealt with later) the quality of selection also depends on the caliber of candidate willing to accept an offer of employment.

It is patently obvious that recruitment procedures should be conceptualized as a two-way process, but it remains uncertain as to why research in this area has for so long been predominantly one-sided.

THE SELECTION INTERVIEW

Despite numerous reviews spanning several decades that consistently concluded that the interview has unacceptably low validity and reliability (e.g., Arvey & Campion, 1982; Schmitt, 1976; Ulrich & Trumbo, 1965; Wagner, 1949; Wright, 1969) it is still overwhelmingly popular in the U.K. (Fletcher, 1981; Gill, 1980; Herriot, 1985) and elsewhere.

In recent years, the overall trend in published interview research has been for studies to become more microanalytic in approach. Monahan and Muchinsky (1983) reported a marked decline since the 1950s in studies adopting a macroanalytic strategy.

Validating the Interview

Guion (1976) provided the classic article applying the principles of psychological measurement to personnel selection, particularly to test validation. Reviewing developments in testing prior to 1950, he propounded the "tenets of orthodoxy" in selection and argued that both criterion-related validities (i.e., predictive and concurrent) and descriptive validities (i.e., content and construct) must be considered. He concluded that "validity is not singular, and it is erroneous to speak of 'the validity.'"

Nevertheless, in a major departure from the previously accepted approach to validating the interview primarily by actuarial means, Herriot (1984) advocated a wider perspective. Through applying attribution theory and role theory to the interview, he argued that the interview should not be "conceptualized as a psychometric device . . . [but] as a social episode with somewhat ambiguous rules." Low interview validity coefficients (e.g., Reilly & Chao, 1982) results from "confusion about roles and objectives." Certainly, other research supports Herriot's argument that the expectations of both parties may differ considerably (e.g., Fletcher, 1981, 1985; Taylor & Sniezek, 1984). Interestingly, Herriot and Rothwell (1983) concluded that both parties expected the other to talk for a greater proportion of the time than they actually did, and so as a result their expectations were commonly not met. For Herriot (1984), the interview is an encounter and should be validated as a social negotiation, not as a psychometric tool.

Arvey and Campion (1982) outlined reasons why the interview remains so popular despite such adverse validity study findings. These include the suggestion that the interview fulfills wider purposes than merely assessment, such as selling the job to the candidate, as well as the faith of the interviewer in his or her own judgment. Certainly the interview has considerably wider objectives than those pertaining to tests, and so perhaps may not be expected to attain comparable validity coefficients.

Interviewer-Interviewee Interaction

Recent literature on the interview itself contains a more interactive (or "two-way") approach with a few texts (e.g., Bayne, 1982; Shackleton & Fletcher, 1984; Webster, 1982) and several studies adopting this focus. Previous studies suggested the importance of the candidate's verbal and nonverbal behavior on the outcome of the interview (e.g., Forbes & Jackson, 1980; Imada & Hakel, 1977; McGovern & Tinsley, 1978; Rasmussen, 1984) but as Keenan and Wedderburn (1975) and Keenan (1976) concluded, the behavior of the interviewer is significantly influential also. More recent findings indicate that any positive nonverbal behavior emitted by the interviewer tends to increase the desire of the candidate to accept a job offer and, most important, is often construed by the candidate as being indicative of their chances of success (Campion, 1980; Rynes & Miller, 1983).

Snyder (1974) and Snyder and Simpson (1984) have proposed the construct of "self-monitoring." This is defined by Snyder (1974) as "self-observation and self-control guided by situational cues to social appropriateness." It seems likely that self-monitoring would enhance both the interviewer's and the interviewee's performance. We can probably expect research to be forthcoming on its application to the selection interview.

Lewis (1980) considered a counseling skills approach to be an effective interview style. He argued that interviewers should be both "supportive" and "confronting" in their behavior. Although

Lewis (1985) described three major interviewer qualities (empathy, genuineness, and sincerity), more specific verbal and nonverbal behaviors were not identified. On the other hand, Herriot (1984) suggested that if interviewers are too informal, the role expectations of the interviewee are not fulfilled, and thus an interactive barrier is created.

Clearly, research in this area is in its early stages of development, but such studies hold considerable academic promise as well as extensive practical applications. It remains to be seen whether more detailed studies can identify more specifically those behaviors that relate to effective performance by both interviewer and interviewee.

Discrimination

Rather surprisingly, racial and sexual discrimination by interviewers has received scant attention by researchers in spite of wide-ranging legislative provisions.

Both Arvey (1979) and Mullins (1982) found black applicants received no less favorable ratings at interviews than white applicants. However, Arvey found that consistently lower evaluations were given to female candidates than to male, and this finding has been replicated by Cann, Siegfried, and Pearce (1981) and Keenan and Logue (1985).

Other areas of interviewer bias remain virtually unresearched, such as the effects of age of applicant and physical or mental disabilities. We would agree with Arvey that this is an area badly in need of more research.

The Situational Interview

One final development in interviewing technique shows particular promise. This is the "situational interview" (Latham & Saari, 1984; Latham, Saari, Pursell, & Campion, 1980). Based on the outcome of systematic job analysis, critical incidents of job behavior are identified. Questions are then formulated based on these incidents of the "what would you do in this situation?" type. Candidates' hypothetical answers are rated by the interviewer on 5-point Likert-type scales. The Latham and Saari (1984) study indicated a significant validity coefficient between candidates' answers and their subsequent behavior on the job. Interrater reliability coefficients of .76 and .79 and validity coefficients of between .30 and .46 have been reported by Latham and associates.

Similarly, Fletcher (1985a) argued for a radical revision of the questioning strategies of the interviewer. He advocated the use of future-related questions, rather than questions requiring the interviewee to justify past behavior. This would clearly entail some fundamental changes to the current style of interviewing favored by many personnel specialists.

SELF-EVALUATION

There is some controversy over whether self-evaluation (or self-assessment) can be recommended as a valid and reliable technique. It is a truism that there is, and always has been, self-evaluation by the applicant in the early stages of recruitment (on the basis of advertisement details, for instance) with only those considering themselves to be competent applying. More recently this technique has been conducted both in the latter stages of recruitment (e.g., by self-score tests prior to interviews) and in the selection interview and subsequent decision-making process itself.

In a review of 55 studies comparing self-evaluation with, for the most part, tests or supervisors ratings, Mabe and West (1982) obtained a mean validity coefficient of .29 with a standard deviation of .25. On the other hand, Shrauger and Osberg (1981) reviewed 43 predictive studies of which 29 found results that favored self-assessment, 10 favored other methods (interviews, biodata, and so on), in three studies the two approaches tied, and in the remaining study the outcome was indefinite.

However, the conditions under which self-evaluation is carried out vary widely (see also Heneman, 1980) and this may fundamentally determine the effectiveness of this technique. Fletcher (1985a) supported the viability of self-evaluation as long as certain conditions are fulfilled. These conditions are synthesized from Shrauger and Osberg and from Mabe and West. They center upon eliciting an honest assessment from the individual through informing him or her of the objectives of the assessor and ultimately through cross-validating any assessment with information gained from other sources and through feedback to the individual. Self-evaluation would also appear to be most effective with intelligent applicants who have a high internal locus of control, Fletcher argues.

Intuitively, self-evaluation seems to have considerable potential, currently underresearched and underexploited. It is our contention that Reilly and Chao's (1982) conclusion "based on the research available, self-evaluation cannot be recommended as a promising alternative" (to psychometric testing) is erroneous. Clearly more research would be beneficial, particularly if its basis were that of predictive validity or assessment-reassessment reliability. The balance of existing evidence, however, supports Fletcher's (1985) opinion that "we should make more use of self-assessment or, at the very least, experiment with its use" (p. 10).

BIODATA

Muchinsky (1983) has said that if Academy Awards were given for the most consistently valid predictor, then biodata would be the winner. Biodata (short for biographical data) can be defined as historical and verifiable pieces of information about an individual (Asher, 1972) in a selection context, usually reported on application forms.

The test-retest reliability of biodata is good (Owens, Glennon, & Allbright, 1966) though whether they are accurate in the sense of not being faked by applicants is more open to dispute (Cascio, 1975; Goldstein, 1971).

Studies of the criterion-related (mostly concurrent rather than predictive) validity of biodata has continued to show impressive results, supporting the statement by Muchinsky quoted above. Reilly and Chao (1982) reviewed a large number of different selection procedures and concluded that only biodata and peer evaluation had validities to match those of tests.

Two rather different ways of using biodata exist in Britain (Savage, 1985). One relies on statistical modeling and prediction equations based on multiple regression, factor analysis, and the interaction of moderator variables to link individual responses to criterion measures. A problem with this method is that the equations frequently prove much less valid when cross-validated (Zedeck, 1971). An alternative approach, described by Matteson (1978) and Brush and Owens (1979), is less rigorously empirical and has a simpler method of assigning item weights. It sets behavioral criteria of job performance and designs the questionnaire on similar patterns of behavioral factors. This makes the results more intuitively understandable and the questionnaire more adaptable. Mitchell and Klimoski (1982) reported that this method is equally valid, although the problem of cross-validation remained.

The combined effects of a large number of young people coming into the job market, coupled with very favorable selection ratios resulting from high levels of unemployment, have encouraged some industrial and commercial organizations to conduct biodata studies in Britain since 1980. However, hardly any of these studies are reported in journals. Presumably this is because there is little incentive for such organizations to publish. Also, perhaps they fear that publicity concerning predictor items may lead to cheating, with applicants making use of the information to pick the answer most likely to get them selected. One exception to this lack of published work is an article by Savage (1985). He reported validity results from 13 studies conducted in Britain between 1982 and 1985 and involving 969 people. The method adopted was the second of the two types (i.e., the Matteson, 1978, approach) described above. A weighted mean validity coefficient of .57 with a range from .39 to .87 was obtained. In only two cases was cross-validation attempted, but the results are encouraging. In one case, a concurrent validity of .41 became .51 on cross-validation and, in the other, an initial validity of .50 became .40, a shrinkage of 20% of the predictor variance. Savage concluded that with thorough job analysis and a framework of behavioral categories, biodata validities continue to live up to their earlier promise.

ASSESSMENT CENTERS

An *assessment center* (AC) has been defined in a British review by Fletcher (1982) as consisting of the "assessment of a group of individuals by a team of judges using a comprehensive and integrated series of techniques." A similar, though much more detailed, definition has been published in the United States by leading practitioners in the field (Task Force on Assessment Center Standards, 1980). One essential feature of ACs is their use of multiple-assessment techniques including interviews, psychometric instruments, simulations such as in-basket exercises, written exercises, group exercises, and peer assessment. So it is appropriate that the AC comes late in this review, which has already discussed many of the measures. The assessments are used, though, not only for (usually management) selection, but also for training, promotion, and career development.

One theme in the literature concerns establishing the reliability of ACs. Tenopyr and Deltjen (1982) pointed out that making generalized statements about AC reliability is not a straightforward task, given the variety of different techniques that go to make up a typical AC and its final overall rating of participants. This has resulted in it being a much underresearched area. We are not much further forward than we were after the classic studies of the War Office Selection Board (WOSB) in Britain (Vernon & Parry, 1949) and the AT&T studies in the United States (Bray, Campbell, & Grant, 1974; Bray & Grant, 1966; Moses, 1973). These, plus a small study by McConnell and Parker (1972), are excellent attempts at alternate forms reliability and have given coefficients of about .7.

In fact, such reliability evidence as there is has mostly to come from studies of the separate exercises and ratings that are the component parts of the AC rather than the final overall rating. An interrater reliability study of group exercises by Jones (1981), for example, yielded coefficients of .7, though with increases in reliability after discussion suggesting pooling of judgments. A review of simulation of "work sample" literature by Robertson and Kandola (1982) quoted little reliability evidence but what there was suggested coefficients around .3 for in-basket and dyadic role plays. Reliability evidence on the interview has already been cited, though not all ACs use interviews. Reliabilities of psychometric instruments, on the other hand, are likely to be acceptable.

Unlike reliability, there is no shortage of validity evidence, though much of it concerns content validity. Thus Fitzgerald and Quaintance (1982) quoted a large number of validity studies among their survey of 115 ACs in U.S. state and local government organizations but nearly all were content validity studies. Content validity alone is not enough, especially since it may be better described as "content-oriented test development" (Dunnette & Borman, 1979). Other, criterion-related, validity evidence should be sought.

There have been a number of excellent reviews of the criterion-related validity of ACs, such as Finkle (1976) and Thornton and Byham (1982). Relatively little if any of the research comes up to the standard of the seminal AT&T studies either in scope or methodology. They have often relied on supervisors ratings as the criterion, for example. Bray and Campbell (1968) earlier commented that "the assessment center might have been considered not sufficiently accurate for use if supervisory judgment had been relied upon as the sole criterion." And validity coefficients, though usually quite respectable, have rarely been as high as the AT&T work. Meta analysis by Schmitt, Gooding, Noe, and Kirsch (1984) of 21 ACs showed an average validity coefficient of .407.

A study by Schmitt et al. (1984) used a number of interesting criteria in the AC with school administrators. The AC consisted of simulations, including two in-baskets, a group exercise, and an interview. Administrators' overall ratings from the AC were significantly correlated with performance ratings by teachers and supervisors but not with ratings by support staff or student ratings of school climate. It would seem that AC validity based on supervisors ratings may not be supported when other criteria are employed. This lends weight to the argument that we may be misled in our faith in the AC when many reported validity studies place reliance on a very limited range of criteria.

REFERENCES

Recent research findings support the long-suspected view among organizational psychologists that most references are virtually useless as screening devices. The opinion has been vindicated that reference letters commonly contain little or no specific, relevant information and such details that are included are mostly indefinite and inaccurate.

Muchinsky (1979) considered the question of the value (or the "supplementary validity") of the reference. Quoting Mosel and Goheen's findings (1952, 1959) that 80% of reliabilities fell below .40, while correlation with supervisory ratings was $-.12$, he concluded that the reference is of little real value. Similarly, Reilly and Chao (1982) calculated an average predictive validity of .14 on the basis of the results of ten studies (n = 5,718). Baxter, Brock, Hill, and Rozelle (1981) analyzed the content of 80 references concerning 40 student applicants for university places and found descriptions to be mainly "nondiscriminative, nonconsensual, and nondifferentiative."

Thus it is reasonable to conclude that the effectiveness of the reference letter as a screening device is highly dubious. Its popularity, however, remains unscathed. Beason and Belt (1976) found 82% of responding organizations used references while Kingston (1971) reported 88% of those surveyed either contacted previous employers or requested reference details.

Within the British context, it is probable that the reference is as widely used today as during the 1970s. This is in contrast to the United States, for example, where recent legislative developments have restricted the inclusion of personal details in references.

Our contention is that in the light of the research findings such usage should be limited to factual checks of biographical information (e.g., "Did applicant X hold this position for this period of time as claimed?") to the exclusion of requests for opinions relating to personality characteristics, suitability for the position, and so on.

TESTING

Testing in Britain has not been stifled in the same way as it was in the United States following legal cases on fairness. On the other hand, it has never played quite as large a part in selection as it has in the United States. Sneath, Thakur, and Medjuck (1976) reported that 72% of a sample of 281 British organizations used tests in their selection procedures but only half had tried to estimate the tests' validity in their situation and only 5% had used statistical methods to do so. Yet interest in psychometrics in selection has grown steadily in recent years. One reason is doubtless the relatively large number of unemployed, referred to above, with the preselection problem of screening large numbers of applicants. Second, the influential figure among U.K. managers of Michael Edwardes may have contributed. He is an enthusiast for testing. This was well publicized in the management literature as well as in his book *Back from the Brink* (1983) about his efforts at turning round the loss-making nationalized car manufacturer, British Leyland. Finally, the legal framework surrounding the dismissal of employees makes it a very difficult exercise. This has focused attention on ways of making selection more effective through a professional and scientific approach.

GRAPHOLOGY

In the U.K., graphology (or the analysis of handwriting to infer personality characteristics) is little used as a selection technique. A survey by Gill (1980) reported that 93% of U.K. responding companies rated graphology as "not very useful." In certain continental European countries, though, graphology is more widely used by organizations.

However, since 1980 there has been an upsurge of interest in graphology as a selection technique in the U.K., particularly by personnel consultants, some of whom have added it to their battery of assessment aids. There is still, though, a lack of evidence to support its validity or reliability (e.g., Lester, McLaughlin, & Nosal, 1977; Rosenthal & Lines, 1972; Williams, Berg-Cross, & Berg-Cross, 1977). Further, many of the studies that do show some validity can be criticized for significant methodological flaws and the use of relatively small sample sizes to generate often widely generalized conclusions.

Perhaps typical of the literature advocating graphology as a valid and reliable technique is Lynch (1985), where examples of three scripts were analyzed. Based on mainly positive responses by subjects to the analyses, the article recommended the technique as "cost effective." Fletcher (1985b), in the same journal volume, urged greater caution in the light of inconclusive validity evidence and the probable capacity of individuals to fake their handwriting to suit their purpose.

Some commendable research is, however, at hand. Rafaeli and Klimoski (1983) conducted a detailed comparison between the predictions of ten expert graphologists on 206 scripts written by 103 sales staff. No statistically significant validity coefficients were found, regardless of whether the criterion used was supervisors' ratings or self-ratings. In fact, the professional graphologists achieved no greater accuracy in terms of predictive validity than did a group of undergraduate students who also rated the scripts.

Loewenthal (1982) concluded that it is less expensive and more reliable for organizations to use psychometric tests and interviews in preference to the services of a graphologist.

To summarize, there is virtually no consistent relationship between handwriting and personality. No reliance should be placed on graphology as a selection technique. The tragedy is that this invalid method is so widely used.

OTHER RECENT DEVELOPMENTS

The area of impression formation has also received attention in the literature. Recent research has commenced the mammoth task of unveiling the cognitive processes of the recruiter as a function of impression formation resulting from the application form or resume. Oliphant and Alexander (1982) reported that ratings of applicant characteristics made by 12 personnel professionals (6 male, 6 female) on the basis of resumes were influenced by the specificity of information presented and by sex of rater. Specific details generally resulted in more favorable ratings, but the rating of the female recruiters tended to be more stringent than those of the males.

Herriot and Wingrove (1984) obtained verbalized positive and negative perceptions of seven recruiters as they reacted to application form details (n = 722). It was found that although significant interrecruiter differences emerged (see also Wingrove et al., 1984) the tendency was for inferences to be made more frequently toward the end of applications than during the initial review stages.

Further, it was found that the inferences drawn by individual recruiters were more accurate predictors of hiring decisions than were application form items. Herriot and Wingrove argue that the use of a "decision aid" at this stage, which forces the recruiter to rate application characteristics against established criteria, may prove to be an effective control mechanism.

Another development includes the use of the polygraph or "lie detector." Use of the polygraph as a screening device has been considered recently by some British organizations including Her Majesty's Government in a highly publicized case concerning a government communications headquarters. The British Psychological Society (1984) produced a statement pointing out that there is no sound evidence to support the use of the polygraph in occupational assessment. Similarly, in the United States (Gibbons, 1983), there have been reports of significant error rates where the polygraph is used for screening purposes (see also Ginton, Gaie, Elaad, & Ben-Shakhar, 1982, for a U.S. view of the polygraph).

Finally, benefits resulting from basing the recruitment process on systematic and detailed job analyses have continued to be highlighted. Two separate studies using different techniques (Robinson, 1981; Sparrow, Patrick, Spurgeon, & Barwell, 1982) endorsed this approach in the light of the findings of the Gill (1980) survey.

As Sparrow et al. (1982) observed, two broad approaches have characterized developments in job analysis since the 1960s. First, the "ability requirements approach" centering upon the specification of abilities required to perform jobs using behaviorally anchored scales (e.g., Fleishman, 1967, 1978; Fleishman & Hogan, 1978). Second, the Position Analysis Questionnaire (PAQ) (McCormick, Denrsi, & Shaw, 1979) elicits job elements related to human attributes and has been termed the "job component approach" (Sparrow et al., 1982). Interrater reliabilities, and the reliability of the PAQ in assessing human attributes have been consistent at around .80 (Marquardt, 1972; McCormick et al., 1979; Meechan & McCormick, 1969). The validity of this technique was found by Sparrow et al. to be .91 for the job of setter in the plastics injection molding industry. Patrick and Moore (1985) described a modified British version of the PAQ known as the Job Structure Profile (JSP). Interrater reliability for this version was .90 with retest reliability of .76. This job analysis technique would therefore seem to have considerable promise as a method of anchoring subsequent selection procedures on more dynamic samples of behavior.

7

CAREER DEVELOPMENT AND PLANNING IN ORGANIZATIONS

DONALD SUPER
University of Florida
Gainesville, FL, USA

FRANK J. MINOR
IBM Corporation
Franklin Lakes, NJ, USA

The transition from education to work is often something of a shock to the youth making the transition, and the youth is something of a shock producer for the employer. The movement from the school culture of the world of work often results in culture shock. There is a shift from nurturing the individual to utilizing and developing specific skills needed to satisfy the organization's goals. The individual's personal development, desires, preferences, and needs are considered only within the context of the organization's business needs.

How and when a task is to be performed, where the work is to be done, the hours of work, the place of employment, are now controlled by outsiders. Work shifts, work mates, the work pace, the work place, working conditions, and with them, to a certain degree, the lifestyle are employer determined.

The early years of employment are, for many young people, years of drifting, floundering, or trial; they are sometimes years in which these follow in succession as goals are formulated and clarified; they are sometimes years of exploration in which vague goals are clarified with experience. Students in liberal arts colleges generally have two years in which to try out various subjects and potential majors, really committing themselves to a major field by the time they begin their third year of study (chemistry, engineering, and premedical programs are examples); some are able, thanks to the curricula in some fields (architecture, law, psychology, business, for example) to postpone definite decisions until they graduate and go on to graduate school. But despite exploratory programs in high school and college, despite the increased efforts of career and professional education during the last two decades, there is still a great deal of floundering and trial during the first years of employment.

Some employers recognize this fact, and seek through induction programs to minimize the shock of changing cultures, to facilitate assimilation into the adult working world, and to provide opportunities for exploration and trial within the range of opportunities available in the company or at least in the division, branch, or department.

The Life-Career Rainbow, shown in Figure 7.1, is used to show some of the complexities of a career. The outer ring or arc of the Rainbow depicts the major life stages of Growth (Childhood), Exploration (Adolescence), Establishment (Young Adulthood), Maintenance (Middle Adulthood), and Decline or Disengagement (Old Age). The ages at which transitions from one major life stage to another are shown, not as precise ages, but as approximations: Career development does not progress steadily and according to a calendar, despite the fact that some theorists and researchers would seem to have it so. In Figure 7.2 the impression of the regularity and rigidity of development is unfortunately strengthened, despite the graphic portrayal of transitions. It does have the advantage of bringing out, more than does the Rainbow, the characteristics of the major life stages.

Both figures help to point out that career development in business and industry, and in government, involves a period of transition from education to work. Attending to the transitional needs of exploration (finding out what is there and what it is like) and of trial (experiencing at first hand) is thus an important provision in the planning and conduct of career development programs.

The Life-Career Rainbow makes a number of other important points. First, a career is not just occupational, but involves a number of roles in addition to that of worker or wage earner. A person's first career role is that of child, whose responsibility (aided by parents and others) is to grow physically, intellectually, emotionally, and socially. Then comes the role of pupil or student, then that of pursuer of leisure activities or inactivity, then that of citizen or member of a larger community and its organizations, then those of worker, spouse, homemaker, and parent. There has been much interest, contemporaneous with the first development of the Life-

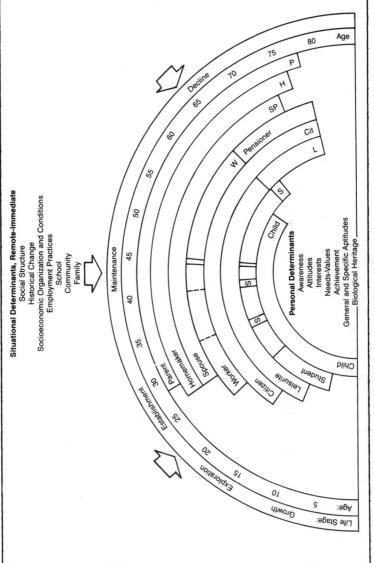

Situational Determinants, Remote-Immediate
Social Structure
Historical Change
Socioeconomic Organization and Conditions
Employment Practices
School
Community
Family

Personal Determinants
Awareness
Attitudes
Interests
Needs-Values
Achievement
General and Specific Aptitudes
Biological Heritage

Figure 7.1 The Life-Career Rainbow: Nine Life Roles in Schematic Life Space

85

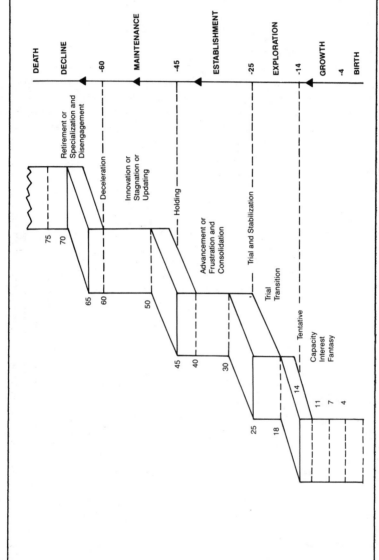

Figure 7.2 Life Stages and Substages: Super's 1957, 1963, 1981 formulation

Career Rainbow, in the coexistence and interaction of these roles. The terms *dual-career* and *dual-wage* family have become common and the impact of both man and wife being wage earners outside of the home on their respective occupational careers, their respective homemaking careers, and the development of their children has become a widespread subject of concern and of research. The Rainbow serves as a heuristic device in research, and in career development programs with both youth and adults it conveys the notions of multiple careers and of their interaction.

The arcs of the Rainbow can be shaded to indicate the temporal importance of each role in the life space, the relative amount of time devoted to it, the increase or decrease of time in the role with changing demands and with changing life circumstances. Thus in Figure 7.1 the taking on of the roles of spouse and of homemaker (male or female) might show a decrease (less shaded space) in the worker role just before and during the early stage of marriage as courtship and marriage leave less time for evening and weekend work.

The depth of color or shading in the arc, in some versions of the Rainbow, is used to show the amount of commitment or involvement, as contrasted with time given to participation, in each role. Used as a teaching device in class, in workshops, and in counseling, blank copies of the Rainbow are used to help people see their own life career roles, their commitments, and their participation more clearly (Super, 1982).

EDUCATIONAL PROGRAMS FOR CAREER DEVELOPMENT PRIOR TO EMPLOYMENT

Although important pioneer work in career development in schools, colleges, and universities was carried on prior to the 1970s, it was in that decade that the terms become household words and that programs in career education and career guidance blossomed. Curricula were *infused* with information about occupations and with opportunities to develop concepts of oneself as a worker, and they were *added to* by the provision of more courses designed to orient students to the world of work and, to a lesser degree, to the concept of evolving and changing careers with age and with socioeconomic changes. Career counseling centers and career placement services in colleges and universities became more numerous and were strengthened in attempts to facilitate the transition from education to work. Work-study and cooperative education programs became more popular.

EVALUATING THE OUTCOMES OF
CAREER EXPLORATION AND PLANNING

There is extensive literature on the evaluation of career education and counseling programs in the United States, and some similar work has been done in Great Britain and in France. The task has proven to be much more difficult than had been imagined, because of the difficulties of selecting appropriate criteria of outcomes and of controlling nonexperimental variables. It takes time for the effects of guidance and counseling to manifest themselves, and in the meantime other unplanned experiences intervene and confuse the picture. Men and women who have come to know themselves and the world of work may be expected to make wiser choices and to be better satisfied with their careers than those who have not, but knowledge comes from informal and unplanned experiences as well as from the formal and planned. Despite these problems there is accumulating evidence that the career development programs of schools and universities do produce graduates who flounder less and who are better satisfied with their careers than those who do not have the benefit of such programs and services. Leibowitz and Schlossberg (1981) have explored some of these issues, with a focus on organizational settings.

CONTINUING CAREER DEVELOPMENT
AFTER EDUCATION LEAVES OFF

When a new employee is hired, it has been pointed out above, an unfinished product is introduced into the organization. The new worker is still in the process of *exploring,* of getting to know his or her abilities and interests, of learning what the organization and its clientele expect of him or her, and of finding out just where and how he or she fits into the scheme of things. This is of course why induction programs, some good and some bad, have been in existence for decades. What in sociology and social psychology is now called the process of socialization proceeds, formally or informally. What may have seemed like an abstract problem of business or professional ethics when in school or university becomes a very real problem of everyday life when dealing with fellow workers, clients, or patients. What may have seemed a trivial problem of personal preference in dress when a student, becomes a very important problem when the budding manager first encounters the expectation of conformity with corporate standards in the selection and wearing of suits, dresses, linens, and accessories.

The induction period is thus clearly a continuation of the exploratory process, even if the inductee is over 25 years of age that is shown in Figure 7.2, the Life-Stages Ladder, as the typical ending of the Exploratory Stage. Indeed, the Career Pattern Study has shown that some 25% of young men are still in this stage at age 25. One of the most successful of the young men in that sample said, in a long discussion when he was 36 years old, that he really had no idea of what he wanted to do until he was about 28, when a conversation with a neighbor opened his eyes to an opportunity that appealed to him and to the means of availing himself of that opening.

The Life-Stage Ladder is worthy of study of this stage and for those that follow, with a focus on the developmental tasks that are encountered in each stage and substage. Super (1984) goes into these in some detail, drawing upon recent research and theory to document their importance and use in career development practice. Much exploration is fortuitous, some is planned; much is random, while some has clear cut objectives; some is prospective in that it takes into account an unfolding future, but some is retrospective as past experience is reviewed for new insights into oneself and one's situation; some exploration is direct, taking place in the real world, some indirect in the observation of others, and some takes place in fantasy, which, when given some direction, can help to clarify feelings and objectives. It is the purposes of induction programs to reduce floundering by guided and evaluated exploration.

The Life or Career-Stage Ladder can be used to stimulate thinking about where one is in one's career, especially the occupational career. Individual deviations from the typical pattern in Figure 7.2 can be plotted to show the developmental tasks with which the individual is coping and the kind of adjustment being made, for example, continuing trial without stabilization, consolidation with frustration due to plateauing, or with advancement resulting from choice of a good launching platform and good use of talents.

After the induction period has passed, the young employee enters the second stage of *establishment*, that of attempting to consolidate the position in the organization and to lay the foundation for advancement. How this is done varies somewhat with the occupation and with the organization: Advancement in academia is based on different criteria and is facilitated in different ways from advancement in selling real estate, which again is different from getting ahead in banking. Career paths in the organization need to be identified and the means of following them learned.

Middle age is the period of *maintenance*: there is a tendency in the middle or late 40s to settle for what one has attained and to seek to maintain it, or, alternatively, to be dissatisfied with what one has attained and to seek to break away from it, seeking "a new career" in which self-fulfillment may be more nearly attainable. This is a stage of stagnation, of updating, or of innovation. Career development then involves finding ways of deriving new satisfactions from what one has been doing or of finding other things to do. If innovation is the inclination of the person in question, what is normally thought of as the maintenance stage may in fact be a continuation of the exploration and establishment stages, with more trying out of new activities, more breaking of new ground, more consolidation of new gains, and more advancement. A good career development program thus needs to help employees to understand their own needs and to find ways of meeting them in their working and nonworking lives.

The last decade of the working career is, for most men and women, a stage of *deceleration*. Energy declines, endurance lessens, and with these changes a process of disengagement from some aspects of one's work is to be expected. The age at which these changes occur varies greatly from one person to another, and so do responses to the changes. Understanding them, and finding suitable ways of coping with them, is important to continued effectiveness and to work and life satisfaction. A well-conceived career development program therefore must involve orientation to and help with the approach of retirement. Deceleration leads to disengagement in the domain of work; it must therefore mean increasing engagement in some other life roles and domains. Career development continues even after retirement from a job.

CAREER DEVELOPMENT TRENDS IN ORGANIZATIONS

In recent years, there has been rapid growth in the introduction and enhancement of career development programs in organizations. The forces that have contributed to the need for the growth of organizational career development programs include:

- *Changing Business Environment.* Rapidly changing technology and new business methods and markets cause ongoing shifts in job duties, skills, demands, and numbers of employees needed. Information about the kinds of shifts expected must be communicated to the work force and management to assure that employee development is responsive to changes in the organization (Minor, 1986).
- *Social Forces.* Organizations are finding that career development programs can help them achieve society's equal opportunity and affirmative action goals. Through such programs, women and minority group members can identify and examine career paths and the qualifications needed for their own growth and development in the organization (Duval & Courtney, 1978). Even without organizational programs more employees seek information about the organization's jobs and career paths in their desire to manage their careers more effectively. Employees are motivated to plan for growth, reduce ambiguity, and find self-realization in their work (Morgan, Hall, & Martier, 1979; Yankelovich, Skelly, & White, 1980).
- *Internal Organizational Pressures.* Informed management recognizes the need for more systematic career development programs, valid job and career information to employees, and more participation by employees in the management of their careers. Formalizing an organization's career development program has advantages for both the employee and the organization. For the employees there is increased satisfaction with their ability to plan for the future and to manage their careers. For the organization there is improved job satisfaction, increased employee commitment to the organization, increased realism in employees' goals and plans, and the enhancement of needed skills in the work force (Minor, 1986; Morgan et al., 1979).

CAREER DEVELOPMENT PROGRAM OBJECTIVES AND METHODS

OBJECTIVES

Organizations plan their career development programs to satisfy their special objectives and needs while responding to societal demands. Objectives common to most organizational career development programs include:

- Develop an employee work force with the skill and experience qualifications needed to perform effectively in their present jobs, as well as to adapt to changing business demands.

- Prevent obsolescence and plateauing.
- Maintain a talent pool of managers or potential managers that can meet future organizational goals.
- Create an organizational climate that enhances employee desire for personal growth, flexibility, self-improvement, and development within the organization,
- Comply with affirmative action goals and guidelines.

The more successful the organization is in achieving these goals, the greater is the likelihood that its employees can adapt to changing business demands. The organization can then more often promote from within and provide employment security through redeployment of employee skill groups in response to demands of the business.

It is worth noting, in view of the differences pointed out between the culture of the school and college, on the one hand, and the business or industrial organization on the other, that the objectives just cited focus on the organization rather than on the individual. When the employee is considered as an individual it is for "self-improvement and development *within the organization*" (italics added), and "outplacement" means, in effect, the constructive dismissal of an unwanted employee. It is not the individual's need for a better growth situation than the company can provide that is being considered. It is of course for this reason, among others, that some companies, as Lancaster and Berne (1981) note, refer some employees to independent, outside, counseling services.

Perhaps one important and positive characteristic of many organizational career development programs is the greater attempt at the coordination of the efforts of many contributors that result from the tendency of businesses to place responsibility, to supervise, to evaluate, and to reward accordingly. The traditions of academia, in which every instructor, every professional by whatever title, is viewed as a member of a "liberal" or free profession, make it more difficult for a dean to coordinate efforts for effective teamwork. To overstate the case, there is, in academic career development work, no bottom line. In business and industry there is, sometimes to the detriment of a program or service, but sometimes to its advantage. The list of employer-assisted programs and services compiled by Lancaster and Berne is more likely to be used as a checklist by which to review one's organization's program in a business setting than it is in an educational setting. The condensed list below should be useful in such a review, and the differences between career planning and career management can lead to new programmatic insights.

METHODS USED IN ORGANIZATIONS
FOR CONTINUED DEVELOPMENT

Career development programs in organizations can be grouped into specific categories that reflect the nature of the service performed (Lancaster & Berne, 1981). Some of the more prevalent categories of service are the following:

- Career planning in seminars and in individualized career counseling conducted by staff counselors and/or managers;
- Career information services that provide employees with data on career paths and ladders in the organization, EEO and affirmative action policies, continuing education and educational assistance programs, training and development opportunities, employment trends, job openings;
- Programs for employee placement and advancement planning, planning, redeployment identification of job skill training needs, and management succession planning;
- Special programs and practices developed to support the special career planning needs of groups such as minorities, women, pre-retirees, midcareer, and handicapped employees.
- Assessment centers for the evaluation of employee management potential, of career interests, and skill and experience development needs to achieve full potential;
- Training and development programs that assist both nonmanagers and managers in the acquisition of basic job-relevant skills (e.g., communication, decision making, technical or business skills).

In a study of career development programs in organizations (Gutteridge & Otte, 1983), the techniques reportedly used by the majority of the organizations were career planning seminars or workshops and individualized career counseling by staff counselors. Most respondents in the study thought a computer-based information system was needed for a comprehensive career development program, one that would contain information about employee skills, career interests, and plans, and could relate them to organization needs.

The career development services provided by organizations can be grouped into two general types of programs: (1) career planning programs and (2) career management programs (Leibowitz & Schlossberg, 1981; Storey, 1981). Career planning programs are designed to help individual employees explore career development avenues.

Career planning programs encourage employees to assess their personal attributes, explore career development options, make decisions about personal objectives, develop plans for the management of their own careers, and communicate their career plans and needs to their managers. The managers' role is to assess and counsel their employees with respect to the realism of their goals and plans. Mutually agreeable goals and plans are then jointly formulated.

Career management programs are designed to help managers make informed decisions about the organization's employees in order to meet the organization's human resource needs. The concerns of career management programs include employee placement, identification of employee skills training needs, development of employees, redeployment of employees to meet changing business demands, and management succession planning (Cloonan & Squires, 1981; Gutteridge, 1986; Gutteridge & Otte, 1983).

Career planning and career management programs, although described separately, are interrelated and complementary. Ideally, the organization should strive to achieve a balance that accommodates both the needs of the individual and those of the organization (Leibowitz & Schlossberg, 1981). Career planning and career management programs are described below with a specific emphasis on innovations brought about through the use of computer-based information systems.

Organizations have found it helpful to use computer-based information systems to manage the increasingly complex career information-handling processes, that is, classifying, searching for, comparing, integrating, summarizing, and updating facts about jobs, careers, training programs, and personal attributes. Two types of computer-based systems have evolved to support organizational career development programs. They are (1) career information and planning systems, to support individual career development activities, and (2) human resource information (HRI) systems to support organizational career management activities.

CAREER PLANNING SYSTEMS

Historically, computer-based systems to support career planning had their origins in high school and college settings, and were designed for use by students (Super, 1970; Minor, Myers, & Super, 1969; Myers & Cairo, 1983). A number of organizations are now using or implementing career planning systems for use by their employees.

The general purpose of an organizational computer-assisted

career planning system is to support the ongoing personal growth and development of its employees. The system communicates job and career information in a form that enables employees to make comparisons between their personal attributes and possible jobs, and to compare selectively different jobs in the organization. These systems are designed to make possible a personalized, interactive, conversation with the employee. The computer serves as an information management tool because of its ability to compare and summarize the numerous complex categories of information used in comparing people and jobs. An information management tool is necessary because neither managers nor their subordinates are equipped to search, link, and integrate all the subsets of information required for exploration and analysis of the detailed facts describing employee attributes, jobs, and avenues of development.

Organizations using or implementing career planning systems report that their systems provide benefits to employees, managers of employees who use the system, and the organization (Minor, 1986).

For employees, they make it possible to identify realistic goals and plans, recognize the various career paths available in the organization, and thus assume greater responsibility in the management of careers. *For managers,* the systems provide a systematic, data-based process for counseling employees, learning about career paths outside their field of specialization, and preparing for counseling sessions with their employee. The systems also relieve the managers of the task of gathering and disseminating career information. *For organizations,* the systems provide a standardized media for communicating to employees information about changing skill demands and job and career content and structures. An additional benefit to the organization is that the system can help employees find a match between their own plans and those projected by the organization's career ladders. The greater the match, as perceived by employees, the more positive is their satisfaction and commitment to the organization (Granrose & Portwood, 1984).

EXAMPLES OF SYSTEMS IN ORGANIZATIONS

A number of organizations have or are in the process of implementing computer-based career planning information systems. Descriptions of their systems and their experiences with them have been reported by the IBM Corporation, Corning Glass Works,

the Cleveland Clinic Foundation, Digital Equipment Corporation, and The Educational Testing Service (Minor, 1986, and others).
Although the systems have similar objectives, they differ in

- the information content and conversational dialogue provided;
- the types of supportive counseling services, orientation workshops, and materials, such as workbooks and videotapes;
- the links between the employees' use of the system and other personnel programs, human resources information systems and the development activities of the organization.

A career planning information system, designed by Minor (1986), is briefly described here in order to provide an example. The system was developed for use by IBM employees and is referred to as the IBM Employee Development Planning System (EDPS). The system is designed as a tool to help employees plan and manage their career and personal growth within the IBM Company. It was developed to be used by employees at all levels, that is, nonexempt employees, exempt professionals, and managers. EDPS is used as an information aid, or tool, to support IBM's existing employee development program and practices. It does not replace or change any of the IBM employee development procedures, or the roles of employees and managers.

The EDPS is organized into a sequential set of modules that lead the employee through an exploration and planning process. Initially, the system helps employees assess their readiness for career development planning and the implications of their individual level of readiness. Employees next create self-descriptive profiles of their work-related interests, abilities, skills, and desired work experiences. These self-descriptions enable the system to search and identify development avenues and job types within the organization that are compatible with employee profiles. System users can learn more about their duties, skills and experience demands, typical lead-in jobs and follow-up jobs, work conditions, and so on. During the analysis the employee expresses likes and dislikes about various aspects of the jobs. Based upon the user's reactions and their planning readiness scores, personalized messages are displayed to the user. The messages describe potential planning problems, consistencies, and inconsistencies in the employee's reactions to the jobs he or she analyzes. A concluding module assists employees to summarize their perceived self-improvement or development needs if they are to achieve the goals and objectives sought. The system enables the employees to skip modules or return to previous modules. The employees then review with their manager their views and preferences about goals, plans, and needs based upon their leaning experiences with the system.

A pilot test was designed to evaluate the impact of EDPS on both employees and their managers (Minor, 1986). Several hundred employees, representing a cross-section of exempt professionals and nonexempt employees, responded to both a presystem-use and a postsystem-use questionnaire. Almost all of the employees found the system highly useful to their career development planning on a variety of criteria. The criteria include improved self-assessment of personal attributes, increased specificity of goals and plans, ability to plan further into the future, identification of personal development needs to achieve objectives, better preparation for career planning discussions with management, greater control of the management of careers, discovery of new job types and opportunities for better jobs, a more systematic approach to career planning, and increased flexibility in development plans and strategies.

Comparisons between employees' responses before and after using the system showed there were no increases in the percentage of employees selecting promotion as their next career objective nor was there any increase in employees' expectations of being promoted. The system thus does not act as a stimulus for raising employees' desires or expectations for promotion. It is important that career planning systems do not raise employees' advancement expectations that cannot be satisfied by the organization.

Correlation analyses show that the more favorably the employees perceive the organization's career development program, their ability to manage their own career, and their satisfaction with their career goals and plans, the greater are their commitment to working for the organization, their satisfaction with their present jobs, and their dedication to their future careers in the organization. These correlations were all highly significant.

Managers of employees who used EDPS were asked to rate the usefulness of the system for their employees. As was the case with employees, almost all of the managers rated EDPS as highly useful to their employees' career development planning and indicated it increased the realism of their goals and action plans. The favorable pilot test results led to the implementation of EDPS for use by IBM employees.

HUMAN RESOURCE INFORMATION SYSTEMS

Another type of computer-based aid to support career development in organizations is the human resource information (HRI) system. HRI systems are designed to help managers make more informed decisions about the development and utilization of their work force for the purpose of satisfying organizational needs. The basic component of an HRI system is an employee data file describing each employee in terms of his or her job position, job level, past work experience, skills, performance appraisals, potential for higher-level positions, educational background, career objectives, skills development needs, and so on. In some applications, an HRI system may include another data file that describes jobs in the organization in terms such as level, prerequisite entry jobs, follow-on jobs, preferred employee qualifications, job locations, positions currently vacant, and so on.

The objectives of some of the major types of applications, which draw upon HRI system data files to support career development programs in organizations include:

- *Staffing*: searching for potential candidates who possess the qualifications needed for a vacant position, or identifying vacant positions that offer the development experiences called for in an employee's development plan (Dunn, 1982; Gutteridge & Otte, 1983; Sheibar, 1979; Sonnefeld, 1984; Walker, 1982).
- *Development Planning*: searching for candidates who can benefit from an available training program or temporary rotation assignment (Gutteridge, 1986).
- *Succession Planning*: identification and placement of managerial talent in positions providing appropriate career development experiences to assure continuing availability of the number and quality of managers needed to meet future organizational goals (Cory, Medland, & Uhlander, 1977; Norton, 1985a, 1985b).

HRI systems and career planning systems can and should complement each other. For example, the employees' goals and personal development activities that result from their use of a career planning system should be used as data in the employee profiles stored in the HRI system (Gutteridge & Otte, 1983).

8

TRAINING

DOV EDEN
Tel Aviv University
Tel Aviv, Israel

This chapter will supplement reviews by Campbell (1971), Goldstein (1980), and Wexley (1984) by examining training worldwide, focusing in particular on Israel, and addressing some general issues pertaining to training.

TRAINING WORLDWIDE

For the foreseeable future, due to population and labor force trends, the developing world, in particular, Asia, will have to carry a much heavier training burden than the more advanced countries of Europe and North America (ILO, 1980). However, judging from published reports, most training, training research, and training innovations appear still to take place in the industrialized countries. The developing nations have not, for the most part, published much training literature, at least not in the universally available English language outlets. Perhaps due to the structure of the economies of most developing nations, where government-owned and public enterprises dominate and leave little to private initiative, they seem to have a relatively strong emphasis on public service management training (Ozgediz, 1983).

TRAINING IN
LESS DEVELOPED COUNTRIES

The direction of flow in the area of training from the industrialized to the developing parts of the world is bolstered by the considerable volume of training conducted in developing nations by multinational enterprises (MNEs). A recent ILO (1981) report reviews the literature of MNE training and concludes that MNEs tend to fashion their training programs in developing host countries after models used in the parent organizations' home countries, a practice that may be dysfunctional. Training of higher-level management personnel is usually done off-site, back in the parent company's country. Even indigenous training can lack local relevance. For example, graduates of business schools in developing countries find it difficult to apply to the local enterprise environment the theoretical knowledge they have acquired based on the conditions prevailing in advanced economies (ILO, 1980).

Paul (1983) has reviewed the published literature on the training of middle- and senior-level public sector managers and administrators in the least developed countries (LDCs). He observed that relevant data are "scanty" and that indicators of training impact are "virtually nonexistant" (p. 21). As shortcomings he cited evaluation of training effectiveness solely on the basis of participant feedback, lack of linkage among training and career planning and promotion, inappropriate needs assessment, dominance of the lecture method, overly academic content, reliance on imported textbooks, models, and approaches, and shortage of qualified trainers. Most of these deficiencies have a familiar ring to Western ears.

Literature on public sector staff training in developing countries is included in a recent annotated bibliography published by the U.N. Department for Technical Cooperation for Development (United Nations, 1983), and a report issued by the ILO Training Department provides information on training in the USSR, Poland, and East Germany (ILO, 1979).

Much training activity in the developing nations imitates approaches pioneered in the industrial West. A recent report (United Nations, 1984) issued by a group of experts meeting under U.N. auspices in San Jose, Costa Rica discusses management training in developing nations. The report reads like an introductory primer on training, spelling out such basics as how to determine training needs, methods, curricula, and program evaluation. The world seems to converge on the need, echoed in unison by many reviewers, to adhere fastidiously to oft-neglected basics.

Useful "how to" guidelines for the effective conduct of training programs, stressing the design of curricula, are contained in the report of a group of international experts who met in Tanzania under U.N. auspices (United Nations, 1982). This report includes relevant references and delineates the important features of effective training that training experts in any country would endorse. It also stresses the importance of tying training design to the national development plan. The idea of a national training plan is alien to U.S. practice. Perhaps the difficult problems being encountered by the American economy during its current post-industrial transition might be abated by a national training policy. This makes sense to the extent that the scale of retraining needed by vast sectors of the American work force is as great as that of newly industrializing countries. Manpower missions of such scale may require coordinated, national planning and policy of the sort used by developing countries, traditional American reliance on individual corporate initiative not sufficing to meet the challenge. This is an area in which the most developed can learn from the developing. Recently, Delaware Governor Du Pont called for just such a national employment and training policy in emerging U.S. industries (Staff, 1983).

The Tanzania workshop (United Nations, 1982) stressed indigenous research as a means of promoting the professionalization of trainers and the relevancy of training programs. In my view, this point is crucial. Technology can be imported effectively; training cannot. Only indigenous research can guide the way to relevant training curricula and methods. For example, while one can admire the accomplishment of Prokopenko and White (1981) in designing a five-volume, modular program to serve as a framework for tailor-made supervisory training to suit the needs of any sector or organization worldwide, it is doubtful that available trainers can utilize such material in the developing countries where the need is most dire. Ayman (1981) has noted that Western psychology has been transplanted to foreign cultures, making it hard to assimilate and apply. To make psychology more applicable, it "should grow out of research, experimentation and practice in each culture" (p. 406). He specifically refers to sensitivity training and programmed learning as examples of technologies that were never properly tested prior to application in the developing countries, with results ranging between satisfactory success and regrettable failure. The same range of results has been observed in the industrialized West, but psychology's low status in developing countries leaves it vulnerable and incapable of sustaining such failures. Ayman called upon the Professional Affairs Committee of the International Association of Applied Psychology to play a more active role in strengthening psychology in the developing countries. But there is a role for psychologists as individuals as well. The most effective way to break the vicious cycle of underdevelopment would be to raise the level of indigenous trainers. If readers of this chapter would spend a sabbatical year in a developing country, training indigenous cadre in training and research methods, the chain effect could result in swift training improvements that would be accomplished by the trained locals themselves.

Due to its timeliness, boldness, and methodological excellence, the InterFace Project conducted by Sorcher and Spence (1982) in South Africa merits special citation as a remarkable training achievement. Using a pretest-posttest randomized experimental design, they assessed the impact of behavior modeling aimed at improving interracial harmony among white supervisors and black workers in a pharmaceutical manufacturing company. Although productivity data could not be used and questionnaires failed to detect any changes, structured interviews revealed improvements in interracial attitudes. Irrespective of how deep or lasting an impact this project may have had in ameliorating that country's seemingly intractable interracial conflict, Sorcher and Spence are to be commended for taking a high risk in applying a training technology to an extremely sensitive issue in such an explosive situation.

TRAINING IN ISRAEL

Although geographically Israel lies in western Asia, scientifically, industrially, and psychologically Israel is part of the industrialized West. Israel is blessed with a vigorous psychological community (Amir & Ben-Ari, 1986), and its I/O research output is respectable by international standards. But, alas, many of the same deficiencies characteristic of training worldwide plague training in Israel too.

As elsewhere, most training is in-house and never published. Similar to armies everywhere, the Israel Defense Forces (IDF) conduct an enormous volume of training, mostly cloaked in secrecy due to security considerations. Nonetheless, the several IDF studies reviewed below reveal a variegated body of high-quality research on cutting-edge training issues. Also, as elsewhere, the multinationals operating in Israel conduct training according to programs developed overseas, usually in the home country, but such imported packages are often supplemented by locally developed materials and local training personnel. Virtually all major Israeli companies have a training unit. Notable are the banks, insurance companies, utilities, publicly owned manufacturing corporations, central and local government, the Civil Service Commission, air, land, and sea transportation companies, medical service organizations, and private industrial firms. Perhaps unique is the large volume of training conducted by the huge Histadrut Labor Federation for its members. Certainly unique is the wide-ranging training that the kibbutz movement provides for it members (and for others) in its own training organizations, where hundreds of courses span the gamut from basic vocational training in occupations such as sheep herding and sewing through computer science, industrial technology, and agronomy, to academic courses in management, education, social work, and business administration. Kibbutz training is an excellent example of local absorption of knowledge through the use of a healthy mix of homegrown experts and outsiders, and development of local training methods and materials, including curricula, cases, and readings. In addition, the kibbutzim have maintained an active program of training personnel from developing countries in a wide variety of fields in which the kibbutzim have achieved world-class expertise. In training, the kibbutzim are a model worthy of emulation.

Additional management training is provided by the Israel Productivity Institute, which is part of the Ministry of Labor, by the universities, and by private consulting firms. The Productivity Institute maintains a varied program of courses for supervisors, technicians, and managers, ranging from one-day specialty workshops to three-year courses granting diplomas. The universities provide training programs for in-service managers, ranging from half-day events to Tel Aviv University's Top Executive Course, which provides as much MBA content as is feasible in an intensive, two-days-a-week, three-semester diploma course for working managers. The training activities of private consulting firms are ubiquitous but elusive due to lack of systematic documentation.

A training problem I have encountered in Israel is that training directors are not, for the most part, professionals. As such, they often do not know what they are buying when they contract with outsiders to provide training services, and they know neither how to diagnose training needs nor how to evaluate training effectiveness. Their efforts are therefore frequently aimed at satisfying their clients, namely, other managers in their organization who participate in training programs, being keenly aware of the political consequences of disgruntled executives returning to headquarters after an unsatisfying training experience. This encourages training directors to seek out popular fads and stage-worthy trainers and to shun effectiveness research. Enthusiastic participant response to the latest training fad then passes for evidence of training success for all concerned.

An allied problem is that an off-site training program, especially one conducted in a five-star mountain or seaside resort complete with swimming pool and tennis courts, is perceived as a bonus. In the absence of sound needs analysis, all managers at a particular rank in the organization demand—and get—this freebie, irrespective of whether or not it will contribute to their effectiveness on the job. One hopes such abuses will diminish as the young professionals trained in Israel's I/O, OB, and MBA programs move into senior positions as training directors, personnel managers, and general managers.

Training fads come and go in Israel as elsewhere, except that in Israel they come a little later, and appear to go quite a bit later. Of the American training fads surveyed recently by Gordon, Lee, and Zemka (1984), sensitivity training, personal-growth labs, TA, psychodrama, MBO, ethics training, and behavior modification have all had a fair run on the Israeli stage, though we seem to have been spared from suggestology and wilderness training. Many Israeli managers get a heavy dose of the latter in annual active reserve duty.

Below, studies of training and training-related issues in Israel are reviewed. The review covers only some articles published in English-language journals after 1979, and therefore exposes only the tip of an iceberg.

TRAINING BASED ON NEEDS ANALYSIS

Zohar (1980) developed an organizational safety climate questionnaire and validated it on a representative sample of Israeli factories in the metals, food, chemical, and textile industries, revealing that the perceived importance of safety *training* programs was the major factor in safety climate, explaining 41% of the variance in the 49 items. Thus the research revealed a clear training need. Perceived importance of training climate showed its importance also by distinguishing best among the factories in terms of their safety climate levels in a discriminant analysis. Zohar and Fussfeld (1981) subsequently applied behavior modification to train Israeli textile workers, who were exposed to average noise levels of 106 dBA, using a token economy to reinforce use of earplugs. During randomly scheduled token dispensing tours, shift managers dispensed one token to each worker who was using earplugs. Accumulated tokens could be used to acquire consumer products priced in tokens. Success of the training was evident in the posttraining earplug use rate of over 90% versus the pre-experimental base rate of only 35%. Two additional indications of the training's success were particularly impressive. High use rates were maintained when reevaluated a year later, even though the token economy had been discontinued after two months. Also, 28 untrained new workers, who joined the department during the follow-up period, all were observed to be wearing earplugs. Rooted in prior organization analysis (Zohar, 1980), Zohar and Fussfeld's (1981) training success demonstrates the crucial importance of organization analysis and content in assessing training needs in order to assure training effectiveness. This issue will be discussed further below.

An additional example of sound needs analysis is Goldberg and Harel's (1984) creation of a tool for designing relevant management training programs in the Israel Electric Co. Dubbed the RPS Index, it is based on three dimensions: job requirements (R), proficiency (P), and self-assessment (S) of training needs, all measured by managers' self-reports. For each of 49 potential training areas, the computed gap between job requirements and present proficiency is weighted by each manager's motivation to acquire more knowledge in the area. Comparisons of summated scores aggregated by department and hierarchical level demonstrated the value of the RPS Index as a tool for revealing differential training needs.

LINKAGE WITH PERFORMANCE EVALUATION

As in the I/O literature at large, performance rating and training intersect in Israel. Shapira and Shirom (1980) introduced some innovative ideas for the use of behaviorally anchored rating scales (BARS) by developing parallel BARS for evaluating the combat effectiveness of tank crews (as opposed to individual soldiers) in an armor training program. Correlations between the ratings and an independent, standard field test of crew proficiency, conducted as a regular part of the training program, speak for the external validity of the scales developed. Tziner (1984) blended training and BARS in another way, showing that "intensive" training (five hours) in both the BARS format and conventional graphic rating scales revealed the superiority of BARS in terms of reduced leniency and halo and greater interrater reliability. Tziner employed a well-controlled, externally valid field experimental design in which civilian managers in an aircraft plant rated their actual subordinates for administrative purposes, as distinct from previous laboratory studies on such scales that have been conducted purely for research purposes. Tziner and

Eden (1985) employed a fractional factorial experimental design that utilized an innovative team effectiveness evaluation procedure developed by Brown, Eden, and Tziner (1978) that solves the statistical problem that arises when each of several judges can rank only a subset of the teams. Tubiana and Ben-Shakhar (1982) developed and validated an inexpensive, paper-and-pencil, self-report questionnaire to measure motivation to serve in the IDF and showed that it was as good a predictor of success in military training as a costly personal interview. Thus Israeli psychologists are working to validate techniques to rate training, to train raters, and to select candidates into training programs.

Tziner and Eden's (1985) field experiment was designed to test the effects of crew composition on ranked performance of armored units on training maneuvers. Crew composition was manipulated by systematically assigning soldiers to three-man tank crews on the basis of all possible predetermined combinations of high and low ability and motivation. Beyond the main effects of ability and motivation on crew performance, there were also crew composition effects for ability. The performance of uniformly high-ability crews far exceeded the level expected on the basis of individual members' ability. The effectiveness of training groups (and other teams) would be significantly enhanced if they were formed in the manner implied by Tziner and Eden's findings.

STRESS AND TRAINING

Two Israeli studies have investigated two previously unresearched types of stress that some trainees, and other personnel, must endure. Eden (1982) studied acute stress among nursing trainees exposed to naturally occurring critical incidents using a multiple-interrupted time series design and found evidence of both psychological and physiological strain in response to acute stress. Sykes and Eden (1985) investigated *transitional stress*, defined as the need to meet the demands of many previously unfamiliar people, tasks, and situations, among American medical students in Israel. Transitional stress necessitates the development of new and appropriate psychological and behavioral responses that gradually turn unfamiliar, stressful demands into routine stimuli. They found relationships among transitional stress, social support, and strain, and proposed the creation of "cultural subcommunities" as a way of reducing transitional stress among sojourner trainees, or others, in a foreign culture.

Friedland and Keinan (1982) and Keinan and Friedland (1984) have addressed the issue of how best to train individuals for maximal performance under stress by testing the relative effectiveness of several methods of training among volunteer candidates for officer training in the IDF. The training methods used in these laboratory experiments differed in the amount of timing of stress introduced into the training process, defined operationally in terms of varying patterns and levels of electric shock administered during training. Their results show that training under increasing levels of stress, mild at first and gradually reaching the level of stress to be experienced during the posttraining performance trials, resulted in the lowest levels of performance. The best performance resulted when no stress accompanied training. Generalization of these findings to combat training should be made very cautiously, if at all, due to the obviously enormous gap between the laboratory and the battlefield. The interesting and crucially important controversy over the extent to which fidelity in training conditions fosters effective posttraining performance can be expected to go on.

HUMAN FACTORS TRAINING

Also based on well-controlled laboratory experimentation, the human factors tradition is alive and well in Israel. This line of research focuses on tasks of varying levels of difficulty that tax different motor and cognitive resources of the trainee. Performance on tasks such as pursuit tracking and digit processing (Gopher & North, 1977) with the addition of letter typing (Gopher, Brickner, & Navon, 1982) is studied, sometimes comparing different training strategies and sometimes using training-to-asymptote to bring subjects to a preliminary baseline level of performance in order to test nontraining hypotheses. The practical applications of this research for personnel training in organizations are in devising efficient training methods for helping workers master the operation of complicated equipment, such as high-tech control panels and cockpits.

ORGANIZATIONAL
AND MANAGEMENT DEVELOPMENT

Eden (1985) has reported the results of a field experiment on team-development training among IDF logistics units. Touted as the most internally valid study to date of the effectiveness of team development, this experiment used randomized experimental and control groups, pretest-posttest comparisons, and unbiased assessments of change based on the responses of subordinates who had not taken part in the training. The results showed no effects of team development. In a quasi-experimental replication among combat units, Eden (in press) found that team development improved teamwork, conflict handling, and information about plans. Although the results of these two studies are contradictory, they demonstrate that well-controlled training evaluation research can be done when the organization is cooperative.

Pazy and Zeira (1983) have described a model of international professional training ambitiously designed to effect organizational change as well as individual professional development. Their description is based on the experience of an Israeli "home organization" that sent groups of engineers for training for periods of between one year and two to an American "host organization" where the trainees learned advanced techniques by working at jobs that are a logical extension of their pretraining jobs. Pazy and Zeira view this "synthetic" approach to training as reaping the benefits of both on-the-job and off-the-job training. They present their model with exceptionally broad scope, revealing explicit cognizance of how the training program interacts with career development, organizational context, and even interorganization relations. This is an excellent example of how a macroperspective can enhance training.

Mailick (1985) has pioneered the introduction of intensive on-the-job senior-level management training in the modular preceptoral format in Israel's public and governmental bureaucracy. For each of several content modules, teams of two or three participants meet biweekly with a preceptor at their work site to discuss ongoing job problems, plan solutions for these problems, discuss brief readings, and evaluate current applications of what was recently learned. The preceptor serves as a facilitator, a coach, a counselor, and a resource person, and works with the participants as a team. Learning is based on guided independent reading, on-the-job application, and preceptoral team analysis, in which the participants' current managerial work constitutes the raw material for learning. In quarterly gatherings all the participants and preceptors engage in an interactive day-long program to reinforce and develop plans to use the module being completed, and to introduce the new module and link it to earlier and future modules in order to integrate, broaden, and generalize learning. Obviously costly due to the high ratio of preceptors to participants, this may be the only format available that enables overloaded top executives to obtain intensive training without disrupting their ongoing work. A sign of its success is that Israel's Administrative Staff College is currently embarking on a new round of preceptoral training for the government's highest-level appointed officials, namely, general managers of ministerial offices and their deputies (Mailick & Hoberman, 1985).

Additional research in Israel with implications for managerial training includes Shapira and Dunbar's (1980) study of Mintzberg's (1973) managerial roles classification using an in-basket simulation among a sample of Hebrew University MBA students and among a sample of managers in an Israeli manufacturing company, and Drory and Gluskinos's (1980) study of Machiavellianism.

THE PYGMALION EFFECT

The Pygmalion effect is a boost in performance on the part of trainees of whom instructors have been led to expect high learning achievement (Rosenthal & Jacobson, 1968; Rosenthal & Rubin, 1978). Babad and his colleagues have conducted a series of studies in which they examined the role of teachers' susceptibility to biasing information in classroom studies of the Pygmalion effect. Reasoning that not all teachers are equally likely to become Pygmalions, Babad (1979) constructed and validated an instrument for estimating an individual's degree of susceptibility to biasing information. Babad and Inbar (1981) then used this instrument to study the personality and teaching behaviors of high- and low-bias physical education teachers-in-training and found that high-bias teachers were more conventional, group dependent, conforming, autocratic, rigid, distant, impulsive, preferential, and untrusting. Babad, Inbar, and Rosenthal (1982a) found that teachers differing in susceptibility to biasing information differ also in the cognitive processing of students' characteristics leading to their nominations into high- and low-expectancy groups. Finally, Babad, Inbar, and Rosenthal (1982b) found that physical education teachers' high expectations—both natural and manipulated—resulted in better student performance in terms of sit-ups and push-ups, broad-jumping, and running speed.

Meanwhile, Eden and his students were conducting field experiments on the Pygmalion effect among IDF trainees. In the first experiment (Eden & Shani, 1982), a random third of the trainees of whom instructors were led to expect more outperformed their control classmates in achievement tests, and reported greater motivation and satisfaction. The second experiment (Eden & Ravid, 1982) replicated the first and also demonstrated the Galatea effect, that is, a boost in learning performance caused by directly raising trainees' own self-expectations. The second experiment also exploited a serendipitous midcourse personnel transfer to discover a "second-generation" expectancy effect, in as much as high-expectancy trainees maintained their high performance under replacement instructors, to whom no expectancy information had been given. Thus training expectancy effects appear to be self-sustaining, as well as self-fulfilling, prophecies (Salomon, 1981). Since much personnel training takes place in the classroom, the Pygmalion effect, and related expectancy effects, deserve more attention than they have received in the training literature. Wexley (1984) cited the Pygmalion research as the only new study of the influence of trainer behavior on trainee learning, an issue that he considers to be in urgent need of empirical investigation. Eden (1984) has published a review and model of the Pygmalion effect in management, a training phenomenon that generalizes to a broad range of supervisor-subordinate relations. A still broader perspective (Eden, 1986) shows the relevance of these expectancy processes for effecting change in the organization as a whole. Pygmalion shares common turf with Bass's (1985) transformational leader and with House's (1977) charismatic leader.

SOME GENERAL TRAINING ISSUES

"CYANAMID FACILITY STEPS UP WORKER TRAINING"

This recent headline on the front page of the *Wall Street Journal* was followed by an article (Meter, 1985) on what American Cyanamid Co. is doing to improve safety in the wake of a spate of chemical-plant disasters and four recent accidents at its Linden, New Jersey plant. "When American Cyanamid Co. held worker-training classes at its plant here last year, employees often missed them. Not this year. Officials are blocking out time for classes and telling workers to be there." The company conducted a study of the plant and "didn't like what it found. Workers were often ill-trained . . . past training methods gave factory personnel little information about how chemical reactions occur." For this company, it took accidents requiring hospitalization of scores of nearby residents to drive home the importance of training. We might wonder whether conventional needs analysis would have detected a similar training need and prevented the 1984 Bhopal calamity. The business community's awareness of the role of training is very partial. Disaster commands attention and headlines, and training might even be a scapegoat in the above case. We never see dramatic headlines attributing outstanding commercial success to personnel training. "Training Averts Catastrophe" would make an implausible banner. When training succeeds, it is usually unglamorous and unnoticed. Training may thus be a game in which you can lose big, but you can't win big.

Why have many of the same maladies afflicted training for so long that reviewer after reviewer cite their predecessors so consistently in pointing out the same shortcomings with a regularity almost unparalleled in social science? This constancy itself is worthy of scientific inquiry.

LACK OF EVALUATION

Throughout the years, those of us who have so eloquently bemoaned the state of training, ourselves engage in training. We administer and teach in degree-granting academic programs in psychology and business administration. To be consistent with what we have been demanding of training directors, we should be conducting evaluation studies of MBA programs by comparing the posttraining managerial performance of trained and untrained managers, using internally valid, randomized designs. Perhaps calls for sound evaluation research have gone unheeded for years because of intractable reasons that are unlikely to change in the foreseeable future. Among these:

(1) It is very hard to do good evaluation research, even under the best of conditions, which rarely prevail.
(2) For all involved—trainers, trainees, and training directors—no evaluation may be preferred to evaluation that is bound to reveal some negative effects. All these stakeholders have a common interest in not revealing shortcomings, each for his or her own reasons. The trainers want to keep their jobs. The trainees do not want to jeopardize the credential value of the training (Bachman, 1983). Training directors do not want to risk a bad showing for their departments. It has been part of my experience to witness trainees mouthing glowing reports in round robin evaluation sessions at the

conclusion of a training program in the presence of the trainers, the training director, and the vice president for personnel, only to have some of those same trainees give more sobering appraisals in private conversations with the trainers, when superiors were out of earshot.

(3) To the extent that training serves an image function for the organization, then being able to say that "we've got" a particular type of program is its raison d'être. Evaluating its effectiveness in terms of subsequent job performance really is not necessary, and may even hinder, its window dressing value.

If the above analysis is correct, then it will take more than review articles to nudge training out of its doldrums.

LACK OF ORGANIZATIONAL ANALYSIS

Wexley (1984) wrote that he was "appalled" at the lack of organization analysis in the training literature despite the continuing call for it as an important aspect of training needs analysis (Bass & Vaughan, 1966; McGehee & Thayer, 1961). Goldstein (1974, 1986) posited organizational analysis as a cornerstone of training needs analysis, and Moore and Dutton (1978) have enumerated the organizational variables that should be considered. Rather than add one more unheeded call, it may be more fruitful to address the question of why psychologists have so consistently ignored organizational variables.

Psychologists by predilection and by training have been oriented to micro Organizational Behavior (OB) much more than to macro OB. Our focus is on the behavior of individuals in an organizational context. We may pay lip service to contextual variables, even viewing organizations as open systems. But we seldom take the organization very seriously. We master psychometrics but we have not yet developed an organometrics. The unit of analysis in much of our "organizational" research remains, appropriately or not, the individual rather than the organization. Training is one I/O specialty, not unlike others, that evidences a pronounced individual bias and relative organizational neglect. A healthier balance of individual and organizational analysis is unlikely to be achieved until we train a new generation of I/O students to be more aware of the importance of organizational context variables and to be more proficient in organizational analysis. This will require including a heavier dose of macro OB in I/O curricula. In short, the lack of organizational analysis in the training literature is a consequence of our relative weakness in macro analysis in general. Students immersed in an integrated program of micro and macro OB will acquire both the awareness and the requisite skills for conducting organizational analysis in training.

LINKAGE WITH STRATEGIC MANAGEMENT

In a similar vein, Zand (1984) has recently called for a linking up of organizational development (OD) and strategic management (SM). Observing how OD has lost ground to SM in recent years as SM has come to dominate management thinking, Zand constructively suggests a rapprochement between the two to achieve an effective synergy. Zand's proposal for OD is generalizable to training. Paraphrasing Zand's observations about OD, training is too often either a stand-alone program designed to remedy a particular operational difficulty or a general program not linked to a strategic plan. Training is not perceived as a useful means of implementing strategy. Training will continue to neglect organizational analysis, remain overly individually focused, and be a short-term, fad-ridden endeavor until I/O psychologists specializing in training begin taking macroapproaches, such as SM, seriously.

Despite the persistent shortcomings discussed above, training will be with us forever. The near future may see dramatic training breakthroughs as personal computers come of age, as the accelerating electronics revolution continues to alter the nature of work, and as the emergence of a world economy reshapes the cultural milieu in which training takes place. Billions are committed annually to training. The field beckons the organizational psychologist to come and discover training. It is an old field in which one can still pioneer.

9

TRAINING AND DEVELOPMENT OF BLACK MANAGEMENT

KARL HOFMEYER
University of South Africa
Pretoria, South Africa

In South Africa, the major challenge facing business remains the extent to which it successfully can advance black employees into skilled and management positions. Blacks are not able to compete on an equal footing with whites because of the many restrictions and disadvantages they face in an "apartheid" society. Ironically, South Africa's economic survival now depends to a large extent on meeting high-level manpower shortages with highly trained black employees, and companies are attempting to redress, in a few years, the effects of many years of discrimination and deprivation.

Some of the problems associated with the training and development of black managers will be discussed here and why black employees have difficulty breaking into the managerial ranks. Also considered will be the reactions of different firms to the obvious need to train and develop black managers. The major training activities engaged in by South African companies over the past five years will be analyzed, and, finally, two important new developments in the field will be outlined.

THE ARGUMENTS

The lack of progress in the training and development of black managers has been attributed both in the United States and South Africa to culture, to a lack of educational qualifications and to racial discrimination (Fernandez, 1975; Hofmeyr, 1982). Since these have provided only a partial explanation in the South African context, a fourth explanation has been added: the observation that the black managers occupy, to a greater or lesser extent, a marginal or peripheral position in organizations dominated by whites and that this affects their ability to develop and perform (Human & Hofmeyr, 1984).

Those who use the cultural argument assert that black employees lack the necessary entrepreneurial attitude or ethic, as well as the required ambition, initiative, and reliability to succeed in business (Fernandez, 1975). According to this argument, whites are reared in the culture geared to the profit motive, to ambition, and to individual achievement, whereas the black environment stresses sharing, affiliation, and being part of a community. Particularly in South Africa, this argument has been used as a neat explanation for any number of perceived differences and stereotypes. In the case of black managers it probably has been overstated, since most black managers have grown up in an urban environment in daily contact with Western norms.

The educational argument states that blacks lack the necessary educational background and qualifications to compete with their white counterparts in business. Increasingly integrated schooling in the United States and improved opportunities to obtain further education has weakened this argument in the United States, but in South Africa poor education remains a formidable obstacle to career success. Black and white education are strictly separated in South Africa and the black system suffers from inadequate funding and poorly trained and underqualified teachers. The products of this system have been described as having assimilated a body of facts without properly digesting or properly understanding the material. Those who attend black schools typically have poor proficiency in English. They have difficulty verbalizing thoughts and ideas and dislike criticism. They show a reluctance to ask questions, as well as a tendency to provide answers to questions in a manner calculated to please the questioner (Adler, 1981).

In South Africa only about 2% of black school pupils complete their schooling, and they do so under very disadvantaged circumstances. Understandably, they regard themselves as a special group and often have high expectations. In the workplace they compete for the first time with whites who have had a superior education and numerous other advantages. The realization that they are ill-prepared for success in business results in frustration and a lack of confidence. Thus the educational argument is an important consideration in explaining why there are so few black managers in South African corporations.

The third argument relates to racial discrimination, asserting that this is at the root of black underperformance. Equal employment opportunity legislation in the United States and affirmative action activities have substantially improved the work and advancement opportunities for minorities, although some discrimination still takes place. In South Africa discrimination is a dominant force: It is found in every sphere of life, from legislation such as job reservation that, until recently, prevented blacks from holding certain skilled jobs in industry, to the attitudes of white bosses toward their black employees.

Because of implicit or explicit discrimination, black employees often face second-rate working conditions, poor placement, inadequate training, and white employee resistance. At lower levels of an organization negative attitudes and discrimination are partly motivated by the fear that blacks could advance and threaten the job security of white employees. At more senior levels, discriminatory attitudes are less obvious but express themselves in a lack of commitment to affirmative action.

In the South African context, the educational, cultural, and discriminatory arguments provide important reasons why there are so few black managers. The fourth, and perhaps less apparent reason, is the observation that potential black managers find themselves in a marginal position in the workplace. Human (1981) argues that black managers in South Africa are expected to function in at least three different worlds. First, they are expected to function in the world of the black township and black urban culture. Second, they are expected to function as a nonwhite in apartheid society. Third, they have to contend with the work situation, where they may be expected to function as equals with their white colleagues. Since their position in the workplace is inconsistent with their position in apartheid society, it is understandable that they are confused and that their work performance may suffer as a result. In interviews conducted by Human (1981) many black managers said that in the work situation they feel as though they do not belong. The general feeling evinced was that black managers are living a schizophrenic existence: They are living in a no man's land between two cultural groups; they are partially accepted and partially rejected by the white world in which they are expected to perform; they face the psychological burden of not knowing where they stand; they cannot take the knowledge they require for granted.

Thus in addition to educational disadvantages and racial discrimination, coupled with some cultural differences, potential black managers have to cope with numerous ambiguities and inconsistencies. They cannot simply commit themselves to the task of developing themselves and moving up in the organization; they have to contend with an additional set of limiting variables that often make their behavior tentative.

The observation that the black manager faces particular ambiguities and conflicts is not unique to South African business. Writing about "What it's like to be a black manager" in the United States, Jones (1973) puts forward an argument very similar to those put forward by black managers in South Africa. As a black manager, Jones found himself in a unique position in a white company. He was anxious because of internal conflicts and confused because of external inconsistencies; he could not take his work world for granted; he was never quite sure of how particular individuals were going to react to him and he could never quite dismiss the fact that he was black from his mind.

Although the feeling of "marginality" experienced by a black manager in the United States is probably less today than in 1973, the phenomenon no doubt still exists and can be added to the traditional arguments of culture, education, and discrimination that are used to explain why blacks experience difficulty breaking through into the managerial ranks.

THE REACTIONS OF COMPANIES

In South Africa the arguments have been thoroughly debated and documented, and companies and practitioners profess that they understand the barriers to black managerial advancement. At the same time, manpower statistics are frequently quoted to attempt to convince companies of the need to develop and advance more black employees into skilled and managerial positions. Despite understanding the arguments and acknowledging the needs, South African companies generally have made very little progress. In the minds of executives, the following reasons are used to rationalize away the need to develop and advance black managers more actively:

(1) Until fairly recently some companies were able to point to legislation such as job reservation and the Physical Planning Act (which dictated ratios of white to black employees in certain industries) to explain why they had not been able to make more progress. This was largely a smoke screen to hide other concerns, because enlightened companies have been able to achieve results despite the legislation.

(2) The management of some companies simply is not alarmed by the manpower forecasts, and argue that they have managed to staff the company with whites in senior positions in the past and can continue to do so in the future.

(3) Given the disadvantages with which the black employee enters the workplace, a company may have to invest substantially more in the training and development of this employee than in the case of a white employee. In particular, smaller companies use this economic argument to justify their position.

(4) Past experience and the possibility of a white "backlash" are often quoted. Managers use the failure of an advancement program or the poor performance of a black manager as evidence promotion of blacks into more senior positions does not work. At lower levels of the organization, white workers and supervisors may resist advancement of blacks and the potential risk of a backlash is often emphasized.

Over the past five years these arguments have been cited frequently to explain away the need for a policy and strategy for black advancement. However, companies are now beginning to experience real shortages of manpower, particularly in the skilled job categories, and the pressure is mounting to advance more blacks into these positions.

There has been a relatively small percentage of enlightened companies who have paid more than lip service to advancement efforts, and their reasoning may be contrasted with that described above:

(1) Some larger companies acknowledge a real shortage of managers that, in the longer term, cannot be avoided. There would be companies that take heed of the published manpower forecasts and who realize that their future growth is dependent upon employing blacks, coloreds, and Indians in more senior positions. The alternatives to advancing other races would include (a) deliberately curtailing expansion, (b) being increasingly prepared to appoint younger, less experienced, or less competent white people into management positions, or (c) increasing the responsibility of the existing executives so that they manage, for example, larger areas and more people.

(2) Some companies acknowledge a responsibility as South African employers to ensure that all races are represented in the management hierarchy. Meaningful efforts to advance black managers may reflect a value system among senior management that dictates that equal opportunities for advancement should be made available to all races. This, in turn, may involve additional time and resources

being allocated to disadvantaged groups to ensure that programs involving equality of opportunity are meaningful.

(3) Some multinational companies engage in affirmative action activities, partly as a result of the pressure placed on them by their parent companies and employment codes such as the Sullivan code of employment practice. American multinationals, in particular, are under intense pressure to be seen to be advancing black employees and some of them are at the forefront of attempts to find innovative and workable approaches.

(4) Finally, in some companies, management foresees a new political arrangement coming into being in the future with a different distribution of power, and may wish to start sharing leadership of their companies in preparation for the future.

The set of reasons given earlier that argue for the maintenance of the status quo needs to be contrasted with the more enlightened view taken by some companies. The range of arguments reflects the diversity of opinions on this problematical, and often emotional, issue.

TRAINING AND DEVELOPMENT THEMES

The response of companies has also included an investment in training and development programs for blacks. These have varied in their nature and objectives, but four of the major themes that have emerged over the past five years are behavior modeling, achievement training, bridging education, and mentorship.

Five years ago, personnel and training practitioners were arguing that to change the attitudes of managers toward their black subordinates, one had to change their behavior first. Largely influenced by writers such as Goldstein and Sorcher (1974), many companies embraced behavior modeling as the key to improving interpersonal and supervisory skills that would result in improved attitudes and the development of employees. Some considerable amounts of time and effort were committed to behavior modeling-based training, but for reasons of inadequate follow-up or support, or the deep-seated nature of attitudes and values, limited success was achieved.

The early 1980s also saw the advent of "achievement training" programs. Based on McClelland's (1961) model, these programs were predicated on the argument that a fundamental reason why black employees were not advancing was that their orientation was affiliation, rather than achievement-based. For example, Tabane

(1979) argued that among blacks, "a 'group mind' and extended family system have tended to keep dormant the need for achievement that otherwise might have emerged." In the programs, high-potential employees are exposed to exercises, lectures, games, role plays, and assignments designed to stimulate increased individuality, assertiveness, and risk-taking propensity. Achievement training programs may have achieved some limited success with individual participants, but they have not substantially altered the advancement patterns in organizations. They have also been subject to some criticism by black managers who reject the notion that potential black managers should be treated differently from white and that they are less achievement motivated.

In the last five years, numerous companies have also developed "bridging education" programs designed to prepare black school leavers or graduates for entry into the business world. A typical program lasts for three months (full time) and covers areas such as the following: learning skills, interactive skills, basic business principles, problem solving, and decision making. Again, these programs have been criticized by some black managers. In interviews (Hofmeyr, 1982), black managers commented that bridging courses and other "blacks only" programs encouraged what they referred to as a "negative self-fulfilling prophecy": If potential black managers were repeatedly told that they were "disadvantaged" and needed "special training," they would begin to accept this and perform less well than they might. One manager expressed the opinion that bridging programs can become an end in themselves if companies concentrate on the courses and not on developing black employees through meaningful responsibility and job experience.

A further identifiable theme has been the emergence of "mentorship programs." Since programs such as those described above seemed to suffer from the weakness that, typically, they were conducted "off-the-job" and relatively little learning was transferred onto the job, it seemed important to link the trainee's manager into the development process. Mentorship programs provide training for the manager, who is then given responsibility for coaching, counseling, and, in other ways, "mentoring" the trainee. Some companies claim impressive results with mentorship programs, but there are also those who criticize them as being paternalistic. Some academics and practitioners argue against the notion that one can formally create mentor-protégé relationships, claiming that, by definition, these relationships can develop naturally only over time between two people who have an affinity for each other and who can learn from each other.

NEW DIRECTIONS

The programs and themes that have characterized the period 1980-1985 represent an operational or ad hoc response to the problems of affirmative action. They address individual aspects of performance and, at best, lead to improvements in interpersonal skills, assertiveness, supervisory skills, and the like. They had not led to significant increases in the numbers of black managers.

This realization has led to a new perception of what is required. First, top managment has to become involved if progress is to be made and, second, more attention needs to be paid to problems associated with the black manager's marginal position in companies.

Addressing the first observation, there is a growing awareness in South African companies that affirmative action has to be based on a holistic approach that involves all employees and is directed by top management. The activities have to move from an operational level to a strategic level. The major reasons for this fact follow:

- At this level, longer-term manpower issues and requirements are given the attention they deserve.
- The attention and support of top management can be ensured.
- Affirmative action plans can be built into the organization's strategic plans.
- Top management and not the human resources specialists dictate the direction and pace of the advancement plans.

The top management of some companies is starting to acknowledge its responsibility for making affirmative action a reality. They realize that as long as responsibility for black advancement rests with the human resources department and depends on training programs, very little will change. Chief executive officers are beginning to verbalize their commitment and build affirmative action targets into their strategic plans.

The second theme that is emerging is the attempt by some companies to understand and deal with the black manager's tentative position in organizations. It was noted earlier that the inconsistencies, ambiguities, and conflicts confronted by the black managers seem to affect their performance and may result in lower productivity, tension, and dissatisfaction. The recognition of this problem has prompted some companies to move the focus of their development activities from skills and other training programs to finding ways to reduce the uncertainty that many black managers experience. A return to some basic issues, such as clarifying job descriptions, key result areas, and standards of performance, is recognized as fundamental to the advancement process. In these companies, behavior modeling and achievement training programs are being replaced by improved systems of goal setting and performance appraisal.

To alleviate the marginal position of the black manager, these companies have also recognized that "cross-cultural training" is needed to improve understanding and communication between groups. They recognize that black managers need to feel more comfortable and accepted in the company and white managers need to provide the same support and encouragement given to high-potential white employees.

CONCLUSION

The new directions discussed above may improve the effectiveness of South African advancement programs. However, progress is likely to continue to be slow.

International experience has shown that class systems and occupational hierarchies tend to be rather stagnant, and there is considerable inertia in the meaningful upward mobility of disadvantaged groups. (See, for example, Neath, 1981). Furthermore, South Africa's political and social policies will severely affect the achievements of organizations in this area. Attitudes, communication, and interpersonal relations are all influenced by the policy of racial separation, and since management development, to a large extent, depends on a supportive environment, there remain fundamental constraints on what can be achieved.

10

MANAGEMENT DEVELOPMENT IN INDIA AND SPAIN

JAIME C. FILELLA
*Escuela Superior de Administración
y Dirección de Empresas (ESADE)*
Barcelona, Spain
Xavier Institute of Management
Bombay, India

The winds of change are blowing well beyond the limits of the Anglo-American and North European world in the way people approach their work situation.

Major changes have been observed in the practice of management development in countries such as India and Spain. The two countries display both similarities and differences to provide a basis for comparison and reflection.

First of all, India and Spain are similar in that they have clearly defined cultural traditions to be acceptable sounding boards to stimulate reflection. Second, the Indian and the Spanish cultural traditions are oral, that is, cultures where people like to talk and to relate with one another in face-to-face situations. Third, both peoples show traits of an idealist temperament: People are intelligent and intellectual with the resulting danger that once they have solved problems mentally, the problems have ceased to exist in reality. Fourth, both have strong regional divisions. The Galicians, Basques, and Catalans of Spain are matched by the Punjabis, Tamils, and Bengalis of India. India is more complicated in that the regionally disparate Spaniards are all Catholic, and likely to speak Spanish as a second or first common language, but their Indian counterparts are likely to be a mix of Hindus, Moslems, Sikhs, and so on with a regional first language followed by one or more possible common languages such as English and Hindi.

The differences between India and Spain are no less clear. They belong to two different streams of Indo-European language development, Sanskrit and Latin, respectively. Second, the size of their population is considerably different, Spain representing hardly 6% or 7% of the Indian population. While Spain was being forged in the 800 year Reconquista, India was being structured by Brahmin ideology, and Moslem empire building as well as overseas cultural and trade expansion toward Southeast Asia. For most of the last 300 years while Spain was climbing down from world power status, India was becoming a colony of Britain. Spain is just emerging from 40 years of autocratic dictatorship with continuing economic uncertainties. Economically also, India and Spain differ significantly, although both countries show wide discrepancies in the way wealth is distributed.

Literacy and industrialization are also different. Suffice what has been said to make the point that although both countries are outside the Anglo-American and North European cultural stream and are markedly different in some respects, they are similar in others and thus provide a sound basis for comparison.

MANAGEMENT DEVELOPMENT
AND THE NEW WORK ETHOS

With the exception of Japan in recent times, industrial progress has been concentrated where Protestantism was born, nurtured, and developed. Despite its obvious negative undertones in some quarters, the White-Protestant culture is an object of admiration and even envy. The spirit of work and the stable dedication to one's profession are often associated with the European value system and social structure. The process by which work has become integrated into the fabric of human societies suggests a continuity (see Wren, 1979) through three stages:

—work as a means of survival all over the world

—work as a tool of ecological change through technology

—work as organized activity

The first two aspects of work became fairly universal. With the development of sophisticated technology, the nations north of the Pyrenees, and the United States began to emerge as clear winners. The organization of work became a very distinctive feature of the same nations in the course of the nineteenth century. It is within this perspective that management development made its appearance in the United States, either in very formally structured educational programs or in fairly loose and short courses. The basic inspiration seems to have been to ensure adequate management for today's complex firms. To this end, managers had to develop as persons and as professionals. Training departments evolved from simple sections within the Personnel Division meant to upgrade senior workers in their technical skills, into highly sophisticated operations, often calling for total autonomy from the personnel manager. Varney (1981) has described three stages in this development process. Bennis (1981) went further and suggested that the training function should be moved from Personnel to join with OD programs and Public Relations under the common name of "Institutional Department."

The creation of such a department may reinforce the trends mentioned by organizational scientists. For instance, Lawler (1985) has spoken of "high-involvement organizations"; Walton (1985) has identified some characteristics typical of what he called "high-commitment organizations"; and a set of other writers have addressed themselves to the transforming effects of leaders within organizations with climates favoring results and satisfaction beyond expectation (Bass, 1985; Roberts, 1985; Tichy & Ulrich, 1984).

Management development in such organizations is a far more complex task than it was a few years ago. To the traditional activities of preparing managers or managers-to-be for the needs likely to occur within a foreseeable future in an organization, new concerns have been added in view of making firms more pliable to the changing environmental conditions either within or outside the firms. Firms, too, have to be made more responsive to the expectations of managers about their professional development and in keeping with their career plans. It would appear that today people begin to look upon their work situation less as a means of livelihood or as a moral obligation than as a chance for them to express what they consider to be worth expressing in their lives. Naisbitt (1982) stresses the growing awareness among working people as people with "work-rights" and not merely human rights, one of the megatrends affecting modern societies in the West.

Work is conceived and experienced today in ways markedly different from the past. Postindustrial countries are far from experiencing work as "binding" whether one subscribes to Max Weber's or Tawney's or to some other explanation proposed to account for the work ethic. Work situations are less binding, more stimulating, and more creative. An obvious question is whether

these changes are confined to the modern industrialized world, or
are observable in other countries such as India and Spain as well?

MANAGEMENT DEVELOPMENT IN INDIA

In a cross-cultural survey, Roberts and Boyacigiller (1983) identified worker motivation, entrepreneurship, and human resource
development as the most significant management research issues in
India. This is as it should be in a country whose major asset is its
population. Actually, India's Five-Year Plans of Development from
the 1950s to the present have kept to policies that are labor—rather
than capital—intensive. Although issues relating to this policy are
socioeconomic in nature, they do not have an impact on the
management and administration of firms as a whole. In the many
"in-company" training programs the Xavier Institute of Management in Bombay runs for private and public firms, we have
identified a set of problems that clearly reflect a host of bureaucratic
side effects in people. Uneven distribution of personnel across
departments, excessive staff for simple tasks, endless discussions
over the exact nature of one's job, vague performance standards,
transfer policies across departments or from one region to another
experienced as punitive, resistance to new technology as a fear
reaction to possible causes of inefficiency or even retrenchment,
clear-cut expectations that promotions will be made from within
the organization, and the like make the point quite clear: People
problems are the great bottleneck in Indian firms.

Much of this situation is due to endless hassles between
management and unions. The situation is at its worst in public sector
companies, although transnational corporations do not have a
cleaner slate (Bhattacharya, 1983). The problem is more than
organizational. It appears to be one of attitude and mentality. Data
available from the use of the Myers-Briggs Type Indicator with
engineers (Pereira, personal communication, 1985) and bank employees, educational administrators, and officers insurance companies (Filella, 1985) show a significant "imbalance" in the Indian
profiles. While the percentage of "negotiators" in the United States
seems to be about 40%, the percentage in the Indian groups ranges
from 4% to 19%. Similarly, while the percentage of "stabilizers" in
the U.S. data accounted for about 40% , the Indian groups had
percentages oscillating between 46% and 80% with a mean of about

65%. There is some reason to wonder at the chances for organizational change when the abundance of stabilizers is further compounded by the absence of negotiators. Although a more systematic analysis is well in order, the trend is disquieting, especially if it is to be interpreted against the proverbial Hindu stereotype of tolerance and of peaceful coexistence.

Here is where the need for training in general and for management development is felt most poignantly. After a thorough survey of research in the organizational behavior area in India, Ganesh and Rangarajan (1983) detected a promising trend in the expectations of major potential users of organizational behavior knowledge. They proposed a model of organizational behavior research in close touch with economists leading to a development of indigenous theories of human behavior, using the industrial revolution forcibly induced by colonialism in the last century as a point of reference. They suggest that the cooperation between economists and organizational psychologists can stimulate mutual understanding and support.

The challenge is directed to organizational behavior researchers and economists. It should also be considered by trainers in the country. Pontes (1983) attributed the dismal industrial performance of India in 1982 (ironically, the U.N. Year of Productivity) largely to the trainer. She felt that trainers had failed in their duty by their lack of adequate qualifications, lack of commitment, and the abundance of self-imposed bureaucratic constraints.

Rajiv Gandhi's Government has unequivocally emphasized the need for training as part of its determination to lead India into a prosperous twenty-first century. Such pronouncements have not fallen on deaf ears. The more adventurous and professionally alive companies, such as Larsen and Toubro, Hindustan Petroleum, Hindustan Levers, and Unit Trust of India, have ambitious programs to develop their personnel. Such companies are well represented in the public and private sectors. What is interesting is to see that the training programs are of different types and have been chalked out one or two years in advance. In addition, consultants and training institutions have become more discriminating in their practices. For instance, at the Xavier Institute of Management, Bombay, we agree to conduct "in-company" programs on conditions that a long-range plan for training be made with definite budgets earmarked for it, and that training programs include a wide range of organizational levels from supervisory to senior management levels along with their assistants. After several years of very rewarding relationships with client firms, we have moved toward very specialized programs of 4 to 15 days duration covering such areas as

—people in managerial positions but with still a clerical mentality due to a policy of internal promotions;

—"natural" groups of senior managers with at least one of their immediate assistants;

—programs for management-union leaders conducted immediately after new contracts have been signed;

—programs specifically meant for socially underprivileged groups (referred to in the Indian Constitution as "scheduled tribes and castes") who are the beneficiaries of the so-called reserved seats. By law, a certain percentage (as high as 15% to 20%) of the posts available in companies have to be assigned to such socially oppressed groups—more or less like the U.S. affirmative programs for disadvantaged minorities.

The need is overwhelming. Three problems have to be mentioned in this connection: the problem of numbers, the problem of communication, and the problem of social/educational differences. The problem of numbers can be easily understood if training is to be imparted to several hundreds and at times even thousands of managers in an organization in batches of 20 or 25. This problem is further aggravated by the language problem. Among older staff and in urban centers English can take care of most problems of instruction. In areas away from large metropolitan centers and among staff below of 30 to 35 years of age, regional languages are absolutely essential for instruction. It is not easy to find a team of trainers belonging to various language groups who have succeeded in developing a common approach to training.

The third problem is a bit more complex. Social differences in a country such as India are really kaleidoscopic. It is not a problem of caste, or economic status, or education. It is an ubiquitous problem with multiple manifestations. To put it simply, a management trainee in Bombay can know as much and be as qualified as his or her counterpart in any country in the world. The fact that his or her knowledge and fluency in English is as good as any one in the United Kingdom, the United States, or Canada complicates the situation even further. The type and standards of education in many an Indian management institute are such that what is published in English anywhere in the world is widely publicized and read, although there is no guarantee that it may become professionally functional in practice because of diverse sources of organizational resistance. The outcome is disastrous for the self-image of the Indian manager: having up-to-date knowledge according to international standards and not being able to put it into practice.

In view of reducing this gap between knowledge and practice, B. K. Singh organized a very daring and novel seminar in August 1985 with the participation of over 600 delegates from all over the country. The topic was "Creativity and Innovations in Personnel Management" and was meant to report on the 40 or 50 projects that had been identified by a team of experts as creative, daring, and had proved successful after at least 2 or 3 years of sustained implementation. A quotation from the convention brochure will convey better than any other information what the program was about.

> India, as a developing country, cannot merely look at the Western or Japanese models of Personnel Management if it has to make rapid progress. It has to look inward, learn to multiply its own successes in these areas and develop its own indigenous methods of participation or negotiation. The knowledge and awareness of successful indigenous experiences in different aspects of Personnel Management would enable the multiplication of benefits accruing from them and would go a long way in the development of the country. It would also be of great use in evolving strategic models for harmonious employee relations in organizations.

Many participants felt the convention was a landmark in the development of indigenous forms of managing people in Indian organizations. The projects ranged from successful industrial relations programs largely in politically restless and hostile areas such as West Bengal, to employee or worker participation in the solution of "off the job" problems in the western region. Curiously enough, there was a report of a company run along Gandhian principles that, after some spectacular successes, had gotten into serious trouble; the company was officially closed down as economically unviable.

Reflection on what is being done in India to develop managers commanding India's limited resources and its many "barefoot managers" suggests that management development is not a matter of rendering assistance to people to develop themselves into managers, so that they can climb the organizational ladder with greater professional competence and confidence. Rather it assists all managers to develop a functional outlook. In other words, the problem is not to have good ideas or up-to-date knowledge. Due to English as the lingua franca of Indian business, almost too much is known by Indian managers to make them feel comfortable in the practice of management. What is needed is the application of indigenously developed ideas to the Indian reality.

MANAGEMENT DEVELOPMENT IN SPAIN

Two impressions stand out. First, more is being done in Spain for the training of managers than is publicized. Second, there is a secret feeling that Spanish managers are all right personally; they need to possess the right tools and to be taught the right techniques. Whatever the cause, the description of many a sound and seemingly coherent training program is accompanied by the apologetic, and yet self-righteous, tone of the statements about it.

The paucity of the published material may be largely due to the fact that Spain is an oral society. People will easily talk for hours on end, but their fingers get cramped when it comes to putting the same thing in writing. The second impression regarding the natural qualities of Spanish people as potential managers is more difficult to substantiate. The following remarks may give an inkling into this complex problem and into what is professionally acceptable or unacceptable in management development programs in Spain. Let me pursue this matter more explicitly.

Many a Spaniard secretly harbors the feeling that Mediterranean people have kept their capacity to enjoy life and are willing to grant that people in the United States, Britain, and Northern Europe have developed the skill of negotiating with reality through the use of high technology (Racionero, 1985). This assumption may explain the unquestioned attitude of having to learn relatively little about the quality of life in Spain and of having to learn a lot about technology. Baruel (1978) suggests that Spain's industrial development lies in the prudent transfer of euro-technology and the more effective use of its largely untapped human resources. "Curiously enough," he remarks, "creativity is available in large supply in Spain where imagination and initiative are traits very congenial to the Spanish character, at least in some regions" (p. v). This remark is in keeping with the skill to empathize found among Latin peoples (Alexander, Barrett, Bass, & Ryterband, 1971) and more specifically with the profiles of more than 60% of Spanish managers that are characterized by their strong human relations orientation at the cost of a concommitant task orientation (Filella, 1980). Fontela (1980) has suggested that Spain's growth as an industrial country rests squarely with the creation of a climate conducive to more orderly and incisive entrepreneurial and managerial activities. Underlying all the above observations there seems to be the assumption that the problem is basically, if not exclusively, structural and cultural (*coyuntural* is the Spanish word for it) and not personal as such.

How are training programs affected by these assumptions? How do training specialists approach the formation of those who have to steer Spanish firms into the European community? Management development programs reflect an ambiguity between concentrating on the strengths of Spanish managers and "giving" them what they lack. Many of the available reports of what is being done are about techniques (quality circles, to mention one) rather than development of people (Yela, 1985). Yet most successful training programs have evolved from a genuine effort to help people learn and personally grow. Three such projects were at BIMBO, a food producer, VULCA, a rubber factory, and LA CAIXA, a savings bank.

When BIMBO was in the grips of a hostile strike, Marcet (1981) took over as director of industrial relations. After some patch-up work, Marcet proposed a thorough training program to cover the whole company, and more specifically its executives. After five years, BIMBO is now seen as an exemplary firm for its healthy climate and the spirit of cooperation that prevails among its employees. The change seems to be largely due to the steady effects of a well-designed and implemented training program. The basic approach reflects an OD philosophy, putting people through a process of self-reflection along three channels: technical knowledge in keeping with the firm's policy to expand in the markets of southern Europe, self-knowledge as a first step toward personal growth, and team building. Two features in the program call for specific mention. First of all, training programs are run by internal staff as "in-company" programs along with the option for people to register in long educational courses conducted by management schools in the region. Second, people in BIMBO are encouraged to have ambitious career plans with the full assurance that the company will back them up if the plans are in line with the company's policy or, at least, will not interfere with them if they are only for the benefit of the employee. It is this combination of freedom and respect for the individual (so central to the Spanish ethos), along with a clear policy, that accounts for the success of the program.

VULCA is a rubber firm that, like a phoenix, rises from the ashes, flies again, and very high indeed. In 1981 the company was deep in the red. There was talk of selling the company off to some multinational or other. Under the leadership of a newly appointed chief executive, an ambitious policy of insertion into the European markets was evolved and today VULCA is a very profitable organization. The key to the success is to be found in the ability of the chief executive to combine an up-to-date technology with a very thorough training program. Training, however, is not confined to technical skills. On the contrary, it all began with a four-day seminar with the top management group. Lower levels were then covered with two aims in mind, to give them a sense of identity and a chance to react to the top management policy. An open climate has evolved that has allowed the company to reach where it is now. The chief executive makes no bones about his basic philosophy: Resourcefulness matters more than resources. This is especially evident in the way he has organized the R & D department with a very definite effort to create a "mentality" (Puyuelo, 1986).

The third example is the program of management development designed for the 960 branch managers of LA CAIXA, which has already been taken by 200 of them. LA CAIXA is a savings bank with deep roots in the history of Catalonia in the northeastern part of Spain. LA CAIXA was established in 1904 for the specific purpose of safeguarding the financial interests of old and retired people after the protracted general strike of 1902 that had reduced many families to misery. Today, LA CAIXA is the strongest financial institution in this region with 960 branch offices within 16,000 square miles. Training is not new to LA CAIXA. In the period 1984-1985, as many as 8,000 employees were given courses for a total of over 17,000 hours by 405 instructors over a period of 11 months. It is within this matrix of training projects that an Executive Development program was elaborated by Sole, Sala, and Roma (1984) over a period of 6 months and with the help of two external consultants. The program's specific objective is not to impart knowledge, but to help people reflect on the proper use of what they know in order to run a branch office effectively. The program runs through two modules of 24 hours each with an intervening period of one month between the two modules. The "break" of one month is meant to increase the chances that the participants will reflect on their performance and get a deeper insight into their ways of handling day-to-day problems. Three features are worth mentioning after more than 10 programs have already been conducted. First of all, participants get deeply involved in the process of self-reflection. Second, their immediate superiors in the various regional offices feel also responsible for the results of the program. Third, the program has brought to the fore and into bolder relief the impact of the socialization process at work in LA CAIXA.

This last feature accounts for the success of the program. People in LA CAIXA develop a mentality of their own characterized by the faithfulness to one's job and moral integrity along with a flat structure and a minimum set of norms from headquarters regarding company policy, objectives, performance, and the like. LA CAIXA runs; it is not being run. A very strong socialization process seems to be at work.

Summing up, much is happening in the field of management development in Spain today. Nevertheless not much is published or made known about it. The better known programs are those run by multinationals in Spain (IBM, Standard Electrica, Fasa Renault, and the like). In addition, there are excellent attempts by indigenous Spanish firms to develop their programs in keeping with their specific needs and requirements, and always in close touch with the available resources rather than trying to make up for what people lack. It is in this area that much work is still to be done. Spaniards today are in a mood of "becoming European" and of putting an end to the feeling that "Spain is different." This may be all right as a slogan to promote tourism, but not as a way of life. Becoming European is not just a matter of being part of the European community; it is a process of knowing what one's identity is in order to be able to assimilate what is needed. A process of search is underway.

At ESADE a model is being developed that may guide our search with special reference to management development. The model seeks to integrate three forces at work in the practice of management: the dynamics of power, the dynamics of reason, and the dynamics of trust. The model assumes that the most managers need a balanced combination of these types of dynamism. Discussions with Spanish managers seem to suggest that the issue of whether a manager is born or made is often only partially resolved. Those who favor the view that managers are born seem to have in mind issues involving power and power problems; those in favor of training and education as a way of preparing managers pay attention to the need for technical knowledge. In most discussions, the issue of trust is totally ignored. We are going on the hunch that the "natural gift" of managers (Spanish and others) is the spontaneous self-expression that creates an environment of openness and trust. Spaniards, in general, and managers, in particular, may find in this point something worth reflecting upon.

CONCLUSION

There are some indications that work today is being experienced less as a socially binding economic necessity than as a chance for people to express their talents in socially useful ways. Such changes have an effect on management development programs and in the relationship within organizations of the training function as a whole with the personnel departments. It has nowadays become difficult to think of training independently of organization development, and even of the public image of the firm in society. In addition, it is clear that these trends are not confined to America or northern Europe.

In India, human resources development has been the focus of attention in recent times, with specific reference to worker motivation and to the entrepreneurial spirit among young managers. In large companies many programs are organized for junior managers who have been inducted as management trainees or have been promoted from the ranks. Many of them reflect a clear interest in making firms less bureaucratic and rigid, despite of the resistances from the "old ways" so rampant among managers, union leaders, and working people in general. Government policies have recently encouraged training as an integral function of management in an effort of leading India into the twenty-first century. There is more in this policy than a slogan.

In Spain, too, the winds of change have been felt. The transition from Franco's regime to democracy has been successfully achieved. The entry of Spain into the European community has been looked upon by many as an official recognition of a process well underway. Much had to be dismantled indeed, and much more had to be refocussed. Today, after many traumatic experiences of total overhauling of large firms ("reconversion industrial" as it is called), of painful closures, and humiliating absorption of family concerns by multinationals, the economy seems to be stronger and poised for better times. Training has a role to play, and it is playing it well. Its main function seems to be directed to the improvement of work life, as is evident in the reports presented in national conventions. A guided search beyond the more elaborate programs of the large multinationals reveals training efforts well- planned and very much in touch with the needs of managers in Spain today. I think that a climate is evolving in which training is perceived less as a way of imparting information and of teaching techniques from "the other side of the Pyrenees" than as learning. It may sound simple. In practice, however, this shift may mean to stop thinking that Spaniards are different and have to start facing the fact that learning means change, and not just the acquisition of new techniques. It is perhaps through this roundabout process that the actual freeing of the human resources available to the Spanish manager may be finally possible.

Part II

The Work and Organizational Environment

11

JOB AND TASK ANALYSIS

JEN A. ALGERA
Vrije Universiteit
Amsterdam, The Netherlands

In this chapter, main trends in developments in job and task analysis will be reviewed; European developments will be emphasized. First, conceptual and taxonomic issues will be discussed. Second, methodology of task analysis will be covered. Third, specific fields will be discussed in which task analysis is used for rather diverse purposes such as personnel selection, training, and task design. Although some methods appear to be useful for different purposes, in fact, most task analysis methods have been developed and tested for a single purpose. Finally, new technologies are changing existing jobs and this is affecting methods of task analysis.

CONCEPTUAL AND TAXONOMIC ISSUES

Definitions of the concept *task* vary. Companion and Corso (1982) emphasized that the level of analysis used for the definition of the concept of task is the main cause for definitional disagreement. What is considered in one situation as a task can be a task element in another analysis. Companion and Corso (1982) stressed the necessity of a general definition of *task* that is appropriate at all levels of analysis. Wallace (1983) also remarked that variation in the unit or level of analysis employed in current job analysis research is a main source of problems in the interpretation of research results in a more broad conceptual system. He called for more concern with taxonomies and construct validity and he presented a scheme, elaborated from Pearlman (1980), that specified a hierarchy of seven explicit levels of job analysis.

A second source of variation in definition of a task depends on the degree the task performer is redefining an externally imposed

137

task. Thus tasks can be defined as subjectively perceived by the performer, or may be defined in terms of external stimuli, imposed on the performer.

Four approaches to task analysis (Algera, 1984; Companion & Corso, 1982; Fleishman, 1982; Fleishman & Quaintance, 1984) include:

(a) *Behavior description.* In this approach, task analysis is based on description of what operators actually do while performing a task. Most emphasis is placed on the task performer's overt behavior, for example, dial setting, meter reading.

(b) *Behavior requirements.* This approach focuses on the responses that should be made in order to achieve a successful outcome. The emphasis is on the intervening processes between stimulus and response, for example, scanning, short-term memory.

(c) *Ability requirements.* In this approach tasks are analyzed in terms of the human abilities required to perform the task. This approach is empirically based; that is, abilities are derived from correlations among human task performance, for example, deductive reasoning. Guilford's (1967) well-known Structure-of-Intellect Model belonged to this ability requirements approach. He classified intellectual abilities along the three dimensions of operations (e.g., memory), contents (e.g., visual), and products (e.g., relations).

(d) *Task characteristics.* Here, task analysis is in terms of the intrinsic properties of the task, apart from the responses that should be made (behavior requirements), or are made (behavior description), or the abilities required to fulfill the task (ability requirements). The focus is on the intrinsic, objective properties of tasks, for example, goal clarity.

Fleishman and Quaintance's (1984) seminal book *Taxonomies of Human Performance* presented such new developments as the "criterion measures approach," the "information-theoretic approach," and the "task strategies approach." All three used behavior requirements. Both the criterion measures approach and the information-theoretic approach stemmed from the same definition of a task as a transfer of information between components.

Four major classes of tasks characterizing the transfer of information between person and machine components of a system are as follows: machine-person, person-machine, machine-machine, and person-person. Task activities (e.g., searching, coding) are operationally defined by dependent measures (e.g., probability of detection, percentage correctly coded responses), hence the label "criterion measures." In the information-theoretic approach, human and machine tasks are both defined as an information transfer between an information source and a receiver. The taxonomy for classification of tasks is grounded on input (source) and output (receiver) constraints of a system. An important difference between the information-theoretic approach and the criterion measures approach is that the former is of a deductive nature, based on a theoretical model, while the latter is of an inductive nature, starting with empirical observations.

In the task strategies approach, based on the work of Miller (1973), 24 task functions have been defined (e.g., short-term memory), which represent intervening processes of the operator in a sequence of goal-directed behavior. Corresponding to these task functions, task strategies, to be used by the operator to become a more skilled task performer, have been developed. This approach could be useful for systems design and for training.

Companion and Corso (1982), reviewing five taxonomic approaches on ten criteria, came to the conclusion that none of the taxonomies meets the most critical criterion, namely, integration of empirical relationships. They emphasized the importance of this criterion and suggested a strategy for theory development in which the contribution from the empirical relationships is given at least as much consideration as the taxonomy. In their view, attempts to develop taxonomies in essence without regard to empirical relationships are not efficient.

METHODOLOGICAL AND
PSYCHOMETRIC ISSUES

Job and task analysis methods can vary in the technique of data collection, such as the "agent" used in collecting job information and the type of information collected. This, of course, leads to methodological and psychometric questions.

A number of studies have appeared on the issue of the most appropriate statistical procedures for assessing job differences and job similarities. Grouping individual jobs into broader classifications can be very useful for personnel management purposes, such as for selection and for training. A great number of techniques for analysis are available, such as cluster analysis procedures and analysis of variance procedures. But different cluster analyses techniques can lead to different results (Zimmerman, Jacobs, & Farr, 1982).

Arvey, Maxwell, and Gutenberg (1981) conducted a Monte Carlo study to investigate the statistical power of the univariate ANOVA procedure to detect true job differences and to examine the values of the omega-squared estimates for the various effects. Omega-squared estimates appear to be more useful in examining job differences than traditional significance testing. They provided a tentative rule of thumb for the evaluation of omega-squared values for the job $\times$ dimensions interaction. Similarly, Lee and Mendoza (1981) compared univariate and multivariate analysis of variance procedures to test for significant differences. Monte Carlo simulations were used to investigate the power and control for Type I error. The results indicate that the appropriateness of different statistical techniques is dependent on whether assumptions are met or violated.

Stutzman (1983) warned against the assumption that jobs within a single classification are similar. He found statistically significant as well as practical differences across jobs within a single job classification. An "average" profile across a number of specific jobs can misrepresent the profile for each individual job. He suggested that job classification attempts should start at the level of specific jobs (or individual positions). Again, discussing the recent focus on different grouping methods, Pearlman (1980) pointed out the danger of overlooking substantive questions in the search for a statistical solution to a psychological problem. He emphasized that different possible job groupings (dependent on the type of job descriptor and grouping method) should first be evaluated against the practical criterion of interest.

The psychometric properties of newly developed job analyses techniques have been reported by Banks, Jackson, Stafford, and Warr (1983) who developed the Job Components Inventory for the British work setting. The inventory was initially constructed for the analysis of low-skill jobs and intended for use in the development of training schemes for less-qualified young people (Stafford, Jackson, & Banks, 1984). Results of studies on the reliability and validity of five sections of the JCI (use of tools, equipment, physical and perceptual requirements, mathematical requirements, communications requirements, and decision making and responsibility) were reported. In general, the supervisor-job incumbent agreement was satisfactory and the instrument discriminated between jobs. Further research (Banks & Miller, 1984) found high reliability levels for interoffice, interrater, and supervisor-job holder agreement. Patrick and Moore (1985) investigated interrater and retest reliability for both incumbents and supervisors for the Job Structure

Profile, a modified British version of the Position Analysis Questionnaire (PAQ). Both types of reliability results turned out to be quite satisfactory. An additional finding was that the type of rater (job incumbent or supervisor) did not affect interrater or retest reliabilities; hence in practice mixed groups of raters could be used.

Cornelius, DeNisi, and Blencoe (1984a) attempted to replicate Smith and Hakel's (1979) findings on the convergent validity between expert and naive raters. They found lower values between these two types of raters and criticized the earlier conclusions on methodological grounds. Arvey, Davis, McGowen, and Dipboye (1982) manipulated the amount of job information and the degree of job interest exhibited by incumbents. Both types of manipulations had only very minor effect on the PAQ and no effects on the JDS (Job Diagnostic Survey). That job analysts were not biased by incumbents' positive or negative statements about the job is reassuring. However, the fact that no effects resulted from giving more job information is more problematic. It becomes unclear how much job information is needed for accurate description of jobs. If strong agreement between raters rests on stereotypes of jobs, independent of the amount of information, then the accuracy of these stereotypes becomes a central question. For example, in the area of interest measurement, some researchers prefer to use job activity items rather than job title, because reaction to job titles suffers from stereotyped bias. However, Crowley (1981) found little differences between these two types of items (activities versus titles) in comparing two research questionnaires, based on existing British instruments used for career education.

Sackett, Cornelius, and Carron (1981) compared job classification results based on global judgments with a task oriented-approach in which jobs were described by a 237 element profile. The less time-consuming global judgments approach led to the same job classification results as the task-oriented approach. In addition, they found a high correlation between incumbent ratings and supervisor ratings. Of course, whether the global approach will provide enough information depends on the specific purpose of job analysis. Thus Jones, Main, Butler, and Johnson (1982) found that reliable ratings can be derived from narrative job descriptions, on the aggregated level of PAQ job dimensions. However, on the item level, interrater agreement was rather low. Schmitt and Fine (1983) reported high levels of interrater agreement for both correlational and percentage agreement analyses in a study where judges had to rate skill requirements from written job analysis material.

The studies mentioned show that, although agreement between

and within different types of raters tends to be rather satisfactory, some questions still are unanswered. Probably the most interesting issue is the role of job stereotypes in raters' responses. Especially in an era where jobs are changing rather fast because of technological developments, job stereotypes can be inaccurate and could lead to invalid results if they play a major role in the responses of raters who provide job-related information.

JOB AND TASK ANALYSIS
FOR SPECIFIC PURPOSES

As has been stated before, job analysis results are applied in a number of areas. Accordingly, developments in some specific areas will be evaluated. Although a number of studies on job analysis related to occupational choice (e.g., Cunningham, 1983; Gottfredson, 1982; Prediger, 1981, 1982; Winer, 1981) and job evaluation (e.g., Doverspike, Carlisi, Barret, & Alexander, 1983; Gomez-Mejia, Page, & Tornow, 1982; Wallace, 1983) have appeared, far more publications concern job and task analysis for the purpose of personnel selection and task design. Therefore, developments in only these two areas will be covered here. Job analysis for the purpose of training will be touched on in the last paragraph in the section on task analysis and new technologies.

In the area of personnel selection, the most important issue discussed in the last five years is the question of validity generalization. Contrary to former "beliefs," Schmidt, Hunter, and others (e.g., Pearlman, Schmidt, & Hunter, 1980; Schmidt, Gast-Rosenberg, & Hunter, 1980; Schmidt & Hunter, 1981; Schmidt, Hunter, & Perlman, 1981) claimed that observed differences in validity coefficients can be explained by sampling error and other methodological artifacts, such as differences between studies in criterion reliability and degree of range restriction. For example, Schmidt et al. (1981) stated that large task differences between jobs do not produce large moderator effects, and suggest that other potential moderators, such as changes in technology, product, or job tasks over time, age, and applicant pool composition, will not moderate test validities either.

These findings would imply that test validities are not specific to the situation, and that a validity study is not necessary in the case where validity information on similar job-test combinations is available. What has to be shown then is that the job at hand can be considered as belonging to the same class of jobs as the original validity generalization study. Hence the crucial question is what job classification techniques are most appropriate within the framework of validity generalization.

This question has been addressed by several researchers. For example, Pearlman (1980) doubted the usefulness of molecular approaches to job analysis. Based on the results of validity generalization studies using the Schmidt-Hunter procedures, he stated that aptitude test validities generalize across broad occupational areas, and that differences in specific tasks or elements among jobs do not necessarily imply differences in the abilities underlying successful job performance. He advocated the attribute (abilities) requirements approach for job family development. In the same vein, after comparing the results of a simple, holistic approach with an elaborate job inventory approach in classifying jobs into three broad occupational groupings, Cornelius, Schmidt, and Carron (1984b) concluded that a detailed job analysis is not necessary for making job classification decisions for selection purposes.

However, the Schmidt-Hunter procedure for validity generalization has been criticized on several grounds (see, e.g., Algera, Jansen, Roe, & Vijn, 1984; Burke, 1984; Jansen, Roe, Vijn, & Algera, 1985; Roe, 1984; Schmitt, Gooding, Noe, & Kirsch, 1984a, 1984b) and it seems that the debate continues on the proper procedures for validity generalization, including classification rules for jobs and tests.

Above and beyond the question of whether validity generalization eliminates the need for detailing differences between apparently similar jobs, there still remain situations that call for detailed job information. Personnel selection procedures that depend on content validity, such as work samples, situational interviews, and simulations, still require detailed job information for their development. For example, Osburn, Timmreck, and Bigby (1981) suggested, on the basis of results from an experiment with simulated interviews, that the employment interview should be focused on critical job behavior rather than on more general dimensions, which is common practice. In this experiment, experienced employment interviewers were not able to distinguish between the more and less qualified applicants in the general dimension condition, whereas in the specific and relevant dimension condition, applicants could be reliably differentiated.

A procedure for content-oriented personnel selection is illustrated by Robinson (1981). In his job analysis procedure, information about the job performance domain is generated by a panel of experts who examine observable job behaviors. Critical tasks are identified and used as a basis for constructing selection tests. In this case, several work sample tests were developed for the job of construction superintendent, for example, a blueprint reading test, a construction error recognition test, a scheduling test. In similar fashion, Olson, Fine, Myers, and Jennings (1981) used the functional job analysis (FJA) procedure to generate work sample tests for heavy equipment operators. They obtained support for criterion-related validity of the tests, using a concurrent validity approach.

The state of the art in job and task analysis for application to problems of personnel selection thus seems to develop along several lines. From the framework of validity generalizations, central questions concern similarities and differences between jobs and the proper procedures for establishing job groupings. On the other hand, an interest in content-oriented methodologies can be observed. In the United States, this latter orientation is also stimulated by the necessity of adhering to requirements of job-relatedness to meet Equal Employment Opportunity guidelines. A third line seems to be the renewed interest in the synthetic validity approach, both in Europe (e.g., Algera & Groenendijk, 1985) and the United States (Hamilton, 1981; Mossholder & Arvey, 1984; Trattner, 1982). Where in validity generalization the central issue concerns the "transportability" of validity across situations for jobs as a whole, in the synthetic validity approach, jobs are divided into job elements. Here, job analysis is a keystone for determining the proper job elements.

The motivational properties of tasks are the central issue for numerous task design analyses. The Job Diagnostic Survey (JDS), a measuring instrument developed within the framework of the job characteristics model of work motivation (see, e.g., Hackman & Oldham, 1980), has been used in many studies. Translations are now available in German (see, e.g., Kleinbeck & Schmidt, 1983; Schmidt & Kleinbeck, 1983; Schmidt, Kleinbeck, & Rutenfranz, 1981a, 1981b) and in Dutch (Foeken, 1979a, 1979b).

The psychometric properties of the Job Diagnostic Survey and a similar instrument, the Job Characteristics Inventory (JCI), have been reviewed by Aldag, Barr, and Brief (1981). The task characteristics measured include skill variety, task identity, task significance, autonomy, and feedback. Aldag et al. (1981) concluded that the internal consistency reliability and convergent validity of the JDS and JCI are acceptable, but the substantive validity of both instruments is questionable, if the criterion used is affective; the validities are unacceptable, if the criterion used is behavioral.

Roberts and Glick (1981), in their review of the job characteristics approach, criticized the heavy reliance on job incumbents' questionnaire data in many studies. They stated that while many researchers claim to study "situation-person" relationships, they in fact study only "within-person" relationships.

Using only task characteristics as perceived by job incumbents implies that both the observations on the independent variables (task characteristics) and on the dependent variables (behavior and attitudes of task performer) derive from the same source of information. Hence a possible alternative explanation for the high correlations between task structure and dependent variables, cognitive consistency within the individual, cannot be excluded. Aldag et al. (1981) therefore recommended the use of indices of task characteristics that are not dependent on reports from the focal job incumbents. Algera (1981, 1983) used both independent assessments and incumbents' perceptions of jobs as predictors. He found a substantial convergence in the patterns of correlations between job characteristics and workers' responses in the two forms of measurement. He developed graphic scales with empirically derived scale authors for the measurement of 24 task characteristics. The definitions of these task characteristics were less abstract than JDS dimensions.

Roberts and Glick (1981) expressed some doubts concerning the construct validity of the JDS. Similarly, Aldag et al. (1981) stated that the discriminant validity of JDS and JCI is at least questionable. One of the few studies on this last issue is that of Ferratt, Dunham, and Pierce (1981). They investigated the discriminant validity of job design measures and job satisfaction measures. They concluded that these two constructs can be both conceptually and empirically differentiated and that confounding is a problem in measurement rather than a problem of construct definition. Drasgow and Miller (1982), presenting the "fidelity coefficient" to assess the degree of association between the observed scale and the underlying construct, reported that only three of the JCI scales related highly to a single underlying construct. The other three scales (task identity, task variety, and dealing with others) did not provide accurate measurement of the intended construct. Other studies on construct validity of JDS and JCI provided indications of the empirical dimensionality (Griffin, Moorhead, Johnson, & Chonko, 1980; Lee & Klein, 1982; Pokorney, Gilmore, & Beehr, 1980), and in general the dimensionality was supported, although sample-specific deviations of the assumed dimensionality also occurred.

In the job characteristics approach, incumbents' perceived task characteristics are assumed to reflect the objective attributes of jobs, and, accordingly, redesigning tasks will lead to changes in task perceptions and subsequently result in behavioral and attitudinal changes (see, e.g., Hackman & Oldham, 1980). However, in the late seventies, Salancik and Pfeffer (1978) provided another model to explain employee perceptions of the reactions to task characteristics. In their Social Information Processing (SIP) approach it was suggested that, at least partially, social and informative cues in the workplace influence task perceptions.

This discussion on the effects of object task changes and social information cues on task perceptions has been continued (Caldwell & O'Reilly, 1982; Salancik, 1984; Stone, 1984; Stone & Gueutal, 1984). Thomas and Griffin (1983) reviewed 10 studies addressing this question. Both experimental and field research was included. Results indicated that some elements of the perceived task environment are predominantly influenced by the objective task, other elements are primarily determined by both types of determinants. They concluded that the task attributes approach has not been refuted by these studies, but in fact there is support for an overlapping model, rather than support for one or the two models.

Recently, Campion and Thayer (1985) presented the Multimethod Job Design Questionnaire (MJDQ), which is based on approaches stemming from different disciplines. Starting with nearly 700 job design rules found in the literature, four underlying rationales emerged: motivational (from organizational psychology), mechanistic (from classic industrial engineering), biological (from work physiology), and perceptual/motor (from experimental psychology). Analogous to this taxonomy of job design approaches, a taxonomy of job outcomes was generated: satisfaction, efficiency, comfort, and system reliability. The main results from a field study were that different job design approaches produce different outcomes. Campion and Thayer (1985) advocate an interdisciplinary approach so that compromises among conflicting job design approaches and individual versus organizational outcomes can be reached.

TASK ANALYSIS
AND NEW TECHNOLOGIES

New technologies are changing existing jobs. In general, it can be stated that there is an increase in the use of mental instead of motor skills. Ekkers, Brouwers, Pasmooij, and Vlaming (1980) concluded that the tasks of many people who previously did not have direct contact with the computer will be changing so that interactive computer use will be an integral part of their jobs. Card, Morgan, and Newell (1983) emphasized that communication with machines is different from operation of machines. The operator of a machine accomplishes a limited number of tasks and makes use of a limited number of controls. The user who communicates with a computer uses a quite different style of interaction. Both user and computer can interrupt, query, and correct the communication at various points in the process (Card et al., 1983). The same point is touched on by Hollnagel (1983) and Hollnagel and Woods (1983). These latter authors advocate "cognitive systems engineering," an approach that tries to design man-machine systems on the level of cognitive functions.

With regard to the quality of working life and new technology jobs, in a recent Dutch study of jobs requiring the monitoring of display screens (Padmos, Pot, Vos, & Mol, 1984), differences in workers' responses (e.g., satisfaction, psychosomatic and psychic complaints) seemed to covary with classically defined task characteristics from the "motivational approach," such as autonomy, optional interaction, pacing of work, and variety. However, one of these task characteristics, feedback, deserves special attention in situations of new technology where some control acts are performed by the computer, or where the user is in dialogue with the computer (Buchanan & Boddy, 1983). Two types of feedback can be distinguished: outcome feedback and cognitive feedback (Jacoby, Mazursky, Troutman, & Kuss, 1984). Outcome feedback pertains to information about the accuracy or correctness of the response. Cognitive feedback or "diagnostic" feedback relates to the information value of feedback. Jacoby et al. (1984) stated that probably outcome feedback is less useful than diagnostic feedback for cognitive (as opposed to motor) tasks, and further that outcome feedback may be dysfunctional in a complex, dynamic environment.

The most salient aspect of new technology tasks from the viewpoint of task analysis is that there is a change from overt behavior to covert behavior of the task performer. This change seems in particular to have consequences for the development of training schemes (Verhoef, Zwaga, & Koelenga, 1983) and man-machine interface design (Roe, 1985). In terms of the conceptual bases for task analysis discussed before, this means that task analysis methods falling into the category "behavior description approach" are less relevant because emphasis is more on overt than on covert behavior. For example, existing task analysis methods such as the PAQ (McCormick, Jeanneet, & Mecham, 1972), of which also German and Dutch versions are in use, or the "Arbeitswis-senschaftliche Erhebungsverfahren zur Tatigkeitsanalyse (AET)" (Rohmert & Landau, 1979; English edition 1983) are therefore probably less useful.

The "behavior requirements approach" has its focus on the mental processes between stimulus and output response. The "task strategies approach," referred to earlier, offers 24 information-processing task functions and their associated task strategies that could be valuable in analyzing tasks that are characterized mainly by cognitive operations. In evaluating this approach, Fleishman and Quaintance (1984) stated that this descriptive system is useful for systems design. Also the scheme provides guidance to teach trainees the competence associated with skilled performance.

Other schemes, based on an information-processing approach for analyzing covert behavior have been proposed. For example, Hollnagel, Pedersen, and Rasmussen (1981) presented a schematic diagram for various internal data processing mechanisms in which three levels of behavior are distinguished: skill-based (use of highly trained habitual routines), rule-based (use of repertoire of rules and know-how), and knowledge-based (need to exercise functional understanding in causal deduction and planning) behavior. This scheme was used by Hollnagel et al. (1981) in their studies of human performance in high-risk systems to describe operator performance in a chain of events, using a timeline format. Similar schemes, including different levels of regulation of psychological processes, have been presented (see, e.g., Roe, 1985).

Another way to obtain information about the operator's covert behavior is to make use of verbal reports. Leplat and Hoc (1981) noted a revival of the use of verbalization, at least in some European countries, for the analysis of work situations in which a cognitive component is crucial. Verbal reports can take the form of thinking aloud, either while performing the task or after (subsequent report). However, Leplat and Hoc (1981) raise the question of the validity of subsequent verbal reports. Validation is necessary because homomorphism between the cognitive process involved during the task and that revealed in the verbalization does not always exist (see, also, Hoc & Leplat, 1983).

Other researchers have also used verbal protocols for task

analysis. For example, Drury (1983) studied the task of a stock exchange specialist using a verbal protocol technique. Extremely complex flow graphs were constructed that led to many suggestions for task design. Card et al. (1983) used verbal protocols along with videotaped behavior to study human-computer interaction on a computer-aided design task. The verbal protocols turned out to be very helpful for identifying the mental pauses and the phase structure of the total session. Hollnagel et al. (1981), studying operator performance in nuclear power plants, advocated combining data from different data sources, such as research simulators, training simulators, and interviews with plant personnel, for new systems design and for training. Their suggestions would appear to be valuable for the study of tasks in automated systems in other settings as well.

The introduction of new technology has led to a change in the type of skills needed for successful performance. Thus there seems to be a need for task analysis methods that focus more directly on the underlying mental processes of skills than traditional instruments such as the PAQ or the AET. A number of schemes and data collection methods (e.g., verbalizations) have been developed. There are, however, still many questions regarding the reliability and validity of these methods, which remain to be addressed.

12

ERGONOMICS AND COGNITIVE ASPECTS OF COMPUTER-CENTERED TECHNOLOGIES

JEAN-CLAUDE SPERANDIO
René Descartes Université (PARIS V)
Paris, France

The notion of "new technologies" is not a very precise one. However, several new technologies, which differ in the various industrial sectors and that have each evolved in a specific way, do share one principal point in common: the growing use of computers, either directly or indirectly.

One important feature that these computer-centered technologies present for psychologists is that the human work involved becomes less hard in physical terms, but harder or more complex intellectually. Tasks that required a certain physical effort and expenditure of energy are being replaced by tasks that require more attention or more elaborate information processing. It follows that the expected aptitudes of operators are no longer the same. This phenomenon has intensified considerably in the last ten years, and now generates a wealth of research topics and applications for the whole field of work psychology. Although we shall deal only with the ergonomic aspects here, it should be clear that the topics under consideration cover a much larger area.

Another important feature of new technologies is the explicit use of ergonomics in the attempt to resolve certain technical or social problems resulting from the sometimes too rapid installation of such technologies. This intensive use of ergonomics constitutes ipso facto a major impetus furthering the development of ergonomics itself. Accordingly, it may be useful to present the characteristics of the ergonomic approach in general before talking about "the state of the art." This many-faceted subject will be discussed below, and at the end of this chapter we shall describe the state of computer ergonomics in France, although disciplinary developments in France are not particularly different than elsewhere.

THE ERGONOMIC APPROACH

Ergonomics is a multidisciplinary subject. Its originality lies in its wide and unrestricted borrowing from other sciences, not only from psychology. There are data, methods, and theories that each one can offer within its domain for the analysis and improvement of human work. Physiology and psychology are the principal, though not exclusive, contributors.

The main goal of ergonomics is not to develop scientific knowledge concerning the fundamental mechanisms of human performance, but rather to use this knowledge to improve human work. However, since the fundamental scientific knowledge is often inadequate or incomplete, ergonomics has concentrated equally on developing fundamental research and on application necessary for the achievement of its own goals.

For ergonomics, improving work means increasing the qualitative and quantitative performances of the man-machine system in terms of efficiency and reliability according to the system's criteria. Ergonomics also implies the improving of conditions of task realization for the worker, in particular reducing work loads, fatigue, different forms of hardship, including boredom and monotony, reducing the risk of accident, the causes of illness or discomfort, and contributing to an increase in motivation and satisfaction.

These different criteria of improvement complement each other and ergonomics should try to satisfy all of them. There is no scientific theory, no standard that would allow forming a hierarchy of ergonomic criteria that depends on the local characteristics of the sociotechnical systems. It is not surprising to observe differences in the relative importance of these criteria in different countries, different eras, and different areas of application. For example, in western Europe, and particularly in France, there is a tendency to treat as most important those criteria concerning the quality of working conditions, whereas, in countries like the United States or Japan, criteria related to gains in performance and reliability have been seen to be more important. All the same, such differential tendencies have never been exclusive and appear to be evolving now toward a better balance.

THE EFFECT OF COMPUTING
ON THE DEVELOPMENT OF ERGONOMICS

While the evolution of ergonomics is influenced both by the scientific progress in the discipline on which ergonomics depends, and by the evolution of technology, the topics addressed by ergonomics result more from the important technological topics of the day than from ergonomic theories. This is equally true at the geographical level: The observed difference in the ergonomics practiced by different countries is due more to differences in the level of technological development than to political or ideological differences.

The first researches on the ergonomics of computing were carried out in the 1950s, that is very shortly after the birth of the first computers. However, right until the end of the 1960s, computing was marginally mentioned only in congresses on ergonomics. Ergonomists were at that time more concerned with reducing discomfort involved in physical work than with the intellectual and sensory aspects of work that now dominate the majority of man-computer interfaces.

Ergonomics applied to computing (hardware, software, and organizational aspects of computerization) has grown progressively in the last twenty years and now constitutes the most representative and most dynamic of the fields of activity of contemporary ergonomics. This dynamic quality is illustrated by the quantity and the diversity of research in this field. Although the following classification is questionable on the grounds of the numerous interrelations, four main subdivisions may be distinguished:

—ergonomics of hardware and work stations

—ergonomics of software engineering

—ergonomics of programming

—work analysis

ERGONOMICS OF HARDWARE

Up until the end of the 1960s, computing took place mainly in large rooms full of computer devices, where the main ergonomic problems involved temperature regulation and the noise of the printers. These problems concerned only a small number of individuals and very few explicit complaints were made by the operators, who were often considered as privileged. Outside these rooms, the noisy and tiresome work involved in preparing the punched cards often took place in large rooms in an atmosphere of high productivity, and marked an important area of dissatisfaction. There were numerous complaints and numerous conflicts, which were addressed to doctors and physiologists rather than psychologists.

All the same, a few rare ergonomic studies concerned with the computerization of tasks with a high level of intellectual complexity, such as Air Traffic Control, were conducted during the latter 1960s in France and also in the United States and in several countries of western Europe. This type of study exemplifies a tendency that was to develop along with cognitive ergonomics, which is now in full development.

From the 1970s on, computer ergonomics diversified. The approach initially focused largely on work involving cathode-ray terminals. The order of importance of the problems was first visual, second postural, and very occasionally social and psychological. It can be said that the ergonomists oriented to physiology were able to move rapidly and effectively into action, even at the international level, with numerous research programs, publications, and symposia on this topic. This mobilization, made possible only because the fundamental theoretical knowledge in vision and posture research were already well developed, soon gave rise to a large body of data and recommendations for the conception and setting up of new work stations. In addition, it allowed for the medical follow-up of the operators, for which we can find good coverage in the literature (for example, Cakir, Hart, & Stewart, 1980).

Nowadays, and until the advent of new screen technologies that may introduce new problems, there is no longer a need for major research on physiological aspects, even if applications in the field can still be critical. However, in addition to strictly visual problems, working with visual displays also creates problems of information presentation, structuration, coding, color choice, and so on, which constitute perceptual problems dealing with software ergonomics and in cognitive psychology.

Besides visual display terminals, ergonomics has equally studied all the other technological devices by which the user communicates with the computer, and in particular the keyboards. We know that the keyboards currently used in computing, direct descendants of typewriter keyboards, are far from optimal. Various alternatives based on criteria of ergonomic optimization have been proposed, but they have faced a constant objection that has served as a pretext for stasis: the habits of the users. Yet this is not a good reason, since the majority of computer-keyboards users have never seriously practiced typing, and cannot therefore be said to have a preference for traditional typewriter keyboards in the first place. Nevertheless, as with visual display terminals, ergonomics does have at its disposal a large data base that provides designers, buyers, and users with practical recommendations (see Cakir et al., 1980).

More and more pointing devices are being used as a complement to keyboards and screens, which can facilitate communication in certain transactions: light pens, mouse, ball, joystick, and so on, and even direct use of the finger on tactile screens. These different means have been the object of experimental comparisons results of which allow the appropriate choice of technique for a specific task and according to the operator's aptitude and experience.

Communicating with the computer using speech is beginning now to be used in real situations. The computer is now capable of producing a high-quality synthesized voice that even has a good level of prosody. Technology is equally making good progress in the field of voice recognition. These methods are referred to as "natural," but their performance often turns out to be disappointing or too limiting, either for the system or for the operator. In fact, although a number of ergonomic studies have been performed on this subject and notably in France, ergonomists are far from having acquired a sufficient level of knowledge concerning the different factors to be taken into consideration.

We know, however, that the auditory presentation of information by synthesized voice is generally well accepted by the subjects, even when the prosody is far from perfect, as long as comprehension of the message is not too difficult. This method does not always give a better performance than by visual presentation. That depends on the subjects, the type of message, and task conditions, including the noise level. It also depends on the memory processing demanded of the subject and on the occupation of human sensorial channels. Little is known of the long-term effects when the task is prolonged, the subject is tired, or stressful elements are present.

Voice recognition is also still in its infancy. Repeating the same words several times in order to input in the computer the list of words that the machine has to recognize is a tiresome task for poorly motivated subjects. Above all, the reliability of current systems is dependent on a weak intraindividual variability of elocution that is often critical in practice. Also, pronouncing a word can be slower and less effective than the manual designation of the word or the manual activation of a key, especially if emotional factors or fatigue come into play. It constitutes, nevertheless, a future path for the development of man-computer communication, to be followed when the operational circumstances are ready.

ERGONOMICS OF SOFTWARE
(USER CENTERED)

This above expression, which is a little ambiguous since it may be confused with ergonomics of programming (programmer centered), pertains to everything in the man-computer interface that depends on the programs and not on the machines. This area of study comprises the following subdivisions: syntax and management of dialogues, presentation and management of input information, presentation and management of output information and the functions of assistance and documentation (on-line and off-line).

It is neither possible nor useful to go into technical details pertaining to each of these points. Here are a few guidelines that led to practical recommendations in this field:

—adapt the vocabulary used to the needs and cultural level of the user

—adapt dialogue complexity to the user's level of practice

—reduce memory load

—assure that the user remains in contact with the current dialogue and that his actions are explicit

—always give feedback on actions

—protect the user from destructive actions that he or she may inadvertently commit

—give the user the opportunity to correct his or her own errors

—guide the user in his or her learning stages

The two most important factors to be taken into account in the designing of ergonomically satisfactory software and that have been the object of numerous studies are the type of user and the type of task.

Users may differ in a multitude of ways, but the essential criterion is their level of experience: experience with the task and experience in using the computer system. A design chosen for beginners may need to be modified for experienced users. Because a user's experience develops, the ideal software should evolve with this experience, or at least the user should be able to regulate the functioning of programs by variable options to suit him or her better. For example, the degree of initiative and flexibility in the management of dialogues is an important factor that affects ease of learning and final performance. For beginning or occasional users, less flexible dialogues (controlled by the computer) are preferable to user-managed dialogues, but the opposite is true for experienced users. Also, the question/answer mode is the one that incurs the least errors among beginners, but it very quickly becomes boring for experienced users who begin to anticipate the forthcoming questions, especially with a slow system.

This distinction between experienced users and beginner should be kept in mind for the whole of software ergonomics. This is a factor that we also find in many other fields of ergonomics.

The task factor is equally important in determining the desired features of ergonomically adapted software. It must be taken into account in the management of dialogues and in presentation of input and output information. For example, the use of a selection process in "menus" (list of choices) is generally a good solution for the input of orders, but it requires several points to be taken into consideration: use a pointing device adapted to the characteristics of the screen and the task as a function of desired pointing speed; organize the menus so that one does not have to make simultaneous multiple choices in the same menu; do not offer menus with too many items; present the items in a logical order for the task and group them into functional categories; avoid too many branches in tree structures; adopt a common menu presentation for all applications and a common vocabulary that is coherent with the other vocabularies used by the operator.

In the same way, the arrangement of information on the screen should be optimized to concur with the order in which this information will be used within the task, and, if possible, in a way that is compatible with whatever documents are concurrently in use. When several colors are used to code categories of information or objects, the choice of colors should be made with respect to any chromatic significations, if such conventions exist in the context. Furthermore, the sensitivity of the eye to chromatic differences, and also a person's limited capacity to distinguish several colors simultaneously should be considered.

These are only a few elementary examples aimed at introducing here the following fundamental principle: Software ergonomics must begin, not by cataloging universal norms or rules of thumb, but rather by a precise analysis of task and user characteristics. It is after this that we may begin to establish a technical inventory of desired ergonomic specifications.

The principal feature of research in software ergonomics is that it is carried out in the field in the framework of various concrete applications: office computerization, newspaper photocomposition, industrial robotics, centralized process control, air or marine traffic control, piloting aircraft, expert systems, and so on. It follows that the experimental results give the impression of being "sui generis" and scattered about. We therefore need more comprehensive analytical and practical work providing general syntheses of this field.

ERGONOMICS OR PROGRAMMING

Here we shall look at computer programs again, but this time from the point of view of the people who write or modify them. In the last fifteen years in the United States and other countries around the world, notably in France, a small but dynamic field of research has developed at the intersection of experimental psychology and ergonomics, dealing with the cognitive processes involved in programming. Programming is a particular case of problem solving in which its final form is that of a text written following certain conventional rules, the respect of which determines the computer's "understanding." But a program is obviously also meant to be understood by men and women, so that they are able to adapt it in the future, to modify it, or detect possible errors ("bugs"). In this field, cognitive psychology is interested in establishing the fundamental mechanisms involved in discovering the algorithms necessary for effectively solving the problem, as well as the rules of reading and comprehension. Three main categories of factors are studied:

—programmer characteristics: programming knowledge and programming experience, expertise in the field, programming style

—task characteristics: design of new programs, error detection, adapting programs written by others

—program characteristics: structuring, language used, length, complexity, presentation, related documentation, and so on

The research in this field (see reviews of Curtis, 1982; Schneider-man, 1980; Sperandio, 1984) has mainly been carried out in the laboratory with student subjects, but some research was done in the field with professional programmers. The practical benefits of these researches also pertain to the training of programmers. Issues relating to the organization of programming teams are also covered under this field of research.

WORK ANALYSIS

Ergonomics should not limit itself to giving specific recommendations on hardware or software. Without an analysis of the work, ergonomics can generally provide very little help, other than some general principles of little operational use. Any ergonomics study in the field necessarily includes a detailed analysis of the task's characteristics; of the operator's characteristics (physical, social, cultural, intellectual, motivational, and so on); and the conditions in which the work is to be done (constraints of the physical environment, qualitative and quantitative criteria of performance, schedules, specific stress, and so on).

Since ergonomic practices and procedures must be viewed jointly within the context of the above considerations, clearly the analysis is primarily a question of methodology. We shall not say more about this here, since this ergonomic methodology is not new and has been widely published, but for the benefit of non-ergonomist readers we shall stress the fact that this work analysis is a fundamental step in the ergonomic process for all applications of some importance. Failure to undertake this analysis or a bad analysis may make the ergonomic intervention inoperative, unnecessarily costly, and even damaging.

During the conception process, it is preferable that future users be able to participate directly in the design of the system. More than simple opinion surveys, which are frequently disappointing, the organization of work groups, expression groups, or quality circles may give good results. Not only can future users bring the designer's attention to "bugs," but they can also contribute in establishing a sociotechnical list of the advantages and disadvantages at the level of performance as well as that of working conditions that we expect from the future organization of the new system or the new technology. This survey, which should also include factors such as new competencies and qualifications to be acquired versus the old ones, new staff status and leaders, new work loads and constraints, and so on, is necessary for understanding the mechanisms of resistance to technological change.

THEORETICAL TRENDS AND
LINES OF RESEARCH

The main theoretical trends of cognitive ergonomics do not differ from those of fundamental cognitive psychology. There are no specific theories, but rather a greater sensitivity for the study of certain factors and mechanisms through the analysis of intellectual activity in the field. In particular, cognitive ergonomics can integrate, if necessary, factors that traditionally belong to physiology and sociology.

Under the influence of behaviorism, ergonomic psychology was not really interested in human information processing up until the 1960s. Considering the operator as a "black box" that receives information and produces adequate responses in function of appropriate learning, ergonomics was principally interested in the factors allowing information presentation and response execution to be optimized. This out-dated conception nevertheless provided ergonomics with a status of justified effectiveness. Two significant ergonomic approaches to human cognition may be examined.

First, from the 1960s on, by analyzing intellectually complex tasks, ergonomists began to pay attention to certain processes of filtering and organizing of information during the operator's cognitive activities, processes that depend on the particular objectives set by the operator. One of the first contributions was provided by Ochanine (see "In Memoriam," 1981) who demonstrated that the "operative" mental image was selectively incomplete, deformed, and guided by the objectives of the current action. This theory of operativity was then padded out by numerous experimental studies (reviewed in Sperandio, 1984a) in visual perception, memory, and reasoning. Operators select and organize the data they need the most for a given task as a function of their own processing capacities, which depend directly on their prior learning.

For example, by measuring eye movements in various real tasks, several studies have showed that the experienced operator preferentially extracts information from the sources that generally provide the most information (Sperandio & Bouju, 1983). In the same way, studies on "operational" memory have shown that subjects preferentially conserve the information that is the most useful for the task.

We have also demonstrated that this relevant information is stored in what may be referred to as "working memory" and is organized as a function of the most likely order of use (Sperandio, 1975, 1984a). These results have been used notably to optimize the presentation of information on visual display terminals, but above all, on complex work panels (for example, the instrument panels of modern aircraft, traffic control centers, or centralized process control centers).

A second approach of importance, different in its methods and origins, but nevertheless convergent, is the field of research in "problem solving" inspired or derived from the initial models of Newell and Simon. The aim here is to formalize the inferential processes involved in operators' reasonings or heuristics and particularly in tasks characterized by the need to find an optimal solution in limited time. The studies of air traffic control are exemplary of this type of research, but more recent researches are carried out on various cognitive tasks, for example: control of power stations (Drouin, 1976), rail traffic control (Senach, 1984), breakdown diagnostics (Alengry, 1985), medical diagnostics (Sebillotte, 1982), and so on. A new and promising area for the application of studies on operational reasoning and knowledge representation is that of expert systems of which applications in helping with diagnostics are already well developed.

Finally, let us mention the recent connections developed with linguistics and psycholinguistics. The study of natural language, principally in its oral form, has begun to interest ergonomists much more now than in the past, because computing is on the verge of establishing man-computer communication in "almost natural" or "natural limited" language (Scapin, 1982; Sperandio & Letang, 1986). Despite the severe limitations that exist at the moment, this is undoubtedly an important area of research for the future.

It should be clear that the theoretical foundations of cognitive ergonomics are not limited to what has been presented above. For a more developed synthesis, one should consult some recent books on the subject, for example, Leplat (1985), de Montmollin (1984) or Sperandio (1984a). We should also note that research is also done on aspects that are not strictly cognitive, but that are related, such as sensory fatigue, work load, night shift work, and so on.

As ergonomic research is not, as in laboratory research, carried out on the basis of theoretical paradigms selected by the researcher, but more often conducted on the basis of field problems, different theoretical topics generally overlap.

THE RESEARCH TEAMS IN FRANCE

In ergonomics, research and application are frequently imbricated. This overlapping is justified by the topics under study, but it is exaggerated by the fact that research laboratories are now pushed to look for a part of their financing in contracts with companies. In any case, one of the dominant features of research in this field is the significant increase in the number of field studies that aim both at acquiring scientific knowledge and solving concrete problems. Another important feature of research is the tendency to blur the traditional boundaries among the physiological, cognitive, and social areas of the work.

The situation of French research teams in ergonomics applied to computing is modest in terms of the number of teams and the number of researchers. Only one team, directed by Bisseret (with about ten researchers) is really specialized in computer ergonomics: the "group of ergonomics psychology" that is a part of the "Institut National de Recherche en Informatique et Automatique" (INRIA). Some of their main research topics include: control room ergonomics (air traffic, city train traffic), software ergonomics (numerous fields of application), research on programming and programmable robots, and research on dialogues in limited natural languages.

Apart from this team, the researchers working in computer ergonomics are generally scattered among laboratories or research teams whose specializations cover a much larger area, for example: occupational psychology or psychophysiology or general ergonomics. The teams mentioned here are all more or less associated with universities or with important research institutes. Contrary to what may be seen in other countries, and notably in the United States, there are no private research teams in this field, except in companies who manufacture computer equipment (only some researchers). There are also several military research teams specialized in ergonomics, including cognitive ergonomics, and they are occasionally interested in aspects of computing.

Let us begin with the teams situated in Paris. The laboratory of occupational psychology, directed by Professor J. Leplat, is supported by the "Centre National de Recherches Scientifiques" (National Science Research Council) and by the "Ecole Pratique des Hautes Etudes" (EPHE). This team is not limited to ergonomics and is not particularly specialized in computing, but does contribute to several topics, in particular: studies of human reliability, programming, teaching of programming, computer-aided drawing, computer-aided teaching, and, more generally, in studies of problem-solving tasks.

The laboratory of ergonomics, supported by the "Conservatoire National des Arts et Metiers," and directed by Professor A. Wisner, has a long history in ergonomics that has principally been oriented toward physiology and more recently toward psychology as well. This laboratory was one of the first to provide an in-depth analysis of the technical mutations in the press industry (newspaper photocomposition), not only on a physiological level (visual constraints', night work, and so on), but also on the cognitive and social level. This laboratory also does research in software ergonomics.

At the University of PARIS XIII, Professor M. de Montmollin leads a team that is specialized in the study of communication. Certain topics and fields of research within this domain concern computerization and automatization, and especially their organizational and sociotechnical aspects.

At the University of PARIS V (René Descartes), in the laboratory of Applied Social Psychology, a research team, directed by Professor J. C. Sperandio, is specialized in computer ergonomics. The present researches concern work in the computerized control rooms for chemical processes, man-computer communications with speech components (synthesis and recognition), programming, computerization of schools, and so on.

Outside of Paris, several teams are integrated into larger laboratories in those universities where occupational psychology or ergonomics are taught. In particular, the team led by Y. Queinec in the laboratory of psychophysiology at the University of Toulouse. The main topics include ergonomics of control rooms, visual constraints of CRT-terminals, and shift work. In this team particularly, the traditional boundaries among psychology, sociology, and physiology have been set aside.

Ergonomic psychology is equally present, although in limited numbers of researchers and teachers, at the Universities of Aix-Marseille, Grenoble, Poitiers, Rennes, Lille, and Bordeaux. We cannot describe each one individually here, but we can point out that students and young researchers in cognitive psychology are demonstrating a significant attraction to an ergonomic approach to the questions we have discussed here that gives hope for a greater development of this field in the near future.

13

FROM SOCIOTECHNICAL TOWARD PURPOSEFUL VIABLE SYSTEMS DESIGN

LEOPOLD VANSINA
LUC HOEBEKE
THARSI TAILLIEU
*International Institute
of Organizational and Social Development
and
University of Leuven
Leuven, Belgium*

From our study of the literature and from our experiences as an interdisciplinary team of consultants, three major conclusions have emerged that have changed our approach to organization- and work-systems design.

I

Sociotechnical fits cannot be designed. Only conditions can be provided to enable the achievement of such a fit between subsystems of different nature. High-performing systems are characterized by such fits (Vaill, 1982), but in order to be and to remain viable as well as meaningful to others they must achieve a minimal degree of adaptation to the changing conditions of the wider systems in which they operate. Under these conditions, participation in the design phase is not sufficient. Self-managing work units, although having a richer capacity to cope with variances, make sense only in larger systems, for example, organizations, when they continue to take part in the purposing processes of the whole system (Vansina, 1985a). Consequently, design work cannot just be based on democratic or humanistic values. It does require collaborative effort between the various disciplines and the stakeholders of the system concerned, in order to achieve joint optimizational and mutually satisfactory relations, respectively.

Sociotechnical literature, however, has not paid enough attention to real divergencies of interests between parties in the organization (Blackler, 1982), and definitely not enough to the external stakeholders. By and large, the psychological theories and reviews of sociotechnical work focus on the individual, individual job design, and the job characteristic model (Roberts & Glick, 1981). Managers and designers, however, work with aggregates or broad categories of people, not just individuals. The latter have become too volatile due to the increasing changes in the external and internal conditions. Indeed, individuals often move voluntarily within and across organizations. Furthermore, the increasing rate of change within the product-market-technology entity reduces significantly the stability within any job design. Consequently, designing jobs just for individuals has largely become unproductive.

Emery's (1963) statement that the highest levels of productivity can be achieved only in an organization that integrates individual needs in the design of the work itself, becomes equally as questionable in its realization, as the current emphasis on meaningful work. For the "meaningful work" enthusiasts argue that the meaning attributed to the job by the jobholder should be considered more than the actual task characteristics. Individual needs and attribution of meaning, however, evolve and change as people mature. The meaning therefore should primarily come from identification with the particular mission of the organization that provides meaning to the collectivity of work.

It is therefore not surprising to hear Den Hartog and Van Eynatten (1982) state their *disbelief in standard solutions*. A conclusion they came to after evaluating the experiences with work-structuring experiments, accumulated over 15 years, within the Philips Concern.

Like many other authors from the Sociotechnical School, Susman's (1976) argument applies more to the quality of working life than to the quality of work. Susman talks about only "steady states of performance"; and the advantages of self-regulation for the worker are weighed against acceptable standards of performance.

Economic recession increases our awareness of the intense interrelatedness of personal well-being and the economy, and the relevance for both of the ideal-seeking principle of continuous development of the system and its resources, human and other.

II

Sociotechnical systems' theory would deserve its name better if it offered a more coherent frame of systems constructs to guide practitioners. Its outspoken orientation toward social value appealed to a large number of practitioners, at the expense of theory building. This observation seems to be supported by the conclusion of several authors reviewing their own and others' work. Warrington (1977), for example, advocates an open systems framework for describing and reporting, but concomitant guidelines are lacking for designing and conducting work along these lines.

Pasmore, Francis, and Haldeman's (1982) review of 134 experiments highlighted the nature of sociotechnical interventions and the resulting effects. But the mapping of specific features of totally different scope to particular outcomes did not reveal a systemic framework in the practice. The enumeration of their variables, however, does shed some light on the relationship.

Dependent variables included productivity (60% of studies), absenteeism (23%), turnover (19%), attitudes (54%), safety (6%), grievances (7%), and quality control (24%).

As independent variables, the following are reported: autonomous work groups (50%), technical-skill training (40%), and technological changes (only 16%). The remaining interventions all occurred in less than 10% of the cases. They were minimal critical specifications, feedback on performance, allowing operators to supply themselves, providing managerial information to operators, allowing operators to select their peers, equalizing status differentials, rewarding on knowledge basis, peer reviews or internal group support mechanisms.

Few sociotechnical interventions go beyond the formation of autonomous groups and the development of skills necessary to create changes in related, wider aspects of organizational structure and functioning. But, the relationships among these autonomous work groups and the wider organization and its systemic integration requires further study and theory building.

Indeed, autonomous work groups emerged as a solution to the problem of creating "viable self-maintaining and self-adjusting production units" (Herbst, 1974). But there are few principles available to order and regulate systemic parts within the whole organization. Cherns (1976) does stress the iterative nature of the design process, focusing on the outcome of work in QWL terms.

Some of his principles refer to interaction problems between operational units and hierarchy, but none does so explicitly.

Susman (1976) formulates conditions that are helpful in deciding whether to bring decisions inside, or outside, the boundaries of a group, centralized in roles or handed to the group as a whole to improve or maintain a level of performance. The critical conditions are (a) boundary-transaction uncertainty, which determines whether the regulatory decisions (pertaining to maintaining boundary conditions, allocation, and coordination of resources) can be separated; and (b) conversion-uncertainty, which determines whether the actual operations can be separated from the decision without loss in performance.

De Sitter (1981) seemingly thinking along the same lines as Susman, formulates guidelines and principles about self-regulation at an operational level that are helpful in settling issues between the work group and its supervision.

Hackman (1976, pp. 31, 33), as do most authors in the field of job enlargement, describes the inevitable change in management's role conception: "for the manager to move from managing what goes on within the boundaries of a group to helping the group to manage those boundaries themselves." He does, however, recognize that this principle is not enough to guide design workers:

> Clearly more research on intergroup relations and on boundary maintenance of self-managing groups is required. At present all that perhaps can be said with confidence is that the strength of group boundaries and the way relationships are managed across boundaries, will have important effects on what happens both within the separate groups and in the organization as a whole.

Likert's outdated linch-pin model may still be shaping our minds, thereby preventing us from venturing into the development of a more relevant systemic organizational theory.

The most fundamental insight from sociotechnical systems is the "joint optimization process" (Trist, 1981) between essentially two components, "people" and "things." Each is regulated by its own specific laws. But the concept "sociotechnical system" may equally imprison our minds, confining our thinking to joint optimization processes between people and the hardware technologies. Indeed, most sociotechnical work involves only blue-collar workers, a category that also appeals most to social involvement, while neglecting the joint optimization processes with the more diversified and specific components of the "thing," for example, information, systems' scope, complexity, and time-span properties.

III

Purposeful and viable organizations consist of purposeful, viable subsystems. As experience with sociotechnical redesigns accumulated, the issue of the unit of the work system under focus became unavoidable. Job- and work-system designs are monitored and affected by systems of a higher hierarchical order using Beer's terminology, or by middle and top management (Emery, 1982) or as social and organizational psychologists prefer to call it by their context. Interventions, sociotechnical optimalizations at one level, do not necessarily lead to constructive developments at another level. Consequently, the focus shifted from job and work design to total organization design with an outspoken preference for "green-field-projects"—the sociotechnical design of new factories in virgin territory where one may expect to face only minimal influence from traditional concepts, physical constraints, established expectations, and habits. The ball has not stopped there either. Trist (1983) concluded that "Debureaucratization of single organizations is necessary but not sufficient." Needed are advances in institution-building of "functional social systems that occupy a position in social space between the society as a whole and the single organization."

Such large-scale changes in the ordering of work within society can never be achieved by the individual efforts of an elitist group. A confrontation with changing realities and a failure of old paradigms to cope with them successfully (e.g., the "economic depression," the unemployment issue, the unpayable welfare system) leads to a growing search for new paradigms in a variety of fields: education (Emery, 1982), work (Handy, 1980), information systems (Espejo, 1983), and organizational design.

The pathology of bureaucracy (Acar & Aupperle, 1984) is a consequence of principles derived from a mechanistic model of organizations (Gharajedaghi & Ackoff, 1984). Observed behavioral deviations from this model, called autonomous transactions, are still largely perceived as "things to be brought under control," either through management or technological devices, while in reality these very autonomous transactions are essential responses of a social system to stay alive and be meaningful. One just has to recall some of the examples of "moonlighted research discoveries," small business grown out of the hidden economy, or informally introduced improved work methods, to come up with a list of valued autonomous transactions.

In large organizations, in particular, the composing parts have each separately, must share influence of the whole, and are unlikely to be able to understand and "experience" the whole. A comprehensive theory may enable them to relate their experiences and understandings to the whole.

Systems-thinking seems to serve most often as the new paradigm and as relevant theory. We believe that technological developments, more than any other, will necessitate such systems-thinking. New technology changes the concepts of space and time on which traditional organizational theories for ordering the world of work have been developed. The sociopolitical and economic developments, on the other hand, will push the paradigm shift toward the purposeful or social rather than the organic model.

The essence of this purposeful model is that it recognizes that organizations are not fully determined by their environments, but that they can choose their purpose (mission) and their ways of achieving it, within a set of constraints. In the purposeful system model, development of resources and human need satisfaction capabilities, and not just survival or profit, is the final and overriding objective. Survival is a necessary condition, while profit is like oxygen; it is needed for survival. But profit and survival provide only the minimal requirement for development.

A second, notable characteristic is its other directedness. The whole organization has to set itself a mission, which is internally and externally perceived as meaningful, namely, as fulfilling a valuable function in society. Once the primary work systems and their desired outputs are identified, the organization is then designed in an iterative way, accounting for what the next hierarchical level has to do in order to facilitate the primary work system to remain viable while generating its desired outputs. The same questions are raised to the next higher levels of hierarchical order, up to the very top. The top level sees to it that together all lower levels are able to contribute to the fulfillment of the corporate mission.

As you may have noticed, this other directedness of all hierarchical levels is not completely new: Argyris (1957) and McGregor (1960) have already defined the management's role as creating conditions for subordinate motivation and commitment. In our current thinking, however, each systemic hierarchical level has, besides the tasks of providing the necessary conditions for the lower levels to achieve their respective specified outcomes, its own purpose, time frame, and scope. Systems theory carried by an interdisciplinary team enables us to specify the minimal conditions as well as to stretch them beyond the social sciences into essential areas such as logistics, information (market developments, operations), and technology.

So far, we have highlighted some of the basic gaps, and misleading moves in the search for a more coherent theory of work and organizational design. In the process, we may have stepped on some sacred toes of orthodox sociotechnical authorities. It is not our intent to downgrade their work, but to direct attention to areas needing further development. In the remaining part, we will present some of our current thinking to further construct development as well as to clarify the basis of our interdisciplinary practice.

LINKING SCHOOLS OF THOUGHT
TO FURTHER THE DEVELOPMENT
OF BASIC THEORETICAL CONSTRUCTS

In the 1980s, more theoretical streams from systems design (Beer, 1973, 1981; Checkland, 1981; Langefors & Sungren, 1976; Lundeberg et al., 1981) are meeting—at least in Europe—the theoretical constructs from Herbst (1974) developed from the original pragmatic work with the sociotechnical systems approach.

Where engineering principles, applying the "hard" sciences, are meeting sociotechnical principles, applying the "soft" sciences, an as yet poorly explored domain of theory formation and action research becomes visible. The relevance of developing these domains further for the changing environments becomes more obvious each day for operations researchers (Eden, Jones, & Sims, 1983; Tomlinson, 1981) and system designers (Bemelmans, 1984; Lundeberg, Goldkuhl, & Nilsson, 1981). A number of negative experiences resulting from the introduction of new technologies have opened the mind of some "hard" systems designers toward the social aspects of the work in which they are involved. With the exception of a few (e.g., Hoebeke, 1984; Klein, 1974; Mumford, 1979), social scientists are not much aware of the need engineers and system designers have for a body of knowledge that has been accumulated by the sociotechnical school of thought.

VARIANCE AND COMPLEXITY

Three sources of variance are increasing continually. On the input side, the market demands more flexibility in differentiated and updated products. At the same time, there is a trend toward global product-markets.

Technology is moving forward in using more and more composite materials and devices for all kinds of application. Both developments are thereby broadening the spectrum of wanted variance or needed flexibility in output. In the car industry, for example, the development of new materials such as ceramics and fiberglass as substitutes for steel, opens up choices, but at the same time, it increases the uncertainty over the direction in which the market will move.

The introduction of automated systems, and the strong trend toward integrated manufacturing, such as integrated flows (e.g., continuous glass production) have as a consequence that the transformation processes generate increasingly wanted as well as unwanted variances. The latter are deviations from the expected outputs, and lead to a growing concern about total quality control and/or safety.

At the output side, Western industries are countering the competition of low-salary countries by producing more "customized" products or by increasing the added value technologically, and by upgrading their post-sale-services; thereby adding to the already rich wanted variances. The textile industry, for example, is responding in a manner similar to that of the chemical industries, where a shift can be observed from bulk chemicals toward specialties. The through-put, or transformation processes of organizations are, consequently, becoming more and more complex.

Cybernetics has already calculated the factorially increasing variety—a measure of complexity—stemming from the increasing numbers of interdependencies within a system and the increasing rate of change of these interdependencies in time.

Coping with this increasing amount of complexity by generating an equal amount of complexity in response (Ashby, 1956; see Ashby's law of requisite variety) increases the skill and competence requirements for tasks that can no longer effectively and safely be analyzed and subdivided by Taylor's principles. The "people system" is the only one able to match the complexity generated by such processes (Janssens, Hoebeke, & Michiels, 1984). In nuclear power stations, the researchers observed that the operators became involved in process-management functions, thereby taking de facto control of decisions and autonomous actions. These and other observations seem to lead to the conclusion that semiautonomous work groups and job enlargement are essential in running complex transformation processes.

The research on "human failures" (Rasmussen & Rouse, 1981) and "normal accidents" (Perrow, 1984) provides further support for and insight in work- system design. The first study supports one of the key principles of sociotechnical work, namely, that work design should be considered a collaborative process between the operators and the designers. Although this principle was by and large inspired by democratic or power-sharing values, research highlights the necessity for operators to learn about work systems as they develop through their inevitable start-up problems. Learning to operate the system under normal conditions does not enable the operators to understand it and consequently to intervene properly when conditions become abnormal.

Many technologically one-sided designers enter into a vicious circle of technological fix upon technological fix in an attempt at correction when things start to go wrong, and become too complex in response to the threat of potential danger and the economic health of the firm, or for life on earth at large. These technological "security" measures are tempting because they are at the same time anxiety reducing, and responsibility avoiding, while maintaining the myth of technological advancements and the supremacy of an elite group of experts who must be trusted.

The evidence from "normal accidents," however, suggests that whenever these technological systems do not "fit" specific human requirements (individual or group) the process will lead to "disasters."

In this context it must be said that psychology is neglecting an increasingly important field of mental ergonomics, namely, the mental processes of human beings and their limitations to handle complexity.

Although collaboration between social scientists and engineers is becoming more fashionable, it is still too rarely achieved. Most of the work done is by trial and error when catastrophes and near-misses occur (Three Mile Island, Bhopal); namely, the work occurs after the expert technological designs have been completed and have generated unwanted variances.

Most likely there are a variety of reasons that can serve to explain this situation, as pointed out earlier. From our experience, at least two need to be mentioned. First, rigid academic discipline inhibits the development of a body of knowledge necessary for the design of technologies fitting human beings. Second, the sociotechnical approach often takes the form of an ideology, be it "industrial democracy" or the "humanization of work," thereby rubbing most "hard" scientists the wrong way. Now that we have ample evidence that advanced technology necessitates sociotechnical work, these very efforts no longer need to be energized by ideology. This does not mean, however, that human values need to be substituted by technocratic values. On the contrary, human values are an essential part of successful organizations (Peters & Waterman, 1982; Vaill, 1982; Vansina, 1982), but a solid base for leverage is emerging from the technological and the socioeconomic developments.

VIABLE SYSTEMS DESIGN AND CRITICAL SPECIFICATION DESIGN

Both the Sociotechnical School of the Tavistock Institute, and the Viable System Model of Stafford Beer originated in the United Kingdom after World War II. Strangely enough, it took more than three decades before their approaches met in systems thinking (Emery, 1981) and in consultant practices (Janssens et al., 1984). From two different frameworks—the abstract concepts of viability, presented by a cybernetician, and the pragmatism of the socio-technical work—one arrives at the same conclusions: "Viable systems consist of viable subsystems" and "complexity can be dealt with through interactions between semiautonomous units at different hierarchical levels."

In the context of this chapter, it suffices to sketch the correspondence and complementarity of the two frameworks in the hope that it may be further developed on a more solid theoretical basis for organization and work-systems design.

The concept of hierarchical decoupling of Beer (1981) into systemic hierarchical levels or "recursion levels" can best be described by the analogy of a Russian Doll: When one opens the doll, one discovers that inside it contains a similar smaller doll and so on. This concept is very similar and complementary to the realities behind the Herbst principle of "minimal critical specification design." Each design level specifies only the boundary and the boundary transactions of a system, leaving the necessary degrees of freedom within the system to regulate and determine itself; in other words, to enable it to become self-managing.

"The decoupling principle" deals with the linking problem between autonomous groups and the next hierarchical level, or in more theoretical terms, between systemic hierarchical levels. "Minimal critical specification design" is a more general applicable design principle. Applied to a particular systemic hierarchical level it leads to design of work systems, in which only the critical properties are specified.

Both principles are essential to enable work systems and the overall organization to become self-regulating while reducing complexity in a relevant way. The value of both principles becomes clear in the light of the great number of sociotechnical experiences aborted because one stumbled over the "higher" echelons, even in greenfield projects. One of the deeper reasons resides in the lack of conceptual tools and the subsequent inability to replace old mechanical models. Indeed, in organizations where the basic organizational metaphor remains a "mechanism," and where the design of degrees of freedom is seen as a contradiction in terms, one is bound to face incredible difficulties trying to link functionally semiautonomous work systems to controlling hierarchical levels.

Along which dimensions can the decoupling most effectively be designed? Beer advances environmental scope, as expressed in the analogy of the Russian doll. Jaques (1983) provides empirical evidence for still another hierarchical decoupling dimension, namely, time span. From our consulting experiences, we observed a third dimension, namely, purpose. The differences in the work activities of the decoupled systemic hierarchical levels cannot be described in terms of strategic, executive, or operational activities, since these take place at each level, but in terms of purpose proper to the environmental scope and the given time span. Each systemic hierarchical level has within its own scope and time frame, the responsibility for providing appropriate conditions for the lower systemic hierarchical level to generate its specified output, and fulfill its purpose. In addition, each level has its own purpose to be defined in the context of the specificities of the organization concerned.

ROOT DEFINITIONS
AND TRANSFORMATION PROCESSES

The previous section showed a first way to amplify sociotechnical concepts for use in organizational design. The uncoupling of the various hierarchical levels in a hierarchical order of systems makes it possible as well as necessary to define in an iterative way the basic transformation process (the purpose) of each system.

Checkland (1981) has, in a broad action research program, worked on what he calls root definitions of human activity systems. He came to the conclusion that well-defined systems consist of six basic components (root definitions) indicated by the mnemonic CATWOE: Clients, Actors, Transformation Process, Weltanschauung, Owners, and Environmental Constraints. Starting from these root definitions it becomes possible to differentiate the transformation processes and their environments for each systemic hierarchical or recursion level. The transformation processes of a simple cement-producing plant, for example, can be ordered on three levels and described as:

   on a first level: transforming the raw materials to cement;

   on a second level: transforming process specifications into the development and maintenance of production facilities; and,

   on a third level: transforming customers orders into timely deliveries of quantitatively and qualitatively adequate goods.

The higher level sets the boundaries within which the lower level needs to perform its own task, and at the same time determines the degrees of freedom for that level.

The degrees of freedom of each systemic level can be determined through the other components of the CATWOE mnemonic. The specification of each of these root definitions in practice implies choices within given sociotechnical system requirements and the minimal requirements for success in that type of business. The fact that the higher systemic hierarchical level sets the boundaries for the lower level does not mean that the organization and its constituent work systems must be designed top-down. Once the mission of the overall organization and its strategy is defined one can start with the primary work systems and move upward. It is evident that such a design process is essentially iterative. If not, one risks skewing the design in favor of one or another systemic levels and its occupants.

Checkland's method gives an alternative to the traditional task and job descriptions that resulted in complete specifications and outdated reward systems. As each viable subsystem of the organization defines its purpose in relation to the other subsystems and to the overall mission, technological and/or socioeconomic developments do not require an elaborate redefinition of tasks and jobs.

In the example of the cement plant, the operators running the plant may find themselves shifting from level-one activities toward level-two activities in the process of getting the plant fully automated. The technique of responsibility charting, first described by Galbraith (1973), can then be used within the framework of the various transformation processes to schematize changing interdependencies between the actors of the various processes.

TOTAL QUALITY CONTROL (TQC) AND ACTION RESEARCH AS A CHANGE STRATEGY

Once TQC has passed beyond the quality circle fad (Lawler & Mohrman, 1985), it will become perceived as the control of all the transformation processes of an organization necessary to satisfy the customers' needs in the most economical way. Only then will its correspondence with sociotechnical work systems and organizational design become visible. Both these approaches focus on the analysis of process variances, input and output variances, and ways of eliminating or coping with them. Both approaches perform system changes through a series of methodological steps very similar to decision making and implementation steps (Hoebeke, 1984).

Furthermore, they build upon the knowledge base available in the people who are running the processes and let them participate in the design of process and system changes. It is sufficient to cite here, as an illustration, the first key principle of Tribus (1983): "Workers work in the system, managers should work on the system to improve it with their help!"

Both approaches have essentially an open-systems approach toward work systems stressing boundary roles and/or environment-system interactions: Customers and suppliers of the work systems are involved, to a certain degree, in these quality improvements. These approaches provide a strong link between product quality, the quality of the processes to produce, the service of the customer, and the quality of working life for the social system running these processes. Vansina (1984, 1985b) integrated both approaches using concepts of Tribus (1983) and Emery (1978). This integration is seen, to some degree, in Japanese management. For in some Japanese enterprises the sociotechnical approach, and organization development, are brought together in their quality-improvement activities, although not necessarily with the same labels (Fukuda, 1983).

The TQC has widened the domain of sociotechnical work beyond the shop-floor level into which it has largely been confined to areas beyond the visible boundaries of the organization, namely, to establish mutual satisfactory relations with all its stakeholders. Ackoff (1981) defines *stakeholders* as all the entities that have a recognizable influence on the survival and the development of the organization. TQC has, as such, the explicit aim of gearing the whole organization toward quality. Putting into practice the concepts outlined above in the framework of TQC is a task in which we are actively involved. Linking the various approaches and disciplines mentioned here is already showing results. Some of these will be reported during 1986.

CONCLUSIONS

New theories, based on new paradigms, are needed to enable practitioners to design viable work systems appropriately linked to the systemic hierarchical levels, each having its proper purpose, time span, and environmental scope. The effect must be multidisciplinary.

The design practice, furthermore, must restrict itself to the definition of the degrees of freedom, and the inevitable interdependencies to enable work systems, as well as organizations, to adapt themselves to the external and internal changing conditions, allowing for joint optimization necessary to achieve a fit between components for different natures.

The dominant values upon which most of the pragmatic work of the sociotechnical school is based seems to be shifting from "participation and industrial democracy" to "joint responsibility, and learning from complementary information"; and from "the satisfaction of work" toward the pursuit of "continual improvement."

14

THE CLIMATE METAPHOR IN ORGANIZATION THEORY

GÖRAN EKVALL
The Swedish Council for Management and Work Life Issues
Stockholm, Sweden

The concept of climate to describe psychological conditions in a social "region" is popular in our everyday language as well as in the social and behavioral sciences. "Organizational climate" has become a well-established subject of research in recent years.

ORGANIZATIONAL CLIMATE AS A SCIENTIFIC CONCEPT

During the last twenty years or so there have been at least a dozen extensive English-language reviews of theory and research in the field of organizational climate (Schneider & Reichers, 1983). In the Norwegian and Swedish languages, reviews have appeared during the 1980s (Baklien, 1983; Ekvall, 1985). In Belgium, a research group has produced reviews and research reports on the concept both in English and in Dutch (Bouwen, De Cook, & De Witte, 1980; De Cook, 1980). A glance at the various reviews makes it immediately evident that there are two theoretically distinct approaches to the concept of organizational climate; one is realistic and objectivistic, the other subjectivistic and phenomenological.

According to the objectivistic view, climate exists as a reality in the organization; it can be observed and studied in various ways. *Climate* is defined by typical behaviors, attitudes, and feelings in the organization; patterns that are consistent both with regard to individuals and to situations. In this perspective, climate is an attribute of the organization that exists *independently* of the organization members' perceptions and apperceptions. It is an objectively existing part of the organizational reality.

According to the subjectivistic approach, the organizational climate is regarded as a perceptual and cognitive structuring of the organizational situation common to the organizational members.

In the organization there is a continual flow of events and actions, of routines and processes. Individuals encounter these various phenomena and try to interpret them so that the surrounding world becomes comprehensible. They create a "cognitive map" for themselves; with its help they can place what they see and hear, thus becoming able to see more meaning in it. When the members of the organization interact with one another, there is an exchange of experiences and apperceptions; their many personal cognitive maps confront one another and are modified. In this way, common ways of perceiving and interpreting what happens in organizations arise. According to this approach, the organizational climate consists of the common apperceptions that evolve in the course of time and events.

Theoretically speaking, the distinction is quite clear. But on the empirical side it has not been kept distinct, and in the various research reports we often find the authors alternating between the two views. In practice, that is to say when conclusions about the life of organization are to be drawn from the research results, the theoretical distinction is perhaps not all that important. Most studies of organizational climate have made use of questionnaires in which the individual organization members have been asked to describe the climate by answering what is usually a large number of questions regarding conditions in the organization. The questions have been much the same, regardless of whether the researcher has adopted a realistic or a phenomenological view of climate. The individual descriptions have then been aggregated to produce climate scores for the whole organization, or for that part of the total organization to which the description applied.

What is more important than the ontological distinction is the fact that both approaches regard climate ecologically, as a "molar" variable; as an overall attribute. The climate concept is concerned not with adjustment to the individual task or relations with a particular colleague, but with the total social-psychological situation. It is also significant that however theoretically different their starting points may be, both approaches see perceptions and cognitions rather than attitudes, feelings, or abilities as the mediating links between situations and behavior.

RESEARCH METHODS

Research on organizational climate has in most cases been based on perceptions and descriptions provided by the organization members, which have been aggregated to produce organizational parameters. Researchers have constructed questionnaires containing a number (often a large number) of statements about life in the organization. The individual organization member has been asked to react to these statements and to mark on a scale the extent to which he or she believes them to apply. The answers to sets of questions concerned with the same phenomena (e.g., trust, risk taking, autonomy) have been combined into points for these variables, and the points of all the members have then been combined (generally as arithmetic means) to produce organizational measures.

The phenomenological approach allows for no other strategy, although question techniques and the nature of the statistical analysis to obtain common perceptions may of course vary. All members of the organization, or a representative sample, must participate and provide descriptions, since according to this approach it is the general or common perception that constitutes the organizational climate.

In the realistic tradition, the individual in the organization is regarded as an observer and potential reporter of the prevailing climate rather than as a creator or carrier of the climate in the cognitive sense. This means that the researcher can select a number of people in the organization as his or her reporters on quite other grounds than their representativeness. He or she might choose some organization members who have shown a capacity for observation and an understanding of the meaning of the climate concept. Baklien (1983), for instance, employed external consultants to judge the climate in eight companies. These consultants had worked as "change agents" on OB projects in the companies. The agreement between the descriptions of the consultants and of the personnel was good. Ekvall, Arvonen, and Nystrom (1985) made a study of the climate in four independent divisions in an industrial corporation. They asked a group of centrally located personnel officers to describe the climate in the divisions, to complement and control the validity of the descriptions provided by the divisional personnel. The personnel officers occupied staff positions and provided service to the divisions; they therefore had good opportunities for observing the climate in these organizational units.

When the aggregated perceptions of the organization members are used as a measure of climate in the realistic tradition, the more or less explicit logic behind the measurement is as follows: The individual's description of the climate is determined by three factors—(a) the climate as it actually exists, (b) the individuals' personality, intelligence, and personal frame of reference that affect the way they interpret and judge what they see and hear, and (c) the actual experiences that individuals have been able to have in the organization; the focus and extent of the contacts they have had there. Since people vary as regards to their personalities and their experiences in the organization (b and c above), it is assumed that descriptive differences depending on these things will tend to cancel each other out when the descriptions are aggregated to produce organizational measures. Variations between organizations can therefore be assumed to reflect to a great extent real differences in climate. The logic behind the aggregation of individual perceptions by phenomenologically oriented climate researchers to obtain one "composite" perception is that in the course of interaction the organization members create a common cognitive map, which constitutes the organizational climate in this sense. An aggregated score, be it a means, a median, or a mode, is assumed to represent this common climate construction.

ORGANIZATIONAL CLIMATE AND "PSYCHOLOGICAL CLIMATE"

James and Jones (1974) proposed a conceptual classification that has met with a good deal of response among researchers in this field. First, they emphasized the importance of the distinction between climate as an organizational attribute and as an individual characteristic. They then suggested that climate as an organizational attribute should be designated as "organizational climate" and climate as an individual characteristic as "psychological climate." The concept of organizational climate would then include the variant of the operational definition that is based on the mean values of the organizational members' perceptions and descriptions. The concept of the "psychological climate" would be used only in studies where the individual descriptions are used as units of analysis, without any attempt at aggregation to produce an organizational measure. This elucidation of the concepts proved to be very helpful. It clarified the contents and the positions adopted in the previously somewhat confused debate. It also generated a new line of research in which researchers are concerned with what has come to be called "climate discrepancy." It is assumed that the difference between the individual's perceptions and description of the climate, on the one hand, and the descriptions common to all organizational members, on the other, does affect behavior. In other words, what is studied is the difference among each individual's "psychological climate" and the organizational climate, and the effect of this difference on the individual's attitudes, feelings, and behavior in the organization. Some studies of this concept suggest that the discrepancy in the perception of climate does affect job satisfaction and work performance (Joyce & Slocum, 1982).

The concept of psychological climate is closer to the concept of job satisfaction than to organizational climate, since both psychological climate and job satisfaction are attributes of the individual, whereas organizational climate is a characteristic of the social system. But this does not mean that the conceptual borderline between psychological climate and job satisfaction is unclear, even if some of the operationalizations have been, as Johannesson (1973) and Guion (1973) have claimed. Psychological climate refers to individuals' perception and description of an organizational situation, while job satisfaction is defined as their affective reaction to this, their attitudes and feelings about their job and their work situation. Climate descriptions are nonevaluative statements about conditions in the organization, based on individuals' perceptions as a participant in the life of that organization. Job satisfaction is concerned with emotionally colored experiences of the situation, and it is generally studied in terms of attitudes to tasks and other elements in the job situation. Researchers in the field appear to agree on this distinction.

THE GENESIS OF
ORGANIZATIONAL CLIMATE

Organizational climate arises in the confrontation between individuals and the organizational situation. Routines, rules, procedures, strategies, policies, and physical environment—all such factors in the organizational situation evoke reactions in the people involved. It is these reactions in the form of behavior, feelings, and attitudes that constitute the climate in the realistic sense. But we also have to count the people themselves as part of the organizational situation. Individual A is a factor in B's environment, and vice versa. Thus the interaction between organization members is an important part of the climate. Phenomenologically speaking, it is the individual's apperceptions of these conditions and factors and events in the organization that constitute the climate. It is their way of assigning meaning to procedures, policies, and events that comes to constitute the climate.

Schneider and Reichers (1983) speak of "practices, procedures and events" as the conditions in the organization that the individuals observe and interpret in climate terms. Campbell, Dunnette, Lawler, and Weick (1970) claim that climate derives from "the way the organization deals with its members and its environment." Pritchard and Karasick (1973) say that climate is the result of "the behavior and policies of members of the organization, especially top management." Payne and Pugh (1976) present a model of the major influences on organizational climate. The model is based on the idea that structural variables largely determine climate. They found two variables that exhibited more consistent correlations with climate in the research reports surveyed, namely, decentralization and the size of the organization. De Cock, Bouwen, De Witte, and De Vish (1985) have an organizational climate model where the causal factors are "context," "structure," "personnel policies," and "management strategy."

An exhaustive model of the etiology of organizational climate would have to be extremely complex. Many different kinds of variables affect climate. Moreover, the relations between some of these variables can also exert an influence on climate; for example, an equivalent degree of decentralization can generate quite different climates in two organizations because the age composition of the work forces is not the same. In an all-embracing model the role of the individuals—as articulators, creators, and describers of the climate—must be clarified. The effect of external factors such as technology, markets, ownership conditions, assets, and so on must also be taken into account as modifying influences on the relations between other variables and climate. And not least, both strategic and personal leadership must be directly included in the model.

The relation among the basic values and beliefs of the corporate culture on the one hand, and climate on the other, should also be subjected to theoretical elucidation and empirical study. Payne and Pugh (1976) see them as part of the climate concept. "These processes reflect the members' values, attitudes, and beliefs which thus have become part of the construct." Pritchard and Karasick (1973) on the other hand, seem to regard values as a determinant of climate: "Two organizations having widely diverging value orientations would be expected to have markedly different organizational climates."

The major impact of leadership on organizational climate has been well documented in several experimental studies whereby different management styles have been introduced into artificial or real working units. Many researchers have treated management style as part of the climate concept. Dimensions referred to as "closeness of supervision," "leaders' psychological distance," "management concern for employee involvement," and similar descriptive terms are included in several of the more frequently used climate-measuring questionnaires. However, there are various grounds for questioning this procedure. James and Jones (1974) point out that "closeness of supervision" is a "leadership process variable," and that it should be treated as such, nothing is to be gained by bringing it into the climate concept. Another stronger objection is that the manager and the type of leadership affect the organizational climate as a whole, in all its varied aspects and dimensions. It is consequently not reasonable to regard leadership style as an ordinary climate dimension along with others such as trust, challenge, risk-taking, humor, and freedom. Ekvall and Arvonen (1984) studied the relationship between leadership styles (self-ratings) and organizational climate (as described by subordinates). The result suggests that about 65% of the variance in climate between the 25 units studied is connected with the manager's leadership style.

CONSEQUENCES OF CLIMATE

Climate affects organizational and psychological processes such as communication, problem solving, decision making, conflict handling, learning, and motivation, and thus exerts an influence on the efficiency and productivity of the organization, on its ability to innovate, and on the job satisfaction and well-being that its members can enjoy. The individual organization member is affected by the climate as a whole, by the general psychological atmosphere, which is relatively stable over time. No single separate event produces this more lasting influence on behavior and feelings; it is the daily exposure to a particular psychological atmosphere. It is because of this overall and lasting effect that the climate concept is of interest and importance to our understanding of organizational life.

Research on the consequences of climate has followed two main lines. In one, the analysis is located at the organizational level, and organizational climate (generally the average value of the members' descriptions) has been compared with assessments referring to the whole organization—for example, productivity, sales results, or worker satisfaction. In the second case, the analysis is made at the individual level, and the climate description of the individual ("psychological climate") is compared with his or her work performance and job satisfaction. The results are then often reported as correlation coefficients, based on the values of all the employees in the two variables.

It is important to keep these two types of analysis apart in any attempt to form an opinion of the state of research in this field. A good deal of the confusion that is still to be found regarding the concept of organizational climate as well as about the importance of the concept depends on failure to bear this difference in mind when studying the research reports.

Abbey and Dickson (1983) studied the R & D departments of eight companies in the electronics industry in the United States. They compared the climate in these departments, measured as the average of descriptions provided by researchers active there, with an independent valuation of the company's innovativeness. Strong and significant rank correlations were obtained between the two, climate variables and innovativeness, namely, risk taking/flexibility and the emphasis on performance in the system of rewards. Other climate dimensions showing positive but somewhat weaker correlations were freedom, psychological support, and performance ambition.

Ekvall, Arvonen, and Waldenstrom-Lindblad (1983) studied the organizational climate in two divisions of a large Swedish corporation. One division was regarded by management as having been very innovative and successful over the last few years, while the other was thought to have stagnated and to be unable to adapt to changing environmental conditions. The climate measures were the average values of the descriptions made by the work force. The successful division had significantly higher average values than the stagnating one on the following climate dimensions: challenge, support for ideas, freedom, and dynamism. The value was also higher for trust/openness in the successful division but not as noticeably.

Studies of the kind referred to above are of limited value, since the direction of causality has not been clarified. These studies describe relationships that already exist. We cannot be sure whether the differences in climate between two organizations contributed to the differences in their success, or whether success or failure created the climate. There are probably always forces pulling in both directions. For this reason we need to complement the descriptive studies by experiments and longitudinal research projects in which changes in climate can be studied over time.

Several experiments have been described in the literature. The most frequently discussed is that performed by Litwin and Stringer (1968). They constructed three artificial companies for experimental purposes, and created three quite different climates in these by varying the management style. The result was three climates that produced very different results in terms of job satisfaction, innovation, and productivity.

Another study was carried out by Marrow, Bower, and Seashore (1967). This was an action research project in which the climate was altered by various actions on the part of management, by changes in technology, training programs, and reward systems. The climate changes were accompanied by an increase in productivity and a drop in staff turnover.

The extensive literature of organizational development reports many cases in which various ways of promoting climates of greater openness and trust have had effects on job satisfaction and productivity. As several writers have pointed out, however, the results are by no means unambiguous.

In experiments and action research of this kind, climate is treated theoretically as an "intervening" variable (Likert, 1967). Changes are made in an independent, experimental variable, such as leadership, the reward system, or organizational structure, and effects in productivity, job satisfaction, personnel turnover, innovations, and so on are measured. The climate is then regarded as an organizational attribute affecting this causal chain, as something that, to a certain extent, determines the effects of the changes imposed.

The great theoretical and methodological problem here is the difficulty of actually verifying the importance of climate as a moderating variable. So far there have been no definitive studies, and there is no given research strategy. We know from innumerable evaluation studies that management training and education programs at lower and middle levels remain empty gestures unless the climate as a whole is favorable to change. It is also a well-known phenomenon that any attempt to introduce suggestion schemes or quality circles to exploit employees' ideas will utterly fail if there is a climate of mistrust and tension among different groups in the company. But we know all this from practical experience rather than from systematically acquired knowledge. So far no studies have clearly shown the mediating role of climate in the life of organizations.

Hellriegel and Slocum (1974) stated that several studies clearly indicated the existence of a relation between climate and job satisfaction. They cite both studies based on analysis at the individual level and others concerned with the organizational level. They also claimed to have found many studies demonstrating significant relations between climate and performance. But they also pointed out that these relations are neither as easy to interpret nor as convincing as those referring to job satisfaction.

TOTAL CLIMATE OR SUBCLIMATE

What is a "region" in the case of the emotional/social climate? Does it include the whole company, even if this is geographically scattered? Is it a locally defined part of the company? Is it a functional unit? Is it a certain level in the corporate pyramid? These questions are frequently discussed in research reports. Some researchers have presented results suggesting that climate should be regarded as an attribute of the whole company, and they would like to see the concept of organizational climate referring to characteristics common to the total system. Other researchers have demonstrated differences between departments or levels; they claim that if we wish to understand the behavior of, or in, organizations, we should preferably study the climate in a sub-system. And still others argue that some climate dimensions are more general while some are bound to the local environment; both total climates and subclimates exist.

Payne and Mansfield (1973) studied climate in 14 different organizations. They found that the climate varied between hierarchical levels in 15 of the 20 climate dimensions measured. People at higher levels described the climate as less authoritarian, more friendly, more stimulating, and more likely to promote innovation than people at lower levels.

A study often quoted in discussions of total versus subclimate is Drexler (1977). Drexler found much greater differences in climate between whole organizations than between subdivisions, but he also found a certain variation between departments.

Johnston (1976) studied a young company with a largely academically trained staff. The company was a consulting and research institute that had grown rapidly. At the time of the study it employed 180 people; three years earlier it had employed 12. Johnston found that there were two very different climates in this company. The first generation of employees who had been involved in building up the company, perceived and described an informal, flexible atmosphere lacking any element of authoritarianism. But the second generation of employees who had arrived since the company began to grow so quickly, described a more formalistic, authoritarian, and efficiency-oriented climate. This study shows that different climates may exist side by side under the same roof—climates relating to groups of people and not to organizational units or functions or levels in the hierarchy.

An article by Joyce and Slocum (1984) is interesting in connection with the issues raised by Johnston's results. They introduced the concept of the "collective climate." By this they meant climate perceptions that are common to a group of individuals in an organization, regardless of whether or not the people concerned form a unit in any formal organizational sense. Instead of aggregating the climate descriptions of individuals belonging to the same unit or function, they started from the other end, from the climate descriptions themselves. Individuals whose descriptions are similar come to constitute a "collective climate." In light of a study of their own, the authors claimed that collective climate is related to both work performance and job satisfaction.

This reverse method of aggregating individual descriptions and obtaining a measure of organizational climate has the advantage of providing another kind of opportunity for studying the etiology of climate in different types of organizations. By investigating what the members in the collective climate have in common in the way of situational and individual characteristics, as Joyce and Slocum have done, it is impossible to throw light on covariations among climate and other variables.

Arvonen (1983) studied the climate in nine departments in a large Swedish company in the manufacturing industry. He found significant departmental effects in the variance analysis in all seven climate dimensions measured. Furthermore, he found effects related to hierarchic level in five of the variables. On the other hand, there were no significant interaction effects. Thus the climate varied between departments, and there was a difference between managers and nonmanagers across departments.

Ekvall, Nystrom, and Waldenstrom-Lindblad (1983) studied the climate in three departments in a young innovative company that develops and manufactures automatic bank dispensers. The three departments covered by the study were R & D, marketing/sales, and administration. The climate in the R & D department clearly deviated from the climate in the other two units. In the R & D department it was in all respects more positive. The reason for the difference was that the corporate culture—the basic values prevailing in the company—and the management exercised by the entrepreneur/business leaders were appropriate to development operations but not equally adequate to marketing and administration.

Schneider (1975) closed his long essay on the concept of organizational climate with a number of conclusions, one of which is that organizations do create different subclimates, perhaps according to work group, to functions, or according to positions.

CLIMATES FOR DIFFERENT CONTEXTS

Over the last few years there has been a growing realization in the field of organizational climate research that climates exist in relation to different spheres. For instance, we speak of the service climate, the caring climate, the safety climate, and the innovative climate. Two companies may have similar service climates but completely different safety climates. Schneider (1983) referred to this line of research and the recognition of this phenomenon as one of the most important advances in climate research.

Zohar (1980) provided an example of climate research along these lines. He studied the environmental and safety climate in 20 industrial companies in Israel. Ekvall et al. (1983) provided another example of studying a special climate. They constructed a questionnaire to measure creative organizational climate.

From researchers' point of view, the focus on climate as relating to a certain sphere coincides with their choice of "effect variable." The advantage gained is that researchers construct special instruments for measuring those aspects of climate that are relevant to their question. In climate research the tendency used to be to adopt a more general climate questionnaire. Several of these are described in the literature, and the individual researcher usually chose one of them. But even these broad climate instruments must have stemmed from certain goals and values. More or less consciously, the constructor would have selected questions and variables with a particular organizational effect in mind, perhaps productivity or job satisfaction. Consequently, the questions and variables were not immediately relevant to other more specific criteria. The climate concept acquires greater theoretical and practical importance when the link between the studied climate dimensions and the effect variables is more direct. As we move from general to more specific dimensions, we are better able to understand and predict behavior in organizations on a basis of the climate concept.

IMPORTANCE OF
THE CLIMATE CONCEPT

The concept of organizational climate has not been without its critics. It has been claimed that the concept has simply resulted in a repetition of job satisfaction research, and that as a concept it is vague. No critical article has been quoted as often as Guion's (1973) "A Note on Organizational Climate" in *Organizational Behavior and Human Performance*. Guion raised both types of objections: the risk that the research will produce nothing new but will simply "rediscover the wheel"; and that the concept is a "fuzzy" one. Paradoxically, a justification of the importance of the climate concept in organizational research can be based on the same article. Reading it in the original rather than noting differences and quotations, one finds that Guion did not attack the concept itself even if he criticized the research that had been done up to that time as well as the way the concept of organizational climate had been formulated. On the contrary, he proclaimed the value of studying the kind of superordinate all-embracing environmental aspects that climate represents.

In every organization there are certain relatively stable psychological conditions, whether we regard them as an objective reality that is "in the air," or whether we prefer to adopt a subjectivistic view, seeing the climate as the cognitive map of the psychological conditions that the organization members have created together and that they share. Behavior in the organization is influenced more by pervasive and stable conditions than by transient events.

Schneider (1983) is one researcher who has stringently and persistently argued that climate is a concept important in understanding and explaining behavior in organizations. His thesis is that explanations in terms of motivation, concerned as they are with perspectives and driving forces at the individual level, are not sufficient. Group and organizational phenomena have not received the attention they deserve when it comes to explaining behavior at work. The climate approach starts from perceptions and can thus provide an alternative and a complement to motivational explanations of behavior. To Schneider's argument could be added that not even motivation theory combined with job adjustment approaches gives a sufficient model of behavior in organizations.

Perceptions as the link between organizational conditions and behavior apply equally well to both approaches we have discussed. In both cases it is perceptions and cognitions about conditions in the working environment that effect behavior and feelings. As has been shown, there is very little difference in the role of climates as a determinant of behavior, neither through perception nor through cognition. The difference in the two approaches appears more clearly when it comes to ways of measuring climate.

The climate approach does not exclude motivational models as explanations of behavior. Individuals who experience and interpret the climate will draw their own conclusions from this and will act accordingly. The conclusions they draw depend, to some extent, on their needs and motives. One and the same climate can therefore generate different behavior in different people. Motivation and aptitude theories can help us to explain individual differences in behavior and attitudes. Knowledge about climate and about the way in which people with different personalities, value systems, needs, and motives react to different kinds of climate can help us to a better understanding and explanation of behavior in organizations.

In an overall organizational model, climate can be seen as an intervening variable in the process between input and output, and one that had a modifying effect on this process. Climate affects organizational and psychological processes, and thus acquires an influence over the results of organizational operations. Or we could say that climate determines the result that the organization will be able to enjoy from its resource input, in the form, for example, of profit, innovations, or job satisfaction.

15

ORGANIZATIONAL STRUCTURE

JOSÉ M. PEIRÓ
University of Valencia
Valencia, Spain

Interest in the topic of organizational structure has been increasing for several reasons and in several ways. First, studies on structural dimensions of organizations and their typologies have shown their importance in explaining behavior in organizations. Second, a new emphasis in a multiple-level approach to the study of structure has brought the topic nearer to psychologists' interest. Third, the sociocognitive approaches to organizations have emphasized that the concept of organizational structure includes framework aspects and also the interactions between elements that shape them. Finally, a strong emphasis on structuring and organizing has shown structure to be a dynamic reality.

Furthermore, the multiple theoretical perspectives developed in organizational theory and design (Van de Ven & Joyce, 1981) point to the difficulty of a comprehensive definition of the topic of organizational structure but such multiple perspectives also show its relevance for understanding and explaining organizational behavior (Mohr, 1982).

STRUCTURAL DIMENSIONS AND
CONFIGURATIONS: RECENT DEVELOPMENTS
OF THE RATIONAL PARADIGM APPROACH

Since the 1970s, several authors have tried to clarify the paradigmatic model characterized as the "rational or goal paradigm" (Benson, 1977). According to this model, the design of an organization is guided by the goals it tries to attain. Methodologically, it is positivistic, centered in the measurement of organizational charac-

Author's Note: *I would like to acknowledge the useful comments made by Professor Carpintero, Dr. Prieto, and S. Monleon.*

teristics whose complex reality is taken for granted. Here we shall mention the most relevant lines of investigation that have been pursued within this paradigm.

THE DIMENSIONS OF
ORGANIZATIONAL STRUCTURE

Taking Weber's ideas about bureaucracy as a starting point, several authors have tried to clarify the main dimensions of organizational structure so that they could be empirically studied. During the 1960s and 1970s many efforts were developed by authors such as Blau, Schoenherr, Thompson, Hage, and Perrow. In Europe, the Aston Group produced important contributions to the study of structural dimensions, their relationships with its context and environment, and their effects on members' behaviors, attitudes, organizational effectiveness, and climate. Also included were cross-cultural aspects (Mansfield, 1984; Pugh, 1981).

These contributions increased the emphasis on quantitative methodology generating a large number of instruments subjective and objective in nature (Payne & Pugh, 1976). Furthermore, some of their concepts and methods have been incorporated into new organizational assessment packages (Seashore, Lawler, Mirvis, & Cammann, 1983; Van de Ven and Ferry, 1980). However, several conceptual and methodological aspects have been criticized by Starbuck (1981).

In sum, these approaches look at the structures as "organizational frameworks or skeletons that provide coherence and continuity over time often differentiated from processes." Moreover, "the experienced reality of structure in organizations resides in its impact, in the pattern and regularities that it imparts to the behavior of the organization and its members" (Stein & Kanter, 1980, p. 247). These are realistic approaches that emphasize the framework of organizational structure and its relationships with other contextual and environmental variables.

CONTINGENCY FACTORS AND
ALTERNATIVE PERSPECTIVES

The study of structural dimensions has been developed together with that of the forces and constraints leading to particular structural arrangements adopted in given cases. Technology and size have been the internal contingency factors more frequently considered, and environment, the external one.

Recent works dealing with the *technology-structure relationships* have continued within the line of a technological determinism. The size-technology debate has been involved as well. Some reviews (Gerwin, 1981; Veen, 1984) have pointed out the complexity of the "technology" metaconcept and the variety in its operationalization. Taken together with the large number of indexes about organizational structure, a complex panorama emerges of the relationships between these two sets of variables. The need for a multiple level of analysis (organizational, unit, and task technology) to clarify the relations among technology, size, and structure brings forth anew some old methodological problems such as the desired degree of data aggregation and subjective versus objective measures. Strong technological differences have been found in the wide array of organizations studied: manufacturing, services, and voluntary organizations (Mills & Posner, 1982), and it posits new complexities in the study of the relationships between technology and organizational structure. Differences in the operationalizations and measures, in the organizational level focused, and in the kind of organizations studied can contribute to explaining some of the contradictory empirical results obtained and show the risks in generalizing (Fry & Slocum, 1984). In addition, some authors have recently pointed out the need of a longitudinal approach to the study of technology-structure relationships (Kimberly & Evanisko, 1979) and some promising studies carried out with this methodology have appeared (Dewar & Hage, 1978).

An alternate point of view to technological determinism, characterized by Gerwin (1981) as a system design approach, maintains that "structure and technology are seen as interdependent aspects of a sociotechnical system" (p. 4). In it, emphasis is placed on strategic decisions that may reflect management's own values. Such decisions influence an organization's technology and structure. Tavistock Institute has been a conspicuous advocate of this approach (Trist, 1981).

Studies of *size as a contingent factor of structure* show similar tendencies to the ones pointed out for technology. Size seems to have been defined too globally and is increasingly considered a multidimensional construct (Gupta, 1980). "Alternative operational measures of size are not, in many cases, tapping the same underlying phenomenon" (Kimberly & Evanisko, 1979, p. 279). In general terms, empirical studies have found that size and structure of organizations show significant relationships, but information about more specific relationships between the two sets of variables that operationalize these concepts is needed (Paulson, 1980). Studies on the moderating effects of size on the relations between technology and structure (Carter, 1984), on different aspects of this relationships for manufacturing and service organizations (Glisson & Martin, 1980), and longitudinal designs to determine possible causal relationships (Denton, 1982) are being developed.

In the frame of the contingency approach, several models have been worked out to explain the complex relationships among size, technology, and structure. The ones of Aldrich, Hilton, Aston Group, and Blau-Schoenherr have been reviewed by Gerwin (1981). As an alternative approach, Child (1972) includes the strategic decisions as the basis to explain the relationships between these context variables (size, technology) and structure. He thus rejects the determinism held by the contingency models.

Environment has been the external contingent factor of organizational structure most widely studied. Since the classic studies of Burns and Stalker (1961) and Lawrence and Lorsch (1967), a large number of works, aimed at clarifying the way in which environmental characteristics affect organizational structure (Lawrence, 1981), pay special attention to uncertainty (Argote, 1982) and dependence (Koot, 1983).

Micro and macro level of analysis have been differentiated in current studies. At the micro level, some authors have emphasized the specific relations of specific departments with some environmental subsectors. "The interaction between an environmental sector and an organizational subsystem will be an important determinant of each subsystem's attributes" (Tosi & Slocum, 1984, p. 15). The macro-level approach has been strongly developed with the organizational ecology model (Carroll, 1984; Freeman & Hannan, 1983). The ecology model shares with the contingency model a deterministic view, but both differ in the fact that "organization change is a product of internal adaptation for system structuralists while it is the product of external selection in the natural selection view" (Van de Ven & Astley, 1984, p. 438). So, for the ecologists it is important to develop organizational taxonomies to improve the description and classification of organizational forms. More homogeneous groups are defined and the limited conditions are specified under which predictions may be expected to hold true (McKelvey & Aldrich, 1983).

Also in this aspect, an alternative approach is represented by the strategic choice view. According to it, environment is not viewed as a set of intractable constraints, as it can be changed and manipulated through political negotiation to fit the objectives of top management (Lorange, 1980), but as an "enacted" reality (Weick, 1979a).

In short, during the past few years deterministic studies of structure as a function of technology and environment have been proliferating, at the time alternative views have surfaced pointing out that strategic decisions are the critical element in the determination of organizational structure.

CONTINGENCY MODELS VERSUS STRATEGIC DECISIONS MODELS

The contingency theory has been predominant during the 1970s although the need of a methodological and conceptual clarification has been progressively assumed. Hazewinkel (1984) characterizes this view as a "confusing picture" that includes contextual determinism, the congruency approaches, and the natural selection model. Schoonhoven (1981) intended to clarify the issue calling for the formulation of contingency theory that will include interactive, nonmonotonic, and symmetrical relationships between structure, technology, and environment. In a study of the operating room suites in 17 hospitals, he found multiplicative forms of interaction between technology and structure that were symmetrical (lower values of a dimension of structure, when coupled with lower values of technological or environmental uncertainty, should produce effective organizations) and nonmonotonic (effects of structure on effectiveness are not constant over the values of technological or environmental uncertainty). Fry and Slocum (1984), furthering Schoonhoven's contribution, distinguished among effect, general, and functional congruency to clarify the form of "fit" between congruency factors. Effect congruency "suggest a more-is-better perspective in which it is assumed that variance explained will continue to be improved as additional independent variables . . . are added" (p. 243); general congruency "hypothesizes interaction effects and emphasizes the similarity and matching of levels of independent variables as determinants of performance" (p. 243); and functional congruency suggests that "either one or the other independent variable may be sufficient to lead to high levels of effectiveness, but the joint occurrence of both may do little to improve [it]" (p. 243). These authors conclude that although congruency has been the dominant paradigm in the literature, perhaps it needs to be reconstructed.

Others have pointed out the insufficiencies of the contingency model and have advocated for the alternative position represented by the strategic choice view (Egelhoff, 1982). Organizations are not totally dependent on their environment, but they can influence it (Schreyögg, 1980), even enact it (Weick, 1979a).

Also, the holders of the resource-dependence model are against environmental determinism as environment can be changed through political negotiation. Astley and Van de Ven (1983) have reviewed the differences between those views and suggested ways to eliminate them, and Hazewinkel (1984) has pointed out: "What we have here is, in fact, contingency of higher order. A strict contingency theory with its deterministic character is applicable to small organizations fighting for their life in a very competitive market. If the situation is less threatening and less hostile, the strategic choice or the resource dependence model become more relevant" (p. 768). Thus further research is needed to establish the organizational and environmental conditions in which each model becomes more relevant.

ORGANIZATIONAL TYPOLOGIES AND STRUCTURAL CONFIGURATIONS

The typological approach has a long tradition in organizational theory. Weber described bureaucracy as an ideal type of organization. Later, several authors enlarged and corrected Weber's formula. Burns and Stalker (1961) distinguished between mechanical and organic forms; this typology is still widely used in spite of criticisms and failure of its predictions in a number of situations. Hull and Hage (1982) typology expanded the Burns and Stalker dichotomy into four categories: traditional, mechanical, organic, and mixed. Based in empirical studies, the Aston Group typology is grounded in a three-dimensional model that focuses on the following dimensions: structuring of activities, decision-making authority, and means of control. Seven types of organizations were found as a function of these three dimensions. They were designated by the researchers as full bureaucracy, nascent full bureaucracy, workflow bureaucracy, nascent workflow bureaucracy, preworkflow bureaucracy, personnel bureaucracy, and implicitly structured organization (Pugh, 1981).

In the last decade, a configurational approach has been developed. Khandwalla (1973) pointed out that the "gestalt or configuration of an organization is likely to be a more potent determinant of its effectiveness than any of the individual components of its configuration" (p. 493). But it was Mintzberg (1979, 1983) who gave a broad conceptual basis for this hypothesis. Five structural configurations (simple structure, machine bureaucracy, professional bureaucracy, divisionalized form, and adhocracy) are derived from an organizational model made up of five basic components (strategic apex, middle line, operating core, techno-structure, and support staff) linked to each other by authority, raw materials and information flows, and decision processes. The emerging configurations also depends on nine design parameters and on the contingent factors of age, size, technical system, environment, and power. With these nine design structural para-meters the number of possible combinations would grow rather large, nevertheless, the five just mentioned configurations, with that of "missionary" added later (Mintzberg, 1983), are enough to describe adequately the existing varieties of organizations.

Mintzberg's typology has merited considerable attention. An analysis of citations received by *The Structuring of Organizations* (1979) offers the following figures: 1980, 4 citations; 1981, 3 citations; 1982, 32 citations; 1983, 37 citations, and 1984, 44 citations (plus 5 citations to Structure in Five).[1] A glance at the citations shows special concern with professional bureaucracies: schools, hospitals, courtrooms, and libraries. Criticisms have been leveled at Mintz-berg for his lack of empirical validation (Miller, 1983). Miller and his colleagues have tackled the problem both conceptually (Miller, 1981) and empirically (Miller & Friessen, 1980, 1982). Miller (1983) offers validation data for simple structure, machine bureaucracy, and adhocracies, renamed by Miller as simple firms, planning firms, and organic firms.

In sum, contingency theory and typological approach are well represented in recent research being the most representative lines of investigation using the rational paradigm of organizational structure.

THE STRUCTURING OF ORGANIZATIONS:
BEYOND THE RATIONAL PARADIGM

The insufficiencies of the classic rational paradigm in the theory of organizations have been pointed out (Zey-Ferrell, 1981). Benson (1983) described the situation as one of paradigmatic crisis. He reviewed the proponents of alternate paradigms: demythologizers, politicizers, ecologizers, and totalizers. Others, from a multi-paradigmatic view of organizational theory have placed the rational paradigm in a broader framework. So Morgan (1980) presents functionalist, interpretive, radical humanist, and radical structuralist paradigms. Van de Ven and Astley (1981) look at the system structural view, the strategic choice view, the natural selection view, and the collective action view.

Several authors have analyzed the metaphors used in theories about organizations and their structure. Besides the classical mechanistic and organismic metaphors, others have been proposed such as "information processing systems," "cultures," "social contracts," "negotiated orders," "loosely coupled systems," "organized anarchies," and so on (Fine, 1984; Morgan, 1980). Facing such a plurality of metaphors, some have tried to develop integrative theories (Fombrun, 1985), others have questioned its utility (Pinder & Bourgeois, 1982). Nevertheless, these alternative formulations to the rational paradigm, especially the interpretive or the strategic choice view, have been the basis for a new conceptualization of organizational structure.

SOCIOCOGNITIVE AND POLITICAL
VIEWS ON ORGANIZATIONAL STRUCTURING

It is possible to find some antecedents of sociocognitive approach to the study of organizations (Peiró, 1985), however, it was Weick (1969) and Silverman (1970) who developed it. In their well-known analysis of the Utrecht Jazz Orchestra, Weick and his colleagues pointed out that "in a social structure it is not the objective content of variables but the structure of causality among them that determines the fate of the system.... Social settings are defined and must be analyzed in terms of the participants' epistemology: organization problems are mind-environment problems" (Boughon, Weick, & Binkhorst, 1977, p. 622). Consequently, Weick (1979b) has characterized organizations as a body of socially shared thoughts.

In this context, several authors have enlarged the concept of organizational structure. Traditionally considered as *framework*, they now also add to the meaning of structure the *interactive aspects* known sometimes as "informal structure." For Ranson, Hinings, and Greenwood (1980), structuring is a process influenced by social power and reached by recreating meanings within some contextual constrictions. Willmott (1981) felt that Ranson's position failed to overcome the dualistic conception of structure as formal or informal. More recently, Fombrun (1985) has distinguished among *infrastructure* ("underlying resource dependencies which the organization faces as it struggles to both produce and reproduce itself over time"), *structure* ("formal and informal relationships in organizations"), and *superstructure* ("ideational size of the organization and its symbolic representations and interpretations of collective life"). In this way, he was able to integrate the resource-dependence, politics, and culture metaphors. In his own words, "Structure is, therefore, the repository of organizational learning, the organizations' unique and cumulative 'memory' of successes and failures . . . and structuring is, in aggregate, a historical process of 'sedimentation.'. . . It is a process that relates the legitimization of action in the superstructure to its assertion in structures of dominance that are simultaneously translated into—and come to signify—the pursuit of efficiency in the infrastructure" (pp. 16-17).

Some common themes characterize these contributions: (1) the emphasis on the sociocognitive construction of organizational structure, (2) the interpretive approach to organizational phenomenon, (3) the emphasis on the structuring processes and on the active role of individuals, and (4) the relevant role given to power games and politics.

Empirical work has been carried out within this fourfold perspective. Boughon et al. (1977) studied the causal-cognitive maps of the members of an orchestra, and Ford and Hegarty (1984) studied the causal perceptions of managers and of graduate business students; these perceptions were consistent with contingency theory tenets. Cognitions of work units were investigated by Blackburn and Cummings (1982), who demonstrated that people perceive five dimensions in such cognitions: bureaucratic, affective, interaction, function, and size. Focus on subjective elements have been joined to classical aspects in these examinations. Also, the incorporation of a new technology has been analyzed from a political perspective emphasizing the ritual function in information system design (Robey & Markus, 1984). Brief and Downey (1983) have described the role of implicit theories of organizing and their functions: structuring, interpretation of intents, interpretation of organizational characteristics, and social fabric. Thus empirical study has included analysis of organizational cognitions (Weick, 1979b), power games and organizational politics (Hickson, Astley, Butler, & Wilson, 1981), causal attributions, and organizational paradigms (Brown, 1978) incorporating new research strategies and methodologies.

NETWORK ANALYSIS, ORGANIZATIONAL STRUCTURING, AND STRUCTURE

Social network analysis views a social system "as composed of social objects (people, groups, organizations) joined by variety of relationships and seeks to identify both their causes and consequences" (Tichy, 1980, p. 121; Tichy, Tushman, & Fonbrun, 1979). This approach has been used in recent times for the study of organizations at different levels: interorganizational (Aldrich & Whetten, 1981; van Gils, 1984), organizational (O'Really & Pondy, 1979; Pettigrew, 1973), and groups (Tichy, 1973).

In the study of organizational structure, network analysis has been seen as a promising candidate to replace Weber's structural analysis carried out in the frame of rational paradigm. As Tichy and Fombrun (1979) pointed out, "Whereas neo-Weberian analysis has tended to treat process as a black box and examine structure for its own sake, network analysis explicitly focuses on the interpersonal processes in organization" (p. 925). For some authors, network analysis is more useful in explaining the relationships between structure and performance than contingency theories (Pearce & David, 1983). The previous views look at the attributes of structural elements while the network approach pays attention to the attributes of the relationships among those elements (Moch, 1983). As a result, the analysis of emergent networks are incorporated besides the analysis of the prescribed and formal network. Attention is focused not only on the stable elements but also on the structuring processes that have generated and changed them. Furthermore, analysis can be focused on technical, political, or cultural systems (Tichy, 1980, 1981), that is, on infrastructure, structure, or superstructure, and also on determining the congruency among them.

With the technological advances produced by the third computer generation, which have allowed computational analysis of large volumes of data, it has been possible to measure complex organizational structures with a network methodology (Moch, 1983; Tichy, Tushman, & Fombrun, 1980). Within this general context, some empirical research on organizational structure has been carried out. Tichy and Fombrun (1979) reanalyzed the data from Payne and Pheysey (1973) with a network methodology. They obtained "a richer and empirically more useful set of results." A study of the friendship relations and interactions between employees in a packaging plant obtained nominal position measures and measures of individual position within clusters of work, offering new ways of applying network analysis technique (Moch, 1983). Fombrun (1984) studied the correspondence between formal and governance structures in a medium-sized medical instrument, R & D laboratory, showing the interdependence of various structural levels.

These network studies explicitly raise the need to study the relations between structuring processes and their resultant structure. They represent a step forward in understanding organizational structure but they are still far from providing a deep analysis of the problem.

ORGANIZATIONAL STRUCTURE AND INDIVIDUAL ATTITUDES AND BEHAVIORS

The relations among organizational structure and behaviors and attitudes of their members is a core question in organizational theory if we wish to overcome the gap between the micro- and macro-level approaches (Staw, 1984). Research on this issue has been carried out basically within the frame of the rational paradigm, but some works have been developed in the alternative theoretical framework that emphasizes the structuring process of organizations. Here we will review recent contributions on relationships among structure, attitudes, and behaviors developed within each of these two paradigmatic approaches.

ATTITUDES, BEHAVIOR, AND ORGANIZATIONAL STRUCTURE FROM THE RATIONAL PARADIGM PERSPECTIVE

Porter and Lawler (1965), Berger and Cummings (1979), and James and Jones (1976) have reviewed the large number of empirical and conceptual studies on this topic that used the rational paradigm. These reviews were based on an underlying concept of structure that included seven dimensions: (1) organizational level, (2) line and staff hierarchies, (3) span of control, (4) subunit size, (5) total organizational size, (6) tall or flat shape, and (7) centralized or decentralized shape. In general, the reviewed works aimed to determine the effects of these structural dimensions on one or more attitudes (mainly satisfaction) and behaviors (performance, turnover, absenteeism, and employee-grievance rates) of their members. Research within this approach has continued during the

1980s (Jablin, 1982; Nicholson & Goh, 1983; Srivasta, 1984, among others) and an increased interest in the organizational structure and individual stress relationships is noticeable (Parker & de Cotis, 1983; Van Sell, Brief, & Schler, 1981). In their review, Berger and Cummings (1979) pointed out several methodological problems and, interestingly enough, they observed that "we are at point at which inductive empiricism cannot advance the state of our knowledge much further without the accompaniment of sound conceptual analysis. Simply the explicit awareness that many studies leap from the aggregate macro organizational level (as independent variables) directly to the individual level of analysis (as dependent variables) should warn us that causality cannot be direct and simple cross-sectional bivariate relationship between these two discrepant levels of analysis will not provide adequate explanation" (p. 202).

Not only structural dimensions but also structural configurations and types have been studied as independent variables to determine their effects on individual attitudes and behaviors. The studies that take configurations or types as independent variables assume that global differences between organizational structures are more salient than the variability of their dimensions in explaining behavioral and attitudinal changes. Most of the studies in this approach have employed, rather intuitively, the Burns and Stalker typology in looking for differences in behavior and attitudes of organizational members. But "neither organic nor mechanistic styles are unidimensional constructs, and empirical findings of a lack of uniform application of these styles . . . indicate that elite pick up and choose various aspects of them" (Dewar & Werbel, 1979, p. 428). Some works have specified the structural aspects that serve as criteria for classification (Moch et al., 1979; Sherman & Smith, 1984). Recently, Mintzberg's typology has also inspired some interesting research on this problem.[2]

An additional problem related to the study of the relationship between structure and attitudes-behaviors within the rational paradigm is the differential usefulness of universalistic and contingency predictions. The latter states that structural effects on behaviors and attitudes are moderated by contextual or environmental aspects. Dewar and Werbel (1979) offered empirical results that partially supported both approaches, and in contrast with several recent studies their results indicate "that contingency variables are frequently as good as, or even better than universalistic variables as predictors of satisfaction and conflict" (p. 426).

THE STRUCTURING OF ORGANIZATIONS
AND INDIVIDUAL ATTITUDES AND BEHAVIORS

In a wider perspective of structure that includes interactive patterns (power, communication, contact, work flow, and so on) and superstructure (culture, values, organizational paradigms, and myths), several intermediate processes are relevant between organization and individuals' behavior. The analysis of these processes may contribute to clarifying the influence of organizational structure on individual behaviors and attitudes and also to the structuring processes of organizations. There is a mutual and partial determination between individuals and organizations.

Within this general perspective, the mediating character of social interactions and networks have been emphasized in several empirical studies. Thus Brass (1981) has shown that characteristics of structure and the attitudes and behaviors of members are mediated by job characteristics arising from the job's location of members within the network of work flow transactions. Pearce and David (1983) have pointed out that "organization level characteristics first affect group structural properties which, in turn, have a direct impact on performance" (p. 436). Oldham and Hackman (1981) found support for the job modification model. According to it, structural properties of organizations affect the characteristics of an employee's job, which, in turn, affect the employee's reactions.

Other authors have pointed out the central role of intermediate levels of analysis in order to explain individual behavior. Delruelle-Voeswinkel and Robert (1980) showed the influence of organizational structure on social relations in the work place and also the influence of these social relations on behaviors and attitudes of job holders. Blau (1982) studied the effects of network properties of organizational units in a psychiatric hospital on individual empowering. The capacity of a unit to empower its members is contingent upon its integration in organizationwide communication networks. Finally, Moch (1980) found that workers who were well integrated in their job networks showed greater internal motivation than isolates.

All these works show the importance of social interactions and of relational aspects of organizational positions as influential elements on individual attitudes and behaviors. They also emphasize the mediating role of such social interactions and position relationships between organizational structure and individual behaviors. It is through these mediating elements that structure affects behavior and attitudes of an organization's members.

Individual actions and attitudes are also seen to affect organizational structuring and structure. It does not mean that this influence always happens, nor that all members have the same probabilities of exerting it. It also does not mean that this influence should be the only determinant of organizational structure. It means that social interaction processes among members will contribute to pattern or change structure as other environmental influences do. Such interaction processes are, in turn, influenced by sociocognitive aspects as values and organizational culture. Dominant coalitions and resource dependencies within the organization also play an important role in this structuring process.

Some recent empirical investigations have tried to clarify aspects of these complex processes of structuring. Bartunek (1984) studied the changes in interpretive schemes in a religious order and the reciprocal changes in its organizational structure. Blau and McKinley (1979) obtained data that suggest the influence of members' ideas on organizational complexity and innovation. "Structural complexity and task diversity depend on size in organizations with uniform tasks but are also, and perhaps primarily, affected by cognitive ideas and professional orientations in organizations with nonuniform tasks" (p. 215). Probably the question that has attracted more attention is the role of cognitions and values of managers in strategic decisions and their influence in the process of structuring organizations. Hambrick and Mason (1984) showed the influence of values and cognitions of dominant coalition members on strategy and effectiveness of organizations, and Latouche (1983) pointed out the managers' role in the continual redefinition of organizational culture.

SPANISH CONTRIBUTIONS

The study of the psychosociology of work has a long tradition in Spain although the Spanish Civil War represented a hiatus that took more than two decades to overcome (Peiró, 1984). During the last decades, organizational psychology and industrial sociology have developed extensively. Even so, some topics have received more attention than others. Organizational psychology has paid more attention to individual and group behaviors and attitudes; industrial sociology has focused on the social framework of industrial organizations, that is, on occupational structure and the stratification of social classes, markets, and bureaucratic society (Garmendia, 1984).

In this context, organizational structure has received little attention. Twenty years ago, De Miguel and Linz (1964) presented technology innovation and bureaucracy as the main structural trends in Spanish enterprises but similar studies did not follow it. During the past few years, organizational structure has been tangentially considered in studies about the industrial system or in others on workers' attitudes and behaviors. So the contributions of Tavistock Institute and that of the industrial democracy movement in Europe have received some attention in our country (Lucas, 1984; Medina, 1985a, 1985b; Prida, 1984). The latter has been related to cooperative work organizations ("cooperativas de trabajo asociado") in which the workers own the enterprise. From a comparative perspective, Rull (1980) has studied the size of Spanish enterprises. New technologies (Escudero, 1984; Navarro, 1984) and new ways of work organization (Castillo, 1984; Castillo & Prieto, 1983) have been treated in the more wide framework of industrial systems.

Some attention has also been paid to structural dimensions of work organizations in the surveys about workers' behaviors and attitudes. Lucas (1981) found a positive linear relation between work satisfaction and workers' professional level, and a curvilinear one between the organizational size and work satisfaction. Workers in medium-sized enterprises showed a higher level of satisfaction than did the workers in small or in very large organizations. Tezanos (1983) obtained negative relations among size, formalization, and satisfaction. Significant differences were also found as a function of technology. Mass production technology produced the lowest levels of satisfaction.

The sociocognitive approach and relational analysis also received some attention in our country (Peiró 1985). Meliá and Peiró (1985) studied focal persons' perceptions of their power relationships, communication, and conflict with the members of their own role set in work organizations. Also, Navarro et al. (1985) found a significant effect of such perceived relationships in the role set on stress and work satisfaction of focal persons.

In sum, there has been little research about organizational structure in Spain as such. However, the incorporation of Spain to the European Common Market will probably require more attention to this question in order to support the changes that many of our enterprises will have to face in their structure, technology, and ways of management.

NOTES

1. Data have been obtained from Social Science Citation Index (1980-1984).
2. Storr, Winnubst, and De Wolff are carrying on a study about differences in stress related to the five types of organizations formulated by Mintzberg (personal communication).

16

DECISION MAKING

FRANK A. HELLER
Innovative Climates
The Tavistock Institute of Human Relations
London, U.K.

JYUJI MISUMI
Osaka University
Osaka, Japan

The term *decision making* is now used by a considerable variety of disciplines and covers a wide range of topics, including risk taking, decision aids for computer application, organizational choice, problem solving, the psychology of cognition, judgment, and inference. Much of the classical work takes place in laboratories, under controlled conditions or makes theoretical probabilistic assumptions from which certain deductions can be made.[1]

Decision making grapples with the elusive issue of rationality and predictability. A decision may be predictable if it follows a given logical algorithm or a statistically calculated trade-off between expected cost and expected benefit (or cost variance). It may also be predictable if the rules of nonrationality or even irrationality are known. The important work of Nisbett and Ross (1980), Kahneman, Slovic, and Tversky (1982), and Pitz and Sachs (1984) addresses itself to these issues. A similar debate based on experimentation and theory has developed in Japan with Saeki (1981) and Kondo (1981) emphasizing rationality, while Toda (1980) uses a theory based on emotion and sentiment, and Tao (1982) stresses the importance of relatively complex organizational and environmental determinants that do not fit a rational model.

Even within the area of formal decision theory, important differences in approach have to be considered. A "new theory of social choice" has been put forward by Collingridge (1982) based on Popper's views on falsification and the criterion of demarcation that states that the defining characteristic of a scientific claim is the possibility of its clash with experience (Popper, 1959, Section 6). A new theory or model is better than a previous one not because of "a higher empirical content" but because it meets three conditions: (1) it must ensure the redundancy of the previous theory, (2) it must make some novel prediction(s), and (3) at least some of the new predictions must be corroborated by experiment (Collingridge, 1982, p. 80).

An approach entirely different from formal algorithmic or probabilistic theories owes more to the tradition of social psychology and anthropology (Bass, 1983). It either constructs models based on field observation and experimentation or relies on grounded theory to build up toward a model from emergent reality (Koopman, Drenth, Bus, & Kruyswijk, 1984). These are the principal areas covered by organizational decision-making studies and they sometimes border on the field of leadership research (see Andriessen and Drenth, 1984, and the next chapter by Misumi and Peterson in this book). Research in Europe and Japan provide examples of recent work with organizational decision models.

A LONGITUDINAL APPROACH TO
ORGANIZATIONAL DECISION MAKING

The Decisions in Organizations project (DIO) is a three country study based on seven companies: two in Britain, three in the Netherlands, and two in Yugoslavia. The research has five major characteristics:

(a) The unit of analysis is a sample of 217 medium and long-term decisions;

(b) In each case the process of decision making that lasted from one month to nearly three years was monitored through four phases: (1) start up, (2) development, (3) finalization, and (4) implementation;

(c) A number of quantitative measures were taken in each phase in addition to ethnographic field material;

(d) The Influence-Power-Continuum (IPC) is a major variable in the Decisions in Organizations model. It is measured through six defined alternatives varying from having no information and therefore no influence, via various degrees of participation, to delegation and autonomy (see, also, IDE, 1981, p. 59); and

(e) Among the other variables in the model illustrated in the diagram, the underutilization of competence and status power have special theoretical and policy relevant importance.

The DIO research grew out of a series of previous studies using contingency models, starting with an analysis of top management

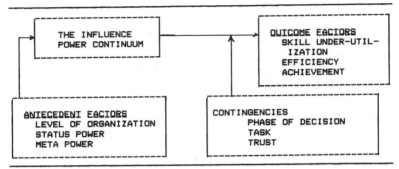

Figure 16.1 The Model

decision making in two American samples (Heller & Yukl, 1968; Heller, 1971) and an eight country (mainly European) comparative study (Heller & Wilpert, 1981). A more ambitious twelve country research called Industrial Democracy in Europe (IDE) was published in 1981 and analyzed decision making at all levels of organization. The DIO longitudinal study (DIO, 1979; DIO, 1983; Heller, Drenth, Koopman, & Rus, in press), which also covers all levels, was designed to complement and extend the IDE research that had used a cross-sectional design (IDE, 1981a; IDE, 1981b).

THE IMPORTANCE OF PHASES

Certain important dimensions of decision making, influence, and power, in particular, vary significantly from phase to phase. The six alternative positions on the Influence-Power-Continuum (IPC) are measured for each level in the organization during each of the four phases of the decision cycle.

The findings show that lower levels of the organization rarely have influence over phase 1 (start up) and phase 3 (finalization). Those two phases tend to be dominated by management. On those occasions when lower-level employees make a contribution to the decision process, it tends to be in phase 2 (development) and phase 4 (implementation).

On theoretical as well as practical considerations, these phases are not equal. Phases 1 and 3 have more determining power than the other two. The start up phase sets the agenda; a new machine is to be bought, a new product developed, or a committee set up. The power to agree that these decisions are accepted or refused comes from the finalization phase. The role of the other two phases is important, but less incisive: searching out alternatives and putting forward options or suggestions and testing out these ideas is the role of the development phase, but the main impetus and direction has already been given in phase 1. The implementation phase is often complex and frequently leads to frictions but it follows on from finalization and usually leaves only limited room for maneuver.

Since the study also collected ethnographic data, it can incorporate the power differences by phases on a descriptive level, but it is also possible to weight the scores differently and arrive at an adjusted overall statistical estimate of total influence for each level in the organization.

There is a more general methodological issue relating to the validity of cross-sectional data about events that occur over time. In most cross-sectional decision-making studies a single score is obtained, but we do not know what respondents have uppermost in their mind when they give their answer. Do they attempt to average out what happens in the various phases, or do they remember particularly well what happened during the longest phase or the most recent one or in the phase during which a crisis occurred? The error variance of cross-sectional scores about longitudinal events is likely to be very large.[2]

THE UNDERUTILIZATION OF COMPETENCE

Competence is the totality of a person's job-relevant experience and skill. It seems that organizations find it very difficult to use the existing reservoir of competence (O'Brien, 1983; Thurley, 1982; Sokolowska, 1984). In the eight country research with senior managers, underutilization of skill was estimated (on average) to be close to 20% (Heller & Wilpert, 1981, pp. 116-122) and "successful" managers underutilized subordinate competence less than "unsuccessful" managers. High underutilization correlated with job dissatisfaction and with autocratic decision methods. In the longitudinal Decisions in Organizations study, the underutilization of the existing human potential emerged as one of most powerful variables in the decision model and was best described as the consequence of low information sharing and top management autocracy (Heller et al., in press). In organizations where consultative committees exerted above average influence on the decision process, underutilization was significantly reduced.

STATUS POWER

Status power (SP) is the formal amount of authority and power assigned to a given level of organization or committee. Company policy documents and committee constitutions often describe and limit formal authority in writing. In other cases, long-established custom and practice contains the relevant information. Status power can be quantified on a continuum similar to the IPC (DIO, 1979; DIO, 1983). The results show that de facto informal influence sharing as well as participation in representative consultative committees is significantly predicted by status power (Heller et al., in press).

The conceptualization of status power bears some resemblance to the formal legal structures of the industrial relations system that was measured at the level of the country in the IDE (1981a, chap. 6). The results show that this formal norm was also a significant predictor of de facto influence sharing at the shop floor level. It can therefore be argued that if participative decision making is to be increased, some changes in the formal policy prescriptions at national and/or organizational level are desirable and functional.

BEYOND PARTICIPATIVE DECISION MAKING

The term *participative decision making* (PDM) is often used in the literature to suggest an optimum method implying the achievement of consensus. This idea derives from the original and very influential research at the University of Michigan under Rensis Likert (1961, 1967), but in practice this method is not widely used and there are some difficulties in its conceptualization. If PDM is used by management primarily to improve subordinate satisfaction, then pseudo or inauthentic participation is just as good as genuine participation (Etzioni, 1969; Heller, 1971, pp. 97-98; Verba, 1961). Pseudoparticipation can take several forms but most usually occurs when consultation takes place after a decision has already been taken or when there is no intention of allowing the consultation to change the predetermined outcome.

Pseudoparticipation is not effective if the primary objective is to improve the quality of the decision, but better decisions do not require consensus; instead they encourage better use to be made of available competence. Decisions about the purchase of a word processor or some other item of equipment can be taken at quite low levels of the organization where the relevant experience exists. Decisions about improvement in quality are frequently most effective if they are left to semiautonomous groups at shop floor level. These examples require devolution of power, or delegation of authority, and can be achieved without joint decision making or consensus with senior management.

To recognize the existence of valid decision methods beyond PDM, the various research projects described above have used an Influence-Power-Continuum that allows for delegation and autonomy at lower levels (see Heller & Yukl, 1969). Vroom and Jago (1974) have also experimented with an extension of PDM, but in general these distinctions are not understood (for instance, Locke & Schweiger, 1979). We will see that the mistaken association between PDM and group consensus also applies to Japanese decision procedures.

META POWER AND TRUST

The DIO research defined *meta power* as influence from outside the focal organization, for instance, the head office, the parent company, banks, government. In practice, most scores related to head office. *Trust* was defined as the amount of confidence higher and lower levels of the hierarchy had in each other and the absence of suspicion in each other's motivation.

Contrary to our hypothesis, meta power was more frequently supportive rather than restrictive of the decision process inside the focal organization and was positively correlated to achievement.[3]

Trust operated as a contingency between status power and outcomes. It correlated significantly with achievement as well as efficiency.[4]

The part of the DIO research reported here concentrated on medium-term tactical and long-term strategic decisions. Several important dimensions, such as power and timing, are significantly different under these two task conditions; lower levels of the organization have more influence over tactical than over strategic decisions.

PARTICIPATIVE
DECISION MAKING IN JAPAN

Although Japan emerged as a modern state with the Meiji restoration about one hundred years ago, it developed as a major industrial power only in the last three decades. It is even more recently, after Japan overtook other advanced western nations, that interest in its idiosyncratic decision-making system began to preoccupy managers and social scientists. While many books and articles have been published, some after very superficial study, the reality of the Japanese methods are still only dimly apprehended. The following account is based on Jyuji Misumi's chapter in the 1984 Yearbook of Organizational Democracy.

To begin with, Misumi shows that not all Japanese decision methods follow the group consensus model. In theory and to an increasing extent in practice, the final authority rests with upper levels of the organizational hierarchy; two surveys conducted by the Ministry of International Trade and Industry document some of this change. The famous ringi system of initiating decisions at middle or lower levels and gradually obtaining approval with higher management had, in many cases, become transmuted to something resembling record keeping and reporting rather than decision making.

THE RINGI METHOD OF DECISION

The *ringi* system has a long history and has been extensively adapted to cover a large variety of situations. It started "as a means of asking the higher authority for instructions under the cabinet system in the early days of the Meiji era" (Misumi, 1984, p. 529). The suggestions that were initiated by lower officials were not matters of tactical or strategic importance but concerned themselves with fairly routine administrative details.

After 1950, the *ringi* method, which was widely used in business organization, was often criticized by foreigners because of its alleged slowness and some Japanese also thought that it would have to give way to more "modern" top-down methods.

However, the finer characteristics of the method are not always clearly understood, particularly by western observers. In the first place, the *ringi* is as much a system of communication as a method of making decisions. A person at a lower level of the organization has an idea and introduces a suggestion that he or she helps to circulate to various people at higher levels and finally to the highest level at the apex of the organization to get approval. However, the original idea does not have to come from the initiator of the *ringi*, it can come from a colleague or from a higher level. The *ringi* is usually written down and circulates as a paper, even if it starts at the first line supervisory level. As it moves up the chain of command it frequently changes content. It may receive additions or the originator may be asked to accept changes. It may also be stopped at any level if there is considerable disapproval. If it finds favor and receives endorsement, this is shown by the signature of each person in the *ringi*. The signature is usually a seal of "hanko" and the method is often known as *"ringi seido."*

Since the method starts at lower levels and meanders upward, it is often referred to as a "bottom-up" management and contrasted to the "top-down" system widely assumed to be the most efficacious method in the United States and Europe. Takamiya (1981) has drawn attention to this important distinction by saying that the *ringi* procedure, compared with the typical European or American procedure where decisions are made largely on the authority of a superior without approval by other persons who could be concerned with the decision, is "as different as chalk from cheese" (Misumi, 1984, p. 529).

It is important to draw attention to five distinguishing features of *ringi*. In the first place, it operates as a method of communication and this means that many people who are directly or indirectly involved learn about the proposal. Second, the *ringi* achieves a degree of consensus among many members of the organization by the time it reaches top management. Third, the method assures an extensive utilization of experience and knowledge of all the people involved and may change in structure and content from the original proposal. Fourth, and as a consequence of this utilization of many people's experience, it is likely to end up as a better quality decision than the original concept.

Finally, since the ideas in the *ringi* initiative are widely disseminated and—in their original or altered form—have obtained approval from the critical actors, implementation can be very rapid. The criticism that *ringi* is very slow is largely due to the misconception that a decision ends with a command or the signature on the document. In the West, implementation is often a very slow process. In the DIO research described earlier, the implementation phase was sometimes longer than the other three phases combined and was frequently punctuated by conflict and resistance because there had been no working through.

Under *ringi* the person who drafts the original proposal and then steers it through the organization has a special interest to see that the decision is rapidly implemented. In this task, he or she is helped by the shared responsibility of the other members who have put their "hanko" on the document. In this sense, decision making by *ringi* takes the form of group decision making; it also has a subtle training or management development function.

In spite of these characteristics, as we have already mentioned, the *ringi* procedure has been criticized. A detailed case study reported on 73 companies using *ringi* was published after World War II (Yamashiro, 1956). This survey took place before Japanese manufacturers had helped the country to reach spectacular rates of growth. It was also a time when Japan was keen to copy Western management principles and practices. The report denounced *ringi* as inefficient, irrational, and primitive. One of the objections was due to its assumption of collective power that made no provision for delegation of authority and responsibility to individuals on lower levels.

However, Misumi points out that the *ringi* method is part of a system that has helped Japan to survive 100 years of rapid change and there can be little doubt that this method of decision making is associated with the period of unprecedented economic growth after 1960. At the same time, it has played a positive role in small-scale family paternalistic companies (Ono, 1960).

The consensus approach to decision making has also made it difficult for Japan to adopt the "line and staff" principle of management that was taken over from the division of function in the armed services in western countries. The initial *ringi* proposal has the character of a staff task, but when it comes back to the initiator for implementation, he or she carries out a line responsibility. In general, Japanese managers carry out both line and staff functions and it is interesting to reflect on the fact that recent modern organization theory in western countries seems to have largely abandoned the line-staff distinction, while research has often failed to obtain empirical support for it (Heller, 1971).

OTHER JAPANESE DECISION AIDS

Both supporters and opponents of the *ringi* system sometimes fail to see that Japanese decision making has more than one string to its bow. Although consensus is highly valued, there are established formal procedures of catharsis that allow dissent and criticism to come to the surface when necessary. *Sake* parties after working hours bring together a boss and his or her subordinates in a nearby bar, which also serves some food. During *sake* parties subordinates can say what they like in the presence of their superior and it will not be counted against them. *Sake* parties are a ritual that permit frustrations and criticism to be brought to the attention of higher levels without loss of face. Subordinates get rid of tensions, while their boss can learn about problems from which, in their hierarchical position, he or she is otherwise remote. In western organizations, senior managers often complain about "the loneliness of high places"; they hear only what subordinates think they want to hear.

Nemawashi is another important decision aid that can work as an addition or as an alternative to *ringi*. *Nemawashi* is an informal preliminary sounding out of opinions. It gives minority views an adequate hearing and prepares the ground for consensus or for a formal vote. The method allows everybody, even dissenters, to come out of the decision process without public humiliation or shame and this is a very important achievement in a culture where "losing face" is particularly abhorrent. However, *nemawashi* has limits; it works better with simple routine matters and becomes noticeably less effective when opinions are sharply divided on matters of considerable importance. In such cases, *jyomukai* or executive meetings tend to be used.

Nemawashi in Japanese means to prepare for transplanting a large tree by cutting off most of the main roots a year or two before it is transplanted. Transplanted into the sphere of decision making, it means that before putting an important formal proposal to a board or committee meeting, the initiator tries informally to discover who might oppose the suggestion so that, through discussion and persuasion, the opposition can be cut off, reduced, or eliminated. *Nemawashi* tries to achieve consent before major decisions have to be reached. In western countries a similar procedure is something called "lobbying," but it is less ritualized because unanimous agreement is not a requirement in the same way that it is in Japan where *nemawashi* has become the standard procedure preceding formal meetings. As a consequence, formal meetings may degenerate into stylized predictable patterns and discussion can drag on for long periods. If, as a result of an emergency, there had been no time for *nemawashi*, agreement might become impossible.

Misumi believes that Japanese decision makers have a higher frustration tolerance than American or European participants in long drawn out meetings, but even in Japan, *nemawashi* may fail if views are sharply divided. In such cases, majority voting procedures are used as they are in western countries, although in Japan less use is made of naked power maneuvers, the objective of consent is less quickly abandoned and more attention is given to the arguments of the minority. Even in the context of hierarchical relations, the decision process retains a sociopsychological orientation sustained by friendly day-to-day personal contacts.

CONCLUSION

Decision making is a complex phenomenon. It has been investigated by psychologists and other social scientists and many worthwhile results have been achieved, but the use of a considerable variety of distinct models and methods has so far prevented the achievement of substantial insights from cross-disciplinary findings.

Our review has concentrated on the study of real life decision processes in modern organizations based, for the most part, on recent research in Europe and Japan. This area of work is beginning to show some cohesion in spite of cultural diversity (Hickson et al., 1986).

Organizational decision making is a process that requires a space-time analysis. The space dimension covers the area within the triangle that symbolizes the structure of hierarchical organizations, while the time dimension is needed to trace the longitudinal events from initiation of the process to its *denouement*.

The decision processes we have reviewed came from very different socioeconomic settings and the evidence was collected by a variety of methods. Nevertheless, the three country Decisions in Organizations research, as well as the evidence from the Japanese decision process, have three features in common in addition to the space-time framework. They both use a contingency approach and a dimension of influence or power that includes consensus decision making, and in different ways they both stress the importance of skill utilization.

Contingencies are specified circumstances that lead to, or require, different behavior. The Japanese *ringi*, for instance, is not a monolithic, standardized, or invariant procedure. It can start at different levels, and its exact passage through the organization is a function of the nature of the issue. A financial initiative will have a different path from a suggestion to change an aspect of the production process. To obtain consensus, which is its main objective, it may sometimes operate on its own and at other times call on *nemawashi* to obtain a higher degree of agreement. On very controversial and divisive issues, neither *ringi* nor *nemawashi* are effective and majority voting can be resorted to.

In the Decisions in Organizations research we described three contingencies: phase of decision, trust, and decision task, but our short summary concentrated on the important behavioral differences that occur during the four phases of a typical decision cycle. It emerged that the amount of influence top management or lower levels have is a function of the decision phase, and other dimensions, such as conflict and meta power, also vary by phase.

Trust is an important contingency leading to achievement. The importance of task as a contingency has again been demonstrated in the DIO study and strongly confirms the results of previous research (Heller, 1971; Heller & Wilpert, 1981; Vroom & Yetton, 1973). These findings are still underestimated by the people who plan or make decisions in organizations and who prefer to look for some simple universal prescription or a checklist to achieve uniform results.

A recent review by Payne (1982) summarizes a large body of evidence that shows that information processing in decision making and other areas of cognition is highly contingent on the demands of the task; even minor changes in tasks lead to significantly different judgments. These findings should also be recognized by decision scientists who, such as the practical man in the field, looks for invariance to help in the search for underlying principles that can serve as the basis for normative prescriptions. Payne's review also stresses the need to move away from cross-sectional research techniques: "We are just beginning to understand . . . the underlying psychological mechanisms that lead to contingent decision behavior . . . that understanding is likely to be advanced by adopting a time dependent (process) view" (Payne, 1982, p. 400).

One of the important findings from the DIO project was the central role of competence and its underutilization in all three countries (Britain, the Netherlands and Yugoslavia). Underutilization was causally related to top management's unrelenting dominance supported by high status power and an absence of consultation. Misumi's account of the Japanese *ringi* method supports this finding by arguing that a major consequence of the elaborate "bottom-up" decision style was to use the experience and skills of all those involved in the process.

The cost in time and effort of using participative mechanisms such as *ringi* and *nemawashi* and the use of semiautonomous groups to improve the quality of products are thought to achieve benefits in speed of implementation, better decisions, and the psychological advantages of avoiding conflict and frustration. At the same time, senior management retains control where it is necessary and can resort to majority voting if opinions are excessively divided.

The Japanese decision methods handle power differently from most western countries, but the critical role of power in the redistribution of influence remains central to an understanding of *ringi* and *nemawashi* as well as western styles.

NOTES

1. An example of this work can be found in the papers to the Tenth Research Conference on Subjective Probability, Utility and Decision Making (Helsinki, August 1985).

2. In the top management research (Heller, 1971; Heller & Wilpert, 1981) a method was used that might have reduced the error due to cross-sectional data. Each manager could describe the amount of influence and power for each decision by distributing 100 points over the Influence-Power-Continuum and only 1% of our sample gave 100 points to a single alternative on the IPC.

3. *Achievement* was defined as the extent to which the original objectives and expectations relating to a given decision were obtained.

4. Efficiency was conceived as an input-output ratio between effort and cost invested in each decision and the outcome of that decision.

17

SUPERVISION AND LEADERSHIP

JYUJI MISUMI
Osaka University
Osaka, Japan

MARK F. PETERSON
Texas Tech University
Lubbock, TX, USA

The early 1980s has been a particularly dynamic half decade from the standpoint of international interest in leadership. During this period, intense Western interest in things Japanese has been combined with efforts in the United States to reconstruct the leadership field following a period of service criticism (e.g., Hunt & Larson, 1977). Much of the Western literature concerning Japanese management deals broadly with management policy, human resources strategy, and organization culture. The present chapter does not maintain such a broad orientation, but focuses instead on three objectives. The first is to provide an update on the PM Theory of Leadership, a Japanese research program spanning much of post-World War II Japan (Misumi, 1985; Misumi & Peterson, 1985). The second purpose is to highlight some of the newer leadership research programs in Japan. Third, the chapter summarizes leadership trends developing outside Japan, especially those reflected in U.S. journals, and considers the contribution that Japanese research makes to these trends. Significant empirical studies grounded in thorough reviews of related European research emphasizing cross-national comparisons of managerial decision making are described by Heller and Wilpert (1981), Hofstede (1984), and Drenth and Koopman (1984).

THE PM THEORY OF LEADERSHIP

The PM Theory of Leadership has perhaps the longest continuing theory of leadership research programs in Japan. It is organized around the concept of two basic leadership functions, the performance (P) function, and the maintenance (M) function. The P function is that which is directly oriented toward accomplishing work, while the M function is oriented toward maintaining social stability. The distinction is closer to a task function versus relations function distinction than to a participative versus directive distinction (Bass, 1981, chaps. 18, 20). The theory postulates that the M function facilitates the work-promoting aspect of P leadership, especially by encouraging subordinates not to rebel against P, and by reducing the stress that can be produced through an exclusive P function emphasis. The PM theory is held together by this basic conceptual formulation rather than by any single empirical research approach.

GENERAL MORPHOLOGY
ISSUES IN PM RESEARCH

The most basic component of the research program is the "general morphology" of leadership. This component postulates four basic patterns of leader behavior. These patterns are (1) leadership placing high emphasis on both the P and M functions, or PM-type leadership, (2) leadership emphasizing only the P function, or P-type leadership, (3) leadership emphasizing only the M function, or M-type leadership, and (4) leadership emphasizing neither function, or PM-type leadership.

Japanese PM research often uses leaders trained to represent these four leadership types as experimental conditions. Experimental manipulation checks indicate that the intended types are accurately reflected both in systematic observers' records and in subjects' perceptions. In field studies, the four types are ordinarily represented by dividing survey measures based on subordinates' descriptions into "high" and "low" levels for each function, and dividing leaders into four groups accordingly. Given the close correspondence between intended experimental conditions and subjects' responses, it was assumed until recently that actual leader behavior corresponded quite closely to perceived leader behavior under field conditions.

However, PM research since 1980 has yielded a more complicated picture of the PM general morphology. It was long known that factor analyses of field surveys often revealed one or more factors besides the primary, largely uncorrelated factors ordinarily used to represent the P and M functions. The P factor most independent of M, the one that has been emphasized in field measures of the P function, involves pressing subordinates to work harder, longer, or better. This "pressure P" component is also the aspect of P leadership emphasized in the laboratory. A "planning P" factor deals with being responsive to the work needs encountered by subordinates through guiding subordinates when they need it, and organizing and planning to make their work easier to accomplish effectively. The "planning P" factor, when constructed as a separate index in field studies, is often correlated with M measures to about the same degree that it is with the "pressure P" measure. Recent research, however, shows that leadership behavior changes and leadership perceptions are transformed as pressure to work hard is increasingly combined with the maintenance function. When these two functions are provided simultaneously, many leader behaviors are experienced as reflecting elements of both P and M rather than being distinctly one or the other.

Evidence for these hybrid forms of experienced leadership came to light in a reanalysis of data concerning the relationship between the usual survey P and M measures in a sample of 36,000 employees working in a variety of industries (Misumi & Arima, 1983). The two variables showed a curvilinear relationship such that pressure-P scores tended to be highest when M leadership was either very high or very low. This finding encouraged speculation about the kinds of actual and experienced leadership that might occur given different combinations of M and pressure-P.

An experiment was carried out to test the hypothesis that two qualitatively distinct aspects of actual M behavior may correspond to low and high levels of P leadership (Onodera & Misumi, 1984). One aspect of M leadership, labeled "situation conserving" M leadership, was postulated as occurring most often toward the low half of the P scale. It involves helping subordinates solve their personal problems and trying to reduce their stress or tension. The other facet of M, labeled "expectative and supportive M" involves expressing personal interest and concern, but for a subordinate's work situation as well as their nonwork situation. The results of the study indicate that "situation conserving" M leadership reduces subordinates' anxiety, but also reduces their problem-solving and goal-achievement efforts. It blunts the effects of any given level of pressure-P leadership. Expectative and supportive M, however, seems to create a constructive anxiety that the leader's high expectations and support might be jeopardized if a subordinate were to perform poorly. Thus the earlier field result may mean that the kind of M leadership associated with low perceived pressure-P is of the situation conserving type. The expectative and supportive form of M behavior is more compatible in subordinates' experience with a leader who shows high pressure-P. Although the two forms of M leadership are not always distinguishable in subordinates' phenomenology as shown in questionnaire responses, they are found to evoke different reactions when manipulated in the laboratory. Work is continuing to clarity the behavioral and phenomenological aspects of the basic PM morphology.

SPECIFIC MORPHOLOGY AND LEADERSHIP DYNAMICS ISSUES

The emphasis in the preceding discussion has been on advances in the most basic area of PM research—the PM general morphology. However, it is not assumed that the P and M functions are fulfilled through a single, fixed set of behaviors under all circumstances. Studies of specific leadership morphology have identified a number of P and M behaviors that are typical of particular settings. Interestingly, aspects of leadership reflecting Talcott Parson's (1960) four-part action framework have been independently and simul-taneously identified as key aspects of the senior executive leader-ship morphology in the United States (Sashkin & Fulmer, 1986) and Japan (Misumi, 1986). The chief executive "adaptation" and "goal attainment" functions are conceptually related to the P concept, while the "interpretation" and "latent pattern maintenance" function discussed by Parsons are related to the corporationwide M function.

Other research is addressing the cross-national specificity of PM types. The consistent association found among the four PM types and a variety of attitude and performance measures in Japan (Misumi & Peterson, 1985) contrast sharply with the inconsistent results using the somewhat similar Ohio State consideration and initiating structure measures in the United States (Schriesheim & Kerr, 1977). A possible reason for the difference is a national specificity in the morphology of leadership. A series of projects is underway to determine (1) whether survey measures of the PM constructs can be developed in other countries that have similar properties to the Japanese measures, (2) what the relationship is between the PM measures and items from the Ohio State scales frequently used in the United States, and (3) what specific supervisor actions do subordinates interpret as reflecting an emphasis on different PM types.

Data from 16,000 employees in mainland China indicate that a Chinese translation of the PM measures has similar factor structure and index averages to those found in Japan (Xu, 1986). Preliminary data collection involving 646 employees in the United States, the United Kingdom, and Hong Kong suggests some degree of national specificity in leadership morphology (Smith, Peterson, & Tayeb, 1986; Smith, Tayeb, Peterson, & Bond, 1986). The English and Chinese translations of the "M" component of the survey measure is consistently identifiable in each country, and appears to be equivalent to the Ohio State "consideration" measure. The "P" component of the survey is closer to the production emphasis dimension in the Ohio State measure, and is somewhat more independent of the "consideration" dimension, especially in the Hong Kong sample, than are the "initiating structure" items. The phenomenological meaning of specific "P," "initiating structure," and "production emphasis" items varies somewhat by country. Other results show significant differences between countries in how specific leader behaviors are interpreted. For example, talking with your boss about work problems is more highly correlated with a consideration/M attribution in the United Kingdom than it is in the United States.

PM research extends beyond studies of the forms of leadership to studies of causal processes—leadership dynamics. The longitudinal analysis of several annual surveys of a bank, for example, indicates that leadership affects work attitudes more than work attitudes affect leadership (Misumi & Mannari, 1985). The ongoing laboratory research component of the PM program is continuing into the study of crisis leadership. Surveys over two decades in a wide variety of Japanese industries and firms involving upwards of 150,000 employees tend to support finding a greater contribution of leaders described as high in both P and M (PM types) to subordinate productivity, creativity, and satisfaction with the leaders. Lowest in contribution to such outcomes are leaders low in both P and M. A number of laboratory experiments confirmed these findings (Misumi, 1985). Some of the PM-based work in this area is noted below in connection with the more general issue of crisis leadership.

OTHER THEMES IN
JAPANESE LEADERSHIP RESEARCH

JAPANESE TESTS OF
FIEDLER'S CONTINGENCY THEORY

Beginning shortly after the publication of Fiedler's Contingency Theory of Leadership (Fiedler, 1967), research began to be conducted in Japan to determine the theory's generalizability. This research has continued with mixed success into the 1980s, just as it has in the United States.

Several studies have addressed Fiedler's initial problem of how leader personality, as measured by such indicators as the least-preferred coworker score (LPC), is reflected in group performance and satisfaction. Although reviews of U.S. contingency theory research indicate that the LPC-performance and LPC-satisfaction relationships are the most consistently supported aspects of Fiedler's model (Rice, 1978, 1981), less support has been found in Japanese studies (Shirakashi, 1968, 1969). Given that the "high" and "low" levels of LPC depend on the scores found in a particular sample, this divergence may indicate, for example, that "low" LPC in Japan does not mean the same thing as "low" LPC elsewhere (Kennedy, 1982). In any case, the results have not encouraged extensive follow-up research.

Other Japanese research has investigated the psychological and behavioral implication of LPC and related leader personality measures. Tanaka (1975), for example, found that under low task structure conditions, leaders who described their least-preferred coworker in relatively favorable terms (high-LPC leaders) showed M behaviors more frequently than did other leaders. Shima (1968, 1972) used one of Fiedler's measures to develop two separate indicators of "tolerance for others," an aspect of cognitive style. A "DP" measure was constructed by calculating the variance in ratings for the leader's preferred coworkers. A "DN" score was constructed to represent the variance in ratings for nonpreferred coworkers. Shima found that these measures reflected cognitive differentiation better than does the LPC score. These studies, however, have not resulted in a clarification of the behavioral or cognitive meaning of LPC.

OTHER CONTINGENCY STUDIES

Several studies have been conducted in Japan to test contingency models besides Fiedler's (e.g., Misumi & Seki, 1971). Recently, Hachiya (1981) studied the moderating effects of personal and task characteristics on the effects of leadership. He found a negative relationship between leadership emphasizing task achievement and followers' satisfaction when followers had low growth needs and tasks allowed little autonomy. No relationship between leadership and satisfaction was found under other circumstances. The relationship between a leader's group-maintenance behavior and follower satisfaction was especially high for followers having low growth needs regardless of other situational factors. However, for those having high growth needs, this relationship was found only where cooperation was required for task performance.

STUDIES PREDICTING
LEADER BEHAVIOR

Several Japanese researchers have used expectancy theory to predict leader behavior. Furukawa (1979), for example, found that managers tend to evaluate their situation and set appropriate management goals. Subsequently, these goals regulate the manager's behavior. When goals are task oriented, the manager tends subsequently to display task-oriented behavior. When the goals emphasize group maintenance, the leader displays maintenance-oriented behavior. Other research conducted in Japan and published in English has been quite successful in predicting leader behavior based on expectancy constructs (e.g., Matsui & Ohtsuka, 1978). The emphasis a Japanese leader places on consideration or initiating structure depends on their belief that these behaviors will have consequences that they desire.

MANAGER CAREER DEVELOPMENT
AND VDL RESEARCH

Graen's (1976) vertical dyad linkage model is being applied to managerial career development in Japan (Wakabayashi & Graen, 1984; Wakabayashi et al., 1980). This research program indicates that the quality of the exchange that a new employee develops with their first supervisor substantially affects the person's subsequent career success. The effects of leadership appear to be at least as strong in Japan as they are being found to be in the United States.

LEADERSHIP IN CRISIS SITUATIONS

Japanese leadership research has also moved outside work organization settings to the emergent leadership situations produced by crises. Little research has been available about the actual role of leadership in emergencies.

Some of the crisis leadership studies have involved experimental simulations conducted as part of the PM research program. Kugihara and Misumi (1984), for example, placed subjects in the position of escaping from a maze that was displayed on a video screen to represent what a person would see if they were inside the maze. Subjects were told that they would receive a painful shock if they did not escape within a specified time period. Leadership conditions representing the four PM types were established by training leaders to provide directions, emphasize escape, and express support in different ways. The subjects escaped most quickly when leaders combined directions about key turning points with expressions of support. In another crisis situation experiment, it was found that even within the PM leadership type, it was especially important initially to provide support and encouragement followed by directions, rather than the reverse (Misumi & Sako, 1982).

Several studies have compared leadership by giving directions about how to escape in an emergency with leadership by physically showing where to escape (Sugiman & Misumi, 1984; Sugiman, Misumi, & Sako, 1983). One of these studies involved Fukuoka city employees who were placed in a simulated emergency situation in the underground shopping area of Hakata railroad station. The leaders were employees working in the shopping district. Under the "follow-direction" condition, leaders were trained to guide the evacuation by giving instructions about where the subjects should go. Under the "follow-me" condition, leaders were trained to take the subjects to the exit. Evacuation occurred more quickly using the latter method. Other studies using a similar experimental design indicate that such factors as the ratio of leaders to followers, and the evacuation setting affect the comparative superiority of the "follow-directions" versus "follow-me" condition in crisis situations.

PARADIGM STRUGGLES IN
U.S. LEADERSHIP RESEARCH

The potential for interchange between United States and Japanese research is affected by recent developments in U.S. research. Signs of a "scientific revolution" in the leadership field became evident during the late 1970s. Kuhn (1970) describes scientific revolutions as periods when established theoretical and methodological paradigms cease to be followed. Instead of the "normal science" process of incremental advances along established lines of research, substantially different research directions come to be followed.

The leadership field in the United States clearly has not had a single accepted research paradigm in the second half of the twentieth century, except perhaps for a general adoption of empirical positivism. However, it did have a small number of "accepted" research themes during the 1970s. Schriesheim and Kerr (1977) reviewed the status of these themes. Their review covered three paradigmatic research themes, two semi-revolutionary themes, and several apparently emerging revolutionary themes. The paradigmatic themes were (1) Fielder's (1967) contingency theory and the LPC measure on which it is based, (2) path-goal structure measures typically used to test it, and (3) four-factor theory (Bowers & Seashore, 1966) and associated measures of leadership. These themes have affected the more established Japanese research programs noted above. The semi-revolutionary themes were the vertical dyad linkage model (Graen, 1976) and the Vroom and Yetton (1973) decision-making model.

The truly revolutionary challenges, some of which Schriesheim and Kerr identified as topics of the future, challenged these latter two emerging normal science paradigms as well as the established ones. These involved challenges (1) to develop an attribution-based reconstruction of subordinate perceptions of leadership and reactions to it, (2) to place leadership in the context of other managerial processes and organizational functions, and (3) to replace survey and personality operationalizations of leadership. Challenges to normal science traditions in U.S. leadership research included criticisms of their methodological validity and attempts to replace them. In effect, an earlier social-industrial psychology approach to organization behavior has been threatened by sociological, anthropological, and even newer social psychological paradigms. The potential cross-contributions of Japanese and American leadership research are affected by these changes in content emphasis and methodological orientation.

SURVEY RESEARCH

The number of studies and reviews dealing with the psychometric properties of "consideration" and "initiating structure" measures has declined during the 1980s compared to the end of the 1970s (e.g., Schriesheim & Kerr, 1977; Schriesheim, Kinicki, & Schriesheim, 1979). This reduction corresponds to findings indicating difficulties in interpreting the usual measures of consideration and initiating structure. Laboratory experiments pursuing implicit leadership themes have also used measures of these variables to demonstrate biases in subordinate descriptions of leadership (e.g., Phillips, 1984).

Similarly, the one recently published report based on the survey of organizations, the other leadership survey instrument frequently used through the 1970s (Schriesheim & Kerr, 1977), is directed at biases affecting it (Weiss & Adler, 1981).

Rather than examining psychometric properties of the Ohio State measures, recent survey studies have tried to incorporate them in tests of more comprehensive theories. Most notable among these are studies based on substitutes for leadership models (Howell & Dorfman, 1981; Pierce et al., 1984) and path-goal theory (e.g., Fulk & Wendler, 1982; Schriesheim & Schriesheim, 1980). However, even here change is evident in that measures of "instrumental leadership" or "achievement-oriented leadership" are being used. Supervisor self-descriptions are also reappearing after having once been discredited (Korman, 1966). While based on prior Ohio State measures, these appear to be used in response to difficulties indicated in earlier work or to criticisms from implicit leadership theory. Since survey-based paradigms are increasingly multivariate and complex, data analysis methods—notably the use of path analysis and canonical correlations—to test these models are designed to accommodate increased complexity. Two survey-based models are being actively pursued, which require somewhat less complex statistical analysis. These involve Graen's (1976) vertical dyad linkage model, and the study of performance-contingent leader behavior (e.g., Podsakoff, Todor, & Skov, 1982). As noted above, Japanese research is contributing very directly to testing the VDL model. The topic of performance-contingent leader rewards and punishment needs to be pursued in Japan where both kinds of actions may have different implications than they do in the United States.

The number of special-purpose survey measures being developed in the United States continues to be extensive. One trend among these is to try to represent Mintzberg's (1973) ten managerial roles in survey form. Attempts at this endeavor have been directed toward testing the leadership substitutes model (Sheridan, Vredenburgh, & Abelson, 1984) and indicating the importance attributed to particular roles (e.g., Pavett & Lau, 1983).

EXPERIMENTAL RESEARCH

The renewed pursuit of leadership using experimental research is one of the major developments of the late 1970s and early 1980s. Laboratory methods are most evident in research concerning cognitions involving subordinate or group performance. The main themes are implicit leadership theories linked to performance perceptions (e.g., Phillips, 1984) and causal attributions by supervisors concerning subordinate performance (reviews by Larson, 1984; Podsakoff, 1982). Laboratory research continues to be needed. As increasingly specific aspects of leadership are identified, laboratory manipulation becomes more possible. Laboratory tests of leadership substitutes hypotheses appear to be a next logical step. Laboratory studies of leader goal setting are already beginning to appear. Laboratory studies appear to be more promising for drawing causal inferences than were the longitudinal survey studies that began to appear during the late 1970s. The long tradition of experimental leadership research in Japan, including controlled studies done outside the laboratory, provides a potential basis for contributing to the increasing U.S. interest in experimental work.

OBSERVATIONAL AND
QUALITATIVE FIELD RESEARCH

Proponents of observational and qualitative research advocated these approaches beginning in conferences during the late 1970s. The Center for Creative Leadership sponsored one conference focusing on such nontraditional research (McCall & Lombardo, 1978). Considering the great prescriptive emphasis given to observational and qualitative methods at leadership conferences during the late 1970s, it is noteworthy that such approaches have not subsequently been vigorously pursued. Perhaps such methods are being pursued but are being disseminated outside academic journals. The Center for Creative Leadership, like several other organizations committed to changing supervision and leadership, continues to use the results of observational and qualitative research in their training materials. Bennis (1984) has published his interview-based analysis of 90 chief executive and senior leaders outside the domain of traditional academic journals. Several sophisticated, popular management books, notably Theory Z (Ouchi, 1981) and In Search of Excellence (Peters & Waterman, 1982) deal in part with leadership and have been substantially affected by the general Japanese management literature. These works rely primarily on qualitative methods.

A traditional review of academic leadership research, such as the present one, may miss a real revolution in leadership theory. It may be that the development of models and programs through sophisticated consulting companies and in-house human resource departments is "substituting" for work coming from academic institutions. Paralleling the paradigm shift toward cognitive social psychological models may be a pragmatic, quasi-scientific paradigm drawing force from consultants and supported by managers. Perhaps a merging of the strengths of academic work coming from several countries, including Japan and the United States, can make an effective, carefully documented contribution to leadership and management theory, even within the popular press. The current status of U.S. leadership research and interest in Asia makes the present an opportune time for comparative qualitative and observational leadership research, as well as comparative laboratory research.

18

PARTICIPATION AND INDUSTRIAL DEMOCRACY

BERNHARD WILPERT
Technische Universität
Berlin, Germany

Participation in its broadest sense denotes the linking of decisions to the interests of affected system members by means of systemic conditions, structures, and processes. Thus it covers a broad topic going under the guise of many terms such as *democratic leadership, industrial democracy, economic democracy, worker self-management, participation in decision making, power equalization, autonomous work groups.* For purposes of this chapter I have juxtaposed *participation* and *industrial democracy* to refer to two distinct subforms, which probably cover the major part of the problem area: *participation* is here, in its more limited sense, understood as the personal involvement of employees in organizational decision making without any formalized regulatory norms; *industrial democracy*, on the other hand, refers to statutorily regulated forms of direct-personal or indirect-representative employee involvement in organizational decision making. Such statutory norms may be based in laws, collective agreements, or formalized managerial statutes.

While comprehensive treatments of both forms in standard reference works on organizational psychology were previously virtually nonexistent (e.g., Dunette, 1976), this is slowly changing with recent European-based reference books (Crouch & Heller, 1983; Drenth & Groenendijk, 1984; Endruweit, Gaugler, Staehle, & Wilpert, 1985; Hoyos, Kroeber-Riel, Rosenbstiel, & Strumpel, 1980; Wilpert & Sorge, 1984) and international reviews (e.g., Ishikawa, 1981; Strauss, 1982) or new journals (economic and industrial democracy, since 1980). In fact, it appears that the field is so fertile that only drastic self-restriction and confinement to a limited time period will be possible within this present review. My chapter will, therefore, cover publications relating to studies in Germany, an excursion to important Norwegian developments, and major international comparative studies with an emphasis on the period from 1980-1985. This review will be preceded by some reflections on the status of the concept of participation in its wider sense in terms of theory development and organizational practice.

THE CONCEPT
OF PARTICIPATION

Given that some authors consider participation as "the most vital organizational problem of our time" (Mulder, 1981) it is quite surprising to note how little theoretical attention it has attracted in general and in organizational psychology (Mulder being himself one of the few notable exceptions, 1977). One could—and should—pursue the issue on at least three levels: the individual, organizational, and societal level.

The theoretical significance of participation from an individual psychological perspective could probably benefit most from relating participation to the affectance or competence motivation identified by White (1959) in his seminal review article on motivation. By competence motivation he describes the motivational states of an individual who experiences his or her ability to influence and control one's environment, "making things happen" as desired, an experience that appears to be a necessary condition for personal self-esteem and openness to learn and grow (Argyris & Schön, 1974). In this light, effective participation in its wider sense may indeed be viewed as a crucial contributing factor to individual growth, a conceptualization of equal importance for theorizing about human development as for the practical design of jobs and work organizations.

From an organizational perspective the concept of participation can be integrated in two perspectives (Dachler & Wilpert, 1978, 1980): participation as a universal and fundamental principle of all organizing (no organization can be conceived without some participation) and participation as a social technology to attain particular goals and objectives. It is to Mulder's credit (1977) to have formulated a rather comprehensive theoretical framework that combines both perspectives as well as linking them to an individual-level perspective: The universal search for exercising power (= affectance?) keeps members of a social system busy reducing experienced power distance to higher positions. "Participation as a means of reducing power differences in small groups, large organizations and society" thus also becomes a central social problem (Mulder, 1977, p. 79).

The most comprehensive theoretical treatments of participation have been carried out in view of its societal significance by political scientists and social theoreticians. Pateman, from a democratic theory position, considers education to be the main function of participation, because it is a prerequisite to develop "the necessary individual attitudes and psychological qualities" for democracy (Pateman, 1970, p. 42). From a socialist perspective, participation is seen to be a central means to activate and free exploited and alienated workers in the process of redesigning society (Vanek, 1975).

This short excursion on the theoretical and practical significance of the concept of participation suggests, on the one hand, that previously little has been done so far in psychological theorizing about antecedents and consequences of participation and, on the other hand, that the very problem nature of participation in its wider sense requires a pluridisciplinary openness that is also reflected in subsequent inclusion of studies from business administration, sociology, political science, and psychology.

SELECTED COUNTRIES

FEDERAL REPUBLIC OF GERMANY (HENCEFORTH GERMANY)

For more than thirty years German companies have attempted to implement a legally introduced system of industrial democracy: *Mitbestimmung*—awkwardly translated as *codetermination*. While there was a certain hiatus of empirical research in the late 1960s and the 1970s on its organizational implementation and effects (Wilpert, 1975), research activities have considerably increased in recent years. This may be mainly attributed to two factors: the introduction of expanded codetermination legislation in the 1970s (1972 Works Constitution Act, 1976 Codetermination Act) and the public discussion surrounding the launching of a gigantic governmental "humanization of work" program in 1974 (for a description of the program and its first twenty publications see Wilpert and Ruiz Quintanilla, 1984). The dominance of a legalistic approach in introducing and safeguarding codetermination in Germany has been noted widely (IDE, 1981b). It necessarily raises the question as to what degree de jure norms have been implemented de facto and what its unintended consequences are (for the hitherto best review in English language see Streeck, 1984). Some of the main findings of recent empirical studies can be summarized as follows:

● The Works Constitution Act of 1972, expanding codetermination rights of individual employees and works councils, although focusing on workplace issues, has tended to extend codetermination to issues of the whole enterprise such as appointment of supervisory board vice chairmen, labor directors in the management board, personnel planning, and the introduction of new technologies (Kirsch, Scholl, & Paul, 1984; Witte, 1982).

● The extension of the codetermination agenda took place partly through enterprise specific collective bargaining agreements, partly through dual membership of employees in works councils and in supervisory boards, thus establishing "supralegel codetermination" (Witte, 1982, p. 169) that also strengthened the position of internal works councils vis-à-vis external union bodies.

● Formalized internal agreements and procedures correlate highest with the expansion of the works council's influence range (Witte, 1980), a finding that corroborates the main result from an international comparative research (IDE, 1981a).

● Although overall unionization in German industry oscillates around 40%, the works councils have become de facto union bodies (Streeck, 1982). Occasionally we can note differences of opinion between works councils and external union bodies (Streeck, 1984), however, works councils are, in practice, the prolonged arms of unions.

● The continuing general consensus orientation of German employee-employer relationships is reflected in the fact that supervisory board decisions are usually reached through consensus decisions (Witte, 1982).

● In companies for which the law stipulates that labor directors are to be appointed with the consent of employee representatives on supervisory boards, their success has increasingly been influenced by their capacity to act in a boundary-spanning manner, linking management, works councils, and unions (Zander, 1981).

● Existing normative prescriptions for certain intensities of participation are sometimes underutilized. Or, sometimes they are extended by works councils, which are in a position to exert influence beyond what is required by law. The latter is often true in social and personnel issues (Schultze-Scharnhorster, 1985; Wilpert & Rayley, 1983), the former in technical or more long-range matters such as company policies and investments.

• Works councils by and large may be classified into an organizational typology reflecting their status within the enterprise (Kotthoff, 1981): "ignored works council" (mainly in smaller enterprises with 70-150 employees), "isolated works council" (usually 300-600 employees, usually victim of managerial distrust and repression), "works council as instrument of management" (usually in companies with patriarchic-benevolent leadership, about every fourth enterprise irrespective of size, roughly 25%), "works council as cooperative counterpower" (strongly oriented toward interest representation, very rare), "respected steadfast works council" (bargaining oriented, usually in middle-sized enterprises with 600-800 employees, about 11%), "respected ambivalent works council" (characterized by strategies of anticipatory conflict regulation, mainly larger enterprises, above 1,000 employees, about 17% of all works councils).

• Several studies analyze and discuss the connection among qualification, social competence, competence acquisition, and participation, partly in the context of a cross-sectional analysis (Wilpert & Rayley, 1983), partly by way of action research-oriented case studies (Hoppmann & Stotzel, 1981; Stiftung, 1981), partly in an attempt to develop a theoretical model of the relationship (Kissler, 1980).

• The mutually supportive effect of several institutions of codetermination (works council, supervisory board representation, labor director in management board) and structural variables (unionization) upon the effectiveness of employee influence has been one of the important findings of a study comparing companies in different industrial sectors (Kirsch et al., 1984). Regression analyses of the same study show that level of involvement of employee representatives in organizational decision making is the best predictor of quality of work life followed by profitability of the establishment and employee orientation of management.

• An issue of growing concern is the relationship between participation and profitability (Cable & FitzRoy, 1980; Rosenberg & Rosenstein, 1980; Witte, 1981). The issue is sometimes also linked to profit sharing and employee ownership as new bases of participation (Hammer & Stern, 1980; Strack, 1984). In cases of high levels of employee participation, it has been shown that personnel and social policies of the enterprise are affected (fewer layoffs, high fringe benefits) and that economic performance is positively related to high codetermination patterns irrespective of enterprise size and general economic conditions of the firm (Witte, 1981).

• Finally, the growing introduction of new technologies in work organizations has posed new and intriguing challenges to codetermination in German enterprises. A growing number of studies address the issues involved (Dirrheimer & Wilpert, 1983). They show that existing codetermination norms are frequently inadequate to cope with the problems of introducing new techniques since their long-term consequences for job performance requirements and organizational structures and processes are hard to evaluate for both management and affected employees or their representatives.

In the literature review of codetermination research of some ten years ago Wilpert (1985) noted the predominance of questionnaire and interview approaches in relatively simple cross-sectional research designs. The picture has changed somewhat since. Although questionnaires and interviews are still the royal road to the study of participation in Germany, more complex variable relationships have been adopted in longitudinal case study approaches; participant observation and document analysis are also included.

NORWAY

As in Germany, the 1970s have brought two important legal changes of the industrial democracy scheme in Norway: the new Company Act of 1973 (relating to the creation of supervisory boards with 1/3 employee representation) and the Work Environment Act of 1977 (mainly relating to employee participation in the design of working conditions). An excellent review of the lessons learned from the Norwegian experiences and studies in connection with strategies of work organizations was written by the late Einar Thorsrud (1984), one of the driving intellectual leaders in the Norwegian Industrial Democracy Program. "The *general conclusion* from the studies of employee representation in Norway is that no fundamental change has occurred in the functioning of the boards. For workers the most important effect has been an extra channel of information which unions could use to put political pressure on the board" (Thorsrud, 1984, p. 342). Intraorganizational transformation of communication structures and, hence, changed bargaining and influence potentials seem to be the most notable consequence. Another important lesson seems to be the perceived need of Scandinavian researchers to change the traditional paradigm of the noninvolved "objective" researcher to higher levels of researcher involvement in the process of creatively helping to induce democratization through a joint learning process among researchers and members of the given target organization. This research model approaches what has been advocated before by Argyris and Schön (1978).

The research projects stimulated by the national work environment program (Gustavson & Hunnius, 1981) are still not yet fully evaluated to draw a general conclusion as to the effects the program has had on changing the Norwegian industrial democracy scene and restructuring working conditions on a large scale. What is striking, however, is the same spirit of joint learning of researchers and employees in the conduct of action programs that pervades these research efforts as well (Gustavson, 1983).

MULTINATIONAL STUDIES

So far this review has been mainly confined to studies relating to a specific country. In order to broaden and complement this focus somewhat, I shall look at the more recent international comparative studies of participation and industrial democracy and try to evaluate what major insights we have gained from them.

One of the most massive international comparative organization studies ever conducted is undoubtedly Hofstede's (1980). It was designed to investigate attitudes and values defined as "a broad tendency to prefer certain states of affairs over others." Although not specifically addressing participation or industrial democracy, his questionnaire surveys at two different times (1967-1969, 1971-1973), about 60,000 employees of a U.S.-based multinational company in 39 subsidiaries using eighteen different languages have nevertheless some bearing on the topic. The dimension of greatest interest here is Hofstede's "Power Distance Index (PDI)" measured by three rather broad items:

—subordinate perception of being afraid to disagree with the superior

—subordinate perception about the superior's decision-making style (e.g., autocratic)

—subordinate's preference for a specific decision style (autocratic versus democratic)

Low PDI scores are then an aggregate of low fear of disagreement, perceived high participativeness of the boss, and a personal preference for such a style. The PDI-aggregates of respondents per country result in distinct national differences, which Hofstede shows to relate to such macroindexes as, for example, gross national product. Besides, different countries seem to fall into distinct "cultural" clusters quite comparable to the now classic study of Haire, Ghiselli, and Porter (1968): Latin and Asian, Middle Eastern, Germanic, Anglo, Nordic.

It remains a moot question whether the PDI truly measures power differentials between hierarchical levels. Based on the items used, one might rather suggest that it is more a measure of a leader-led climate (Drenth & Groenendijk, 1984). In other words, the PDI is exclusively dealing with self-reported perceptions and espoused attitudes and values regarding superior-subordinate relations or participation in its limited connotative sense defined in the introduction to this chapter. Being an attitudinal measure, it corresponds to similar measures in Haire et al., and comparability of findings may be a consequence of measurements used. The PDI correlations with national economic performance measures are difficult to interpret as causal chains.

The eight-country study by Heller and Wilpert (1981) also focused on superior-subordinate relations but in the making of specific decisions as measured in a behaviorally anchored "in-fluence-power-continuum" ranging from "own decision (of boss) without explanation—own decision with explanation—prior con-sultation-joint decision making—delegation (to subordinate)." Res-pondents were 1,600 senior managers (among them 625 boss-subordinate dyads) of large successful companies matched in eight industrial sectors. The research centered on the particular organi-zational and personal circumstances that are conducive to parti-cipative decision making. The method of data collection was group feedback analysis (Heller, 1969).

A high degree of flexibility was observed adjusting decision-making practices to specific situational characteristics such as objective and perceived skills in boss-subordinate dyads or environ-mental turbulence and organizational constraints. This flexibility of behavior, under the assumption of relative stability of espoused attitudes regarding participation, raises considerable doubts about attitude-behavior consistencies. Furthermore, although significant country differences could be demonstrated (Israeli managers were significantly more characterized by centralized, autocratic decision making than Swedish managers) these differences do not fall into typical cultural clusters identified by other researchers. The fact that

North-American managers do not differ significantly from their European counterparts is interpreted as a refutation of the claim that there exists a transatlantic managerial gap in participativeness and lends some support to the convergence thesis of managerial behavior coexisting with the persistence of differences in espoused attitudes (Drenth & Groenendijk, 1984).

One step further to link individual, organizational, and contextual (environmental) variables systematically was made by the twelve-country comparison of the impact of existing normative prescriptions for participation on the organizational distribution of employee involvement and influence in specific decisions (e.g., workplace, personnel, investment decisions) (IDE, 1976, 1981a, 1981b). The data base consisted of interviews from close to 1,000 key respondents and roughly 8,000 randomly selected employees from 134 enterprises matched in technology and size.

An important methodological advance was made in the IDE study by systematically measuring, for the first time, written-down rules and regulations pertaining to the legally/normatively required involvement of employees or their representatives in organizational decision making (de jure industrial democracy). Thus the methods lend themselves to measurement-based international or organizational comparisons of given industrial democracy schemes that go beyond hitherto predominating qualitative comparisons of legal prescriptions (for a similar approach, albeit not related to organizational or behavioral measures, see King and van de Vall, 1978).

The inclusion of organizational characteristics (structure, technology, personnel aspects) and individual variables (biographic, educational, perceptions of informal leadership, attitudes and evaluations regarding participation) enabled the IDE team to investigate relatively complex variable relationships across various systems levels (individual-organizational-environmental).

The highest level of formalization of industrial democracy (de jure dimension) was found in Yugoslavia as opposed to the United Kingdom and Israel. The de facto involvement and influence was shown to be quite similar across countries: rather low, with the exception of Yugoslav enterprises. The impact of hierarchy on participation differentials could be shown to be universal. The most important predictor of de facto involvement and influence turned out to be the intensity of prescribed (de jure) involvement, followed by "employee mobilization" (unionization and percentage of present/former representatives in the work force) and informal participative leadership. Positive evaluation of the industrial democracy system correlated highly with de facto influence of employee representative bodies (e.g., works councils, shop stewards' committees). Again, although national differences could be identified, more behaviorally anchored measures of the IDE study did not yield "cultural clusters."

Another recent advance in the direction of widening research perspectives in terms of extending research methodologies was the study of "Decision Making in Organizations" (DIO, 1983; Heller, Drenth, Koopman, & Rus, 1977), which basically employed the IDE model to a longitudinal three-country comparison and the study by Maurice, Sorge, and Warner (1980), which investigated the "production of industrial hierarchies" in three countries with qualitative techniques relating organizational structures to encompassing societal, educational, and social stratifications. Both studies show striking and enlightening national differences.

19

RECENT DEVELOPMENTS IN ORGANIZATIONAL PSYCHOLOGY IN CHINA

XU LIANCANG
Institute of Psychology
Chinese Academy of Sciences
Beijing, People's Republic of China

Organizational psychology as an independent discipline was introduced into China in the end of the 1970s. But before this, a lot of work relevant to organizational psychology was carried out in the fields of industrial psychology and engineering psychology.

Industrial psychology had its beginnings in early research completed on personnel assessment and on job satisfaction. Also, Frederick W. Taylor's classical organization theory was introduced in Chinese industry and enterprise. But the big impetus to the development of industrial psychology was after 1949 when the People's Republic of China gave strong support to the development of psychology and worked out plans to make the science capable of service to China's socialist construction. The board of directors of the Chinese Psychological Society appealed to its members to "go all out, aim high and achieve more," and to do research that has practical implications to contribute to the construction.

In industrial psychology, the main studies ranged from improving the rationalization of work to safety control. To sum up the experiences of advanced workers, psychologists from the Institute of Psychology, in the 1950s, collaborated with administrators and engineers to investigate the standard operating methods of textile workers and punch press workers (Executive Committee, 1982). Some standards were assigned by the Ministry of Textiles and widely distributed. Psychologists also studied the creative process in technical innovations (Industrial Psychology Section, 1959a). They came to the conclusion that more innovations may be generated collectively rather than individually. The atmosphere in an innovation group may help the individual in developing his or her inspiration for innovative ideas (Industrial Psychology Section, 1959b). Psychologists also examined the problem of motivation—how a group of workers can be encouraged to show high productivity. Field experiments were carried out on the assembly line in a factory. Feeling responsible for the outcomes of the team's work was seen to be the critical psychological state that increases worker motivation (Xu Liancang, 1960). In a study of safety control, psychologists surveyed accidents in factories and mines and investigated the psychological and organizational factors causing the unfortunate events (Li Jiazhi & Xu Liancang, 1957). The working environment also was investigated to seek ways and means of increasing efficiency and reliability in man-machine systems. This study included the monitoring of workers to evaluate fatigue and the effects of shift work. Also studied were loading capacity of monitoring tasks and engineering designs to help the human operator to increase his or her efficiency (Richang & Jiazhi, 1966). A review of the investigations of industrial psychology in China was published in the *Acta Psychologica Sinica*, and an English translation can be found in *Chinese Sociology and Anthropology* (Ruixiang, 1980).

RENEWAL

Industrial psychology, and organizational study in particular, met with difficult problems in the ten-year turmoil from 1966 to 1976 in our country. The influence of the left deviation at that time invaded psychology. Psychology became increasingly criticized as a pseudo-science. Research as well as teaching was stopped; laboratories were closed. During the "Cultural Revolution," there was a misunderstanding that organizational psychology was a social science without the possibilities of any common ground for studies in the socialist countries and the West. If so, Chinese psychologists should not and could not exchange experiences with foreign colleagues. Therefore, they lost the opportunities for the assimilation of their work with that of the world at large. This misunderstanding disappeared when the Chinese government adopted a new policy—the policy of opening China again to the outside world. The new policy directed us to learn from the experiences of developed countries and to absorb their scientific achievements. However, we must fit these ideas with our needs and make organizational psychology serve the modernization of China.

Economic reform in China has resulted in the rapid development of organizational psychology in recent years. The focus of the state has resolutely shifted to economic construction. The general objective of China's economy for the two decades between 1981 and the end of this century is to quadruple the gross annual value of industrial and agricultural production from 710 billion yuan in 1980 to 2,800 billion yuan or so in 2009. The government has made a major policy decision—we must take two steps in our strategic planning: in the first decade, to aim mainly at laying a solid foundation; and in the second, to usher in a new period of vigorous economic development.

THE EFFECT OF ECONOMIC REFORM

To attain its objective, our state must create the necessary conditions to accumulate strength in the economy. Successes on the agricultural front in recent years were made as a consequence of heightened enthusiasm of peasants for production resulting from the adoption of a new incentive system in the rural areas. Economic reform is going on also in industrial management. While the state economy remains paramount, at the same time, it is necessary to develop diverse economic forms for industry.

Diversity in economic forms provides wide possibilities for management practice that in turn requires a scientific theoretical base for explaining facts and events. Principles of organizational behavior have been introduced into China through a variety of channels. Organizational behavior theory is attracting the attention of psychologists, sociologists, factory directors, government officers, and economic experts.

ORGANIZED EFFORT

Psychologists are the mainstream in organizational behavior study. In recent years, the focus of work in industrial psychology has been shifted to organizational psychology—managerial psychology, as it is usually called in China. A meeting to plan the further development of organizational psychology in China was held in 1983. It was sponsored by the Committee of Industrial Psychology of the Chinese Psychological Society, in cooperation with other societies of behavioral sciences and management sciences.

A new society was established—the Chinese Behavior Science Society. At meetings held at Beijing in 1981, 1983, and 1985 and at meetings in other cities, hundreds of papers and reports were presented. In China, there are 24 or more societies or associations involved with organizational behavior studies. For example, within the Chinese Industrial Economic Society, there is a section of organizational behavior sciences and similar sections may be found in many other industrial and engineering societies. The general office of the Chinese Behavior Sciences Society is located in the Institute of Sociology of the Chinese Academy of Social Sciences.

QUESTIONS OF INTEREST

Chinese scientists are interested in discussing several theoretical questions, such as the following.

First, how should we evaluate and make use of Western organizational behavior theory? Organizational behavior study in Western countries is based on psychology, sociology, anthropology, economics, and political science. We need to understand the scientific foundations of organizational behavior study to come to grips intellectually with the discipline. But we must pay attention to the social and political forces involved. Human behavior in industrial production, in business, and in its management always have been conditioned, determined, or regulated by the influence of social class. For example, an important issue in Western organizational behavior study is trying to resolve the conflicts between employee and employer. Understanding the difference in economic forms between the West and China, we can learn from the experience and from organizational behavior theory of the West but should not expect to copy it.

Second, how can we construct an organizational behavior theory suitable to the Chinese society? Integration of theory with practice is the guiding principle directing the research work of Chinese scientists. We study both the applications of organizational behavior and carry out research to construct our theory. At the same time, we continue to learn from the outstanding achievement of foreign scientists.

Third, what should be the core issues in organizational behavior study? At the 1985 conference of the Chinese Behavior Sciences Society at Beijing, 15 core problems were suggested:

(a) the problem of motivation in the socialist context
(b) how to promote the collective consciousness

(c) how to improve solidarity in organizations
(d) the problem of incentives: material and nonmaterial
(e) human needs and their structure in the socialist context
(f) alignment of the goals of state, group, and individual
(g) styles of leadership and styles of management
(h) characteristics of mental work and its management
(i) the assessment method in personnel management
(j) the regulation of interpersonal relationships
(k) organizational development and the regulation of organization structure
(l) soft technology in management as operations research
(m) psychological problems in the distribution systems of wages, salaries, and bonuses
(n) team work
(o) the role of the behavioral sciences in economic reform

RESEARCH WORK IN
ORGANIZATIONAL PSYCHOLOGY

Some of the large number of industrial organizational psychology studies in China have been carried out by institute psychologists, but most have been completed in plants, where the management staff itself had conducted the investigations. In the past five years, more than 700 meetings and workshops were conducted in different cities in China to discuss the problem of how to use the behavioral sciences in management practice, as well as how to introduce overseas experience in this field. Issues have been examined, such as the motivation and needs of workers, leadership and personnel selection, quality of working life, group work and communication, organizational development, counseling, and management performance diagnosis. Questionnaire surveys are becoming increasingly popular in order to get information about workers' needs and comments on management issues. In a plant in northeastern China producing automobile gears, the needs of workers were surveyed by research staffs. A total of 2,700 individual needs were categorized (see Figure 19.1). For example, workers wanted the factory administration to help them to rent an apartment from the factory with a low payment. This was a "right need." If they asked the factory to give every family an apartment free of charge, that was considered as a "wrong need." According to the living level in China, a newly married couple may apply to the administration to rent an apartment with one bedroom. This is a "rational

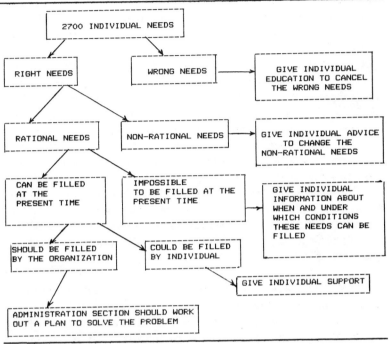

Figure 19.1 Taxonomy of Needs and Suggestions for How to Meet Them

need," while asking to get a two or three bedroom apartment was classified as an "unrational need" although it is a "right need."

Figure 19.1 shows an outline of the work to study workers' needs. Positive effects emerged from this effort, because most workers were satisfied to receive feedback information from the management administration section. Even those who did not get a positive resolution of their needs were able to get their feelings known and to receive explanation from the leadership of the plant.

LEADERSHIP AND MANAGEMENT RESEARCH

Leadership study is one of the key areas of research in China. Managers of factories and enterprises now must also be leaders. They are given more freedom and greater authority in running their own firms. Overcentralization from the top was seen to be one of the causes of poor management performance in the factories and now the factory manager's role is being reformed. The state has called on organizational scientists to make a contribution to implementing this reform in required leadership in factory management.

A research group at the Institute of Psychology of Chinese Academy of Sciences concentrates on the study of leadership. Misumi's Performance and Maintenance Measurement Scale (PM) (see chap. 17) was translated into Chinese and revised initially through a pilot study. High internal consistency, as well as construct and discriminant validity, were found. The PM survey questionnaire was used for counseling and diagnosis. At the same time, the PM scores were adopted as a self-appraisal measure, enabling their use in training and educating managers and middle-level executives. At the end of 1985, the research group had carried out leadership assessment in 53 factories with 16,260 respondents. In total, 93% of all respondents assented to the survey and the contents of the questionnaire.

There was particular interest in comparing our data with the Japanese experience. Cross-cultural differences were expected because Japan already is highly industrialized while China is developing its industry. Also, there are differences in social structure and ideological background. But if we look on each of our ancient civilizations, there is a lot we share in common in history and cultural heritage. For example, the ancient philosophy of China has affected the thought of management in both China and Japan. Research results show that the value of performance and maintenance in our study is about on the same level with reference to the Japanese study. Overall, P(erformance) and M(aintenance) means here were as follows:

Scale	Japan	China
P	34.4	33.2
M	31.3	29.8

However, many interesting differences showed up in the situational factors. The following mean differences appeared (significant at the .1% level) for items illustrating each situational factor (with the Chinese mean shown first): motivation, 3.25 versus 3.10; satisfaction with salary, 2.64 versus 1.70; mental hygiene, 3.26 versus 3.00; teamwork, 3.43 versus 3.10; efficiency of meetings, 2.52 versus 3.20; communications, 3.00 versus 3.20; and performance standards, 3.32 versus 3.20. Responses about the working environment tended to reveal less differences. Thus, except for meeting efficiency of meetings, Chinese employees seemed more satisfied than their Japanese counterparts.

ACTION RESEARCH

In some factories, researchers have carried out experiments attempting to activate organizational development using the revised PM survey questionnaire as an instrument for the action research. The procedure was as follows: (1) Reach an agreement with the factory or enterprise to start the OD research project; (2) explain the research objectives to make clear that this study would not interfere with organizational or personnel operations; (3) survey by questionnaire; (4) data processing by computers; (5) feedback main results to the top leaders and give a report of our research findings to the middle- and first-line managers with the participation of representatives of workers and the administrative staff; and (6) establish OD groups to play an active role in the process of reform. Any good achievement by them should result in awards from the factory.

In a Beijing factory producing artificial diamonds for industrial use, after one year of such OD research, considerable increases in performance were registered (Ping & Liwei, 1986):

(a) increase in gross annual value of production—18.27%
(b) increase in income from market sale—26.28%
(c) increase in profit rate—37.21%
(d) increase in productivity—20.76%

Organizational development is a new field in management science in China, so many factories are interested in our research. In 1984 and 1985, the organizational psychology group was invited to take part in OD research in more than 30 factories.

ACADEMIC ACTIVITIES

In some universities there are research groups or sections for organizational behavior study. For example, the Department of Psychology in Hangzhou University has an active organizational psychology research group. Postgraduate students are studying such issues as attribution theory, reward systems, and job performance. The course in "managerial psychology" is offered to university students as well as factory personnel and government staffs. From 1980 until now, hundreds of students and employees have participated. Organizational behavior studies are initiated when the personnel return to their factories. Recently, the researchers in Hangzhou University joined with the personnel section of their province in creating a unique kind of personnel appraisal standard. Four main criteria were involved: moral standard, knowledge structure, separate abilities, and work performance.

The teaching of organizational psychology also takes place in the management school in the Communication University in Shanghai. Within the school, the section of Human Resources Study conducts research on job analysis and personnel selection. Intellectual, specific aptitude, and work sample tests are used. The work sample or situational decision-making tests present the applicant with a series of hypothetical situations and ask him or her to give the appropriate reaction as in a real work condition. Computer center and software staffs handle the data processing.

Organizational psychology as a course has been taught in many other universities, such as Beijing Normal University, East China Normal University (in Shanghai), and other universities where there are schools or departments of management or business. Because of the long period when organizational psychology remained undeveloped in China, it will be difficult to meet the demand that exists for experienced teaching staff over the next few years. To help fill the gap, many overseas experts in this discipline have been invited to Chinese universities under the sponsorship of the Ministry of Education or scientific exchange agreement. For example, the senior managerial training program opened in Dalian, organized by the National Center for Industrial Science and Technology Management Development, an institution sponsored jointly by China and the United States. So far, 75 American business management professors and ten nonscholar specialists have lectured there for up to ten weeks at a time. Similar schools have been started in China by West Germany, the European Community, and Japan.

NEW ROOTS

Organizational psychology originated in the West. To adopt it to serve the needs of economic management in China, we must be fully aware of the necessity to put down new roots for this discipline in China. Chinese scientists need to search for these roots in China's traditional cultural legacy of concern about interpersonal relations and organization dilemmas. Over the three thousand years of history since the beginning of the Zhou dynasty, rich resources of philosophical and psychological ideas appeared in Chinese literature. For example, according to Confucius and Mencius, human relations were the core principle for administering a country. Confucius, in his classic book *Lun Yu*, stressed harmony in interpersonal relations. Mencius also emphasized collaboration in work. Similar to Japan in this respect, in China, harmony is a principal idea in management. The principle of reaching unanimity through consultation and coordinating activities through common effort will maintain the stability and unity in organizations.

China is now undergoing the process of modernization in industry, agriculture, science and technology, and defense. Along with the process of the four modernizations, the reform of the management system is bound to have great significance. Organizational psychology will be at the forefront of such developments.

20

COMPARATIVE MANAGEMENT:
A Developmental Perspective

SIMCHA RONEN
RAJESH KUMAR
New York University
New York, NY, USA

We begin this chapter with an overview of comparative management. We then focus on the discipline's goals, and evaluate the extent to which the existing literature has met them. Next we deal with some of the methodological problems that jeopardize these goals, and finally point to some directions in which future research should proceed.

Only recently has a substantial body of literature began to emerge in the field of comparative management. Although necessary, it is, by itself, no indication of a discipline's maturity. Even though many empirical studies have been conducted, they are flawed by weak conceptualizations and operationalization of measures, by problems in their level of analysis, by inappropriate borrowing from other disciplines, and by an inadequate definition of culture (Roberts & Boyacigiller, 1983). Cross-cultural interaction poses perhaps the greatest dilemma, both from a theoretical and an applied perspective. A critical shortcoming of much of existing comparative management literature is because it is not interactional. Adler (1983) has made a similar observation. Although some studies seek to demonstrate differences in managerial and employee attitudes across cultures, few studies (if any) have tried, for example, to show what happens when a manager from culture A interacts with his or her counterpart from culture B or with an employee from that culture. One can make certain predictions about the consequence of such interactions (based on existing content differences), but it would be more helpful if such consequences were more specifically analyzed.

A FRAME OF REFERENCE

Although comparative management borrows from a wide variety of disciplines—from sociology, anthropology, political science, and psychology—the focus of our review will be primarily psychological, with some attention paid to sociological and anthropological factors that may affect our conceptualizations. The greater emphasis on individual psychological factors as opposed to macro-level factors is supported by Roberts and Boyacigiller's (1983) survey and by Child's (1981) argument that macro-level variables (organizational structure and technology) are tending to become similar across cultures, while micro-level (psychological) variables (values, attitudes, and needs) continue to be culturally distinctive. Greater attention to conceptual and methodological problems is necessary both to achieve a greater paradigmatic consensus and to develop a coherent set of policy implications. The current lack of consensus derives in part from the diverse theoretical origins of researchers. Although such diversity has many advantages, it makes the task of achieving consensus much harder. Notwithstanding the obvious difficulties involved, attaining such a consensus may be a critical first step in developing an integrated body of work.

THE CHALLENGES OF COMPARATIVE MANAGEMENT RESEARCH

Comparative management theory and research have several different goals: extending the range of variables believed to affect organizational functioning, assessing the values assigned to the same variable in different cultures, examining the nature of the interaction among variables in different cultures, improving and understanding of contextual factors surrounding organizations across cultures, and examining the universality of theories prevailing in the Western world.

Without doubt, an improved appreciation of the context is a critical precondition for realizing most goals within comparative management. Roberts and Boyacigiller's (1983) review of work done by Hofstede (1980), Heller and Wilpert (1981), and England (1978), among others, noted that the primary approach adopted by these researchers is statistical. Ethnographic studies are perhaps equally important because they illuminate the context of behavior. Only upon knowing the latter can researchers feel more confident in the results of current survey instruments. Although the problem of context has been studied by cross-cultural researchers (e.g., Berry, 1981; Brislin, 1983; Whiting, 1976), the impact of the problem on comparative management research remains unclear. (Berry, 1981, supports the notion that an ecological context provides a framework for human action.)

An interesting question concerns the critical distinguishing feature of comparative management research. Do similar variables operate in different cultures even though the values that they take differ when different societies are compared? Or are the variables (and/or their interactions) themselves different? Both from the perspective of theoretical advancement and from the standpoint of devising policy recommendations, it would be useful to answer these questions.

Testing the universality of the theories is another benefit stemming from comparative research. Because the range of independent variables is far wider in cross-cultural research, a theory may have a far better chance of gaining support under such circumstances. For example, Aram and Piraino (1978) have shown that in Chile, Maslow's need hierarchy theory was much better supported than typically demonstrated in industrialized countries.

MODELING

Farmer and Richman (1965) were the first researchers to propose a conceptual model delineating environmental variables (sociological, psychological, and economic) with the potential for significantly affecting managerial functioning. Among the cultural (psychological) variables that they emphasized were achievement orientation, risk preferences, and needs. Although the model has a deterministic and a contingency perspective—a ground for which it has been frequently criticized (Negandhi & Prasad, 1971; Schollhammer, 1969)—it established a framework for the emerging field of comparative management at the time.

A model offered by Negandhi and Prasad (1971) differed from Farmer and Richman's in that Negandhi and Prasad did not give as much importance to culture as to management philosophy. Kelley and Worthley (1981) designed a study to compare the Farmer and Richman (1965) model with Negandhi and Prasad's. They studied the managerial attitudes of Japanese, Caucasian Americans, and Japanese-American managers who worked in Hawaii, and concluded that their study supported the Farmer and Richman model.

However, Ronen (1986) noted that the role of management philosophy as an independent variable has yet to be implicitly tested. Although Kelley and Worthley (1981) documented the importance of culture, they did not adequately differentiate between the effect of culture and that of management philosophy. Alternatively, while culture may be the primary variable from a theoretical standpoint, its impact depends on how well it fits within the managerial philosophy. The emerging task in comparative studies still remains to operationalize culture, designate mediating variables, and identify the independent variables.

DETERMINANTS OF LEADERSHIP
STYLE ACROSS CULTURES

Two major areas in which comparative studies have been most fruitful are leadership style and employee attitude. Although the functions of leadership are probably similar in organizations in different cultures, specific leadership behaviors are likely to vary as a function of cultural content and context differences. Thus Margaret Mead illustrated how the pattern of the appropriate leader-subordinate behavior varies across cultures. For example, the Bachinga in Central Africa were noted for their individualism, their lack of political integration, and their general tendency toward noncompliance with their leaders. In contrast, the traits exemplified by the Bathonga were obedience, respect for the chief, and cooperation (Bass, 1981).

Cross-culturally, a contingency theory would seem made to order. Using Fiedler's contingency model, Bennett (1977), for example, found that while high-performing bank managers in the Philippines had a low LPC score, comparable successful managers in Hong Kong had high scores. However, still needing to be undertaken is the exploration of systematic cultural differences, mediating variables, and the resulting divergences in leadership style. Meanwhile, underlying the differences in leader behavior are the leader's values, needs, beliefs, and attributions, which can help in the exploration. Although both England and Lee (1974), and Bass and Burger (1979), observed that managers are pragmatic across cultures, specific value differences still exist between them. For example, Indian and Australian managers give greater importance to employee welfare than to profit maximization.

Closely associated with managerial values are managerial needs.

While the former directly affect an organization's performance, the latter do so indirectly by influencing managers' satisfaction with their existing jobs. Cross-cultural studies of need achievement have employed Maslow's need hierarchy framework as well as McClelland's framework, which focuses on the needs for achievement, affiliation, and power.

A landmark study utilizing Maslow's framework was carried out by Haire, Ghiselli, and Porter (1966), who found that higher level needs, such as self-actualization and self-esteem, were important to all sets of managers, yet the extent to which these needs were important were less than what they expected. The area of self-actualization provided the greatest potential for increasing managerial satisfaction in all the countries. Bass and Burger (1979) confirmed this proposition; the researchers also found self-actualization was the most sought-after managerial goal. Maruyama (1974) and Redding (1977) questioned the universality of Maslow's hierarchy. In opposition to Maslow, they suggested that the hierarchy is ethnocentric. Nevertheless, with reference to values, managers seem to be a more uniform class across cultures than people in general.

McClelland (1961, 1985) found that although some variation in need for achievement exists in developed countries, it is far lower than that prevailing in developing countries. In any case, differences in need strengths have a direct impact on the nature of the managerial style. For example, in cultures where safety and security are the primary needs, cautious behavior is more likely to be the rule. More risk innovative behavior is more likely to occur in cultures where achievement and self-actualization predominate.

In contrast to needs and values, beliefs are a reflection of individuals' conception of what the world is really like. Differences in belief systems lead to differences in how people construct social reality; the latter in turn affect behaviors. Smith and Thomas (1972), for example, found that Indian managers were cynical. A central aspect of their belief system was the notion that one must often compromise one's ethics to accomplish a task.

A central aspect of a managerial belief system is the attitude toward participatory leadership practices. Managers may tend to view these practices favorably, yet they may also believe that an average worker wishes to be directed and wants to avoid any responsibility. This finding, which originated in the work of Haire et al. (1966), has been replicated by other researchers in other countries (Ajiferuke & Boddewyn, 1970; Argyris, 1967; Barrett & Bass, 1976; Clark & McCabe, 1970; Cummings & Schmidt, 1972; Heller & Wilpert, 1981; Roberts, 1970; Vardi, Shirom, & Jacobson, 1980). Some cultural variation nevertheless appears even here. For example, American managers are more inclined than others to believe that individuals can exercise initiative and display leadership behavior.

Participative leadership has attracted much attention among researchers. The reason is that many beneficial effects (greater agreement, acceptance of decisions) are believed to be closely associated with it—at least in the United States. While a participative style blends in fairly easily in western culture, it can and often does pose problems in other cultures. In many Middle Eastern countries, for example, it is the people at the top who make decisions; even minor issues are "delegated" from the top (Pezeshkpur, 1978). The Turks favor a directive leadership in a task-oriented setting (Kenis, 1977); the Thais are also inclined toward close supervisory practices (Deyo, 1978).

Some studies are fairly consistent in their findings; others seem less so. Although Meade (1967) and Sinha (1976) concluded that an authoritarian style is optimal in India, Kakar's (1971) and Jaggi's (1977) results led to a different conclusion. Conflicting results in leadership studies may also reflect the variation in people's skills and abilities. In a survey of British, Israeli, and German managers, Heller and Wilpert (1981) found that more centralized decision making occurred when subordinates lacked skills.

ATTRIBUTIONAL PROCESSES

Not only do some cultures use more attributions than others (Triandis, 1977), cultures also differ in their propensity to use a situational (the equipment is worn out) or a dispositional (my subordinates are lazy) attribution (Miller, 1984). The question of whether cognitive or motivational factors can best explain attribution bias is still unresolved (Tetlock & Levi, 1982), yet such systematic cultural differences, both in the content and extent of attributions, may profoundly affect interpersonal dynamics. White and Marsella (1982) question the applicability of an attributional framework developed in a western culture to a nonwestern one, but we feel that the question is one of degree of applicability and not whether the model is or is not applicable.

EMPLOYEE ATTITUDES AND MOTIVATION

To the extent that employees' motivational bases differ across cultures, differing leadership and motivational policies may be necessary. In addition, work values offer a useful theoretical link between cultural context and work behavior.

MEANING OF WORK

Understanding the meaning of work is critical in studying the dynamics of work motivations across cultures. A fundamental assumption is cross-cultural studies of work meaning is that such meaning is a subjectively constructed phenomenon.

An international research group, "Meaning of Work" (MOW, 1986), recently concluded a comparative study of work meaning in eight countries. A three-level model was developed to explain the formation, existence, and impact of the meaning of work. The first level identified the factors that cause certain patterns of meaning to emerge; the second measured the different patterns of meaning; the third identified the impact of different MOW patterns. A key concept was work centrality, which was defined as the degree of general importance that working has in an individual's life at any given time. To the extent that work meaning is an indicator of individuals' goals, one would expect that a high score on work centrality would indicate a high involvement and commitment to work. Empirically, the team found that Japan scored the highest on this dimension; England was at the bottom of the scale.

MOTIVATIONAL MODELS

Again, as with managerial motivation, Maslow's hierarchy of needs and McClelland's need for achievement have figured markedly in this line of investigation dealing with workers' motivations. Controversy exists regarding whether western-based motivational models (Maslow, Herzberg et al.) can be applied cross-culturally. Redding (1977) has raised questions about the applicability of western "ego-centered paradigms." Tannenbaum (1980) suggests that the assumption that organizational members respond to rewards and incentives offered by the organization may not be universally valid.

Ronen (1979) undertook a study to determine whether, and if so to what extent, motivational models are applicable across cultures. He noted that structural similarity in work-related value systems does exist, at least within developed countries. His results affirmed the usefulness of the intrinsic-extrinsic dichotomy and Maslow's need categorizations in studying work motivation value systems. Ronen's data consisted of ratings of fourteen work goals by employees of a multinational electronics company in five industrialized nations. The sample consisted of well-trained male employees, none of whom occupied managerial positions. The fourteen work goals clustered in a manner that was consistent with Maslow's conceptualization. In addition, the extrinsic aspects showed a significant overlap with Maslow's basic needs, while the intrinsic aspects were subsumed under needs of self-esteem and self-actualization.

The difference between McClelland's and Maslow's hierarchies and the intrinsic-extrinsic dichotomy is less a matter of the theoretical constructs that are employed, but more a matter of the level of analysis employed. While Maslow's work has direct applicability at an organizational level, McClelland tried originally to relate the presence or absence of achievement motivation with a country's rate of economic growth.

Bhagat and McQuaid (1982) cite a number of studies that empirically confirm the generalizability of McClelland's need for achievement theory cross-culturally (e.g., Hines, 1973, 1974; Melikian, Greinbsberg, Gucegloglu, & Lynn, 1971). Some evidence to the contrary exists as well (Iwawaki & Lynn, 1972; Krus & Rysberg, 1976), but Bhagat and McQuaid (1982) suggested that these researchers may have made the incorrect assumption that motivation is manifested similarly across cultures. As Kornadt, Eckensberger, and Emminghaus (1980) noted, achievement motivation may take on different forms in different cultures. Bhagat and McQuaid (1982) observe that the mix of "culture-specific experience, cognitive structure and values of each person will ultimately determine the area in which achievement motivation will develop, the causal attributions of success or failure, and the learned pattern of reacting to them" (p. 669). The fact that achievement motivation may manifest itself differently in different cultures has implications for the cross-cultural manager. First and foremost, the manager must avoid attributing a lack of motivation to someone who is simply motivated differently. He must therefore use different methods to motivate subordinates in different cultures.

While the intrinsic-extrinsic dichotomy and Maslow's need hierarchy are grounded in theoretical conceptualizations, Hofstede's (1980) work was an empirical attempt to derive certain core variables that seem to affect leadership behavior and employee motivation. Data matrices from 116,000 employees of a major multinational corporation revealed the existence of four dimensions: power distance, uncertainty avoidance, individualism versus collectivism, and masculinity versus femininity. Notwithstanding the many methodological limitations associated with Hofstede's work (Drenth & Groenendijk, 1984; Roberts & Boyacigiller, 1984), and noting also in Chapter 2 Shouksmith's problems in New Zealand with Hofstede's concept of masculinity, a major implication of his work is that organizations in various societies are heavily culturally patterned. Moreover, because Hofstede's cultural dimensions were derived empirically, they challenge and energize further validations. Critical in understanding leadership style are the dimensions of individualism and power distance. As contrasted with the United States, where leadership theories rest on the premise that each individual seeks his or her own interest, leadership in the Third World is primarily a group phenomenon. From the perspective of understanding motivational dynamics, the individualism-collectivism dimension offers a promising line of investigation in operationalizing cultural differences in comparative studies.

Although it is likely that the relative differences among cultures may diminish as a function of industrialization (Kao & Levin, 1978; Machungwa & Schmitt, 1983; Nambudiri & Saiyadain, 1978; Ronen & Shenkar, 1985; Weber, 1969), the question of how long it will take for such differences to diminish still remains very much open. In the interim, culture does retain its salience as a factor affecting motivation. Both researchers and practitioners must recognize its influence.

METHODOLOGICAL AND
RESEARCH CHALLENGES

As an interdisciplinary field, comparative management research is plagued not only by problems that beset each of these individual disciplines, but is also confronted with problems arising from the attempt to integrate these disciplines. But there are also other, more specific, issues.

CULTURE AS THE
INDEPENDENT VARIABLE

Ajiferuke and Boddewyn (1970) have commented that "culture is one of these terms that defy a single all purpose definition and there are almost as many meanings of culture as people using the term." Among the outcomes of this situation is the fact that culture is often used as a residual variable.

Goodman and Moore (1972) noted that to determine the role of culture successfully, researchers must demonstrate which components of culture have main effects, which have no effect, and which ones display an interactive effect. To the extent that cross-cultural management researchers have sought to define culture in the past, however, they have primarily relied on an anthropological definition. For example, Negandhi (1983) suggests that Kluckhohn and Strodtbeck's definition, in which the central hallmark is the concept of value orientation, is useful for cross-cultural management research. Contrarily, Triandis's (1972) more psychological definition of culture stresses that a particular social group reacts to its social environment. Central to Triandis's definition are conceptions of differences in belief structures, attitudes, stereotypes, norms, roles, ideologies, values, and task definition. Triandis's psychological approach permits a relatively more precise operationalization of the term *culture*. Anthropological approaches serve a necessary sensitizing function, yet they do not lend themselves to adequate operationalization. The utility of a psychological perspective is also inherent in Segall's (1984) work. He suggests that meanings associated with artifacts are psychological since they are individual cognitions, although shared to a high degree with others.

We have now reached a point in the field where we need to concentrate on the consequences of interactions between different meaning systems across cultures. Different meaning systems raise the possibility of incorrect attributions and interaction errors. Rice (1980) observed, for example, that in a cross-cultural context, in situations where the speaker's and the listener's schemata are different, divergent interpretations are likely to be the rule rather than the exception.

Cognitive psychology provides a useful tool for studying how content differences, combined with certain specific assumptions about how people process information, can lead to incorrect attributions. Attributions are important not only in the context of cross-cultural negotiations (Fisher, 1979), but also in the context of supervisors making incorrect attributions about the behavior of subordinates from another culture. Current work on cognitive schemata and accessible constructs (Abelson, 1981; Higgins & King, 1981; Rice, 1980; Schank & Abelson, 1977; Taylor & Crocker, 1981;

Wyer & Shrull, 1984) may provide a useful direction for cross-cultural researchers.

NATION VERSUS CULTURE

Comparative management researchers have tended to use the nation state as the unit of analysis (e.g., England, 1978; England, Dhingra, & Agarwal, 1974; Granick, 1972; Haire et al., 1966; Hofstede, 1980; Ronen & Kraut, 1977; Whitely & England, 1977). In the process they have implicitly identified each nation with a distinct culture. Several researchers (Berry, 1979; Elder, 1976; Poortinga, 1977; Roberts & Snow, 1973) are critical of this implicit assumption. Their criticism follows from Triandis's (1972) work, which emphasized that cultural differences exist even among groups within one country. Moreover, the critics argue that in some cases there may be greater similarity of subjective culture across nations than between various groups within a nation. Nevertheless, Ronen and Punnett (1982) noted that there are many good reasons for identifying the nation state with culture or, at least, using the nation state as a unit of analysis: Most nations are political expressions of cultural similarity, and both nation and culture are associated with similar variables—political system, religion, language, geography, economy, education, legal system, labor laws, and mass communication. Again, because most multinational firms function in a nationalistic world, a firm is likely to utilize the nation state as a unit of analysis in conducting its environmental analysis. Because the nation state has been chosen as a unit of analysis in any case, analyzing cultural characteristics in the same unit may offer the advantages of simplicity and pragmatism as a trade-off for the more challenging (and vague) criteria of cultural identity.

PROBLEMS IN ACHIEVING VALIDITY

Cross-cultural researchers should give more attention to pitfalls that limit the generalizability of the results or their elaboration. Reviews of relevant validity problems, and the methodological issues that arise from them, can be found in the writings of cross-cultural psychologists, anthropologists, and, more recently, in the international management literature (e.g., Adler, 1983, 1984; Berry, 1979, 1980; Sekaran & Martin, 1982). Our purpose here will be to focus on some key issues.

One important problem is how to combine the emic (within cultures) and etic (across cultures) levels of analysis. Although we wish to study the uniqueness of a set of behaviors, we also wish to compare such behaviors with each other. Anthropologists have long been cognizant of this problem, yet it is unclear whether comparative management researchers have adequately dealt with it, though cross-cultural psychologists, such as Malpass (1977), have suggested procedures for doing so.

Another important issue is the extent to which measures developed in one culture can be used in another (Sekaran, 1983). Although Sekaran and Martin (1982) found that measures of organizational climate transferred well across cultures (India and the United States), an assumption of transferability cannot and should not be made a priori. Related to this is the issue of data collection (e.g., formatting of questions). Heller (1975) suggests that whether or not cultural effects are demonstrated depends heavily on the format of the question. Broad questions that do not use specific behaviors are the ones that show cultural effects. According to Heller (1975), Haire and his colleagues' (1966) study used broad questions.

Sampling of cultures poses another critical problem. A common criticism against much cross-cultural research is that cultures have often been selected expediently rather than on the basis of any sound theoretical rationale. Related to this problem is that of selecting representative samples from different cultures. It is unclear which of the subjects are the most representative within a given culture. For example, how representative are employees of a multinational company in a given culture? When choosing countries for comparison, the clusters identified by Ronen and Shenkar (1985) may offer a guideline.

What also hinders researchers' ability to draw inferences about the role of culture as a causative factor is the fact that any other variable correlated with culture could also provide a potential explanation for differences in the populations. Malpass (1977) suggested that researchers should obtain data on as many rival explanations as possible. His suggestion may provide the correct theoretical strategy, yet its practicality is uncertain. Causal inferences, which are always uncertain, may be even more uncertain in comparative work.

TRENDS IN CROSS-CULTURAL MANAGEMENT RESEARCH

Nancy Adler (1982) has sought to identify alternative approaches characterizing the cross-cultural management research area. She distinguishes six kinds of studies: parochial, ethnocentric, poly-centric, comparative management, geocentric, and synergistic. The few articles in American management journals that do emphasize the importance of culture, focus on only a single culture, or else seek to compare organizational practices in two cultures (Adler, 1983). Most important—and consistent with what we said earlier—Adler found very few studies that have studied cross-cultural interaction. Moreover, most reported research has been parochial.

In claiming that culture affects managerial functioning we do not wish to rule out the importance of occupational, organizational, and individual factors. Rather, we are primarily interested in isolating the main effect of culture. This has been demonstrated in various studies. Haire et al. (1966) showed that about a third of the variance in work goals and managerial attitudes could be explained by such differences. England (1978) and Griffeth, Hom, Denisi, and Kirchner (1980) observed that culture/country differences account for between a third and half of the variance. The largest source of variance in Bass and Burger's (1979) 12-nation study of managers' responses to simulated organizational problems was cross-national. As Ronen (1986) observed, "The degree of similarity between countries is not determined on an absolute scale, but is relative to the level of dissimilarity with other countries, and therefore is influenced by the number of countries included in the clustering" (p. 261). Although England and Negandhi (1979) stated that the cross-national differences were exaggerated, not only are there real, magnitudinal differences, more important, these differences allow the clustering of countries on the basis of work values, as evidenced in the review and synthesis of eight cluster studies (Ronen & Shenkar, 1985).

The ability to cluster countries on the basis of some dimensions has important implications for practicing managers as well as for researchers in this area. Ronen and Kraut (1979) suggest that clustering enables managers to place international assignees more affectively, to establish compatible regional units, and to predict the results of policies and practices across national boundaries. From the academicians' perspective, clusters set a limit on the extent to which results can be generalized to other countries.

Variables such as values, used in cross-cultural research, originate in one culture and are then examined in others. New variables across cultures have not surfaced. In part that is because at an etic level any emic differences can be reconciled. Moreover, most cross-cultural comparative research has generally been based on western models. For instance, much of the empirical work in

comparative management has either implicitly or explicitly bor-
rowed from these models. Not only should we be careful when
taking such models for granted; we should also question the
assumptions underlying such models. Given the prominence of a
particular paradigm it is unlikely that any new variables can be
uncovered within it. A solution may lie in the use of multicultural
teams of investigators, particularly investigators trained in the
different cultures.

As noted earlier, interactional processes have important implications for understanding a wide variety of phenomena; cross-
cultural negotiations are one of the important applications. Additionally, and more practically, knowledge of such processes can aid
us significantly in developing appropriate staffing policies for
multinational companies. Attributional processes play an important
role in negotiations in that they determine one party's response
toward another. Using a culture assimilator (Fielder, Mitchell, &
Triandis, 1971) may help in preventing such schematic errors. To the
extent that one can systematically identify how the interaction
process differs across cultures, one can choose expatriates who
would be most comfortable with that particular kind of interaction.
Moreover, because of the inherent ambiguity in interaction processes when one crosses cultures, managers may wish to choose
expatriates as individuals who exhibit higher cognitive complexity.
People who score higher on this dimension have a better tolerance
for ambiguity—a key aspect of many cross-cultural encounters.

Bhagat and McQuaid (1982) suggest the use of both multicultural
and multidisciplinary research teams, also as a way to promote a
paradigmatic consensus. The use of a multicultural team (e.g.,
MOW, 1986) may aid in the appropriate utilization of emic and etic
perspectives, and may reduce such methodological problems as
equivalence and back translation. Nevertheless, the advantages of a
multidisciplinary team may be affected by the problems of integration.

Comparative management researchers are also well-advised to
pay more attention to distinguishing between independent and
quasi-independent variables. Although such a distinction may not
be of much heuristic value for applied purposes, it is critical for
theoretical development. Culture as an independent or quasi-
independent variable has an unsettled ontological status. Although
in reality a complex interrelationship exists between culture and
other sociological and economic variables, we believe that researchers must make an attempt to untangle its role either as an
independent or a quasi-independent variable.

21

CONCLUSIONS AND FUTURE PERSPECTIVES

PIETER J. D. DRENTH
Vrije Universiteit
Amsterdam, The Netherlands

During the last 15-20 years, organizational psychology, similar to many other specializations in the social sciences, has been growing strongly, sometimes even explosively, and not only as an applied science containing a number of papers describing recent noteworthy advances in organizational psychology, further supporting this observation. In almost all parts of the world organizational psychology can be observed to have deepened, differentiated, and elaborated its methods, domains, and approaches.

FROM INDUSTRIAL PSYCHOLOGY TO (WORK AND) ORGANIZATIONAL PSYCHOLOGY

In many countries, the subdiscipline discussed in this book went or still goes by different names. Frequently they included the adjective "industrial" (German: "*Betriebs,*" i.e., "company"). As the 1960s wore on, the designation "work and organizational psychology" or even merely "organizational psychology" began occurring more often (witness the title of this book and also the name of the relevant Division of the International Association of Applied Psychology). This change of name is not without significance; it indicates a number of shifts in both the discipline itself and in its orientation.

First, the area of interest widened. Already, in 1961, Leavitt argued in favor of a merger of classical "industrial psychology" with "organizational psychology." Similar signals could be detected in the chapter of Leavitt and Bass in the 1964 *Annual Review*. Porter, in his Annual Review Chapter of 1966, expressed the hope that a marriage between the "personnel-differential" and the "social organizational" orientation and interests would take place. In fact, that is exactly what happened in the following years and that is correctly reflected by the change of name.

A second shift occurred when the attention and research of "industrial" psychologists reduced their emphasis on profit-making production and sales organizations. Nowadays, service organizations (schools, hospitals, banks, insurance companies), government agencies, and other institutions (member associations, sport organizations) fall as often within the scope of work and organizational psychology.

Third, the orientation, value system, and guiding principles of work and organizational psychologists working in the 1980s are somewhat different from those of industrial psychologists of the 1960s and before. They no longer work exclusively on behalf of company management, but rather have turned their attention to the proper functioning of the (interaction) processes in the organization as a whole. In the classic dilemma of "client" versus "organization" (e.g., in personnel selection, performance appraisal, industrial relations, conflict management) today's work and organizational psychologists are less inclined to think in terms of an "either-or" option (and consequently to allow the organizational or management point of view to prevail), but rather to prefer an "and-and" option. They try to think of the client system as encompassing both the individuals (with their needs, expectations, and interests) and the organization (with its requirements, expectations, and interests). Psychologists thus put themselves in a position where they serve both parties, rather than just one of them.

In fact, all three shifts are indicative of the diversification in the scope, fields of interests, and approaches in work and organizational psychology. This diversification is illustrated also by the number of pages devoted to the various topics in leading texts and handbooks. In comparing, for example, a textbook on industrial psychology widely used in the 1960s (Tiffin & McCormick, 1965) with Dunnette's handbook published in the 1970s (Dunnette, 1976), the shift becomes apparent. We find a distinct increase of interest in theory and methodology, a diminished emphasis on classical subjects such as selection, engineering psychology, consumer behavior, motivation, and satisfaction, and little change where subjects such as motivation to work, leadership, and group behavior are concerned. New subjects, however, such as organization characteristics, organization development, management, and decision-making processes take up more than 40% of the total number of pages.

In a recent published handbook on work and organizational psychology (Drenth, Thierry, Willems, & Wolff, 1983), the sections "interaction between person and work" and "interaction between person and group," sections in which mostly traditional topics are discussed, take up nearly 500 pages. However, the section "interaction between organization and environment," dealing with subjects that generally represent new developments, take up even more pages.

The present volume provides illustrations of developments in the field of work and organizational psychology as described above. Of course, this book can by no means pretend to present a comprehensive, representative overview of all recent developments, if only because of its near objectives to both cover the field as well as to provide some insight into developments taking place in various parts of the world. The one objective is fulfilled almost at the expense of the other. Nevertheless, we feel that a reasonable compromise has been reached. Together, the various chapters quite satisfactorily cover the various issues dealt with by today's scientific and professional organizational psychologists and also present some interesting insights into regional developments and preferences. Not only does this overview inform the reader about the present state of the art in organizational psychology, but it also gives descriptions of the "couleur locale" in a number of important regions.

OLD AND NEW SUBJECTS

As appears from the present book, the traditional subjects are still with us. Obviously, there is continuity in a number of core activities of the industrial psychologist. The marriage between personnel psychology and organizational behavior studies has not led to a clear dominance of the latter or to a languishing of the former.

Almost all fields in which industrial psychologists have traditionally been interested originated from the discrepancy between person and task. There were, on the one hand, the organization's demands as to job requirements and expected performance and commitment and, on the other hand, the skills, capacities, behavioral styles, and energies of the individual. In view of the great differences between jobs as well as between people it would be surprising if any group of individuals were to measure up exactly to the psychological demands of the jobs to be fulfilled. Most of the classical contributions of industrial psychologists have focused on removing these person-job discrepancies.

First of all, the discrepancies must be identified and analyzed. In other words, a careful and systematic assessment of how people perform should provide insight into the possible (in-) consistencies between the demands of the job and the input of the worker. This subject is treated in the main chapter on performance appraisal. As Kavanagh, Borman, Hedge, and Gould state in Chapter 5, performance appraisal not only plays a central role in the identification of person-job mismatches, but also provides the key dependent variable against which most personnel decisions are validated.

Second, three types of procedure (corresponding with three further specializations in work and organizational psychology) are applied to reduce person-job discrepancies. One can try to compensate for deficiencies on the part of individuals through training, or one can try to single out the individuals best qualified for each function, as is done in selection, or one can try to analyze and modify the task so that it becomes optimally adapted to the individual who has to perform it (task analysis and ergonomics).

In several chapters, attention is paid to these three procedures. Eden's chapter on training demonstrates that this classical subject is still highly relevant. Indeed, the fast and substantial changes in work environment and task requirements, due to often revolutionary developments in technology and information processing, call for continued attention to the need for training, retraining, and updating of the skills, knowledge, and expertise of personnel. Regrettably, the other feature of training also shows continuity: the lack of adequate empirical or experimental validation of various training methods and techniques. The old arguments still prevail: Research on training in practice is difficult to carry out; negative results of such studies seem to be of no use to any of those involved (trainer, trainee, training director), and in many organizations training often is primarily "window dressing." Here lies an important task for organizational psychology as a scientific discipline.

Shackleton and Anderson (Chapter 6) present a *tour d'horizon* in the traditional field of *selection*. The classical themes of objectivity, predictive validity, and maximal regression are still prominent, but new themes have presented themselves: problems of discrimination in selection, the question whether rising unemployment rates will affect the selection strategies in view of dramatically changing selection ratios, the distribution of responsibilities among psychologists and personnel managers, and the increasing influence of computers in the administration and scoring of tests and in test research.

Algera's (Chapter 11) discussion of the domain of *task analysis* shows that this field is just as central and significant today as it always has been in industrial psychology. Task analysis is a prerequisite for quite a few essential industrial applications, including performance appraisal, training, selection, and remuneration. In itself, task analysis is the first stage in the process of task (re-) design and task structuring in which an attempt is made to achieve an optimal fit between machine and operator. Optimizing this fit is the objective of *ergonomics*, as Sperandio describes in Chapter 12.

On the other hand, this book also presents some new themes in organizational psychology that emerged as a result of particular developments in society or of scientific maturation. A number of these themes may be listed as examples.

Wilpert (Chapter 18) presents *participation* as the key word since the 1970s: the ability to control one's own task and work environment as a means toward personal development and growth. We have by now left behind us the stage where such delicate, often political, issues were measured exclusively by means of traditional instruments such as questionnaires. Nowadays, other means of gathering data—for example, participative observation, analysis of available documentary information, and longitudinal process analyses—are employed.

The same methodological extension of the set of data collection instruments is promoted by Heller and Misumi in their chapter on *decision making*. This subject is itself yet another result of recent advances in organizational psychology. Not too long ago, this research area was claimed by economists and operational research experts, with their complex normative models and optimalization functions. On the basis of the empirical analysis of actual individual or group decision making, psychologists can point out what inconsistent, irrational, and suboptimal decisions are often made and thus make their own contribution. After all, not only are decisions made, but they are made by people. Therefore, to obtain a more complete picture, both the operational and the behavioral dimensions should be taken into account.

The development of new *technology*, particularly of computer-oriented technology, requires other skills on the part of the worker. The shift from tasks requiring hard physical labor to those requiring intellectual and cognitive skills is one of the more salient transitions in job design, as Sperandio (Chapter 12) shows in his analysis of recent developments in ergonomics. At the same time, he also notes the overwhelming evidence for the necessity of observing the principles of social change in introducing and installing new technologies: proper timing, proper preparation, and sufficient involvement of the people concerned.

Shouksmith (Chapter 2) picks up the classical theme of the "meaning of working," but puts it in a daring futuristic framework. His analysis is based on attitudes and values, with respect to working, that are current in an increasing group of members of the labor market—the long-term and indefinitely unemployed. The less central position of working and the stronger appreciation of alternative social activities at first may have been the result of cognitive dissonance tendencies, but they could well become socially accepted, structural views on the place and role of working in society.

Surveying new developments in organizational theories, Peiró shows in Chapter 15 that the studies of organizational structure have made a significant contribution to our understanding of behavior in and of organizations. Here again, we must leave behind the level of simple descriptive analysis: the multi-level approach, interaction between elements, and dynamic analysis will be the new key words.

Stress at the work place and in the worker is another modern development of increasing importance. Its increasing importance is not a fad likely to disappear soon because stress seems to be a product of modern technological developments, the increasing complexity of task requirements, and information processes and the growing inability of workers to cope with these demands. There is no sign that these developments will slow down or stop in the near future. Stress research, as described by De Wolff and Winnubst (Chapter 4), will remain an important field of interest to the organizational psychologist for many years to come.

FUTURE DEVELOPMENTS

Most of the chapters, whether they deal with traditional or with new subjects, reveal certain trends in organizational psychology that not only characterize recent developments but may also represent likely future advances. Some of the more salient tendencies and key concepts associated with them are summarized below.

(1) The first trend is *internationalization*. In the past, many of the developments in industrial and organizational psychology have been of American origin or of mainly American signature. Although it cannot be denied that the United States has played and will continue to play a dominant role in the advancement of this field of applied psychology, there is a growing awareness that social and psychological phenomena are embedded in culture. Recognition of this fact is an essential prerequisite for a real understanding. It is imperative to obtain insight into the cultural contexts in which research is done and its results applied. As Shouksmith makes it clear, one must adapt the methods and procedures used to influence people, to change systems and even those used to research behavioral and organizational processes.

Misumi and Peterson, in Chapter 17, show that simple adaptations of American leadership systems just do not work in Japan. Heller and Misumi demonstrate that the typical Japanese *ringi* method, although it may seem primitive from the perspective of recent Western leadership theories, may well be very useful and relevant in the Japanese context. Eden, in Chapter 8, also remarks on the necessity of incorporating training methods into the national context. For instance, the training techniques popular throughout the Western world are simply not applicable in developing countries. The analysis of organizational psychological developments in China and of their relationships with the historically and politically determined needs of the country, as described by Xu Lian Cang (Chapter 19), provides yet another confirmation of this proposition. Furukawa, in Chapter 3, describes the relationship between the system of Quality Circles and Japanese cultural traditions in organizational development and industrial relations. In fact, it is interesting to read that apparently the system is weakening as these traditions are being replaced by more Western conventions.

Probably, the most pertinent example of the need to understand phenomena as being part of a cultural tradition is Hofmeyer's penetrating analysis in Chapter 9 of problems in training black managers in South Africa. If one fails to understand the black attitudes generated by many years of apartheid, any attempt at finding solution for the persistent lack of black management—a lack so detrimental to political and economic development—is doomed to remain unsuccessful. Cross-cultural research and theorizing, as applied to management behavior by Ronan and Kumar (see Chapter 20), will become ever more important for a real understanding of the behavior in and of organizations throughout the world. To achieve this goal we will have to replace traditional "safari-research" by truly international participative research programs as described by Ronan and Kumar, Wilpert and Heller.

(2) The second trend is *differentiation*. Differentiation is increasing in terms of research methods and analysis procedures on the one hand and of conceptualizations and theoretical models on the other. In methodology we observe not only a further elaboration and extension of data analysis techniques (e.g., through the introduction of large-scale computer support), but also an increasing variety of methods of collecting data. Observation through participation, using the referent as respondent, diachronic process observance, and analysis of available documentary data, for instance, are advocated by Heller and Misumi, Wilpert, Ekvall, and Misumi and Peterson, and will be a welcome addition to the much used, classical questionnaires, tests, and scales.

Differentiation in theoretical approaches is of course manifold. Theoretical progress is inherent in any scientific discipline that relies on fundamental research. This is true even if a large part of the research is applied. An illustrative example of theoretical differentiation is the widely accepted contingency approach. The effectiveness of quality control circles is found to be contingent upon certain environmental conditions and management climate (Furukawa). The impact of participative decision making is contingent upon such factors as phase of the decision-making cycle, the type of decision, mutual trust, and status power (Heller & Misumi). The impact of training is dependent on cultural and political constraints (Eden, Hofmeyer). The effect of scales and procedures rating the quality of performance is contingent, for instance, upon rater motivation and acceptability of the rating (Kavanagh et al.). Ekvall describes many factors that operate as moderators (i.e., contingent variables) with respect to the organizational effects of organizational climate. In most instances, the contingency approach leads to a deepening and further specification of our insight into organizational behavior, which has hitherto been of a too global and general nature.

(3) A third trend is indicated by the key word *integration*. Gradually, organizational psychology has learned how to incorporate loose pieces of research and experience into a better integrated theory or approach. Of course, it still is a long way from

being a comprehensive, all-encompassing theoretical framework and will have to content itself with a fragmentary body of knowledge for some time to come, but already there are signals announcing a more integrative approach. According to Vansina, Hoebeke, and Taillieu the systems approach, one of the earlier attempts at developing a more coherent theory of work systems and organizational design, is still in the process of maturing. Peiró pleads for an integration of sociocognitive and political views that should go beyond what he calls a rational paradigm. Kavanagh et al. emphasizes the need to have the often isolated personnel techniques (such as performance appraisal) embedded in the context of the organizational system. Eden shows how individual training, on the one hand, and organizational development and change, on the other, interact. They should be taken into account simultaneously in order to better understand either one of these processes. Perhaps the strongest case for integration is made by Super and Minor in Chapter 7. Many isolated elements of organizational psychology, such as selection, training, management development, task analysis, and attribution, can be considered in the perspective of an employee's career. This is an integrated and longitudinal perspective. It enables the employee to reflect on and be aware of possibilities and opportunities for advancement in the future. At the same time, it may provide a remedy for organizational problems such as lack of satisfaction or commitment. The career planning system can function then as a guideline for the integration of many kinds of personnel and organizational measures.

(4) A fourth emergent theme is what could be called *multi-disciplinarity*. Today, many of the issues in organizational psychology require a multidisciplinary approach, because practical problems often cross the dividing line between academic disciplines. Interaction between organizations and individuals cannot adequately be covered by monodisciplinary research. In their chapter on stress, De Wolff and Winnubst argue that the best way to approach this subject in research and in taking preventive or curate measures, is to have the various subdisciplines of psychology (e.g., organizational and work psychology, clinical and counseling psychology) join forces. They even advocate the creation of a new type of psychologist, the "clinical work psychologist," who would be best prepared to deal with these problems. Likewise, Vansina, Hoebeke, and Taillieu (Chapter 13) put in a word for multi-disciplinary work in the systems approach: Organization designers, work analysts, and social psychologists should combine their

expertise on behalf of a more complete understanding of the multifaceted complex systems that organizations are. The discussion of other developments in this volume also suggests that such problems can seldom be dealt with by organizational psychologists alone. They have to join forces with sociologists, management scientists, anthropologists, and organization theorists. As yet, however, an *inter*disciplinary approach does not seem feasible in the near future, certainly not in many of the European countries where the traditional division into disciplines is stricter than it is in the United States. Still, a *multi*disciplinary approach could be a good start. Multidisciplinary research teams, in which representatives from each (sub)discipline can contribute from their own experience, should be set up to study the problem fields of organizational science. The psychologists' contribution could then be their specific expertise, such as analytical and methodological competence, insight into both intrapersonal and interpersonal dynamics, and diagnostic and curative skills, and experience with people processes at both the individual and the organizational level. Such a multidisciplinary exercise may well prove to be a phase facilitating the transition to a truly interdisciplinary approach where the dividing lines between disciplines will have been replaced by problem-oriented methods and conceptualizations.

(5) Finally, it appears that organizational psychology is developing a more mature *orientation toward science*. Granted, there still exists a tension between the view of organizational psychology as a discipline directed at practical application and the view in which it is considered a discipline oriented toward scientific research. Eden complains not only of the lack of training research, but also of the apparent absence of need for such research. We read about Kavanagh and his associates' attempt to bridge the still existing gap between research and practice in the appraisal of personnel. In their review of selection devices, Shackleton and Anderson likewise mention some totally invalid methods, such as graphology, among the instruments still in vogue in various countries.

In a more fundamental sense, we may wonder whether organizational psychology has sufficiently freed itself from value systems, ideology, and political norms. This question is related to the issue of "practical" versus "scientific." The more organizational psychology remains or becomes an applied or practice-oriented discipline, the more it may run the risk of becoming an instrument in the hands of ideologists or those in power. Saying this, we are not referring to any ideology or authority in particular. It applies, for instance, to traditional industrial psychologists who may identify completely with company management and put all their "tricks" at the disposal of the personnel manager. In my opinion, it also applies to that orientation in China that takes Marxism as its guide for studying organization and work problems and seeks to integrate such theory and practice (Xu Lian Cang).

Of course, we are not here defending a purely positivistic approach to organizational psychology. We should acknowledge that this scientific discipline, like any other, is embedded in historical and social contexts, and that its reference to application and implementation requires a moral and social responsibility on the part of the scientists, even if he or she is a researcher only. Moreover, it has already been argued that a multimethod approach will lead to better understanding. This is why experimental laboratory research on training may not be sufficient (Eden), why participative observation may uncover otherwise hidden facts and relationships (Heller and Misumi), and why, in addition to a monothetic analysis, a perceptual, phenomenological research approach to concepts with a strongly subjective component (such as organizational climate) deserves attention (Ekvall).

What we are trying to say is that the fundamental requirements for the scientific acquisition of knowledge are apparently becoming more generally and widely accepted in organizational psychology. These requirements concern the unbiased way of asking questions and seeking answers; the necessity for collecting research data in order to confirm or disconfirm a theory; the systematic collection of data; an analysis and interpretation as unbiased as possible; and openness or publicity with respect to the scientific findings.

This last criterion, "openness," may well be one of the most important requirements. Through publicity, one exposes oneself to possible falsification or correction by fellow scientists, that is to say, to the testing of findings and interpretations by the scientific forum. In this way, science becomes what it ought to be: a cumulative product of interaction and communication.

We hope that this book, which tries to describe some of the recent evolution and advances in organizational psychology in various parts of the world, will be a contribution to this scientific communication. We also hope that the trends in organizational psychology, as summarized in this last chapter, will be continued in the years to come.

REFERENCES

Abbey, A., & Dickson J. W. (1983). Work climate and innovation in semiconductors. *Academy of Management Journal, 26*(2), 362-368.

Abbott, M., & Koopman-Boydon, P. G. (1981). Expectations and predictions of the division of labour within marriage. *New Zealand Psychologist, 10,* 24-32.

Abelson, R. P. (1981). Psychological status of the script concept. *American Psychologist, 36,* 715-729.

Acar, W., & Aupperle, K. (1984). Bureaucracy as organizational pathology. *Systems Research, 1,* 157-166.

Ackoff, R. (1981). *Creating the corporate future.* New York: John Wiley.

ACT. (1984). *Discover.* Hunt Valley, MD: Author.

Adler, D. (1981). *The cadet scheme: Anglo American corporation of South Africa.* Unpublished manuscript.

Adler, N. J. (1982). Understanding the ways of understanding: Cross cultural methodology reviewed. In R. N. Farmer (Ed.), *Comparative management: Essays in contemporary thought.*

Adler, N. J. (1983). Cross-cultural management research: The ostrich and the trend. *Academy of Management Review, 8*(3), 226-232.

Adler, N. J. (1986). *International dimensions of organizational behavior.* Boston: Kent.

Adler, S., Skov, R. B., & Salvemini, N. J. (1985). Job characteristics and job satisfaction: When cause becomes consequence. *Organizational Behavior and Human Decision Processes, 35,* 266-278.

Ajiferube, B., & Boddewyn, J. (1970). Culture and other explanatory variables in comparative management studies. *Academy of Management Journal, 13,* 153-165.

Alcalay, R., & Pasick, R. J. (1983). Psycho-social factors and the technologies of work. *Social Science and Medicine, 17*(16), 1075-1084.

Aldag, R. J., Barr, S. H., & Brief, A. P. (1981). Measurement of perceived task characteristics. *Psychological Bulletin, 90,* 415-431.

Alderfer, C. P. (1983). Change processes in organization. In M. D. Dunnette (Ed.), *Handbook of industrial and organizational psychology.* New York: John Wiley.

Aldrich, H., & Whetten, D. A. (1981). Organization-sets, action-sets, and networks: Making the most of simplicity. In P. C. Nystrom & W. H. Starbuck (Eds.), *Handbook of organizational design* (Vol. 1, pp. 385-408). New York: Oxford University Press.

Alengry, P. (1985). *L'activite de diagnostic sur des dispositifs quasi- similaires: Modele mental et caracteristiques de l'expertise.* Paris: Universite Paris V, Memoire de DEA.

Alexander, R. A., Barrett, G. K., Bass, B. M., & Ryterband, F. C. (1971). Empathy, projection, and negation in seven countries. In L. E. Abt & B. F. Riess (Eds.), *Clinical psychology in industrial organizations* (pp. 29-49). New York: Grune & Stratton.

Algera, J. A. (1981). *Kenmerken van werk* [Characteristics of work], (with English summary). Lisse: Swets & Zeitlinger.

Algera, J. A. (1983). "Objective" and perceived task characteristics as a determinant of reactions by task performers. *Journal of Occupational Psychology, 56,* 95-107.

Algera, J. A. (1984). Task characteristics. In P.J.D. Drenth, H. K. Thierry, P. J. Willems, & C. J. de Wolff (Eds.), *Handbook of work and organizational psychology* (pp. 175-195). New York: John Wiley.

Algera, J. A., & Groenendijk, B. (1985). Synthetische validiteit: Een vergelijking van benaderingen [Synthetic validity: A comparison of approaches]. *Nederlands Tijdschrift voor de Psychologie, 40*, 255-269.

Algera, J. A., Jansen, P.G.W., Roe, R. A., & Vijn, P. (1984). Validity generalizaton: Some critical remarks on the Schmidt-Hunter procedure. *Journal of Occupational Psychology, 57*, 197-210.

Andriessen, E.J.H., & Drenth, P. (1984). Leadership: Theories and models. In P. J. Willems & C. J. de Wolff (Eds.), *Handbook of work and organizational psychology*. New York: John Wiley.

Appels, A., Mulder, P., & Van't Hof, M. (1985). Type A gedrag en het hartinfarct: Een 9½ jaar follow-up studie van een klein cohort. *Nederlands Tijdschrift voor de Psychologie, 40(1)*, 20-26.

Aram, J., & Piraino, T. (1978). The hierarchy of needs theory: An evaluation in Chile. *Interamerican Journal of Psychology, 12*, 179-188.

Argote, L. (1982). Input uncertainty and organizational coordination in hospital emergency units. *Administrative Science Quarterly, 27*, 420-434.

Argyris, C. (1957). *Personality and organization*. New York: Harper.

Argyris, C. (1967). Managerial thinking by Maison Haire, E. E. Ghiselli and L. W. Porter: Book review. *Administrative Science Quarterly, 12*, 177-179.

Argyris, C., & Schon, D. (1974). *Theory in practice*. San Francisco: Jossey-Bass.

Argyris, C., & Schon, D. (1978). *Organizational learning*. Reading, MA: Addison-Wesley.

Arima, Y. (1983). *The multiplier effect of P-behavior on M-behavior regarding the number of tapping and the percent correct detection*. Technical report for a grant provided by the Japanese Ministry of Education, Science and Culture (Jyuji Misumi, Principal Investigator), Faculty of Human Sciences, Osaka University.

Arvey, R. D. (1979). Unfair discrimination in the employment interview: Legal and psychological aspects. *Psychological Bulletin, 86*, 736-765.

Arvey, R. D., & Campion, J. E. (1982). The employment interview: A summary and review of recent research. *Personnel Psychology, 35*, 281-322.

Arvey, R. D., Davis, G. A., McGowen, S. L., & Dipboye, R. L. (1982). Potential sources of bias in job analytic processes. *Academy of Management Journal, 25*, 618-629.

Arvey, R. D., Maxwell, S. E., Gutenberg, R. L., & Camp, C. (1981). Detecting job differences: A Monte Carlo study. *Personnel Psychology, 34*, 709-730.

Arvonen, J. (1983). *Studie av kreativt organisationsklimat, ledarskap och struktur i ett indus-triforetag*. Stockholm: Faradet.

Ashby, W. R. (1956). *Introduction to cybernetics*. New York: John Wiley.

Asher, J. J. (1972). The biographical item: Can it be improved? *Personnel Psychology, 25*, 251-269.

Astley, W. G., & Van De Ven, A. H. (1983). Central perspectives and debates in organization theory. *Administrative Science Quarterly, 28*, 245-273.

Aston, J. W. (1978). *Planning for retirement*. New York: Methuen.

Auden, W. H. (1972). Culture and leisure. In G. Bell & J. Tyrwhitt (Eds.), *Human identity in the urban environment*. Harmondsworth: Penguin.

Ayman, I. (1981). Psychologists in developing countries. *International Review of Applied Psychology, 30*, 401-407.

Babad, E. Y. (1979). Personality correlates of susceptibility to biasing information. *Journal of Personality and Social Psychology, 37*, 195-202.

Babad, E. Y., & Inbar, J. (1981). Performance and personality correlates of teachers' susceptibility to biasing information. *Journal of Personality and Social Psychology, 40*, 553-561.

Babad, E. Y., Inbar, J., & Rosenthal, R. (1982a). Pygmalion, Galatea, and the Golem: Investigations of biased and unbiased teachers. *Journal of Educational Psychology, 74*, 459-474.

Babad, E. Y., Inbar, J., & Rosenthal, R. (1982b). Teachers' judgment of students' potential as a function of teachers' susceptibility to biasing information. *Journal of Personality & Social Psychology, 42*, 541-547.

Bachman, J. G. (1983). Schooling as a credential: Some suggestions for change. *International Review of Applied Psychology, 30*, 347-360.

Baehr, A., & Bhagat, R. S. (Eds.). (1985). *Human stress and cognition in organizations.* New York: John Wiley.

Baklien, B. (1983). Organisasjonsklimat: Et frynsete begrep i organisasjonspsykologien. *Nordisk Psykologi, 35*(1), 1-13.

Balchin, N. (1957). The development of industry: Its impact on the worker. In D. C. Thompson (Ed.), *Management, labour and community.* London: Pitman.

Banks, C. G., & Murphy, K. R. (1985). Toward narrowing the research-practice gap in performance appraisal. *Personnel Psychology, 38,* 335-346.

Banks, M. H., Jackson, P. R., Stafford, E. M., & Warr, P. B. (1983). The job components inventory and the analysis of jobs requiring limited skill. *Personnel Psychology, 36,* 57-66.

Banks, M. H., & Miller, R. L. (1984). Reliability and convergent validity of the job components inventory. *Journal of Occupational Psychology, 57,* 181-184.

Barrett, G. V., & Bass, B. M. (1976). Cross cultural issues in industrial and organizational psychology. In M. D. Dunette (Ed.), *Handbook of industrial and organizational psychology* (pp. 1639-1686). New York: Rand McNally.

Bartuneck, J. M. (1984). Changing interpretive schemes and organizational restructuring: The example of a religious order. *Administrative Science Quarterly, 29,* 355-372.

Baruel, J. (1978). Foreword. In R. Hacon (Ed.), *Eficiencia personal y de la organizacion* (pp. i-xv). Barcelona: Editorial Hispano Europea.

Bass, B. M. (1981). *Stodgdill's handbook of leadership.* New York: Free Press.

Bass, B. M. (1983). *Organizational decision making.* Homewood, IL: Richard Irwin.

Bass, B. M. (1985a). *Leadership and performance beyond expectations.* New York: Free University.

Bass, B. M. (1985b). *A new paradigm for training and research in leadership.* Binghamton: State University of New York.

Bass, B. M., & Burger, P. C. (1979). *Assessment of management: An international comparison.* New York: Free Press.

Bass, B. M., & Vaughan, J. A. (1966). *Training in industry: The management of learning.* Belmont, CA: Brooks/Cole.

Bastelaer, A. van, & Beers, W. van. (1980). *Vragenlijst Organisatiestress, Testhandleiding deel 2: Konstruktie en normering.* Nijmegen: Katholieke Universiteit.

Bastelaer, A. van, & Beers, W. van. (1982). *Organisatiestress en personeelsfunctionaris.* Lisse: Swets & Zeitlinger.

Bastelaer, A. van, & Beers, W. van. *Stress and some public background variables: An analysis of variances on replicated data.* Unpublished manuscript, University of Nijmegen.

Baxter, J. C., Brock, B., Hill, P. C., & Rozelle, R. M. (1981). Letters of recommendation: A question of value. *Journal of Applied Psychology, 66,* 296-301.

Bayne, R. (1982). Interviewing. In M. D. Davey & N. Harris (Eds.), *Judging people: A guide to orthodox and unorthodox methods of assessment.* London: McGraw-Hill.

Beason, G., & Belt, J. A. (1976). Verifying applicants' backgrounds. *Personnel Journal, 55,* 345-348.

Beech, H. R., Burns, L. E., & Sheffield, B. F. (1982). *A behavioral approach to the management of stress.* New York: John Wiley.

Beehr, T. A., & Newman, J. E. (1978). Job stress, employee health and organizational effectiveness: A facet analysis, model and literature review. *Personnel Psychology, 31,* 665-699.

Beer, S. (1979). *The heart of enterprise.* New York: John Wiley.

Beer, S. (1981). *Brain of the firm* (2nd ed.). New York: John Wiley.

Bemelmans, T. (Ed.). (1984). *Beyond productivity: Information systems development for organizational effectiveness.* Amsterdam: North-Holland Elsevier.

Bennett, M. (1977). Testing management theorist cross culturally. *Journal of Applied Psychology, 62*(5), 578-581.

Bennis, W. (1981). Interview. *Training and Development Journal, 18,* 324-329.

Bennis, W. (1984). The four competencies of leadership. *Training and Development Journal, 38,* 14-19.

Benson, J. K. (1977). Innovation and crisis in organizational analysis. *Sociological Quarterly, 18*, 3-16.

Benson, J. K. (1983). Paradigm and praxis in organizational analysis. In L. L. Cummings & B. M. Staw (Eds.), *Research in organizational behavior* (Vol. 5, pp. 33-56). Greenwich, CT: JAI.

Berger, C. J., & Cummings, L. L. (1979). Organizational structure, attitudes and behaviors. In L. L. Cummings & B. M. Staw (Eds.), *Research in organizational behavior* (Vol. 1, pp. 169-200). Greenwich, CT: JAI.

Bergh-Braam, A. van der (1981). *De hoofdverpleegkundigen*. Nijmegen: Katholieke Universiteit, Stress Research Group.

Bernardin, H. J. (1982) Relations in a children's psychiatric hospital. *Sociological Quarterly, 23*, 235-251.

Bernardin, H. J., & Cardy, R. L. (1982). Appraisal accuracy: The ability and motivation to remember the past. *Public Personnel Management Journal, 119*, 352-357.

Bernardin, H. J., Cardy, R. L., & Carlyle, J. J. (1982). Cognitive complexity and appraisal effectiveness: Back to the drawing board? *Journal of Applied Psychology, 67*, 151-160.

Bernardin, H. J., Orban, J. A., & Carlyle, J. J. (1981). *Performance rating as a function of trust in appraisal and rate individual differences*. Proceedings of the 41st Annual Meeting of the Academy of Management, San Diego, CA.

Bernardin, H. J., & Villanova, A. (1986). Performance appraisal. In E. A. Locke (Ed.), *Generalizing from lab to field settings* (pp. 43-62). Lexington, MA: D. C. Heath.

Berry, J. W. (1979). Research in multicultural societies: Implications of cross-cultural methods. *Journal of Cross-Cultural Psychology, 10*(4): 415-434.

Berry, J. W. (1980). Introduction to methodology. In H. C. Triandis & J. W. Berry (Eds.), *Handbook of cross-cultural psychology* (Vol. 2). Boston: Allyn & Bacon.

Berry, J. W. (1981, August 16-21). *Textured contexts: Systems and situations in cross cultural psychology*. Paper presented at a symposium at the Conference on Human Assessment and Cultural Factors, Kingston, Canada.

Bhagat, R. S., & Chassie, M. B. (1980). Effects of changes in job characteristics on some theory-specific attitudinal outcomes: Results from a naturally occurring quasi-experiment. *Human Relations, 33*, 297-313.

Bhagat, R. S., & McQuaid, S. J. (1982). Role of subjective culture in organizations: A review and direction for future research. *Journal of Applied Psychology Monograph, 67*(5): 635-685.

Bhagat, R. S., Triandis, H. C. (1986). Cross-cultural dimensions. Unpublished manuscript.

Bhattacharya, S. K. (1983, January 17). Guess who succeeds? *Business India*, pp. 47-64.

Blackburn, R. S., & Cumming, L. L. (1982). Cognitions of work unit structure. *Academy of Management Journal, 25*, 836-854.

Blackler, F. (1982). Job-design and social policies. In J. Kelly & C. Clegg (Eds.), *Autonomy and control at the work-place* (pp. 157-180). London: Croom Helm.

Blau, J. R. (1982). Prominence in a network of communication: Work relations in a children's psychiatric hospital. *Sociological Quarterly, 23*, 235-251.

Blau, J. R., & McKinley, W. (1979). Ideas, complexity and innovation. *Administrative Science Quarterly, 24*, 200-219.

Boal, K. B., & Cummings, L. L. (1981). Cognitive evaluation theory: An experimental test of processes and outcomes. *Organizational Behavior and Human Performance, 28*, 289-310.

Boer, E. J., Verhage, F., & Wolff, C. J. de (Eds.). (1983). *Stress: Uitdaging en bedreiging*. Lisse: Swets & Zeitlinger.

Borman, W. C. (1977). Consistency of rating accuracy and rating errors in the judgment of human performance. *Organizational Behavior and Human Performance, 20*, 238-252.

Borman, W. C., Haugh, L., & Dunnette, M. (1976). *Performance ratings: An investigation of reliability, accuracy, and relationships between individual differences and rater error*. Minneapolis: Personnel Decisions.

Boudreau, J. W., & Rynes, S. L. (1985). Role of recruitment in staffing utility analysis. *Journal of Applied Psychology, 70*, 354-366.

Boughon, M., Weick, K., & Binkhorst, D. (1977). Cognition in organizations: An analysis of the Utrecht Jazz Orchestra. *Administrative Science Quarterly, 22*, 606-639.

Bouwen, R., De Cook, G., & De Witte, K. (1980). *Organizational climate: The meaning and usefulness of the concept.* Centrum voor Organisatie- en personeel-psychologie, KU Leuven.

Bowers, D. G., & Seashore, S. E. (1966). Predicting organizational effectiveness with a four-factor theory of leadership. *Administrative Science Quarterly, 11,* 238-263.

Bowlsbey, J. A. (1984). The computer as a tool in career guidance programs. In N. C. Gysbers (Ed.), *Designing careers.* San Francisco: Jossey-Bass.

Bradaway, M. K. (1980). Role orientations in Middle Eastern executives, a cross-cultural analysis. *Human Organizations, 39,* 271-275.

Brass, D. J. (1981). Structural relationships, job characteristics, and worker satisfaction and performance. *Administrative Science Quarterly, 26,* 331-348.

Brass, D. J. (1984). Technology and the structuring of jobs: Employee satisfaction, performance, and influence. *Organizational Behavior and Human Decision Processes, 35,* 216-240.

Bray, D. W., & Campbell, R. J. (1968). Selection of salesmen by means of an assessment center. *Journal of Applied Psychology, 67,* 3-9.

Bray, D. W., Campbell, R. J., & Grant, D. T. (1974). *Formative years in business: A long-term AT&T study of managerial lives.* New York: John Wiley.

Bray, D. W., & Grant, D. T. (1966). The assessment center in the measurement of potential for business management. *Psychological Monographs, 80*(6).

Breakdown in human adaptation to stress. (1984). Report of the Commission of the European Communities. Boston: Nijhoff.

Brewer, J. M. (1942). *History of vocational guidance.* Boston: Houghton Mifflin.

Brief, A. P., & Downey, H. K. (1983). Cognitive and organizational structures: A conceptual analysis of implicit organizing theories. *Human Relations, 36,* 1065-1090.

Brislin, R. W. (1983). Cross cultural research in psychology. *Annual Review of Psychology, 34,* 363-400.

British Psychological Society. (1984, June). *The use of the polygraph for personnel screening: A statement by the Society issued by the Scientific Affairs Board.* Leicester: Author.

British Psychological Society/Runnymead Trust. (1980). *Discriminating fairly.* Leicester: Author.

Broadbent, D. E. (1985). The clinical impact of job design. *British Journal of Clinical Psychology, 24,* 33-44.

Brown, M. B., Eden, D., & Tziner, A. (1978). *Fractional factorial designs when each judge can rank a subset of the alternatives.* Proceedings of the American Statistical Association.

Brown, R. H. (1978). Bureaucracy as praxis: Toward a political phenomenology of formal organizations. *Administrative Science Quarterly, 23,* 365-382.

Brush, D. H., & Owens, W. A. (1979). Implementation and evaluation of an assessment classification model for manpower utilization. *Personnel Psychology, 32,* 369-383.

Buchanan, D. A., & Boddy, D. (1982). Advanced technology and the quality of working life: The effects of word processing on video typists. *Journal of Occupational Psychology, 55,* 1-11.

Buchanan, D. A., & Boddy, D. (1983). Advanced technology and the quality of working life: The effects of computerized controls on biscuit-making operators. *Journal of Occupational Psychology, 56,* 109-119.

Buhler, C. (1933). *Der menschliche Lebenslauf als psychologisches Problem.* Leipzig: Hirzel.

Burke, M. J. (1984). Validity generalization: A review and critique of the correlation model. *Personnel Psychology, 37,* 93-115.

Burnaska, R. F. (1976). The effects of behavioral modeling training upon managers' behavior and employees' perceptions. *Personnel Psychology, 29,* 329-335.

Burns, H. R., & Sheffield, B. F. (1982). *A behavior approach to the management of stress.* New York: John Wiley.

Burns, T., & Stalker, G. (1961). *The management of innovation.* London: Tavistock.

Cable, J. R., & FitzRoy, F. R. (1980). Productive efficiency, incentives and employee participation: Some preliminary results for West Germany. *Kyklos, 33*(1), 100-121.

Cakir, A., Hart, D. J., & Stewart, T.F.M. (1980). *Visual display terminals.* New York: John Wiley.

Caldwell, D. F., & O'Reilly, C. A. (1982). Task perceptions and job satisfaction: A question of causality. *Journal of Applied Psychology, 67,* 361-369.

Cammock, P., & Inkson, K. (1985). The aspirations of trade apprentices and their implications for apprenticeship. *Journal of Occupational Psychology, 58*, 49-56.

Campbell, D. J. (1982). Determinants of choice of goal difficulty level: A review of situational and personality influences. *Journal of Occupational Psychology, 55*, 79-95.

Campbell, J. P. (1971). Personnel training and development. *Annual Review of Psychology, 22*, 565-602.

Campbell, J. P., Dunnette, M. D., Lawler, E. E., III, & Weick, K. E., Jr. (1970). *Managerial behavior, performance, and effectiveness.* New York: McGraw-Hill.

Campion, M. A. (1980). Relationship between interviewers' and applicants' reciprocal evaluations. *Psychological Reports, 47*, 1335-1338.

Campion, M. A., & Lord, R. G. (1982). A control systems conceptualization of the goal-setting and changing process. *Organizational Behavior and Human Performance, 30*, 265-287.

Campion, M. A., & Thayer, P. W. (1985). Development and field evaluation of an interdisciplinary measure of job design. *Journal of Applied Psychology, 70*, 29-43.

Cann, A., Siegfried, W. I., & Pearce, L. (1981). Forced attention to specific applicant qualifications: Impact on physical attractiveness and sex of applicant biases. *Personnel Psychology, 34*, 65-75.

Cao, R., & Jiazhi, L. (1966). Opinions on the engineering psychology of signal indication of the weak-current, concentrated control in a power station. *Acta Psychology Sinica, 1*, 27-58.

Caplan, R. D., Cobb, S., French, J.R.P., Van Harrison, R., & Pinneau, S. R. (1975). *Job demands and workers' health.* HEW publication (NIOSH), pp. 75-160.

Card, S. K., Morgan, T. P., & Newell, A. (1983). *The psychology of human-computer interaction.* Hillsdale, NJ: Lawrence Erlbaum.

Carroll, G. R. (1984). Organizational ecology. *Annual Review of Sociology, 10.*

Carter, N. M. (1984). Computerization as a predominate technology: Its influence on the structure of newspaper organizations. *Academy of Management Journal, 27*, 247-270.

Cascio, W. F. (1975). Accuracy of verifiable biographical information blank responses. *Journal of Applied Psychology, 60*, 767-769.

Cascio, W. F., & Bernardin, H. J. (1981). Implications of performance appraisal litigation for personnel decisions. *Personnel Psychology, 34*, 211-226.

Casper, R. E. (1985, April). On-line recruitment. *Personnel Journal*, pp. 50-55.

Castillo, J. J. (1984). Las nuevas formas de organizacion del trabajo. *Revista Espanola de Investigaciones Sociales, 26*, 201-212.

Castillo, J. J., & Prieto, C. (1983). *Condiciones de trabejo: Hacia un enfoque renovador de la Sociologia del Trabajo.* Madrid: Centro de Investigaciones Sociologicas.

Chbokar, J. S., & Wallin, J. A. (1984). A field study of the effect of feedback frequency on performance. *Journal of Applied Psychology, 69*, 524-530.

Checkland, P. (1981). *Systems thinking, systems practice.* New York: John Wiley.

Cherns, A. (1976). The principles of socio-technical design. *Human Relations, 29* 783-792.

Child, J. (1972). Organizational structure, environment and performance: The role of strategic choice. *Sociology, 6*, 1-22.

Child, J. (1981). Culture, contingency and capitalism in the cross national. In L. L. Cummings & B. J. Staw (Eds.), *Research in organizational behavior* (Vol. 3) (pp. 303-356). Greenwich, CT: JAI.

Clark, A. W., & McCabe, S. (1970). Leadership beliefs of Australian managers. *Journal of Applied Psychology, 54*, 1-6.

Cloonan, J. J., & Squires, H. F. (1981). Job analysis: Key to integrated human resource system. In D. H. Montross & C. J. Shinkman (Eds.), *Career development in the 1980s.* Springfield, IL: Charles C Thomas.

Collingridge, D. (1982). *Critical decision making: A theory of social choice.* London: Frances Pinter.

Companion, M. A., & Corso, G. M. (1982). Task taxonomies: A general review and evaluation. *International Journal of Man-Machine Studies, 17*, 459-472.

Cook, J., & Wall, T. (1980). New work attitude measures of trust, organizational commitment and personal need non-fulfilment. *Journal of Occupational Psychology, 53*, 39-52.

Cooper, C. L., Mallingen, M., & Kahn, R. (1978). Identifying sources of occupational stress among dentists. *Journal of Occupational Psychology, 51*(3), 227-234.

Cooper, C. L., & Marshall, J. (1976). Occupational sources of stress: A review of the literature relating to coronary heart disease and mental ill health. *Journal of Occupational Psychology, 49,* 11-28.

Cooper, G. L., & Payne, R. (Eds.). (1978). *Stress at work.* Chichester: John Wiley.

Cornelius, E. T., DeNisi, A. S., & Blencoe, A. G. (1984). Expert and naive raters using the PAO: Does it matter? *Personnel Psychology, 37,* 453-464.

Cornelius, E. T., Schmidt, F. L., & Carron, T. J. (1984). Job classification approaches and the implementation of validity generalization results. *Personnel Psychology, 37,* 247-260.

Cory, B. H., Medland, F. F., & Uhlaner, J. E. (1977). *Developing a research based system for manpower management and career progression in the U.S. Army Officer Corps.* Presented at conference on Manpower Planning and Organizational Design, NATO Special Programs Panel on Human Factors and on Systems Sciences, Stresa, Italy.

Cromie, S. (1981). Woman as managers in Northern Ireland. *Journal Occupational Psychology, 54,* 87-91.

Cronbach, L. J., & Meehl, P. E. (1955). Construct validity in psychological tests. *Psychological Bulletin, 52,* 281-302.

Crouch, C., & Heller, F. A. (1983). Organizational democracy and political processes. In *International yearbook of organizational democracy* (Vol. 1). Chichester: John Wiley.

Crowley, A. D. (1981). The content of interest inventories: Job titles or job activities? *Journal of Occupational Psychology, 54,* 135-140.

Cummings, L. L., & Schmidt, S. M. (1972). Managerial attitudes of Greeks: The roles of cultures and industrialization. *Administrative Science Quarterly, 17,* 265-272.

Cummings, L. L., & Schwab, D. (1974). *Performance in organizations: Determinants and appraisals.* Glenview, IL: Scott, Foresman.

Cunningham, J. W., Boese, R. R., Neeb, R. W., & Pass, J. J. (1983). Systematically derived work dimensions: Factor analyses of the occupation analysis inventory. *Journal of Applied Psychology, 68,* 232-252.

Curtis, B. (1981). *Human factors in software development.* Los Angeles: IEEE Computer Society.

Dachler, H. P., & Wilpert, B. (1978). Conceptual dimensions and boundaries of participation in organizations: A critical evaluation. *Administrative Science Quarterly, 23,* 1-39.

Daniel, T. L., & Esser, J. K. (1980). Intrinsic motivation as influenced by rewards, task interest, and task structure. *Journal of Applied Psychology, 65,* 566-573.

D'Arcy, C., Syrotuik, J., & Siddique, C. M. (1984). Perceived job attitudes, job satisfaction, and psychological distress: A comparison of working men and women. *Human Relations, 37,* 603-611.

Davidson, M., & Cooper, C. (1976). *The executive under stress: A research study on stress.* New York: Alexander Hamilton Institute.

Davidson, M., & Cooper, C. (1983). *Stress and the woman manager.* New York: St. Martins.

Deci, E. L. (1975). *Intrinsic motivation.* New York: Plenum.

De Cook, G., Bouwen, R., De Witte, K., & De Vish, J. (1985). *Organizational climate: A provisional model for organizational effectivity.* Centrum voor Organisatie-en personeelpsychologie, KU Leuven.

De Cook, G., De Witte, K., Dullers, A., Engelen, A., Schiepers, M., & Vrancken, A. (1980). *Verkennende studie over organisatieklimaat en over de relatie tussen organisatieklimaat en organisatiestruktuur en organisatiekontekst, Organisatiepsychologische Rapporten: Onderzoeksrapport nr. 1.* Centrum voor Organisatie en personeelspsychologie, KU Leuven.

DeCotiis, T., & Petit, A. (1978). The performance appraisal process: A model and some testable propositions. *Academy of Management Review, 3,* 635-646.

Delruelle-Voswinkel, N., & Georges, R. (1980). Reliance sociale dans les grandes organisations: Bilan d'une etude realisee dans le cadre de Programme National de Recherche en Sciences Sociales. *Revue de l'institut de Sociologie, 2,* 357-369.

De Miguel, A., & Linz, J. J. (1964). *Caracteristicas estructurales de las empresas espanolas: Tecnificacion y burocracia, racionalizacion.* Revista del I.N. de Racionalizacion del trabajo.

den Hertog, F., & van Eynatten, F. (1982). The process of change practical paradigms for redesigning jobs. In J. Kelly & C. Clegg (Eds.), *Autonomy & control at the work-place* (pp. 65-104). London: Croom Helm.

DeNisi, A., Meglino, B., & Cafferty, T. P. (1984). A cognitive view of the performance appraisal process: A model and research propositions. *Organizational Behavior and Human Performance, 33,* 360-396.

Denton, J. A. (1982). Organizational size and structure: A longitudinal analysis of hospitals. *Sociological Spectrum, 2,* 57-71.

De Sitter, L. (1981). *Op weg naar nieuwe fabrieken en kantoren: Productie-organisaties en arbeidsorganisaties op de tweesprong.* Deventer: Kluwer.

Dewar, R., & Hage, J. (1978). Size, technology, complexity and structural differentiation: Toward a theoretical synthesis. *Administrative Science Quarterly, 23,* 111-136.

Dewar, R., & Werbel, J. (1978). Universalistic and contingency predictions of employee satisfaction and conflicts. *Administrative Science Quarterly, 23,* 111-136.

De Wolff, C. J., & van den Bosch, G. (1984). Personnel selection. In P.J.D. Drenth, H. Thierry, P. J. Willems, & C. J. De Wolff (Eds.), *Handbook of work and organizational psychology* (Vol. 1). Chichester: John Wiley.

Deyo, F. C. (1978). The cultural patterning of organizational development: A comparative case study of Thailand & Chinese industrial enterprises. *Human Organization, 37*(1): 68-72.

Dijkhuizen, N. van. (1980). *From stressors to strains: Research into their relationships.* Lisse: Swets & Zeitlinger.

DIO. (1979). Decisions in organizations: A comparative study. *Industrial Relations, 18,* 295-309.

DIO. (1983). A contingency model of participative decision making: An analysis of 56 decisions in three Dutch organizations. *Journal of Occupational Psychology, 56,* 1-18.

Dipboye, R., & dePontbriand, R. (1981). Correlates of employee reactions to performance appraisals and appraisal systems. *Journal of Applied Psychology, 66,* 248-251.

Dohrenwend, B. S., & Dohrenwend, B. P. (Eds.). (1974). *Stressful life events: Their nature and effects.* New York: John Wiley.

Donaldson, G., & Lorsch, G. (1983). *Decision making at the top: The shaping of strategic decisions.* New York: Basic Books.

Doverspike, D., Carlisi, A. M., Barrett, G. V., & Alexander, R. A. (1983). Generalizability analysis of a point-method job evaluation instrument. *Journal of Applied Psychology, 68,* 476-483.

Drasgow, F., & Miller, H. E. (1982). Psychometric and substantive issues in scale construction and validation. *Journal of Applied Psychology, 67,* 268-279.

Drenth, P.J.D., & Groenendijk, B. (1984). Work and organizational psychology in cross-cultural perspective. In P.J.D. Drenth, H. Thierry, P. J. Willems, C. J. de Wolff (Eds.), *Handbook of work and organizational psychology* (pp. 1197-1229). New York: John Wiley.

Drenth, P.J.D., & Koopman, P. (1984). Experience with "werkoverleg" in the Netherlands. *Journal of General Management, 9*(2), 57-73.

Drenth, P.J.D., Thierry, H., Willems, P. J., & Wolff, C. J. de (Eds.). (1983). *Handbook of work and organizational psychology.* New York: John Wiley.

Drexler, J. A., Jr. (1977). Organizational climate: Its homogeneity within organizations. *Journal of Applied Psychology, 62,* 38-42.

Drory, A., & Gluskinos, U. M. (1980). Machiavellianism and leadership. *Journal of Applied Psychology, 65,* 81-86.

Drouin, A. (1976). *Representation mentale et activite operatoire dans un systeme automatise.* Memoire Maitrise Psychologie, Universite. Paris VIII.

Drury, C. G. (1983). Task analysis methods in industry. *Applied Ergonomics, 14,* 19-28.

Dubin, R. (1976). Work in modern society. In K. Dubin (Ed.), *Handbook of work organization and society.* Chicago: Rand McNally.

Dunn, B. D. (1982). The skills inventory: A second generation. *Personnel, 59*(5), 40-44.

Dunnette, M. D. (1976). *Handbook of industrial and organizational psychology.* Chicago: Rand McNally.

Dunnette, M. D. (1983). *Work and non-work in the year 2001.* Monterey, CA: Brooks/Cole.

Dunnette, M. D., & Borman, W. C. (1979). Personnel selection and classification systems. *Annual Review of Psychology, 30,* 477-525.

Duval, B. A., & Courtney, R. S. (1978). Upward mobility: The GF way of opening advancement opportunities. *Personnel,* pp. 43-53.

Edelman, F. (1982, October). Managers, computer systems and productivity. *Interfaces, 12,* 36-46.

Eden, C., Jones, S., & Sims, D. (1983). *Messing about in problems.* Oxford: Pergamon.

Eden, D. (1982). Critical job events, acute stress, and strain: A multiple interrupted time series. *Organizational Behavior and Human Performance, 30,* 312-329.

Eden, D. (1984). Self-fulfilling prophecy as a management tool: Harnessing Pygmalion. *Academy of Management Review, 9,* 64-73.

Eden, D. (1985). Team development: A true field experiment employing three levels of rigor. *Journal of Applied Psychology, 70,* 94-100.

Eden, D. (1986). Team development: Quasi-experimental confirmation among combat companies. Manuscript submitted for publication.

Eden, D., & Ravid, G. (1982). Pygmalion vs. self-expectancy: Effects of instructor- and self-expectancy on trainee performance. *Organizational Behavior and Human Performance, 30,* 351-364.

Eden, D., & Shani, A. B. (1982). Pygmalion goes to boot camp: Expectancy, leadership, and trainee performance. *Journal of Applied Psychology, 67,* 194-199.

Edwardes, M. (1983). *Back from the brink: Apocalyptic experience.* London: Collins.

Egelhoff, W. G. (1982). Strategy and structure in multinational corporations: An information processing approach. *Administrative Science Quarterly, 27,* 435-458.

Ekkers, C. L., Brouwers, A.A.F., Pasmooij, C. K., & Vlaming, P. M. de (1980). *Menselijke stuur-en regeltaken* [Human control tasks]. Leiden: NIPG/TNO.

Ekvall, G. (1985). *Organisationsklimat: Teori och forskning.* Stockholm: Faradet, arbetsrapport.

Ekvall, G., & Arvonen, J. (1984). *Leadership styles and organizational climate for creativity: Some findings in one company* (Rep. 1). Stockholm: Faradet.

Ekvall, G., Arvonen, J., & Nystrom, H. (1985). *Organisation och innovation.* Stockholm: Faradet, arbetsrapport.

Ekvall, G., Arvonen, J., & Waldenstrom-Lindblad, I. (1983). *Creative organization climate: Construction and validation of a measuring instrument* (Rep. 2). Stockholm: Faradet.

Elder, J. W. (1976). Comparative cross national methodology. *Annual Review of Sociology, 2,* 209-230.

Elliot, G. R., & Eisdorfer, C. (Eds.). (1982). *Stress and human health.* New York: Springer.

Emery, E. (1982). New perspectives on the world of work: Socio-technical foundations for a new social order? *Human Relations, 35,* 1095-1122.

Emery, F. (1963). *Some hypotheses about the way in which tasks may be more effectively put together to make jobs.* London: Tavistock Institute of Human Relations.

Emery, F. (1981). *Systems thinking* (2nd ed.). London: Penguin.

Emery, F., & Emery, M. (1978). Participative design work and community life. *Occasional Papers in Continuing Education, 4.*

Emery, F., & Trist, E. L. (1965). The casual texture of organizational environments. *Human Relations, 18,* 21-32.

Endruweit, G., Gaughler, E., Staehle, W. H., & Wilpert, B. (Eds.). (1985). *Handbuch der Arbeitsbeziehungen.* Berlin/New York: de Gruyter.

England, G. W. (1978). Managers and their value systems: A five country comparative study. *Columbia Journal of World Business, 13*(2), 35-44.

England, G. W., Dhingra, O. P., & Agarwal, N. C. (1974). *The manager and the man.* Kent, OH: Kent State University Press.

England, G. W., et al. (1985). *The meaning of work: An international perspective.* London: Academic Press.

England, G. W., & Lee, R. (1974). The relationship between managerial values and managerial success in the United States, India and Australia. *Journal of Applied Psychology, 59*(4): 411-419.

England, G. W., & Negandhi, A. R. (1965). National context and technology as a determinant of employees' perceptions. In G. W. England, A. R. Negandhi, and B. Wilpert (Eds.), *Organizational functioning in a cross-cultural perspective.* Kent, OH: Kent State University Press, 175-190.

Erez, M., & Zidon, I. (1984). Effect of goal acceptance on the relationship of goal difficulty to performance. *Journal of Applied Psychology, 69,* 69-78.

Escudero, E. (1984). Cambio tecnologico y transformaciones en el sistema tecnico de la produccion y del empleo: Algunas hipotesis. *Revista Internacional de Sociologia*, pp. 159-203.

Espejo, R. (1983). Management and information: The complementarity control-autonomy. *Cybernetics and Systems, 14*(1), 85-102.

ETS. (1975). *SIGI.* Princeton, NJ: Author.

Etzioni, A. (1969). Man and society: The inauthentic condition. *Human Relations, 22,* 325-332.

Executive Committee of Chinese Psychological Society. (1982). Retrospect and prospect of 60 years of psychology in China. *Acta Psychology Sinica, 2,* 127-138.

The executive under stress, a research study on stress. (1976). New York: Alexander Hamilton.

Farmer, R. N. (1984). *Advances in international comparative management: A research annual* (Vol. 1). Greenwich, CT: JAP.

Farmer, R. N., & Richman, B. M. (1965). *Comparative management and economic progress.* Homewood, IL: Irwin.

Feldman, J. (1981). Beyond attribution theory: Cognitive processes in performance appraisal. *Journal of Applied Psychology, 66,* 127-148.

Fernandez, J. P. (1975). *Black managers in white corporations.* New York: John Wiley.

Ferratt, T. W., Dunham, R. B., & Pierce, J. L. (1981). Self-report measures of job characteristics and affective responses: An examination of discriminant validity. *Academy of Management Journal, 24,* 780-794.

Ferris, K. R., & Aranya, N. (1983). A comparison of two organizational commitment scales. *Personnel Psychology, 36,* 87-97.

Fiedler, F. E. (1967). *A theory of leadership effectiveness.* New York: McGraw-Hill.

Fiedler, F. E., Mitchell, T., & Triandis, H. C. (1971). The cultural assimilator: An approach to cross cultural training. *Journal of Applied Psychology, 55*(2), 95-102.

Fiedler, F. E., Mitchell, T., & Triandis, H. C., & Wilpert, B. (Eds.). (1979). Kent, OH: Kent State University Press, 175-189.

Fiedler, F. E., Mitchell, T., & Triandis, H. C., Wilpert, B., Richman, B. M. (1965). *Comparative management and economic progress.* Homewood, IL: Irwin.

Filella, J. (1980). *Leadership styles.* Unpublished manuscript.

Filella, J. (1985). *Research data on Jungian types and learning styles.* Bombay: Xavier Institute of Management.

Fine, G. A. (1984). Negotiated orders and organizational cultures. *Annual Review of Sociology, 10,* 239-262.

Fineman, S., & Payne, R. (1981). Role stress: A methodological trap? *Journal of Occupational Behavior, 2,* 51-64.

Finkle, R. B. (1976). Managerial assessment centers. In M. D. Dunnette (Ed.), *Handbook of industrial and organizational psychology.* Chicago: Rand McNally.

Fisher, G. *International negotiations: A cross-cultural perspective.* Chicago: Intercultural Press.

Fitzgerald, L. F., & Quaintance, M. K. (1982). Survey of assessment center use in state and local government. *Journal of Assessment Center Technology, 5,* 9-21.

Fleishman, E. A. (1967). Performance assessment based on an empirically derived task taxonomy. *Human Factors, 9,* 349-366.

Fleishman, E. A. (1978). Related individual differences to the dimensions of human factors. *Ergonomics, 21,* 1007-1019.

Fleishman, E. A. (1982). Systems for describing human tasks. *American Psychologist, 37,* 821-834.

Fleishman, E. A., & Hogan, J. C. (1978). *A taxonomic method for assessing the physical requirements of jobs: The physical abilities analysis approach.* Washington, DC: Advanced Research Resources Organization.

Fleishman, E. A., & Quaintance, M. K. (1984). *Taxonomies of human performance.* Orlando, FL: Academic Press.

Fletcher, B. C., & Payne, R. L. (1982). Levels of reported stressors and strains amongst school teachers: Some UK data. *Educational Review, 34*(3), 267-278.

Fletcher, C. (1981). Candidates' beliefs and self-presentation strategies in selection interviews. *Personnel Review, 10,* 14-17.

Fletcher, C. (1982). Assesment centres. In D. M. Davey & M. Harris (Eds.), *Judging people.* Mainhead, England: McGraw-Hill.

Fletcher, C. (1985a, January). *Interviews, inventories and insight: Chairman's address.* Sheffield: BPS Occupational Psychology Conference.

Fletcher, C. (1985b, March). Comments on graphology: Towards a hand-picked workforce, by Lynch, B. *Personnel Management,* p. 18.

Foeken, H. J. (1979a). Project "arbeidsvoldoening van operators," meetinstrumenten, bewerkingen en resultaten [Project "job satisfaction of operators," measuring instruments, revision and results]. Eindhoven: Technological University.

Foeken, H. J. (1979b). *Arbeidsvoldoening van operators: Het model van Hackman en Oldham nader beschouwd* [Job satisfaction of operators: A closer look at the model of Hackman and Oldham]. Eindhoven: Technological University.

Fontela, E. (1980). *Un estudio prospectivo: Espana en la decada de los ochenta.* Madrid: Instituto Nacional de Prospectiva.

Fombrum, C. J. (1984). Structures of organizational governance. *Human Relations, 37,* 207-223.

Fombrum, C. J. (1986). Structural dynamics within and between organizations. *Administrative Science Quarterly, 31,* 403-421.

Forbes, R. J., & Jackson, P. R. (1980). Non-verbal behaviour and the outcome of selection interviews. *Journal of Occupational Psychology, 55,* 67-72.

Ford, J. D., & Hegarty, W. H. (1984). Decision makers' beliefs about the causes and effects of structure: An exploratory study. *Academy of Management Journal, 27,* 271-291.

Frankenhaeuser, M. (1980). Psychobiological effects of life stress. In S. Levin & H. Ursin (Eds.), *Coping and health.* New York: Plenum.

Freedman, S. M., & Phillips, J. S. (1985). The effects of situational performance constraints on intrinsic motivation and satisfaction: The role of perceived competence and self-determination. *Organizational Behavior and Human Decision Processes, 35,* 397-416.

Freeman, J., & Hannan, M. T. (1983). Niche width and the dynamics of organizational populations. *American Journal of Sociology, 88,* 1116-1145.

Friedland, N., & Keinan, G. (1982). Patterns of fidelity between training and criterion situations as determinants of performance in stressful situations. *Journal of Human Stress, 8,* 41-46.

Friedlander, F., & Margulies, N. (1969). Multiple impacts of organizational climate and individual value systems upon job satisfaction. *Personnel Psychology, 22,* 171-183.

Friedman, M., & Rosenman, R. H. (1974). *Type A behavior and your heart.* Greenwich, CT: Fawcett.

Friedrich, E. S. (1981). *Qualifikation und Beteiligung.* Frankfurt/New York: Campus.

Fry, L. W., & Slocum, M., Jr. (1984). Technology, structure, and workgroup effectiveness: A test of a contingency model. *Academy of Management Journal, 27,* 221-246.

Fukuda, R. (1983). *Managerial engineering.* New York: Productivity Inc.

Fulk, J., & Wendler, E. R. (1982). Dimensionality of leader-subordinate interactions: A path-goal investigation. *Organizational Behavior and Human Performance, 30,* 241-264.

Furnham, A. (1984). Work values and beliefs. *British Journal of Occupational Psychology, 5,* 281-291.

Furukawa, H. (1979). Effects of management objective upon leadership behavior. *Japanese Journal of Experimental Social Psychology, 19,* 15-24 (in Japanese).

Furukawa, H. (1982). Intrinsic and extrinsic work motivation: A review of definitions and interactive relationships. *Japanese Journal of Experimental Social Psychology, 22,* 69-80.

Galbraith, J. K. (1973). *Designing complex organizations.* Reading, MA: Addison-Wesley.

Ganesh, S. R., & Rangarajan, T. (1983). Research review: Organizational behaviour research in India: A critique of the last decade. *Organization Studies, 4,* 357-374.

Gardell, B. (1976). *Arbetsinnehalt och livskvalitet.* Stockholm: Prisma.

Garland, H. (1982). Goal levels and task performance: A compelling replication of some compelling results. *Journal of Applied Psychology, 67,* 245-248.

Garland, H. (1984). Relation of effort-performance expectancy to performance in goal-setting experiments. *Journal of Applied Psychology, 69,* 79-84.

Garmendia, J. A. (1984). Introduction al numero monografico de "Sociologia Industrial." *Revista Internacional de Sociologia*, pp. 7-12.

Geeraerts, G. (1984). The effect of ownership on the organizational structure in small firms. *Administrative Science Quarterly, 29*, 232-237.

Gentry, D., Benson, H., & Wolff, D. J. de. (Eds.). (1985). *Work, stress and health*. Dordrecht: Martinus Nijhoff.

Gerwin, D. (1981). Relationships between structure and technology. In P. C. Nystrom & W. Starbuck (Eds.), *Handbook of organizational design* (Vol. 2). Oxford: Oxford University Press.

Gharajedaghi, J., & Ackoff, R. L. (1984). Mechanisms, organisms and social systems. *Strategic Management Journal, 5*, 289-300.

Gibbons, J. R. (1983). *Testimony before the sub-committee on legislation and national security*. Washington, DC: U.S. House of Representatives, Committee on Government Operations.

Gill, D. (1980). *Selecting managers: How British industry recruits*. London: Institute of Personnel Management/British Institute of Management.

Gils, M. R. van (1984). Interorganizational relations and networks. In P. Drenth, H. Thierry, P. Willems, & C. de Wolff (Eds.), *Handbook of work and organizational psychology* (Vol. 2, pp. 1073-1101). Chichester: John Wiley.

Ginton, A., Gaie, N., Elaad, E., & Ben-Shakhar, G. (1982). A method for evaluating the use of the polygraph in a real-life situation. *Journal of Applied Psychology, 67*, 131-137.

Ginzberg, E., and Associates (1951). *Occupational choice*. New York: Columbia University Press.

Glisson, C. A., & Martin, P. Y. (1980). Productivity and efficiency in human service organizations as related to structure, size and age. *Academy of Management Journal, 23*, 21-37.

Goldberg, A. I., & Harel, G. H. (1984). *The RPS index: Establishing appropriate management training programs*. Haifa, Israel: Technion-Israel Institute of Technology, Faculty of Industrial Engineering and Management.

Goldsmith, W., & Clutterbuck, D. (1985). *The winning streak*. London: Weidenfeld & Nicholson.

Goldstein, A. D., & Sorcher, M. (1974). *Changing supervisor behavior*. New York: Pergamon.

Goldstein, I. L. (1971). The application blank: How honest are the responses? *Journal of Applied Psychology, 55*, 491-492.

Goldstein, I. L. (1980). Training in work organizations. *Annual Review of Psychology, 31*, 229-272.

Goldstein, I. L. (1971). The application blank: How honest are the responses? *Journal of Applied Psychology, 55*, 491-492.

Goldstein, I. L. (1974). *Training: Program development and evaluation*. Monterey, CA: Brooks/Cole.

Goldstein, I. L. (1986). *Training in organizations: Needs assessment, development, and evaluation*. Monterey, CA: Brooks/Cole.

Goldstein, M. S. (1979). The sociology of mental health and illness. *Annual Review of Sociology, 5*, 381-409.

Gomez-Mejia, L. R., Page, R. C., & Tornow, W. W. (1982). A comparison of the practical utility of traditional, statistical, and hybrid job evaluation approaches. *Academy of Management Journal, 25*, 790-809.

Goodman, P. S., & Moore, B. E. (1972). Critical issues of cross cultural management research. *Human Organization, 31*(1), 39-45.

Gopher, D., Brickner, M., & Navon, D. (1982). Different difficulty manipulations interact differently with task emphasis: Evidence for multiple resources. *Journal of Experimental Psychology: Human Perception and Performance, 8*, 146-157.

Gopher, D., & North, R. A. (1977). Manipulating the conditions of training in time-sharing performance. *Human Factors, 19*, 583-593.

Gordon, J., Lee, C., & Zemke, R. (1984). Remembrance of things passed. *Training, 21*(1), 22-39.

Gordon, M. E., Philpot, J. W., Burt, R. E., Thompson, C. A., & Spiller, W. E. (1980). Commitment to union: Development of measure and an examination of its correlates. *Journal of Applied Psychology Monograph, 65*, 479-499.

Gottfredson, G. D. (1982). An assessment of a mobility-based occupational classification for placement and counseling. *Journal of Vocational Behavior, 21*, 71-98.

Gould, R. B., & Hedge, J. W. (1984, August). *Air Force job performance criterion development.* Paper presented at the annual meeting of the American Psychological Association, Anaheim, CA.

Gould, S., & Werbel, J. D. (1983). Work involvement: A comparison of dual wage earner and single wage earner families. *Journal of Applied Psychology, 68,* 313-319.

Graen, G. (1976). Role-making processes within complex organization. In M. D. Dunnette (Ed.), *Handbook of industrial and organizational psychology* (pp. 1201-1245). Chicago: Rand McNally.

Granick, D. (1972). *Managerial comparisons of four developed countries: France, Britain, U.S. and Russia.* Cambridge: MIT Press.

Granrose, C. S., & Portwood, J. D. (1984, August). *A model of individual career strategies: Understanding the organization's impact.* Paper presented at the Careers Division, Academy of Management, 44th Annual National Meeting, Boston.

Greiff, B. S. (1974). Work performance and occupational stress. In A. A. McLean (Ed.), *Occupational stress.* Springfield, IL: Charles C Thomas.

Griffeth, R. W. (1985). Moderation of the effects of job enrichment by participation: A longitudinal field experiment. *Organizational Behavior and Human Decision Processes, 35,* 73-93.

Griffeth, R. W., Hom, P. W., Denisi, A., & Kirchner, Q. A. (1980, August). *A multivariate multinational comparison of managerial attitudes.* Paper presented at the Fortieth Annual Meeting of the Academy of Management, Detroit.

Griffin, R. W. (1982). Perceived task characteristics and employee productivity and satisfaction. *Human Relations, 35,* 927-938.

Griffin, R. W., Moorhead, G., Johnson, B. H., & Chonko, L. B. (1980). The empirical dimensionality of the job characteristic inventory. *Academy of Management Journal, 23,* 772-777.

Guilford, J. P. (1967). *The nature of human intelligence.* New York: McGraw-Hill.

Guion, R. M. (1973). A note on organizational climate. *Organizational Behavior and Human Performance, 9,* 120-125.

Guion, R. M. (1976). Recruitment, selection and job placement. In M. D. Dunnette (Ed.), *Handbook of industrial and organizational psychology* (Vol. 33, pp. 297-300). Chicago: Rand McNally.

Gupta, N. (1980). Some alternative definitions on size. *Academy of Management Journal, 23,* 759-766.

Gustavson, B. (1983). The Norwegian work environment reform: The transition from general principles to work place action. In C.F.A. Heller (Ed.), *Organizational democracy and political processes in international yearbook of organizational democracy* (Vol. 1). Chichester: John Wiley.

Gustavson, B., & Hunnius, G. (1981). *New patterns of work reform: The case of Norway.* Oslo/New York: Oslo University Press/Columbia University Press.

Gutteridge, T. G. (1986). Career development programs. In D. T. Hall (Ed.), *Frontiers in industrial/organizational psychology, careers volume.* San Francisco: Jossey-Bass.

Gutteridge, T. G., & Otte, F. L. (1983). *Organizational career development.* Washington, DC: American Society for Training and Development.

Hachiya, H. (1981). The influence of situational factors on the relationships between leader behavior and subordinate response: An examination of the interaction between subordinate individual characteristics and task characteristics. *Japanese Journal of Experimental Social Psychology, 21*(1), 17-24 (in Japanese).

Hackman, J. (1976). *The design of self-managing work groups* (Tech. Rep. 11). New Haven, CT: Yale University, School of Organization and Management.

Hackman, J. R., & Oldham, G. R. (1980). *Work redesign.* Reading, MA: Addison-Wesley.

Haire, M., Ghiselli, E. E., & Porter, L. W. (1966). *Managerial thinking.* New York: John Wiley.

Hall, D. T. (1976). *Careers in organization.* Pacific Palisades, CA: Goodyear.

Hall, D. T., & Richter, J. (1984). The baby boom in mid-career. *Career Center Bulletin, 4*(3), 15-16.

Hambrick, D. C., & Mason, P. A. (1984). Upper echelons: The organization as a reflection of its top managers. *Academy of Management Review, 9,* 193-206.

Hamilton, J. W. (1981). Options for small sample sizes in validation: A case for the J-coefficient. *Personnel Psychology, 34,* 805-816.

Hammer, T. H., & Stein, R. N. (1980). Employee ownership: Implications for the organizational distribution of power. *Academy of Management Journal, 23,* 78-100.

Handy, C. (1980). The changing shape of work. *Organizational Dynamics,* pp. 26-34.

Harris-Bowlsbey, J. (1983). *Discover for organizations: Human resource development manual.* Hunt Valley, MD: American College Testing Program.

Haynes, S. G., Levine, S., Scotch, N., Feinheit, M., & Kannel, W. B. (1978). The relationship of psychosocial factors to coronary heart disease in the Framingham study, 1, 2, and 3. *American Journal of Epidemiology, 107,* 362-402.

Hazewinkel, A. (1984). Organizational structure and contingency theory. In P.J.D. Drenth, H. Thierry, P. J. Willems, & C. J. de Wolff (Eds.), *Handbook of work and organizational psychology* (Vol. 2). Chichester: John Wiley.

Heath, A. (1981). *Social mobility.* Glasgow: Fontana.

Hedge, J. W. (1982). *Improving the accuracy of performance evaluations: A comparison of three methods of performance appraisal training.* Unpublished doctoral dissertation, Old Dominion University, Norfolk, VA.

Heller, F. A. (1971). *Managerial decision making: A study of leadership styles and power sharing among senior managers.* London: Tavistock.

Heller, F. A. (1975). *Some problems in multinational and cross cultural research on organizations.* Paper presented at the Thirty-Ninth Annual Meeting of the Academy of Management, Atlanta, GA.

Heller, F. A., Drenth, P.J.D., Koopman, P., & Rus, V. (in press). *Decisions in organizations: A three country longitudinal study.* Berlin: Walter de Gruyter.

Heller, F. A., Drenth, P.J.D., Koopman, P., & Rus, V. (1977). A longitudinal study in participative decision-making. *Human Relations, 30*(7), 567-587.

Heller, F. A., & Wilpert, B. (1981). *Competence and power in managerial decision making.* New York: John Wiley.

Heller, F. A., & Yukl, G. (1969). Participation and managerial decision-making as a function of situational variables. *Organizational Behavior and Human Performance, 4,* 227-241.

Hellriegel, D., & Slocum, J. W., Jr. (1974). Organizational climate: Measures, research and contingencies. *Academy of Management Journal, 17,* 255-280.

Helsinki (1985, August 26-29). *Tenth research conference on subjective probability, utility and decision-making.* Helsinki, Finland.

Heneman, H. G. (1980). Self-assessment: A critical analysis. *Personnel Psychology, 33,* 297-300.

Henry, J. W. (1979). Research in multicultural societies: Implications of cross-cultural methods. *Journal of Cross-Cultural Psychology, 10*(4): 415-434.

Herbst, P. (1974). *Sociotechnical design.* London: Tavistock.

Herriot, P. (1981). Towards an attributional theory of the selection interview. *Journal of Occupational Psychology, 54,* 165-173.

Herriot, P. (1984). *Down from the ivory tower: Graduates and their jobs.* London: John Wiley.

Herriot, P. (1985, May). Give and take in selection. *Personnel Management,* pp. 33-35.

Herriot, P., & Rothwell, C. (1981). Organizational choice and decision theory: Effects of employers' literature and selection interview. *Journal of Occupational Psychology, 54,* 17-31.

Herriot, P., & Rothwell, C. (1983). Expectations and impressions in the graduate selection interview. *Journal of Occupational Psychology, 56,* 303-314.

Herriot, P., & Wingrove, J. (1984). Decision processes in graduate pre-selection. *Journal of Occupational Psychology, 57,* 269-275.

Hertog, F., & van Eynatten, F. (1982). The process of change: Practical paradigms for redesigning jobs. In J. Kelly & C. Clegg (Eds.), *Autonomy and control at the work-place* (pp. 65-104). London: Croom Helm.

Hesketh, B., & Shouksmith, G. (1982). Reasons given for being unemployed and the job search process. *New Zealand Journal of Industrial Relations, 7,* 137-144.

Hickson, D. J., Astley, W. G., Butler, R. J., & Wilson, D. C. (1981). Organizations as power. In L. L. Cummings & B. M. Staw (Eds.), *Research in organizational behavior* (Vol. 3, pp. 151-196). Greenwich, CT: JAI.

Hines, G. J. (1973). Cross cultural differences in two factor motivation theory. *Journal of Applied Psychology, 56*(3), 375-377.

Hines, G. J. (1974). Achievement and motivation levels of immigrants in New Zealand. *Journal of Cross-Cultural Psychology, 3,* 37-45.

Hoc, J. M., & Leplat, J. (1983). Evaluation of different modalities of verbalization in a sorting task. *International Journal of Man-Machine Studies, 18,* 283-306.

Hoebeke, L. (1984). *Linking action research and operations research: The use of O.R. models and techniques in organizational interventions.* Paper presented at the 10th IFORS Conference, Washington, DC.

Hofmeyr, K. B. (1982). *The formulation of a model for the development of potential black managers.* Unpublished doctoral dissertation, University of South Africa, Pretoria.

Hofstede, G. (1980). *Culture's consequences: International differences in work-related values.* Newbury Park, CA: Sage.

Hofstede, G. (1984). *Culture's consequences* (Abr. Ed.). Newbury Park, CA: Sage.

Hollnagel, E. (1983). What we do not know about man-machine systems. *International Journal of Man-Machine Studies, 18,* 135-143.

Hollnagel, E., Pedersen, O. M., & Rasmussen, J. (1981). *Notes on human performance analysis.* Roskilde: Riso National Laboratory.

Hollnagel, E., & Woods, D. D. (1983). Cognitive systems engineering: New wine in new bottles. *International Journal of Man-Machine Studies, 18,* 583-600.

Holmes, T. M., & Rahe, R. H. (1967). The social readjustment rating scale. *Journal of Psychosomatic Research, 11.*

Holzman, W., et al. (1985). *Psychology and health.* Prepared for the World Health Organization IUPS/IAAP/IAACP.

Hoppmann, K., & Stotzel, B. (1981). *Demokratie am arbeitsplatz.* Frankfurt/New York: Campus.

House, J. S. (1981). *Work, stress and social support.* Reading, MA: Addison-Wesley.

House, R. (1971). A path-goal theory of leader effectiveness. *Administrative Science Quarterly, 16,* 321-338.

House, R. J. (1977). A 1976 theory of charismatic leadership. In J. G. Hunt & L. L. Larson (Eds.), *Leadership: The cutting edge.* Carbondale: Southern Illinois University Press.

Howard, A., Shudo, K., & Umeshima, M. (1983). Motivation and values among Japanese and American managers. *Personnel Psychology, 36,* 883-898.

Howell, J. P., & Dorfman, P. W. (1983). Substitutes for leadership: Test of a construct. *Academy of Management Journal, 24,* 714-728.

Hoyos, C. G., Kroeber-Riel, W., Rosenstiel, L. von, & Strumpel, B. (Eds.). (1980). *Grundbegriffe der wirtschaftspsychologie.* Munchen: Kosel.

Hullenaar, R.H.J. van, & Koningsveld, D.B.J. van. (in press). *Een onderzoek naar oorzaken van arbeisongeschiktheid dissertatie.* Nijmegen: Catholic University.

Hull, F., & Hage, J. (1982). Organizing for innovation: Beyond Burns and Stalker's organic type. *Sociology, 16,* 564-577.

Human, L. N. (1981). Some tentative comments on the black manager in a white world. *South African Journal of Business Management, 12,* 103-103.

Human, L. N., & Hofmeyr, K. B. (1984). Black managers in a white world: Strategy formulation. *South African Journal of Business Management, 15,* 96-106.

Hunt, J. A., & Larson, L. L. (Eds.). (1977). *Leadership: The cutting edge.* Carbondale: Southern Illinois University Press.

Hutchinson, V. (1984). Alternative employment contracts. In G. Shouksmith & B. Hesketh (Eds). *Planning and training for work and leisure.* Palmerston North, N.Z.: Massey University.

IDE. (Industrial Democracy in Europe International Research Group). (1981a). Industrial democracy in Europe: Differences and similarities across countries and hierarchies. *Organization Studies, 2*(2), 113-129.

IDE. (1981b). *Industrial democracy in Europe.* Oxford: Clarendon.

Ilgen, D. R., & Feldman, J. M. (1983). Performance appraisal: A process focus. In B. Shaw & L. L. Cummings (Eds.), *Research in organizational behavior* (Vol. 5). Greenwich, CT: JAI.

Ilgen, D. R., Nebeker, D. M., & Pritchard, R. D. (1981). Expectancy theory measures: An empirical comparison in an experimental simulation. *Organizational Behavior and Human Performance, 28*, 189-223.

Imada, A. S., & Hakel, M. D. (1977). Influence of nonverbal communication and rater proximity on impressions and decisions in simulated employment interviews. *Journal of Applied Psychology, 65*, 295-300.

Industrial Psychology Section, Institute of Psychology, the Chinese Academy of Sciences. (1959a). Creative thinking as observed in trial manufacture of die automation mechanism. *Acta Psychology Sinica, 2*, 108-115.

Industrial Psychology Section, Institute of Psychology, the Chinese Academy of Sciences. (1959b). Explorative experiences in promoting invention and creation. *Acta Psychology Sinica, 1*, 36-41.

Inkson, J.H.K., & Gidlow, R. (1981). Waterfront workers as traditional proletarians: A New Zealand study. *Australian and New Zealand Journal of Sociology, 17*, 10-20.

International Labour Office. (1979). *Training systems in Eastern Europe*. Geneva: Author.

International Labour Office. (1980). *Training: Challenge of the 1980s*. Geneva: Author.

International Labour Office. (1981). *Multinationals' training practices and development*. Geneva: Author.

Ishikawa, A. (Ed.). (1981). Workers' participation in management in four Asian countries. *Asian and Oceanian Studies in Industrial Democracy, 1*.

Iwawaki, S., & Lynn, R. (1972). Measuring achievement motivation in Japan and Great Britain. *Journal of Cross-Cultural Psychology, 3*, 219-220.

Ivancevich, J. M. (1982). Subordinates' reactions to performance appraisal interviews: A test of feedback and goal-setting techniques. *Journal of Applied Psychology, 67*, 581-587.

Ivancevich, J. M., & Smith, S. V. (1981). Goal setting interview skills training: Simulated and on-the-job analyses. *Journal of Applied Psychology, 66*, 697-705.

Jablin, F. M. (1982). Formal structural characteristics of organizations and superior-subordinate communication. *Human Communication Research, 8*, 338-347.

Jackson, P. R., Paul, L. J., & Wall, T. D. (1981). Individual differences as moderators of reactions to job characteristics. *Journal of Occupational Psychology, 54*, 1-8.

Jackson, S. E., & Zedeck, S. (1982). Explaining performance variability: Contributions of goal setting, task characteristics, and evaluative contexts. *Journal of Applied Psychology, 67*, 759-768.

Jacobson, S. F., & McGrath, H. M. (Eds.). (1983). *Nurses under stress*. New York: John Wiley.

Jacoby, J., Mazursky, D., Troutman, T., & Kuss, A. (1984). When feedback is ignored: Disutility of outcome feedback. *Journal of Applied Psychology, 69*, 531-545.

Jaggi, B. (1977, July-October). Job satisfaction and leadership style in developing countries: The case of India. *International Journal of Communication Sociology*, pp. 230-236.

James, L. R., & Jones, A. D. (1974). Organizational climate: A review of theory and research. *Psychological Bulletin, 81*, 1096-1112.

James, L. R., & Jones, A. D. (1976). Organizational structure: A review of structural dimensions and their conceptual relationships with individual attitudes and behavior. *Organizational Behavior and Human Performances, 16*, 74-113.

Jansen, P.G.W., Roe, R. A., Viojn, P., & Algera, J. A. (1985). *Validity generalization revisited*. Unpublished manuscript.

Janssens, L., Hoebeke, L., & Michiels, H. (1984). The application of cybernetic principles for the training of operator crews of nuclear power plants. In R. Trappl (Ed.), *Cybernetics and systems research* (Vol. 2, pp. 387-389). Amsterdam: Elsevier.

Japanese Industrial and Vocational Training Association. (1982). Research reports on the actual conditions and practices of small group activities in Japan (in Japanese). *Industrial Training, 28*(10), 22-37 (in Japanese).

Japanese Institute for Group Dynamics. (1983). *Reports on the meaning of working life: An international comparison* (in Japanese) (Tech. Rep.). Fukuoka, Japan: Japanese Institute for Group Dynamics.

Jaques, E. (1970). *Work, creativity and social justice*. New York: International University Press.

Jaques, E. (1983). *A general theory of bureaucracy*. London: Heinemann.

Johannesson, R. E. (1973). Some problems in the measurement of organizational climate. *Organizational Behavior and Human Performance, 10,* 118-144.

Johannson, G.N.M., & Aronsson, G. (1984). Stress reactions in computerized administrative work. *Journal of Occupational Behavior, 5,* 159-181.

Johannson, G.N.M., Aronsson, G., & Lindstrom, B. O. (1978). Social psychological and neuroendocrine stress reactions in highly mechanized work. *Ergonomics, 21,* 583-599.

Johnson, C. S., & Figler, H. E. (1984). Career development and placement services in postsecondary education. In N. C. Gysbers (Ed.), *Designing careers.* San Francisco: Jossey-Bass.

Johnston, H. R. (1976). A new conceptualization of source of organizational climate. *Administrative Science Quarterly, 21,* 95-103.

Jones, A. (1981). Inter-rater reliability in the assessment of group exercises at a UK assessment centre. *Journal of Occupational Psychology, 54,* 79-86.

Jones, A. P., Main, D. S., Butler, M. C., & Johnson, L. A. (1982). Narrative job descriptions as potential sources of job analysis ratings. *Personnel Psychology, 35,* 813-828.

Jones, E. W. (1973, July-August). What it's like to be a black manager. *Harvard Business Review,* pp. 108-116.

Joyce, W. F., & Slocum, J. (1982). Climate discrepancy: Refining the concepts of psychological and organizational climate. *Human Relations, 35,* 951-972.

Joyce, W. F., & Slocum, J. W. (1984). Collective climate: Agreement as a basis for defining aggregate climates in organizations. *Academy of Management Journal, 27*(4), 721-742.

Jyuji, M. (1976). *The behavior science of leadership.* Ann Arbor: University of Michigan Press.

Kahn, R. L. (1981). *Work and health.* New York: John Wiley.

Kahn, R. L., Wolfe, D. M., Snoek, J. E., & Rosenthal, R. A. (1964). *Organizational stress: Studies in role conflict and ambiguity.* New York: John Wiley.

Kahneman, D., Slovic, P., & Tversky, A. (1982). *Judgement under uncertainty: Heuristics and biases.* Cambridge: Cambridge University Press.

Kakar, S. (1971). Authority patterns and subordinate behavior in Indian organizations. *Administrative Science Quarterly, 16*(3), 295-307.

Kao, H.S.R., & Levin, D. A. (1978). *Worker motivation in South East Asia: A study of spinning workers.* Paper presented at the Nineteenth International Congress of Applied Psychology, Munich, Germany.

Kapes, J. T., & Mastie, M. M. (1982). *A counselor's guide to vocational guidance instruments.* Washington, DC: National Vocational Guidance Association.

Karasek, R. A. (1979). Job demands, job decision latitude and mental strain: Implications for job redesign. *Administration Science Quarterly, 24,* 285-308.

Karasek, R. A., Baker, D., Marxer, F., Ahlborn, A., & Theorell, T. (1981). Job decision latitude, job demands and cardiovascular disease: A prospective study of Swedish men. *American Journal of Public Health, 71,* 694-705.

Kasl, S. V. (1984). Stress and health. *Annual Review of Public Health, 5.*

Kavanagh, M. J. (1982). Evaluating performance. In K. M. Rowland & G. R. Ferris (Eds.), *Personnel management.* Boston: Allyn & Bacon.

Kavanagh, M. J., Borman, W. C., Hedge, J. W., & Gould, R. B. (1983). *Job performance measurement in the military: A model, literature review, and directions for research.* Unpublished technical report, Air Force Human Resources Laboratory, Brooks AFB, TX.

Kavanagh, M. J., Hedge, J. W., Ree, M., Earles, J., & DeBiasi, G. (1985, May). *Clarification of some empirical issues in regards to employee acceptability of performance appraisals: Results from five samples.* Paper presented at the annual meeting of the Eastern Academy of Management, Albany, NY.

Kavanagh, M. J., MacKinney, A. C., & Wolins, L. (1971). Issues in managerial performance: Multitrait-multimethod analyses of ratings. *Psychological Bulletin, 75,* 34-49.

Kawharu, I. H. (1968). Urban immigrants and *tangata whenua.* In E. Schwimmer (Ed.), *The Maori people in the nineteen-sixties.* Auckland, New Zealand: Longmans.

Keenan, A. (1976). Effects of the non-verbal behaviour of interviewers on candidates' performance. *Journal of Occupational Psychology, 49,* 171-176.

Keenan, A., & Logue, C. (1985, April). Interviewing women. *Personnel Management,* p. 59.

Keenan, A., & Wedderburn, A.A.I. (1975). Effects of the non-verbal behavior of interviewers on candidates' impressions. *Journal of Occupational Psychology, 48*, 129-132.

Keinan, G., & Friedland, N. (1984). Dilemmas concerning the training of individuals for task performance under stress. *Journal of Human Stress, 10*, 185-190.

Keller, R. T., & Holland, W. E. (1981). Job change: A naturally occurring field experiment. *Human Relations, 34*, 1053-1067.

Kelley, L., & Worthley, R. (1981). The role of culture in comparative management: A cross cultural perspective. *Academy of Management Journal, 24*(1), 164-173.

Kemp, N. J., & Cook, J. D. (1983). Job longevity and growth need strength as joint moderators of the task design-job satisfaction relationship. *Human Relations, 36*, 883-898.

Kenis, I. (1977). A cross cultural study of personality and leadership. *Group Organizational Studies, 2*, 49-60.

Kennedy, C. W., Fossu, J. A., & White, B. J. (1983). An empirical comparison of within-subjects and between-subjects expectancy theory models. *Organizational Behavior and Human Performance, 32*, 124-143.

Kennedy, J. K. (1982). Middle LPC leaders and the contingency model of leadership effectiveness. *Organizational Behavior and Human Performance, 30*, 1-14.

Kenny, D. A. (1979). *Correlation and causality.* New York: John Wiley.

Khandwalla, P. M. (1980). Viable and effective organizational design of firms. *Academy of Management Journal, 16*, 481-495.

Kibler, L. (1980). *Partizipation als lernprozess.* New York: Campus.

Kimberly, J. R., & Evanisko, M. J. (1979). Organizational technology, structure and size. In S. Kerr (Ed.), *Organizational behavior.* Columbus, OH: Grid.

King, C. D., & van de Vall, M. (1978). *Models of industrial democracy.* New York: Mouton.

Kingston, N. (1971). *Selecting managers: A survey of current practice in 200 companies.* London: British Institute of Management.

Kirsch, W., Scholl, W., & Paul, G. (1984). *Mitbestimmung in der unternehmenspraxis.* Meunchen: Planungs- und Organisations-wissenschaftliche Schriften.

Klein, L. (1974). *New forms of work organisations.* London: Tavistock.

Kleinbeck, U., & Schmidt, K. H. (1983). Angewandte motivationspsychologie in der arbeitsgestaltung. *Psychologie und Praxis, Zeitschrift für Arbeits- und Organisationspsychologie, 27*, 13-21.

Klimoski, R., & Rafeli, A. (1983). Inferring personal qualities through handwriting analysis. *Journal of Occupational Psychology, 59*, 191-202.

Komaki, J. L., Collins, R. L., & Penn, P. (1982). The role of performance antecedents and consequences in work motivation. *Journal of Applied Psychology, 67*, 334-340.

Kondo, J. (1981). *A method of decision making: Recommendation of PDPC.* NHK Publishing.

Koomen, C. J. (1985). The entropy of design: A study on the meaning of creativity. *IEEE Transactions on Systems, Man and Cybernetics, 15*(1), 16-30.

Koopman, P., Broekhuysen, J. W., & Meisn, M. O. (1984). Complex decision making at the organizational level. In P.J.D. Drenth, T. Thierry, P. J. Willems, & C. J. de Wolff (Eds.), *Handbook of work and organizational psychology.* Chichester: John Wiley.

Koopman, P., Drenth P., Bus, F., Kruyswijk, A., & Wierdsma, A. (1981). Content, process and effect of participative decision making on the shop floor: Three cases in the Netherlands. *Human Relations, 34*, 657-676.

Koot, W. (1983). Organizational dependence: An exploration of external power relationships of companies. *Organizational Studies, 4*, 19-39.

Korman, A. K. (1966). Construction, initiating structure and organizational criteria: A review. *Personnel Psychology, 19*, 349-362.

Kornadt, H. J., Eckensberger, L. H., & Emminghaus, W. B. (1980). Cross-cultural research on motivation and its contribution to a general theory of motivation. In H. C. Triandis & W. Lonner (Eds.), *Handbook of cross-cultural psychology* (Vol. 3). Boston: Allyn & Bacon.

Kornhauser, A. (1965). *Mental health and the industrial worker.* New York: John Wiley.

Kotthoff, H. (1981). *Betriebsrate und Betriebliche herrschaft: Eine Typologie von Partizipationsmustern im Industriebetrieb.* Frankfurt/M., New York: Campus.

Krus, D. J., & Rysberg, J. A. (1976). Industrial managers and Ach: Comparable and compatible? *Journal of Cross-Cultural Psychology, 7*, 491-496.

Kugihara, N., & Misumi, J. (1984). An experimental study of the effect of leadership type on follower's escaping behavior in a fearful emergency maze-situation. *Japanese Journal of Psychology, 55*, 14-21 (in Japanese with English abstract).

Kuhn, T. S. (1970). *The structure of scientific revolutions* (2nd ed.). Chicago: University of Chicago Press.

Lancaster, A. S., & Berne, R. B. (1981). *Employee sponsored career development programs.* Columbus: Ohio State University, National Center for Research in Vocational Guidance.

Landy, F. J., & Farr, J. L. (1980). Performance rating. *Psychological Bulletin, 87*, 72-107.

Lanfefors, B., & Sundgren, M. (1976). *Information systems architecture.* New York: Petrocelli/Charter.

LaRocco, J. M., House, J. S., & French, J.R.P. (1980). Social support, occupational stress and health. *Journal of Health and Social Behavior, 21*, 202-218.

Larson, J. R., Jr. (1984). The performance feedback process: A preliminary model. *Organizational Behavior and Human Performance, 33*, 42-76.

Larson, L. L., Hunt, J. G., & Osborn, R. N. (1976). The great hi-hi leader behavior myth: A lesson from Occam's razor. *Academy of Management Journal, 19*(4), 628-641.

Lassen, C. (1978). *Adjustment in retirement.* Unpublished thesis, Massey University, New Zealand.

Latané, B.W.K., & Harkins, S. (1979). Many hands make light the work: The causes and consequences of social loafing. *Journal of Personality and Social Psychology, 37*, 822-832.

Latham, G. P., & Saari, L. M. (1982). The importance of union acceptance for productivity improvement through goal setting. *Personnel Psychology, 35*, 781-787.

Latham, G. P., & Saari, L. M. (1984). Do people do what they say? Further studies of the situational interview. *Journal of Applied Psychology, 69*, 569-573.

Latham, G. P., Saari, L. M., Pursell, E. D., & Campion, M. A. (1980). The situational interview. *Journal of Applied Psychology, 65*, 422-427.

Lawler, E. E., III (1976). The multitrait-multimethod approach to measuring managerial job performance. *Journal of Applied Psychology, 51*, 369-381.

Lawler, E. E., III (1982). Increasing worker involvement to enhance organization effectiveness. In P. S. Goodman (Ed.), *Change in organizations.* San Francisco: Jossey-Bass.

Lawler, E. E. (1985). Education, management style, and organizational effectiveness. *Personnel Psychology, 38*, 1-26.

Lawler, E. E., & Mohrman, S. A. (1985). Quality circles after the fad. *Harvard Business Review, 1*, 65-71.

Lawrence, G., Cullen, J., Foster, M., Mayer, H. Wisner, A., & Wolff, C. J. de (1981). *Physical and psychological stress at work.* London: European Foundation for the Improvement of Living and Working Conditions.

Lawrence, P. (1981). The Harvard organization and environment research program. In A. Van de Ven & W. Joyce (Eds.), *Perspectives in organization design and behavior.* New York: John Wiley.

Lawrence, P., & Lorsch, J. (1967). *Organization and environment: Managing differentiation and integration.* Homewood, IL: Irwin.

Lazarus, R. S. (1966). *Psychological stress and the coping process.* New York: McGraw-Hill.

Lazarus, R. S., & Launier, R. (1978). Stress related transaction between person and environment. In M. Pervin & R. Lewis (Eds.), *Perspectives in interactional psychology* (pp. 287-327). New York: Plenum.

Leavitt, H. J., & Bass, B. M. (1964). Organizational psychology. In P. H. Mussen & M. R. Rosenzweig (Eds.), *Annual review of psychology, 15.* Palo Alto, CA: Annual Reviews.

Lee, C., & Schuler, R. S. (1982). A constructive replication and extension of a role and expectancy perception model of participation in decision making. *Journal of Occupational Psychology, 55*, 109-118.

Lee, J. A., & Mendoza, J. L. (1981). A comparison of techniques which test for job differences. *Personnel Psychology, 34*, 731-748.

Lee, R., & Klein, A. R. (1982). Structure of job diagnostic survey for public sector occupations. *Journal of Applied Psychology, 67,* 515-519.

Leibowitz, Z., & Schlossberg, N. (1981). Designing career development programs in organizations: A systems approach. In D. H. Montross & C. J. Shinkman (Eds.), *Career development in the 1980s.* Springfield, IL: Charles C Thomas.

Leplat, J. (1985). *Erreur humaine: Fiabilite humaine dans le Travail.* Paris: Armand Colin.

Leplat, J., & Hoc, J. M. (1981). Subsequent verbalization in the study of cognitive processes. *Ergonomics, 24,* 743-755.

Leppin, A. (1985). Social support: A literature review and research integration. In R. Schwarzer (Ed.), *Stress and social support.* Berlin: Free University of Berlin.

Lester, D., McLaughlin, S., & Nosal, G. (1977). Graphological signs for extraversion. *Perceptual and Motor Skills, 44,* 137-138.

Levinson, D. J., et al. (1974). The psychological development of men in early adulthood and the midlife transition. In D. F. Hicks, A. Thomas, & M. Roff (Eds.), *Life research in psychopathology, 3.* Minneapolis: University of Minneapolis Press.

Levinson, D. J., et al. (1978). *The seasons of man's life.* New York: Ballantine.

Lewis, C. (1980). Investigating the employment interview: A consideration of counselling skills. *Journal of Occupational Psychology, 53,* 111-116.

Lewis, C. (1984, January). What's new in selection. *Personnel Management,* pp. 14-16.

Lewis, C. (1985). *Employee selection.* London: Hutchinson.

Li Jiazhi & Xu Liancang (1957). A preliminary analysis of the cause of accidents in industry. *Acta Psychology Sinica, 2,* 184-193.

Li Ping & Yang Liwei (1986, January). Quantitative analysis and evaluation on management performance and leadership in enterprises. *Economics Daily, 2.*

Likert, R. (1961). *New patterns of management.* New York: McGraw-Hill.

Likert, R. (1967). *The human organization.* New York: McGraw-Hill.

Litwin, G., & Stringer, R. (1968). *Motivation and organizational climate.* Cambridge, MA: Harvard University Press.

Locke, E. A., Frederick, E., & Bobko, P. (1984a). Effect of previously assigned goals on self-set goals and performance. *Journal of Applied Psychology, 69,* 694-699.

Locke, E. A., Frederick, E., & Bobko, P. (1984b). Effect of self-efficacy, goals, and task strategies on task performance. *Journal of Applied Psychology, 69,* 241-251.

Locke, E., & Schweiger, D. (1979). Participation in decision making: One more look. In B. Staw (Ed.), *Research in organizational behavior.* Greenwich, CT: JAI.

Locke, E. A., Shaw, K. N., Saari, L. M., & Latham, G. P. (1981). Goal setting and task performance: 1969-1980. *Psychological Bulletin, 90,* 125-152.

Lockwood, D. (1966). Source of variations in working class images of society. *Sociological Review, 14,* 249-267.

Loewenthal, K. (1982). Handwriting as a guide to character. In D. M. Davey & N. Harris (Eds.), *Judging people: A guide to orthodox and unorthodox methods of assessment.* London: McGraw-Hill.

Lofquist, L. H., & Dawis, R. H. (1969). *Adjustment to work.* London: Appleton.

Lohss, W. E. (1985). *A personal communication.* Phoenix: Arizona Public Service Company.

Lorange, P. (1980). *Corporate planning: An executive viewpoint.* Englewood Cliffs, NJ: Prentice-Hall.

Lowenthal, M. F., Thurnher, M., Chiribooa, D. & Associates (1975). *Four stages of life.* San Francisco: Jossey-Bass.

Lucas, A. (1981). Una aproximacion sociologica al estudio de la satisfaccion en el trabajo en la provincia de Santander. *Revista Internacional de Sociologia, 13,* 65-100.

Lucas, A. (1984). Perspectiva sociologica para el estudio de la democracia industrial. *Revista Internacional de Sociologia,* pp. 263-292.

Lundeberg, M., Goldkuhl, G., & Nilsson, A. (1981). *Information systems development.* Englewood Cliffs, NJ: Prentice-Hall.

Luthans, F., McCaul, H. S., & Dodd, N. G. (1985). Organizational commitment: A comparison of American, Japanese, and Korean employees. *Academy of Management Journal, 28,* 213-219.

Luthans, F., Paul, R., & Baker, D. (1981). An experimental analysis of the impact of contingent reinforcement on salespersons' performance behavior. *Journal of Applied Psychology, 66,* 314-323.

Lynch, B. (1985). Graphology: Towards a hand-picked workforce. *Personnel Management,* pp. 14-18.

Mabe, P. A., & West, S. G. (1982). Validity of self-evaluation of ability: A review and meta-analysis. *Journal of Applied Psychology, 67,* 280-296.

Machungwa, P. D., & Schmitt, N. (1983). Work motivation in a developing country. *Journal of Applied Psychology, 65,* 31-42.

MacKinney, A. C. (1967). The assessment of performance change: An inductive example. *Organizational Behavior and Human Performance, 2,* 56-72.

Mailick, S. (1985). *A management development program for Israel.* Jerusalem: Joint Distribution Committee-Israel.

Mailick, S., & Hoberman, S. (1985). Israel's administrative staff college. *Public Personnel Management Journal, 14,* 65-72.

Malpass, R. S. (1977). Theory and method in cross cultural psychology. *American Psychologist, 32,* 1069-1079.

Mangin, G. (1983). *Die behinderten und ihre beschaftigung.* Eurostat, Luxembourg: Statisches Amt der Europaischen Gemeinschaften.

Mansfield, R. (1984). Formal and informal structure. In M. Gruneberg & T. Wall (Eds.), *Social psychology and organizational behaviour* (pp. 119-147). Chichester: John Wiley.

Marcelissen, F.H.G., Weel, A.H.N., & Winnubst, J.A.M. (1983). Organisatiestress en gezondheid: Tussenstand van een longitudinaal onderzoeksproject. *Tijdschrift voor Sociale Gezondheiszorg, 61,* 811-814.

Marcelissen, F.H.G., Weel, A.H.M., Winnubst, J.A.M., Wolff, C. J. de, & Leufting, A. E. (1984). *Het VOS-PBGO project de eerste twee fasen.* Intern rapport KU Nijmegen.

Marquardt, L. D. (1972). *The rated attribute requirements of job elements in a structural job analysis questionnaire: The position analysis questionnaire.* Unpublished master's thesis, Purdue University.

Marrow, A., Bowers, D., & Seashore, S. (1967). *Management by participation.* New York: Harper & Row.

Marshall, J., & Cooper, C. L. (Eds.). (1981). *Coping with stress at work.* Aldershot: Gower.

Maruyama, M. (1974). Paradigmatology and its application to cross disciplinary, cross professional and cross cultural communication. *Dialectica, 28.*

Matsui, T., & Ohtsuka, Y. (1978). Within-person expectancy theory predictions of supervisory consideration and structure behavior. *Journal of Applied Psychology, 63*(1), 128-131.

Matsui, T., Okada, A., & Mizugchi, R. (1981). Expectancy theory prediction of the goal theory postulate, "The harder the goal, the higher the performance." *Journal of Applied Psychology, 66,* 54-58.

Matteson, M. T. (1978). An alternative approach to using biographical data for predicting job success. *Journal of Occupational Psychology, 51,* 155-162.

Maurice, M., Sorge, A., & Warner, M. (1980). Societal differences in organizing manufacturing units: A comparison of France, West Germany, and Great Britain. *Organization Studies, 1*(1), 59-86.

Mayfield, E. C. (1964). The selection interview: A re-evaluation of published research. *Personnel Psychology, 17,* 239-260.

McCall, M. W., & Lombardo, M. M. (Eds.). (1978). *Leadership: Where else can we go?* Durham, NC: Duke University Press.

McClelland, D. C. (1961). *The achieving society.* New York: Van Nostrand Reinhold.

McClelland, D. C. (1985). *Human motivation.* Glenview, IL: Scott, Foresman.

McConnell, J. J., & Parker, T. C. (1972, March). An assessment center program for multi-organizational use. *Training and Development Journal,* pp. 6-14.

McCormick, E. J., Denrsi, A. S., & Shaw, J. B. (1979). Use of the position analysis questionnaire for establishing the job component validity of tests. *Journal of Applied Psychology, 64,* 51-56.

McCormick, E. J., Jeanneret, P. R., & Mecham, R. C. (1972). A study of job characteristics and job dimensions as based on the Position Analysis Questionnaire (PAQ). *Journal of Applied Psychology, 56,* 347-368.

McGehee, W., & Thayer, P. W. (1961). *Training in business and industry.* New York: John Wiley.

McGovern, T. V., & Tinsley, H.E.A. (1978). Interviewer evaluations of interviewee nonverbal behavior. *Journal of Vocational Behaviour, 13,* 163-171.

McGrath, J. E. (1976). Stress and behavior in organizations. In M. D. Dunnette (Ed.), *Handbook of industrial and organizational psychology.* Chicago: Rand McNally.

McGregor, D. M. (1960). *The human side of enterprise.* New York: McGraw-Hill.

McKelvey, B., & Aldrich, H. (1983). Populations, natural selection and applied organizational science. *Administrative Science Quarterly, 28,* 101-128.

Meade, R. (1967). An experimental study of leadership in India. *Journal of Social Psychology, 72,* 35-43.

Medina, J. (1985a). *Modelo de analisis de sistemas sociotecnicos experimentado en un proceso de cambio y desarrollo organizativo.* El Presente y Futuro de la Psicologia del Trabajo en la Empresa, Madrid, Forum Universidad-Empresa.

Medina, J. (1985b). *Tecnologia, territorio y tiempo como barreras de comunicacion interpersonal en un proceso de cambio organizativo.* El Presente y Futuro de la Psicologia del Trabajo en la Empresa, Madrid, Forum Universidad-Empresa.

Meechan, R. C., & McCormick, E. J. (1969). *The rated attribute requirements of job elements in the Position Analysis Questionnaire: Report Number 1.* West Lafayette, IN: Purdue University, Occupational Research Center.

Melia, J. L., & Peiró, J. M. (1985). *Analisis empirico de un modelo bifactorial de poder e influencia en un proceso de cambio organizativo.* En Presente y Futuro de la Psicologia del Trabajo en la *intervencion psicosocial en las organizaciones.* Barcelona: Universidad Autonoma de Barcelona.

Melikian, I., Greinsberg, A., Gucegloglu, D. M., & Lynn, R. (1971). Achievement motivation in Afghanistan, Brazil, Saudi Arabia and Turkey. *Journal of Social Psychology, 83,* 1183-1184.

Mento, A. J., Cartledge, N. D., & Locke, E. A. (1980). Maryland vs. Michigan vs. Minnesota: Another look at the relationship of expectancy and goal difficulty to task performance. *Organizational Behavior and Human Performance, 25,* 419-440.

Meter, B. (1985). Cyanamid facility steps up worker training, revises procedures, slows output. *Wall Street Journal,* pp. 1, 18.

Meyer, J. P., & Allen, N. J. (1984). Testing the "side-bet theory" of organizational commitment: Some methodological considerations. *Journal of Applied Psychology, 69,* 372-378.

Miller, D. (1981). Toward a new contingency approach: The search for organizational gestalts. *Journal of Management Studies, 18,* 1-26.

Miller, D. (1983). The correlates of entrepreneurship in three types of firms. *Management Science, 29,* 770-791.

Miller, D. C., & Form, W. H. (1951). *Industrial sociology.* New York: Harper.

Miller, D., & Friesen, P. H. (1980). Momentum and revolution in organizational adaptation. *Academy of Management Journal, 23,* 591-614.

Miller, D., & Friesen, P. H. (1982). Structural change and performance: Quantum vs. piecemeal-incremental approach. *Academy of Management Journal, 25,* 867-892.

Miller, J. E. (1984). Culture and the development of everyday social explanation. *Journal of Personality and Social Psychology, 46*(5), 961-968.

Miller, J. V. (1984). Career development programs and practices in the schools. In N. C. Gysbers (Ed.), *Designing careers.* San Francisco: Jossey-Bass.

Miller, R. B. (1973). Development of a taxonomy of human performance: Design of a systems task vocabulary. *JSAS Catalog of Selected Documents in Psychology, 3,* 29-30.

Mills, P. K., & Posner, B. Z. (1982). The relationships among self-supervision, structure, and technology in professional service organizations. *Academy of Management Journal, 25,* 437-443.

Minor, F. J. (1978, August). *Computer applications to support employee career planning.* Paper presented at XIXth International Congress of Applied Psychology, Munich, Federal Republic of Germany.

Minor, F. J. (1984, August). *A computer-based employee development planning system.* Paper presented at the Careers Division, 44th Annual National Meeting of the Academy of Management, Boston.

Minor, F. J. (1986). Computer-based systems to support career development programs. In D. T. Hall (Ed.), *Frontiers of industrial/organizational psychology careers volume.* San Francisco: Jossey-Bass.

Minor, F. J., Myers, R. A., & Super, D. E. (1969). An experimental computer-based educational and occupational orientation system for counseling. *Personnel and Guidance Journal, 47,* 564-569.

Mintzberg, H. (1973). *The nature of managerial work.* New York: Harper & Row.

Mintzberg, H. (1979). *Structuring of organizations: A synthesis of the Research.* Englewood Cliffs, NJ: Prentice-Hall.

Mintzberg, H. (1983). *Structures in five: Designing effective organizations.* Englewood Cliffs, NJ: Prentice-Hall.

Misumi, J. (1984). Decision making in Japanese groups and organizations. In B. Wilpert & A. Sorge (Eds.), *International yearbook of organizational democracy, 2.* Chichester: John Wiley.

Misumi, J. (1985). *The behavioral science of leadership.* Ann Arbor: University of Michigan Press.

Misumi, J. (1986). *Organizational psychology and group dynamics in Japan.* Paper presented at the Department of Psychology, University of Michigan.

Misumi, J., & Arima, Y. (1983). *Hypothesis on change of leadership pressure-P feature by multiplier effect of leadership M behavior.* Technical report, Faculty of Human Sciences. Osaka University (in Japanese).

Misumi, J., & Mannari, N. (1985). A longitudinal study of PM leadership effectiveness. In J. Misumi (Ed.), *The behavioral science of leadership* (pp. 284-290). Ann Arbor: University of Michigan Press.

Misumi, J., & Peterson, M. F. (1985). The performance-maintenance (PM) theory of leadership: Review of a Japanese research program. *Administrative Science Quarterly, 30,* 198-223.

Misumi, J., & Sako, H. (1982). An experimental study of the effect of leadership behavior on followers' behavior of following after the leader in a simulated emergency situation. *Japanese Journal of Experimental Social Psychology, 21*(1), 49-59 (in Japanese).

Misumi, J., & Seki, F. (1971). The effects of achievement motivation on the effectiveness of leadership patterns. *Administrative Science Quarterly, 16,* 51-59.

Mitchell, T. W., & Klimoski, R. J. (1982). Is it rational to be empirical? A test of methods for scoring biographical data. *Journal of Applied Psychology, 67*(4), 411-418.

Moch, M. K. (1980). Job involvement: Internal motivation and employees' integration into networks of work relationships. *Organizational Behavior and Human Performance, 25,* 15-31.

Moch, M. K., Bartunek, J., & Brass, D. J. (1979). Structure, task characteristics and experienced role stress in organizations employing complex technology. *Organizational Behavior and Human Performance, 24,* 258-268.

Moch, M. K., Feather, J. N., & Fitzgibbons, D. (1983). Conceptualizing and measuring the relational structure in organizations. In S. E. Seashore, E. E. Lawler, III, P. H. Mirvis, & C. Cammann (Eds.), *Assessing organizational change: A guide to methods, measures and practices* (pp. 203-229). New York: John Wiley.

Mohr, L. B. (1982). *Explaining organizational behavior.* San Francisco: Jossey-Bass.

Monahan, C. J., & Muchinsky, P. M. (1983). Three decades of personnel selection research: A state of the art analysis and evaluation. *Journal of Occupational Psychology, 56,* 215-225.

Montmollin, M. de (1984). *L'intelligence de la tache, elements d'ergonomie cognitive.* Peter Lang: Berne.

Moore, M. L., & Dutton, P. (1978). Training needs analysis: Review and critique. *Academy of Management Reviews, 3,* 532-545.

Morgan, G. (1980). Paradigms, metaphors and puzzle solving in organization theory. *Administrative Science Quarterly, 25,* 605-622.

Morgan, M. A., Hall, D. T., & Martier, A. (1979, March-April). Career development strategies in industry: Where are we and where should we be? *Personnel, 56,* 13-30.

Mosel, J. N., & Goheen, H. W. (1952). Agreement amongst replies to an employment recommendation questionnaire. *American Psychologist, 7,* 365-366.

Mosel, J. N., & Goheen, H. W. (1959). The employment recommendation questionnaire: III. Validity of different types of references. *Personnel Psychology, 12,* 469-477.

Moses, J. L. (1973). The development of an assessment center for the early identification of supervisory potential. *Personnel Psychology, 26,* 569-580.

Moses, J. L., & Ritchie, R. J. (1976). Supervisory relationships training: A behavioral evaluation of a behavior modeling program. *Personnel Psychology, 29,* 337-344.

Mossholder, K. W., & Arvey, R. D. (1984). Synthetic validity: A conceptual and comparative review. *Journal of Applied Psychology, 69,* 322-333.

MOW Team. (1986). *The meaning of work: An international perspective.* London: Academic Press.

Muchinsky, P. M. (1979). The use of reference report in personnel selection: A review and evaluation. *Journal of Occupational Psychology, 52,* 287-297.

Muchinsky, P. M. (1983). *Psychology applied to work.* Homewood, IL: Dorsey.

Muchungwa, P. D., & Schmitt, N. (1983). Work motivation in a developing country. *Journal of Applied Psychology, 68,* 31-42.

Mulder, M. (1971). Power equalization through participation? *Administrative Science Quarterly,* pp. 31-38.

Mulder, M. (1977). *The daily power game.* Leiden: Martinus Nijhoff.

Mullins, T. W. (1982). Interviewer decisions as a function of applicant race, applicant quality and interviewer prejudice. *Personnel Psychology, 35,* 163-174.

Mumford, E., & Weir, M. (1979). *Computer systems in work design.* London: Associated Business Press.

Murphy, K. R., Garcia, M., Kerkar, S., Martin, C., & Balzer, W. K. (1982). Relationship between observational accuracy and accuracy in evaluating performance. *Journal of Applied Psychology, 67,* 320-325.

Murphy, L. R. (1984). Occupational stress management: A review and appraisal. *Journal of Occupational Psychology, 57,* 1-15.

Myers, R. A. (1978, August). *Career development of army officers with computer support.* Paper presented at XIXth International Congress of Applied Psychology, Federal Republic of Germany.

Myers, R. A., & Cairo, P. C. (Eds.). (1983). Computer assisted counseling. *Counseling Psychologist, 11,* 7-75.

Myrtek, M. (1985). Stress und type-A-verhalten, risikofaktoren der koronaren herzkrankheit? Eine kritische bestandsaufnahme. *Psychotherapie, Psychosomatik, medizinische Psychologie, 35,* 54-61.

Naisbitt, J. (1982). *Megatrends: New directions transforming our lives.* New York: Warner.

Nambudire, C.N.S., & Saiyadain, M. S. (1978). Management problems and practices: India and Nigeria. *Columbia Journal of World Business, 13,* 62-70.

Navarro, M. (1984). Maquinismo, trabajo industrial y nuevas tecnologias. *Revista Internacional de Sociologia,* pp. 13-39.

Navarro, R., Peiró, J. M., Melia, J. L., & Luque, O. (1985). *Caracteristicas de los equipos multiprofesionales de servicios sociales y su relacion con el desempeno de los roles que los integran.* Boletin de Estudios y Documentacion.

Negandhi, A. R. (1983). Cross cultural management research: Trends and future directions. *Journal of International Business Studies, 14*(2), 17-28.

Negandhi, A. R., & Prasad, S. B. (1971). *Comparative management.* New York: Appleton-Century-Crofts.

Neider, L. L. (1980). An experimental field investigation utilizing an expectancy theory view of participation. *Organizational Behavior and Human Performance, 26,* 425-442.

Newman, J. E., & Beehz, T. A. (1979). Personal and organizational strategies for handling job stress: A review of research an opinions. *Personnel Psychology, 32,* 1-43.

Nicholson, P. J., & Goh, S. C. (1983). The relationship of organization structure and interpersonal attitudes to role conflict and ambiguity in different work environments. *Academy of Management Journal, 26*, 148-155.

Nisbett, R., & Ross, L. (1980). *Human inference strategies and shortcomings of social judgment.* Englewood Cliffs, NJ: Prentice-Hall.

Norton, L. A. (1985, February). *The Tenneco story: Executive resources.* Fairfield, IA: Corporate Education Resources.

Norton, L. A. (1985, April). *The northern Telecom story: Executive resources.* Fairfield, IA: Corporate Education Resources.

Nunnally, J. C. (1978). *Psychometric theory* (2nd ed.). New York: McGraw-Hill.

O'Brien, E. O., & Kabanoff, B. (1979). Comparisons of unemployed and employed workers on work values, locus of control and health variables. *Australian Psychology, 14*, 143-154.

O'Brien, G. E., & Dowling, P. (1980). The effects of congruency between perceived and desired job attributes upon job satisfaction. *Journal of Occupational Psychology, 53*, 121-130.

Ochanine, D. (1985). (in memoriam). *L'image operative.* Recueil d'articles, Centre d'Education Permanente de l'Universite de Paris, I.

Office of the Data Protection Registrar. (1985). *The data protection act, 1984: An introduction to the act and guide for data users and computer bureaux, Guideline Number 1.* London: Author.

Oldham, G. R., & Hackman, J. R. (1981). Relationships between organizational structure and employee reactions: Comparing alternative frameworks. *Administrative Science Quarterly, 26*, 66-83.

Oliphant, V. N., & Alexander, E. R. (1982). Reactions to resumes as a function of resume determinateness, applicant characteristics and sex of raters. *Personnel Psychology, 35*, 829-842.

Oliver, N. (1984). An examination of organizational commitment in six workers' cooperatives in Scotland. *Human Relations, 37*, 29-46.

Olson, H. C., Fine, S. A., Myers, D. C., & Jennings, M. C. (1981). The use of functional job analysis in establishing performance standards for heavy equipment operators. *Personnel Psychology, 34*, 351-364.

Onglatco, M.L.U. (1985). *Socio-psychological dynamics of quality circle involvement: Research findings based on Japanese and Filipino samples* (Tech. Rep.). Tokyo: Rikkyo University, Graduate School of Applied Sociology.

Onglatco, M.L.U., & Matsui, T. (1984). Organizational and motivatinal correlates of quality control circle involvement: A case study in a Japanese bank. *Journal of Applied Sociology* (Rikkyo University), *25*, 155-178.

Ono, T. (1960). *Japanese management and ringi systems.* Tokyo: Diamond.

Onodera, T., & Misumi, J. (1984). *An experimental study of M 2-factor hypothesis in leadership PM theory.* Technical report, Faculty of Human Sciences, Osaka University (in Japanese).

O'Reilly, C. A., & Pondy, L. R. (1979). Organizational communication. In S. Kerr (Ed.), *Organizational behavior* (pp. 119-151). Columbus, OH: Grid.

Osburn, H. G., Timmreck, C., & Bigby, D. (1981). Effect of dimensional relevance on accuracy of simulated hiring decisions by employment interviewers. *Journal of Applied Psychology, 66*, 159-165.

Ouchi, W. (1981). *Theory Z.* Reading, MA: Addison-Wesley.

Owens, W. A., Glennon, J. R., & Allbright, L. E. (1966). *A catalog of life history items.* Greensboro, NC: Richardson Foundation.

Ozgediz, S. (1983). *Managing the public service in developing countries: Issues and prospects* (Staff Working Paper No. 583, Management and Development Subseries No. 10). Washington, DC: World Bank. .

Padmos, P., Pot, F. D., Vos, J. J., & Mol, E. C. de Vries-de. (1984). *Gezondheid en welbevingen bij het werken met beeldschermen* [Health and well-being in working with VDU's]. Leiden: NIPG/IZF/TNO.

Parisi, D. N. (1985, April). *A personal communication.* Merck & Co., Inc.

Parker, D. F., & Decoths, T. A. (1983). Organizational determinants of job stress. *Organizational Behavior and Human Performance, 32*, 160-177.

Parker, S. R., & Smith, M. A. (1976). Work and leisure. In R. Dubin (Ed.), *Handbook of work organization and society*. Chicago: Rand McNally.

Parsons, C. K., & Linden, R. C. (1984). Interviewer perceptions of applicant qualifications: A multivariate field study of demographic characteristics and nonverbal cues. *Journal of Applied Psychology, 69*, 557-568.

Pasmore, W., Francis, C., & Haldeman, J. (1982). A North American reflection on empirical studies of the seventies. *Human Relations, 2*, 999-1022.

Pateman, M. (1970). *Participation and democratic theory*. London: Cambridge University Press.

Patrick, J., & Moore, A. K. (1985). Development and reliability of a job analysis technique. *Journal of Occupational Psychology, 58*, 149-158.

Paul, S. (1983). *Training for public administration in developing countries: A review* (Staff Working Paper No. 584). Washington, DC: World Bank.

Paulson, S. K. (1980). Organizational size, technology, and structure: Replication of a study of social service agencies among small retail firms. *Academy of Management Journal, 23*, 341-347.

Pavett, C. M., & Lau, A. W. (1983). Managerial work: The influence of hierarchical level and functional specialty. *Academy of Management Journal, 26*, 170-177.

Paxy, A., & Zeira, Y. (1983). Training parent-country professionals in host-country organizations. *Academy of Management Review, 8*, 262-272.

Payne, J. W. (1982). *Contingent decision behavior. Psychological Bulletin, 92*, 382-402.

Payne, R. L., & Mansfield, R. (1973). Relationships of perceptions of organizational climate to organizational structure, context and hierarchical position. *Administrative Science Quarterly, 18*, 515-526.

Payne, R., & Pheysey, D. (1973). Organization structure and sociometric nominations amongst line managers in three contrasted organizations. *European Journal of Social Psychology, 1*, 261-284.

Payne, R. L., & Pugh, D. D. (1976). Organizational structure and climate. In M. D. Dunnette (Ed.), *Handbook of industrial and organizational psychology* (pp. 1125-1172). Chicago: Rand McNally.

Pearce, J. L. (1983). Job attitude and motivation differences between volunteers and employees from comparable organizations. *Journal of Applied Psychology, 68*, 646-652.

Pearce, II, J. A., & David, F. R. (1983). A social network approach to organizational design-performance. *Academy of Management Review, 8*, 436-444.

Pearlman, K. (1980). Job families: A review and discussion of their implications for personnel selection. *Psychological Bulletin, 87*, 1-28.

Pearlman, K., Schmidt, F. L., & Hunter, J. E. (1980). Validity generalization results for tests used to predict job proficiency and training success in clerical occupations. *Journal of Applied Psychology, 65*, 373-406.

Peiró, J. M. (1983-1984). *Psicologia de las organizaciones* (2 Vols.). Madrid: Universidad Nacional de Educacion a Distancia.

Peiró, J. M. (1984). Historical perspectives of work and organizational psychology in Spain. In H. Carpintero & J. M. Peiró (Eds.), *Psychology in its historical context*, pp. 267-282.

Peiró, J. M. (1985). Psicologia organizacional cognitiva: Nuevas aproximaciones al estudio de la conducta organizacional. In J. Mayor (Ed.), *Actividad humana y procesos cognitivos*. Madrid: Alhambra Universidad.

Pen R. (1980). Thirty years of industrial psychology in China. *Acta psychology sinica, I*, 16-21.

Perrow, C. (1984). *Normal accidents*. New York: Basic Books.

Peters, T. J., & Waterman, R. H. (1982). *In search of excellence*. New York: Harper & Row.

Pettigrew, A. M. (1973). *The politics of organizational decision making*. London: Tavistock.

Pezeshkpur, C. (1978). Challenges to management in the Arab world. *Business Horizons, 21*, 47-55.

Phillips, J. S. (1984). The accuracy of leadership ratings: A cognitive categorization perspective. *Organizational Behavior and Human Performance, 33*, 125-138.

Phillips, J. S., & Lord, R. G. (1980). Determinants of intrinsic motivation: Locus of control and competence information as components of Deci's cognitive evaluation theory. *Journal of Applied Psychology, 65*, 211-218.

Pierce, J. L., Dunham, R. B., & Cummings, L. L. (1984). Source of environmental structuring and participant responses. *Organizational Behavior and Human Performance, 33,* 214-242.

Pinder, C. C., & Bourgeois, V. W. (1982). Controlling tropes in administrative science. *Administrative Science Quarterly, 27,* 641-652.

Pirikahu, N., Macpherson, J., Gibbs, L., Kahu, S., & Ponter, B. (1984). The Patea experience. In G. Shouksmith & B. Hesketh (Eds.), *Planning and training for work and leisure.* Palmerston North, New Zealand: Massey University.

Pitz, G., & Sachs, N. (1984). Judgment and decision: Theory and application. *Annual Review of Psychology, 35,* 139-163.

Podsakoff, P. M. (1982). Determinants of a supervisor's use of rewards and punishment: A literature review and suggestions for further research. *Organizational Behavior & Human Performance, 29,* 58-83.

Podsakoff, P. M., Todor, W. D., & Skov, R. (1982). Effects of leader contingent and noncontingent reward and punishment behaviors on subordinate performance and satisfaction. *Academy of Management Journal, 25,* 810-821.

Pokorney, J. J., Gilmore, D. C., & Beehr, T. A. (1980). Job diagnostic survey dimensions: Moderating effect on growth needs and correspondence with dimensions of job rating form. *Organizational Behavior & Human Performance, 26,* 222-237.

Pontes, I. F. (1983, February 26). Training and development: A critical appraisal. *Economic Times Supplement.*

Poortinga, Y. H. (Ed). (1977). *Basic problems in cross cultural psychology.* Lisse: Swets & Zeitlinger.

Popper, K. (1959). *Logic of scientific discourse.* London: Hutchinson.

Porac, J. F., & Meindl, J. (1982). Undermining overjustification: Inducing intrinsic and extrinsic task representations. *Organizational Behavior and Human Performance, 29,* 208-226.

Porter, L. W. (1966). Personnel management. In P. R. Farnsworth, O. McNemar, & Q. McNemar (Eds.), *Annual review of psychology* (Vol. 17). Palo Alto, CA: Annual Reviews.

Porter, L. W., & Lawler, E. E. (1965). Properties of organization structure in relation to job attitudes and job behavior. *Psychological Bulletin, 64,* 23-51.

Powell, G. N. (1984). Effects of job attributes and recruiting practices on applicant decisions: A comparison. *Personnel Psychology, 37,* 721-732.

Prediger, D. J. (1981). Getting "ideas" out of the DOT and into vocational guidance. *Vocational Guidance Quarterly, 29,* 293-305.

Prediger, D. J. (1982). Dimensions underlying Holland's hexagon: Missing link between interests and occupations? *Journal of Vocational Behavior, 21,* 259-287.

Price, R. H., & Bronfman, L. (1984). *Bibliography; unemployment and occupational stress: Risk factors and intervention programs.* University of Michigan.

Price, V. A. (1982). *Type A behavior pattern.* New York: Academic Press.

Prida, B. (1984). El enfoque sociotecnico: Una nueva concepcion para la organizacion del trabajo. *Revista Internacional de Sociologia,* pp. 131-157.

Pritchard, R. D., & Karasick, B. W. (1973). The effects of organizational climate on managerial job performance and job satisfaction. *Organizational Behavior and Human Performance, 9,* 126-146.

Prokopenko, J., & White, J. (Eds.). (1981). *Modular programme for supervisory development.* Geneva: International Labour Office.

Pugh, D. S. (1981). The Aston program perspective. The Aston Program of Research: Retrospect and Prospect. In A. H. Van de Ven & W. F. Joyce (Eds.), *Perspectives on organization design and behavior.* New York: John Wiley.

Puyuelo, L. (1986, Abril-Junio 25). Investigacion y desarrollo. *Revista Fomento de la Comunicacion e Investigacion.*

Quaglieri, P. L. (1982). A note on variations in recruiting information obtained through different sources. *Journal of Occupational Psychology, 55,* 53-55.

Racionero, L. (1985). *La Mediterrania i els barbars del nord.* Barcelona: Editorial Laia.

Rafaeli, A., & Klimoski, R. J. (1983). Predicting sales success through handwriting analysis: An evaluation of the effects of training and handwriting sample content. *Journal of Applied Psychology, 68,* 212-217.

Ranson, S., Hinings, B., & Greenwood, R. (1986). The structuring of organizational structures. *Administrative Science Quarterly, 25,* 1-17.

Rasmussen, J. (1985). The role of hierarchical knowledge representation in decision making and systems management. *IEEE Transactions on Systems, Man and Cybernetics, 15,* 234-243.

Rasmussen, J., & Rouse, W. B. (1981). *Human detection and diagnosis of system failures.* New York: Plenum.

Rasmussen, K. G. (1984). Nonverbal behavior, verbal behavior, resume credentials and selection interview outcomes. *Journal of Applied Psychology, 69,* 551-556.

Reiche, H.M.J.K.I. (1981). *Stress aan het werk.* Lisse: Swets & Zeitlinger.

Reilly, R. R., & Chao, G. T. (1982). Validity and fairness of some alternative employee selection procedures. *Personnel Psychology, 35,* 1-62.

Rice, G. E. (1980). On cultural schemata. *American Ethnologist, 7*(1), 153-171.

Rice, R. W. (1978). Construct validity of the least preferred coworker score. *Psychological Bulletin, 85,* 1199-1237.

Rice, R. W. (1981). Leader LPC and follower satisfaction: A review. *Organizational Behavior and Human Performance, 28,* 1-25.

Ritchie, J. E. (1973). *The employment of minority groups in New Zealand society.* Wellington, N.Z.: Hicks Smith.

Redding, S. G. (1977). Some perceptions of psychological needs among managers in South East Asia. In Y. H. Poortinga (Ed.), *Basic problems in cross cultural psychology* (pp. 333-343). Amsterdam: Swets & Zeitlinger.

Roberts, K. H. (1970). Looking at an elephant: An evaluation of cross cultural research related to organizations. *Psychological Bulletin, 74*(5), 327-350.

Roberts, K. H., & Boyacigiller, N. (1982). *Issues in cross national management research: The state of the art.* Paper delivered at the National Meeting of the Academy of Management, New York, NY.

Roberts, K. H., & Boyacigiller, N. (1983). Research review: A survey of cross-national organizational researchers: Their views and opinions. *Organization Studies, 4,* 375-386.

Roberts, K. H., Boyacigiller, N., & Snow, C. C. (Eds.). (1973). A symposium: Cross national organizational Research. *Industrial Relations, 12*(2), 137-247.

Roberts, K. H., & Glick, W. (1981). The job characteristics approach to task design: A critical review. *Journal of Applied Psychology, 66,* 193-217.

Roberts, N. C. (1985). Transforming leadership: A process of collective action. *Human Relations, 38,* 1023-1046.

Robertson, I. T., & Kandola, R. S. (1982). Work sample tests: Validity, adverse impact and applicant reaction. *Journal of Occupational Psychology, 55,* 171-184.

Robey, D., & Markus, M. L. (1984). Rituals in information system design. *MIS Quarterly,* pp. 5-15.

Robinson, D. D. (1981). Content-oriented personnel selection in a small business setting. *Personnel Psychology, 34,* 77-87.

Roe, R. A. (1984, September 6). *Advances in performance modeling: The case of validity generalization.* Paper presented at the Symposium "Advances in Testing," International Test Commission, Acapulco, Mexico.

Roe, R. A. (1985, April 18-20). *"Acting systems design": An alternative approach to the design of interactive computer systems.* Paper presented at the workshop on Changing Work Structures and Work Meaning in the Context of New Technologies, Bad Homburg, FRG.

Rohmart, W., & Landau, K. (1979). *Das arbeitswissenschaftliche erhebungs verfahren zur tatigkeitsanalyse (AET).* Bern-Stuttgart-Wien: Verlag Hans Huber, English edition published 1983 by Taylor & Francis, London.

Ronan, W. W., & Prien, E. P. (1971). *Perspectives on the measurement of human performance.* New York: Appleton-Century-Crofts.

Ronen, S. (1986). *Comparative and multinational management.* New York: John Wiley.

Ronen, S. (1979). Cross national study of employees work goals. *International Review of Applied Psychology, 28*(11), 1-12.

Ronen, S., & Kraut, A. I. (1977). Similarities among countries based on employee work values and attitudes. *Columbia Journal of World Business, 12*(2), 89-96.

Ronen, S., Kraut, A. I., & Punnett, B. J. (1982). *National or culture: The appropriate unit of analysis in cross cultural research*. Paper presented at Northeast meeting of the Academy of International Business, NY.

Ronen, S., & Shenkar, O. (1985). Clustering countries on attitudinal dimensions: A review and synthesis. *Academy of Management Review, 10*(3), 435-454.

Rosenberg, R. D., & Rosenstein, E. (1980). Participation and productivity: An empirical study. *Industrial and Labor Relations Review, 33*(3), 355-367.

Rosenthal, D., & Lines, R. (1972). Handwriting as a correlate of extraversion. *Journal of Personality Assessment, 42*, 45-48.

Rosenthal, R., & Jacobson, L. (1968). *Pygmalion in the classroom: Teacher expectation and pupils' intellectual development*. New York: Holt, Rinehart & Winston.

Rosenthal, R., & Rubin, D. B. (1978). Interpersonal expectancy effects: The first 345 studies. *Behavioral and Brain Studies, 3*, 377-415.

Ross, J. E., & Ross, W. C. (1982). *Japanese quality control circles and productivity*. Virginia: Boston Publishing Company.

Rothstein, M., & Jackson, D. N. (1980). Decision-making in the employment interview: An empirical approach. *Journal of Applied Psychology, 65*, 271-283.

Ruddy, T. M. (1985). *Performance appraisal: A review of four training methods*. Unpublished Masters' thesis, Rensselaer Polytechnic Institute, Troy, NY.

Rull, A. (1980). El Tamano de las empresas en Andalucia y su comparacion con el resto del pais. *Revista Internacional de Sociologia, 33*, 75-100.

Rushton, J. P., & Sorrentino, R. M. (Eds.). (1981). *Altruism and helping behavior*. Hillsdale, NJ: Erlbaum.

Rynes, S. L., Heneman, H.G.I., & Schwab, D. P. (1980). Individual reactions to organizational recruiting: A review. *Personnel Psychology, 33*, 529-542.

Rynes, S. L., & Miller, H. E. (1983). Recruiter and job influences on candidates for employment. *Journal of Applied Psychology, 68*, 147-154.

Saari, L. M., & Latham, G. P. (1982). Employee reactions to continuous and variable ratio reinforcement schedules involving a monetary incentive. *Journal of Applied Psychology, 67*, 506-508.

Sackett, P. R., Cornelius, E. T., & Carron, T. J. (1981). A comparison of global judgment vs. task oriented approaches to job classification. *Personnel Psychology, 34*, 791-804.

Saeki, Y. (1981). *The theory of decision-making: The invitation to theories of social decision-making*. Tokyo: Tokyo University Press.

Salancik, G. R. (1984). On priming, consistency, and other effects in job attitude assessment: With a note on current research. *Journal of Management, 10*, 250-254.

Salancik, G. R., & Pfeffer, J. (1978). A social information processing approach to job attitudes and task design. *Administrative Science Quarterly, 23*, 224-253.

Salomon, G. (1981). Self-fulfilling and self-sustaining prophecies and the behaviors that realize them. *American Psychologist, 36*, 1452-1453.

Salvendy, G. R., & Smith, M. J. (1981). *Machine pacing and occupational stress*. London: Taylor & Francis.

Saskin, M., & Fulmer, R. M. (1986). Toward an organizational leadership theory. In J. G. Hunt, R. Baliga, H. P. Dachler, & C. A. Schriesheim (Eds.), *Emerging leadership vistas*. Elmsford, NY: Pergamon.

Savage. A. (1985). Biographische Fragebogen als Methode der Personalauswahl. In H. Schuler and W. Stehle (Eds.), *Beitrage zur Organisationpsychologie, Band 2*. Stuttgart: Verlag für Angewandte Psychologie.

Scapin, D. L. (1982). *Conception des langages de commande en langue naturelle restreinte*. These de doctorat de psychologie, Universite de Paris V.

Schank, R., & Abeleson, R. (1977). *Scripts, plans, goals and understanding: An inquiry into human knowledge structures*. Hillsdale, NJ: Lawrence Erlbaum.

Schmidt, F. L., Gast-Rosenberg, I., & Hunter, J. E. (1980). Validity generalization results for computer programmers. *Journal of Applied Psychology, 65*, 643-661.

Schmidt, F. L., & Hunter, J. E. (1981). Employment testing: Old theories and new research findings. *American Psychologist, 36*, 1128-1137.

Schmidt, F. L., Hunter, J. E., & Pearlman, K. (1981). Task differences of aptitude test validity in selection: A red herring. *Journal of Applied Psychology, 66,* 166-185.

Schmidt, K. H., & Kleinbeck, U. (1983). Beziehungen zwischen intrinsischen und extrinsischen Anreizfaktoren der Arbeitsmotivation und Arbeitszufriedenheit (die Zuordnung eines Gultigkeitsbereiches für ein Arbeitsmotivationsmodell). *Psychologie und Praxis, Zeitschrift für Arbeits- und Organisationspsychologie, 27,* 79-86.

Schmidt, K. H., Kleinbeck, U., & Rohmert, W. (1981). Die Wirkung von Merkmalen der Arbeitssituation und Personlichkeitsvariabelen auf die Arbeitszufriedenheit und andere motivationsbezogene Einstellungsvariabelen. *Zeitschrift für Experimentelle und Angewandte Psychologie, 28,* 465-485.

Schmidt, K. H., Kleinbeck, U., & Rutenfranz, J. (1981). Arbeitspsychologische Effekte von Anderungen des Arbeitsinhaltes bei Montagetätigkeiten. *Zeitschrift für Arbeitswissenschaft, 35,* 162-167.

Schmidt, K. H., Schweisfurth, W., Kleinbeck, U., & Rutenfranz, J. (1981). Einige arbeitspsychologische Ergebnisse zur Wirkung von Arbeitsinhaltsveranderungen bei Teilefertigungstätigkeiten. *Zeitschrift für Arbeitswissenschaft, 35,* 101-107.

Schmitt, N. (1976). Social and situational determinants of interview decisions: Implications for the employment interview. *Personnel Psychology, 29,* 79-101.

Schmitt, N., & Fine, S. A. (1983). Inter-rater reliability of judgments of functional levels and skill requirements of jobs based on written task statements. *Journal of Occupational Psychology, 56,* 121-127.

Schmitt, N., Gooding, R. Z., Noe, R. A., & Kirsch, M. (1984a). Meta-analyses of validity studies published between 1964 and 1982 and the investigation of study characteristics. *Personnel Psychology, 37,* 407-422.

Schmitt, N., Gooding, R. Z., Noe, R. A., & Kirsch, M. (1984b). Meta-analyses of validity studies published between 1964 and 1982 and the investigation of study characteristics. *Personnel Psychology, 37,* 407-422.

Schmitt, N., Noe, R. A., Meritt, R., & Fitzgerald, M. P. (1984). Validity of assessment center ratings for the prediction of performance ratings and school climate of school administrators. *Journal of Applied Psychology, 69,* 207-213.

Schneider, B. (1975). Organizational climates: An essay. *Personnel Psychology, 28,* 447-479.

Schneider, B., & Reichers, A. E. (1983). On the etiology of climates. *Personnel Psychology, 36,* 19-36.

Schollhammer, H. (1969). The comparative management theory jungle. *Academy of Management Journal, 12,* 81-97.

Schön, D. (1983). *The reflective practitioner.* New York: Basic Books.

Schoonhoven, C. B. (1981). Problems with contingency theory: Testing assumptions hidden within the language of contingency "theory." *Administrative Science Quarterly, 26,* 349-377.

Schreyögg, G. (1980). Contingency and choice in organization theory. *Organization Studies, 1,* 305-326.

Schriesheim, C. A., & Kerr, S. (1977). Theories and measures of leadership: A critical appraisal of current and future directors. In J. G. Hunt & L. L. Larson (Eds.), *Leadership: The cutting edge.* Carbondale, IL: Southern Illinois University Press.

Schriesheim, C. A., Kinicki, A. J., & Schriesheim, J. F. (1979). The effect of leniency on leader behavior descriptions. *Organizational Behavior and Human Performance, 23,* 1-29.

Schriesheim, J. F., & Schriesheim, C. A. (1980). A test of the path-goal theory of leadership and some suggested directions for future research. *Personnel Psychology, 33,* 349-370.

Schuler, R. S. (1980). Definition of conceptualization of stress in organizations. *Organizational Behavior and Human Performance, 25,* 184-215.

Schuler, R. S. (1985). Integrative transactional process model of coping with stress in organizations. In A. Beer & R. S. Bhagat (Eds.), *Human stress and cognition.* New York: John Wiley.

Schuler, R. S. (1980). A role and expectancy perception model of participation in decision making. *Academy of Management Journal, 23,* 331-340.

Schultze-Scharnhorster, E. (1985). *Partizipationspotential am Arbeitsplatz.* Frankfurt/M.: Peter Lang.

Schwarzer, R. (Ed.). (1985). *Stress and social support*. Berlin: Free University of Berlin, Department of Psychology, Educational Psychology.

Seashore, S. E., Lawler, E. E., III, Mirvis, P. H., & Cammann, C. (Eds.). (1983). *Assessing organizational change: A guide to methods, measures and practices*. New York: John Wiley.

Sebillote, S. (1982). *Les processus de diagnostic au cours du deroulement de la grossesse*. These de doctorat de psychologie, Universite de Paris V.

Segall, O. (1984). More than we need to know about culture but are afraid not to ask. *Journal of Cross-Cultural Psychology, 15*(2), 151-162.

Sekaran, U. (1983). Methodological and analytic considerations in cross national research. *Journal of International Business Studies, 14*(2), 61-73.

Sekaran, U. (1985). The path to mental health: An exploratory study of husbands and wives in dual careers. *Journal of Occupational Psychology, 58*, 129-137.

Sekaran, U., & Martin, H. J. (1982). An examination of the psychometric properties of some commonly researched individual differences, job and organizational variables in two cultures. *Journal of International Business Studies, 13*(1), 51-65.

Sekimoto, M. (1985, April 20). *Salient changes in Japanese workers' organizational commitment* (in Japanese). Article on the Nihon Keizai Shinbun.

Selles, G., Gerrichhauzen, J. en, & Wolff, C. J. de (1985). *De mid career crisis*. Deventer: Van Loghum Slaterus.

Selye, H. (1936). A syndrome produced by divers nocuous agents. *Nature, 138*, 32.

Selye, H. (1976). *The stress of life* (rev. ed.). New York: McGraw-Hill.

Senach, B. (1984). *Assistance automatisee a la resolution d'incident dans les systemes dynamiques*. These doctorat de psychologie, Universite de Paris V.

Shackleton, V. J., & Fletcher, C. (1984). *Individual differences: Theories and applications*. London: Methuen.

Shapira, Z., & Dunbar, R.L.M. (1980). Testing Mintzberg's managerial roles classification using an in-basket simulation. *Journal of Applied Psychology, 65*, 87-95.

Shapira, Z., & Shirom, A. (1980). New issues in the use of behaviorally anchored rating scales: Level of analysis, the effects of incident frequency, and external validation. *Journal of Applied Psychology, 65*, 517-523.

Sheibar, P. (1979, January). A simple selection system called job match. *Personnel Journal, 53*, 26-29.

Sheridan, J. E., Vredenburgh, D. J., & Abelson, M. A. (1984). Contextual model of leadership influence in hospital units. *Academy of Management Journal, 27*, 57-78.

Sherman, J. D., & Smith, H. L. (1984). The influence of organizational structure on intrinsic versus extrinsic motivation. *Academy of Management Journal, 27*, 877-885.

Shiflett, S., & Cohen, S. L. (1982). The shifting salience of valence and instrumentality in the prediction of perceived effort, satisfaction and turnover. *Motivation and Emotion, 6*, 65-77.

Shima, H. (1968). The effects of the leader's modes of interpersonal cognition upon the enforcement of the group norm. *Japanese Journal of Educational & Social Psychology, 8*(1), 87-103 (in Japanese).

Shima, H. (1972). The effects of the cognitive structure of the leader upon the performance of the group. *Japanese Journal of Experimental Social Psychology, 11*(2), 99-108 (in Japanese).

Shirakashi, S. (1968). An experimental study of leadership effectiveness in a small group: A test of the contingency model. *Japanese Journal of Educational & Social Psychology, 8*(2), 249-267.

Shneiderman, B. (1980). *Software psychology, human factors in computer and information systems*. Cambridge: Winthrop.

Shouksmith, G. (1985). *Stress and life in New Zealand*. Palmerston North, N.Z.: Dunmore.

Shouksmith, G., & Hesketh, B. (1986). Changing horses in mid stream: Job and life satisfactions for veterinarians. *New Zealand Veterinary Journal*.

Shrauger, J. S., & Osberg, T. M. (1981). The relative accuracy of self-predictions and judgments by others in psychological assessment. *Psychological Bulletin, 90*, 322-351.

Silverman, D. (1970). *The theory of organizations: A sociological framework*. London: Heinemann.

Sinha, J.B.P. (1976). The authoritarian leadership: A style of effective management. *Indian Journal of Industrial Relations, 2*, 381-389.

Smith, B. E., & Thomas, J. M. (1972). Cross cultural attitudes among managers: A case study. *Sloan Management Review, 13*, 34-51.

Smith, J. E., & Hakel, M. D. (1979). Convergence among data sources, response bias, and reliability and validity of a structured job analysis questionnaire. *Personnel Psychology, 32*, 677-692.

Smith, P. B., Petersen, M. F., & Tayeb, M. (1986). *The validity of Japanese measures of leader style in Western organizations.* Unpublished manuscript, School of Social Sciences, University of Sussex, Brighton, England:

Smith, P. B., Tayeb, M., Peterson, M. F., & Bod, M. (1986). *On the generality of leadership style measures.* Unpublished manuscript, University of Sussex, School of Social Sciences, Brighton, England.

Sneath, F., Thakur, M., & Medjuck, B. (1976). *Testing people at work.* London: Institute of Personnel Management.

Snyder, M. (1974). Self-monitoring of expressive behavior. *Journal of Personality and Social Psychology, 30*, 526-537.

Snyder, M., & Simpson, J. A. (1984). Self-monitoring and dating relationships. *Journal of Personality and Social Psychology, 47*, 1281-1291.

Social Trends. (1977). HMSO. In B. C. Fletcher & R. L. Payne (Eds.). Stress and work, a review and theoretical framework (special issue). *Personnel Review, 9*, 19-29.

Sokolowska, J. (1984). Determinants and consequences of discrepancy between desired and realistic goals in an industrial setting. *Polish Psychological Bulletin, 15*(2), 127-134.

Sole, C., Sala, S., & Roma, J. (1986). *Curs de commandaments de LA CAIXA.* Barcelona: Escola de Formacio de LA CAIXA.

Sonnenfeld, J. A. (1984). *Managing career systems: Channeling the flow of executive careers.* Homewood, IL: Irwin.

Sorcher, M., & Spence, R. (1982). The interface project: Behavior modeling as social technology in South Africa. *Personnel Psychology, 35*, 557-581.

Sparrow, J., Patrick, J., Spurgeon, P., & Barwell, F. (1982). The use of job component analysis and related aptitudes in personnel selection. *Journal of Occupational Psychology, 55*, 157-166.

Sperandio, J. C. (1975). Complements a l'etude de la memoire operationelle. *Le Travial Humain, 38*(1), 41-62.

Sperandio, J. C. (1980). *La psychologie en ergonomie.* P.U.F., Paris.

Sperandio, J. C. (1984). Synthese des recherches de psychologie experimentale sur la lisibilite des programmes informatiques. In *Approaches quantitatives en genie logiciel.* Seminaire AFCET Informatique, Sophia-Antipolis.

Sperandio, J. C., & Bouju, F. (1983). L'exploration visuelle de donnees numeriques presentees sur ecran cathodique. *Le Travail Humain, 46*(1), 49-63.

Sperandio, J. C., & Letang, C. (1986). *Simulation experimentale de la synthese vocale en dialogues grand public.* Rapport IRAP/CNRS (GRECO n'39), Universite de Paris V.

Spurgeon, P., Patrick, J., & Michael, I. (1984). *Training and selection of computer personnel.* Sheffield: Manpower Services Commission.

Srivasta, B. N. (1984). Hierarchical level of managers and their perceptions of actual and desired influence. *Journal of Social Psychology, 112*, 237-244.

Staff. (1983). The retraining challenge: A call to action. *Training*, pp. 68-69.

Stafford, E. M., Jackson, P. R., & Banks, M. H. (1984). An empirical study of occupational families in the youth labour market. *Journal of Occupational Psychology, 57*, 141-155.

Starbuck, W. H. (1981). A trip to view the elephants and rattlesnakes in the Garden of Aston. In A. H. Van de Ven & W. F. Joyce (Eds.), *Perspectives on organization design and behavior.* New York: John Wiley.

Staw, B. M. (1984). Organizational behavior: A review and reformulation of the field outcome variables. In *Annual review of psychology* (pp. 627-666). Palo Alto, CA: Annual Reviews Inc.

Stein, B. A., & Kanter, R. M. (1980). Experiencing organizational structure. In C. P. Alderfer & C. L. Cooper (Eds.), *Advances in experiential social processes* (Vol. 2). New York: John Wiley.

Stone, D. L., & Stone, E. F. (1985). The effects of feedback consistency and feedback favorability on self-perceived task competence and perceived feedback accuracy. *Organizational Behavior and Human Decision Processes, 36*, 167-185.

Stone, E. F. (1984). Misperceiving and/or misrepresenting the facts: A reply to Salancik. *Journal of Management, 10*, 255-258.

Stone, E. F., & Gueutal, H. G. (1984). On the premature death of need-satisfaction models: An investigation of Salancik and Pfeffer's view on priming and consistency artifacts. *Journal of Management, 10*, 237-249.

Stor, T. (1985). *Spanningen bij personeelsfunktionarissen in verschillende organisatie-typen.* Doctoraal scriptie, Nijmegen.

Storey, W. D. (1981). Strategic personal career management. In D. H. Montross & C. J. Shinkman (Eds.), *Career development in the 1980s.* Springfield, IL: Charles C Thomas.

Stouffer, S. A. (1949). *The American soldier.* New York: John Wiley.

Strack, H. C. (1984). *Die Beteiligung von Mitarbeitern an Gewinn und Kapital.* Frankfurt/M.: Peter Lang.

Strauss, G. (1982). Workers' participation in management: An international perspective. *Research in Organizational Behavior, 4*, 173-265.

Streeck, W. (1982). Organizational consequences of corporist cooperation in West German labour unions. In G. Lehmbruch & P. C. Schnitter (Eds.), *Patterns of corporist policy-making* (pp. 29-81). London: Sage.

Streeck, W. (1984). Co-determination: The fourth decade. In B. Wilpert & A. Sorge (Eds.), *International perspectives on organizational democracy: International yearbook of organizational democracy* (pp. 391-422). Chichester: John Wiley.

Stutzman, T. M. (1983). Within classification job differences. *Personnel Psychology, 36*, 503-516.

Sugiman, T., & Misumi, J. (1984). Action research on evacuation method in emergent situation (II): Effects of leader-evacuee ratio on efficiency of follow-direction method and follow-me method. *Japanese Journal of Experimental Social Psychology, 23*(2), 107-115 (in Japanese with English abstract).

Sugiman, T., Misumi, J., & Sako, H. (1983). Action research on evacuation method in emergent situation (I): Comparison between follow-direction method and follow-me method. *Japanese Journal of Experimental Social Psychology, 22*(2), 95-98 (in Japanese with English abstract).

Super, D. E. (1957). *The psychology of careers.* New York: Harper.

Super, D. E. (1964). *La psychologie des interets.* Paris: Presses Universities de France.

Super, D. E. (1965). L'orientation vers une profesion ou vers une carriere? *Bulletin de l'Institut National d'Orientation Professionnelle, 21*, 243-248.

Super, D. E. (1970). *Computer assisted counseling.* New York: Teachers College Press.

Super, D. E. (1980). A life-span, life-space, approach to career development. *Journal of Vocational Behavior, 13*, 282-298.

Super, D. E. (1985a). *New dimensions in adult vocational and career counseling.* Columbus, OH: National Center for Research in Vocational Education.

Super, D. E. (1985b). Coming of age in Middletown; careers in the making. *American Psychologist, 40*, 405-414.

Super, D. E., & Bowlsbey, J. A. (1979). *Guided career exploration.* Cleveland, OH: Psychological Corporation.

Super, D. E., et al. (1957). *Vocational development: A framework for research.* New York: Teachers College Press.

Susman, G. (1976). *Autonomy at work.* New York: Praeger.

Sykes, I. J., & Eden, D. (1985). Transitional stress and psychological strain: A failure of hardiness and social support as buffers. *Journal of Occupational Behavior, 6*, 293-298.

Tabane, A. (1979). *The socio-cultural background of the black South African and its impact on business development.* Unpublished manuscript.

Takamiya, S. (1981). The characteristics of Japanese management. *Management Japan, 14*(2), 6-9.

Tanaka, K. (1975). An experimental study on the effects of changing task structure in the contingency model: An exercise in situational engineering. *Japanese Journal of Experimental Social Psychology, 15*(1), 74-85.

Tannenbaum, A. S. (1980). Organizational psychology. In H. C. Triandis & R. W. Brislin (Eds.), *Handbook of cross cultural psychology: Social psychology* (Vol. 5, pp. 281-334). Boston: Allyn & Bacon.

Tao, M. (1982). Organizational atmosphere and decision-making. In T. Futamura (Ed.), *Human behavior in organizations: An exhortation toward the theory of organizational behavior. Series of current business administration.* Juhikaku.

Task Force on Assessment Center Standards. (1980, February). Standards and ethical considerations for assessment center operations. *Personnel Administrator,* pp. 35-38.

Taylor, M. S., Fisher, C. D., & Ilgen, D. R. (1984). Individuals' reactions to performance feedback in organizations: A control theory perspective. In K. Rowland & J. Ferris (Eds.), *Research in personnel and human resources management* (Vol. 2, pp. 81-124). Greenwich, CT: JAI.

Taylor, M. S., & Sniezek, J. A. (1984). The college recruitment interview: Topical content and applicant reactions. *Journal of Occupational Psychology, 57,* 157-168.

Taylor, S., & Crocker, J. (1981). Schematic basis of social information processing. In E. T. Higgins et al. (Eds.), *Social cognition: The Ontario symposium* (pp. 89-134). Hillsdale, NJ: Lawrence Erlbaum.

Teas, R. K. (1981). A within-subject analysis of valence models of job preference and anticipated satisfaction. *Journal of Occupational Psychology, 54,* 109-124.

Tenopyr, M. L., & Oeltjen, P. D. (1982). Personnel selection and classification. *Annual Review of Psychology, 33,* 581-618.

Terborg, J. R., & David, G. A. (1982). Evaluation of a new method for assessing change to planned job redesign as applied to Hackman and Oldham's job characteristic model. *Organizational Behavior and Human Performance, 29,* 112-128.

Tetlock, P. E., & Levi, A. R. (1982). Attribution bias: On the inconclusiveness of the cognition-motivation debate. *Journal of Experimental Social Psychology, 18,* 68-88.

Tezanos, J. F. (1983). Satisfaccion en el trabajo y sociedad industrial: Una aproximacion al estudio de las actitudes hacia el trabajo de los obreros industriales madrilenos. *Revista Espanola de Investigaciones Sociologicas,* pp. 27-52.

Thomas, J., & Griffin, R. (1983). The social information processing model of task design: A review of the literature. *Academy of Management Review, 8,* 672-682.

Thornton, G. C., & Byham, W. C. (1982). *Assessment centers and managerial performance.* London: Academic Press.

Thorsrud, E. (1984). The Scandinavian model: Strategies of organizational democratization in Norway. In B. Wilpert & A. Sorge (Eds.), *International perspectives on organizational democracy* (pp. 337-369). Chichester: John Wiley.

Thurley, K. (1982, November). *The development and utilization of human resources in the context of technological change and industrial restructuring utilization of human resources: A proposed approach.* OECD Paper, Centre for Educational Research and Innovation, CERI/CW.

Tichy, N. (1973). An analysis of clique formation and structure in organizations. *Administrative Science Quarterly, 18,* 194-208.

Tichy, N. (1980). A social network perspective for organizational development. In T. G. Cummings (Ed.), *Systems theory for organization development* (pp. 115-162). Chichester: John Wiley.

Tichy, N. (1981). Networks in organizations. In P. C. Nystrom & W. H. Starbuck (Eds.), *Handbook of organizational design* (2 vols., pp. 225-249). Oxford University Press.

Tichy, N., & Fombrun, C. (1979). Network analysis in organizational settings. *Human Relations, 32,* 923-965.

Tichy, N., Tushman, M., & Fombrun, C. (1979). Social network analysis for organizations. *Academy of Management Review, 4,* 507-519.

Tichy, N., Tushman, M., & Fombrun, C. (1980). Network analysis in organizations. In E. E. Lawler III, D. A. Nadler, & C. Cammann (Eds.), *Organizational assessment* (pp. 372-398). New York: John Wiley.

Tichy, N., & Ulrich, D. O. (1984). The leadership challenge: A call for the transformational leader. *Sloan Management Review, 26,* 59-68.

Tiffin, J., & McCormick, E. J. (1965). *Industrial psychology* (4th ed.). Englewood Cliffs, NJ: Prentice-Hall.

Tiggeman, M., & Winefield, A. H. (1984). The effects of unemployment on the mood, self-esteem, focus of control and depressive affect of school leavers. *Journal of Occupational Psychology, 57*, 33-42.

Toda, M. (1980). Emotion and decision making. *Acta Psychologica, 46*, 133-155.

Tomlinson, R. (1981). Some dangerous misconceptions concerning operational research and applied systems analysis. *European Journal of Operational Research, 7*, 203-212.

Torrington, D. D., & Chapman, J. B. (1983). *Personnel management* (2nd ed.). London: Prentice-Hall.

Tosi, H. L., & Slocum, J. W., Jr. (1984). Contingency theory: Some suggested directions. *Journal of Management, 10*, 9-26.

Trattner, M. H. (1982). Synthetic validity and its application to the uniform guidelines validation requirements. *Personnel Psychology, 35*, 383-397.

Triandis, H. C. (1972). *The analysis of subjective culture*. New York: John Wiley.

Triandis, H. C. (1977). *Interpersonal behavior*. Monterey, CA; Brooks/Cole.

Tribus, M. (1983, March 2). *Managing to survive in a competitive world*. Paper presented at the Society of Automotive Engineers, Detroit, MI.

Trist, E. (1981). *The evolution of socio technical systems*. Ontario Ministry of Labour.

Trist, E. (1983). Referent organizations and the development of interorganizational domains. *Human Relations, 36*, 269-284.

Trist, E. L. (1981). The evolution of sociotechnical systems as a conceptual framework and as an action research program. In A. H. Van de Ven & W. F. Joyce (Eds.), *Perspectives on organization design and behavior*. New York: John Wiley.

Tubiana, J. H., & Ben-Shakhar, G. (1982). An objective group questionnaire as a substitute for a personal interview in the prediction of success in military training in Israel. *Personnel Psychology, 35*, 349-357.

Turner, J. A. (1980). *Computers in bank clerical functions: Implications for productivity and the quality of working life*. Unpublished doctoral dissertation, Columbia University.

Turner, R. (1960). Sponsored and contest mobility and the school system. *American Sociological Review, 25*, 855-867.

Tziner, A. (1984). A fairer examination of rating scales when used for performance appraisal in a real organizational setting. *Journal of Occupational Behavior, 5*, 103-112.

Tziner, A., & Eden, D. (1985). Effects of crew composition on crew performance: Does the whole equal the sum of its parts? *Journal of Applied Psychology, 70*, 85-93.

Ulrich, L., & Trumbo, D. (1965). The selection interview since 1949. *Psychological Bulletin, 63*, 100-116.

United Nations. (1982). *Curricula design for management development*. New York: United Nations Department of Technical Co-operation for Development.

United Nations. (1983). *Annotated bibliography on staff training and development in the public sector and on public finance management, accounting and audit*. New York: Author.

United Nations. (1984). *Management training of scientific and technical personnel in the public services of developing countries*. New York: Author.

Vaill, P. (1982, Autumn). The purposing of high performing systems. *Organizational Dynamics*, pp. 23-39.

Van de Ven, A. H., & Astley, W. G. (1981). Mapping the field to create a dynamic perspective on organization design and behavior. In A. H. Van de Ven & W. F. Joyce (Eds.), *Perspectives on organization design and behavior*. New York: John Wiley.

Van de Ven, A. H., & Ferry, D. L. (1980). *Measuring and assessing organizations*. New York: John Wiley.

Van de Ven, A. H., & Joyce, W. F. (Eds). (1981). *Perspectives on organization design and behavior*. New York: John Wiley.

Van Sell, M., Brief, A. P., & Schler, R. S. (1981). Role conflict and role ambiguity: Integration of the literature and directions for future research. *Human Relations, 34*, 43-71.

Vanek, J. (1975). *Self management: Economic liberation of man*. Harmondsworth: Penguin.

Vansina, L. S. (1982). *Developing organizations through their top performance: Findings on how general managers think and manage*. Presented at the Annual Convention of the American Psychological Association, Washington, DC.

Vansina, L. S. (1984). Quality control of . . . total quality control programmes. *Krilons-Gruppens Arsbok*, pp. 65-79.

Vansina, L. S. (1985a). Decentralisatie van de onderneming door opsplitsing in zelfstandige eenheden: Wat kunnen wij ervan leren? [Decentralisation of the company into autonomous units: What can we learn from the experiences?] *Permanente Educatie Managers, 1*, 51-66.

Vansina, L. S. (1985b). Kwaliteitsbeheersing van . . . integrale kwaliteitsbeheersingsprogramma's. *Sigma, 2*, 13-19.

Vardi, Y., Shirom, A., & Jacobson, D. (1980). A study on the leadership beliefs of Israeli managers. *Academy of Management Journal, 23*, 367-374.

Varney, G. H. (1981). Productivity in the 80's: Are you ready? *Training and Development Journal, 18*, 13-17.

Vecchio, R. P. (1982). The contingent-noncontingent compensation controversy: An attempt at a resolution. *Human Relations, 35*, 449-462.

Veen, P. (1984). Characteristics of organizations. In P.J.D. Drenth, H. Thierry, P. J. Willems, & C. J. de Wolff (Eds.), *Handbook of work and organizational psychology*. Chichester: John Wiley.

Verba, S. (1961). *Small groups and political behavior*. Princeton, NJ: Princeton University Press.

Verhoef, L., Zwaga, H., & Koelenga, H. (1983). *Training operators for complex supervision and control systems: A literature review and principles for the design of a training course*. Utrecht: Psychological Laboratory, State University.

Vernon, P. E., & Parry, J. B. (1949). *Personnel selection in the British forces*. London: University of London Press.

Voges, K. E., Long, N. R., Roache, M. S., & Shouksmith, G. (1982). *The perceptors of stress by prison officers and their wives*. Popnesku North: Massey University.

Vroom, V., & Jago, A. (1974). Decision making as a social process: Normative and descriptive models of leader behavior. *Decision Sciences, 5*, 743-769.

Vroom, V. H., & Yetton, P. W. (1973). *Leadership and decision-making*. Pittsburgh: University of Pittsburgh Press.

Vucht Tijssen, J. van e. a. (1978). *Middenkader en stress*. Den Haag: Commissie Opvoering Productiviteit van de Sociaal Economische Raad.

Wagner, R. (1949). The employment interview: A critical summary. *Personnel Psychology, 2*, 17-46.

Wakabayaski, M., & Graen, G. B. (1984). The Japanese career progress study: A 7-year follow-up. *Journal of Applied Psychology, 69*, 603-614.

Wakabayaski, M., Minami, T., Hashimoto, M., Sano, K., Graen, G., & Novak, M. (1980). Managerial career development: Japanese style. *International Journal of Intercultural Relations, 4*, 391-420.

Walker, A. J. (1982). *HRIS Development*. New York: Van Nostrand Reinhold.

Wallace, M. J. (1983). Methodology, research practice, and progress in personnel and industrial relations. *Academy of Management Review, 8*, 6-13.

Walton, R. L. (1985). From control to commitment in the workplace. *Harvard Business Review, 64*, 76-84.

Warrington, A. (1977). *Organizational behaviour and performance*. London: Macmillan.

Watts, A. G., Super, D. E., & Kidd, J. M. (Eds.). (1981). *Career development in Britain*. Cambridge, UK: Hobson's.

Webber, R. H. (1969). Convergence or divergence. *Columbia Journal of World Business, 4*(3), 75-83.

Webster, E. C. (1982). *The employment interview: A social judgment process*. Schomberg, Ontario: SIP.

Weick, K. E. (1969). *The social psychology of organizing*. Reading, MA: Addison-Wesley.

Weick, K. E. (1979). *Cognitive processes in organizations*. Greenwich, CT: JAI.

Weiss, H. M., & Adler, S. (1981). Cognitive complexity and the structure of implicit leadership theories. *Journal of Applied Psychology, 66*, 69-78.

Welsch, H. P., & LaVan, H. (1981). Inter-relationship between organizational commitment and job characteristics, job satisfaction, professional behavior, and organizational climate. *Human Relations, 34*, 1079-1089.

Wexley, K. M. (1984). Personnel training. *Annual Review of Psychology, 35*, 519-551.

Wherry, R. J., & Bartlett, C. J. (1982). The control of bias in ratings: A theory of ratings. *Personnel Psychology, 35*, 521-551.

White, G. M., & Marsella, A. J. (1982). Introduction: Cultural conceptions in mental health research and practice. In A. J. Marsella & G. M. White (Eds.), *Cultural conceptions of mental health and therapy*. Holland: D. Ridel.

White, R. W. (1959). Motivation reconsidered: The concept of competence. *Psychological Review, 66*(5), 297-333.

Whitely, W. A. (1979). A cross national test of England's model managers' value systems and their relationship to behavior. In G. W. England, A. R. Negandhi, & B. Wilpert (Eds.), *Organizational functioning in a cross cultural perspective* (pp. 19-47). Kent, OH: Kent State University Press.

Whitely, W. A., & England, G. M. (1977). Managerial values as a reflection of culture and the process of industrialization. *Academy of Management Journal, 20*(3), 439-453.

Whiting, B. B. (1976). The problem of the packaged variable. In K. Riegal & J. Meacham (Eds.), *The developing individual in a changing world* (Vol. 1). Den Haag: Mouton.

Williams, M., Berg-Cross, G., & Berg-Cross, L. (1977). Handwriting characteristics and their relationship to Eysenck's extraversion-introversion and Kagan's impulsivity-reflectivity dimensions. *Journal of Personality Assessment, 41*, 291-298.

Willmott, H. (1981). The structuring of organizational structure: A note. *Administrative Science Quarterly, 26*, 470-474.

Wilpert, B. (1975). Research on industrial democracy: The German case. *Industrial Relations Journal, 6*, 53-64.

Wilpert, B. (1984). Participation in organizations: Evidence from international comparative research. *International Social Science Journal, 367*(2), 355-366.

Wilpert, B., & Rayley, J. (1983). *Anspruch und wirklichkeit der mitbestimmung*. Frankfurt, M./New York: Campus.

Wilpert, B., & Ruiz Quintanilla, S. A. (1984). The German humanization of work programme: Review of its first twenty publications. *Journal of Occupational Psychology, 57*, 185-195.

Wilpert, B., & Sorge, A. (Eds.). (1984). *International perspectives on organizational democracy: International yearbook of organizational democracy, 2*. Chichester: John Wiley.

Winer, J. L. (1981). Worker functions and intraoccupational specialty in psychology. *Vocational Guidance Quarterly, 30*, 50-60.

Wingrove, J., Glendinning, R., & Herriot, P. (1984). Graduate pre-selection: A research note. *Journal of Occupational Psychology, 57*, 169-171.

Winnubst, J.A.M. (in press). Time anxiety and type A behavior. In L. D. Spielberger, I. G. Sarason, & P. B. Defares (Eds.), *Stress and anxiety* (Vol. 10). New York: John Wiley.

Winnubst, J.A.M., Marcelissen, F.H.G., Bastelaer, A.M.L., van Wolf, C. J. de, & Leufting, A. E. (1984). Type A behaviour pattern as a moderator in the stressor-strain relationship. In A. M. Koopman-Iwema & R. Roe (Eds.), *Work and organizational psychology: European perspectives*. Lisse: Swets & Zeitlinger.

Winnubst, J.A.M., Marcelissen, F.H.G., & Kleber, R. J. (1982). Effects of social support in the stressor-strain relationship: A Dutch sample. *Social Science and Medicine, 16*, 475-482.

Winnubst, J.A.M., Marcelissen, F.H.G., & Kleber, R. J. (1983). Social support as a moderator of stressor-strain relationships in industrial organizations. In M. Horvath & E. Frantic (Eds.), *Psychophysiological risk factors of cardiovascular diseases*. Basel: Karger.

Witte, E. (1980). Der Einfluss der Arbeitnehmer auf die Unternehmenspolitik. *Die Betriebswirtschaft, 40*, 541-59.

Witte, E. (1981). Die Unabhängigkeit des Vorstandes im Einflusssystem der unternehmung. *Zeitschrift für betriebswirtschaftliche Forschung, 33*, 273-296.

Witte, E. (1982). Klassenkampf und gruppenkampf in unternehmen. Abschied von der konfliktideologie. In H. D. Ortlieb et al. (Eds.), *Hamburger Jahrbuch für Wirtschafts- und Gesellschaftspolitik, 27*, 167-182.

Wolff, C. J. de (1981). *Werk en Gezondheid*. Report for Wetenschappelijke Raad voor het Regeringsbeleid, Catholic University Nijmegen.

Wolff, C. J. de (1982). Werk en Gezondheid. In *Kwaliteit van de Arbeid, publication V27 Wetenschappelijke Raad voor het Regeringsbeleid*. Den Haag: Staatsuitgeverij.

Wolff, C. J. de (1985). *Directory of work and organizational psychology.* Nijmegen: Catholic University.

Wood, S. (1982, November). Has the recession revolutionized recruitment? *Personal Management,* pp. 40-42.

Work in America. (1973). *Report of a special task force to the Secretary of Health Education and Welfare.* Cambridge: MIT Press.

Wren, D. A. (1979). *The evolution of management thought.* New York: John Wiley.

Wright, O. R. (1969). Summary of research on the selection interview since 1964. *Personnel Psychology, 22,* 391-413.

Wyer, R. S., & Srull, T. (Eds.). (1984). *Handbook of social cognition* (Vols. 1-3). Hillsdale, NJ: Lawrence Erlbaum.

Xu Liancang (1960). Labor psychology in China. *Problems of Psychology, 3,* 179-184.

Yamashiro, A. (Ed). (1956). *Case studies on rationalization of ringi system.* Tokyo: Diamond.

Yankelovich, Skelly, & White, Inc. (1980). *A continuing study of changing work values and employee motivations: Signal 1980 overall findings.* New York: Author.

Yela, M. (1985). *Presente y futuro de la psicologia del trabajo en la empresa.* Madrid: Fundacion Universidad-Empresa.

Young, D. M., & Beier, E. G. (1977). The role of applicant nonverbal communication in the employment interview. *Journal of Employment Counseling, 14,* 154-165.

Zajonc, R. B. (1965). Social facilitation. *Science, 149,* 269-274.

Zand, D. (1984, Winter). Organization development and strategic management. *Academy of Management OD Newsletter,* pp. 1, 7.

Zander, E. (1981). Personalwirtschaftliche Konsequenzen der unternehmensverfassungsrechtlichen Mitbestimmung. In K. Bohr et al. (Eds.), *Unternehmensverfassung als Problem der Betriebswirtschaftslehre* (pp. 309-328). Berlin: Erich Schmidt.

Zedeck, S. (1971). Problems with the use of "moderator" variables. *Psychological Bulletin, 71,* 295-310.

Zey-Ferrell, M. (1981). Criticisms of the dominant perspective on organizations. *Sociological Quarterly, 22,* 181-205.

Zimmerman, R., Jacobs, R., & Farr, J. (1982). A comparison of the accuracy of four methods for clustering jobs. *Applied Psychological Measurement, 6,* 353-366.

Zohar, D. (1980). Safety climate in industrial organizations: Theoretical and applied implications. *Journal of Applied Psychology, 65,* 96-102.

Zohar, D., & Fussfeld, N. (1981a). A system approach to organizational behavior modification: Theoretical considerations and empirical evidence. *International Review of Applied Psychology, 30,* 491-505.

Zohar, D., & Fussfeld, N. (1981b, August). *Textured contexts: Systems and situations in cross cultural psychology.* Paper presented at the symposium at the conference on human assessment and cultural factors, Kingston, Canada.

NOTES

NOTES

NOTES

NOTES